Third Edition

The Sociology of Education in Canada

Terry Wotherspoon

OXFORD
UNIVERSITY PRESS

OXFORD
UNIVERSITY PRESS

8 Sampson Mews, Suite 204, Don Mills, Ontario, M3C 0H5
www.oupcanada.com

Oxford University Press is a department of the University of Oxford.
It furthers the University's objective of excellence in research, scholarship,
and education by publishing worldwide in

Oxford   New York

Auckland   Cape Town   Dar es Salaam   Hong Kong   Karachi
Kuala Lumpur   Madrid   Melbourne   Mexico City   Nairobi
New Delhi   Shanghai   Taipei   Toronto

With offices in

Argentina   Austria   Brazil   Chile   Czech Republic   France   Greece
Guatemala   Hungary   Italy   Japan   Poland   Portugal   Singapore
South Korea   Switzerland   Thailand   Turkey   Ukraine   Vietnam

Oxford is a trade mark of Oxford University Press
in the UK and in certain other countries

Published in Canada by Oxford University Press

Library and Archives Canada Cataloguing in Publication

Wotherspoon, Terry
The sociology of education in Canada : critical perspectives / Terry
Wotherspoon. — 3rd ed.

Includes bibliographical references and index.

ISBN 978-0-19-542660-1

1. Educational sociology—Canada—Textbooks. I. Title.

LC191.8.C2W67 2009   306.430971   C2008-906516-6

Cover image: STOCK4B-RF/Blend Images/Getty Images

Printed and bound in Canada.

3 4 — 12 11

MIX
Paper from
responsible sources
FSC
www.fsc.org   FSC® C004071

The Sociology of Education in Canada

Contents

Each chapter ends with Annotated Further Readings, Key Terms, and Study Questions

List of Figures, Tables, and Boxes   vii
Preface   xi

1   The Sociological Analysis of Education 1
Introduction   1
The Sociological Understanding of Educational Problems   1
Sociology and Its Relation to Other Disciplines   4
The Nature of Sociological Inquiry   5
Sociological Perspectives   9
Emerging Directions in the Critical Analysis of Education   14
Conclusion   16

2   Sociological Theories of Education   20
Introduction   20
Structural Functionalism and Liberal Theory   20
Interpretative Analysis of Schooling   28
Critical Analysis   33
Guidelines for Research and Analysis in the Sociology of Education   50
Conclusion   51

3   Historical Dimensions of Canadian Education   54
Introduction   54
The Historical Development of Education in Canada   55
Conclusion   74

4   The Structure of Canadian Education Systems   78
Introduction   78
An Overview of Educational Activities in Canada   78
School Choice and the Educational Marketplace   88
The Governance and Financing of Canadian Education   94
Comparative Educational Growth   101
Conclusion   106

5   The Process of Schooling   109
Introduction   109
The Multi-faceted Nature of Educational Practices   110
The Contribution of Schooling to the Development of Human Subjects   112
Regulation and Resistance in Schooling   116
Streaming   118
Official Knowledge   125
Hegemony   130
Silencing in Educational Processes   131

Student Response and Resistance   135
Youth Cultures and Moral Panics   137
The Concern for Safe, Inclusive Educational Environments   142
Conclusion   143

6   Teachers and Teaching   145
Introduction   145
Teachers and Teaching in Canada   147
Teaching as a Profession   148
Gender and Teaching   153
Proletarianization and Intensification of Teaching   168
Conclusion   175

7   Schooling and Work   179
Introduction   179
Contemporary Demands for Educational Reform: The 'Mismatch'
    between Schooling and Jobs   180
The Relationship between Schooling and Work   188
The Contributions of Schooling to Work and the Economy   189
Discontinuities in Relationships among Schooling, Work,
    and Economic Activity   198
Education and Work in Canada   202
Conclusion   221

8   Educational Opportunity and Social Reproduction   224
Introduction   224
The Nature and Causes of Social Inequality in Canada   225
Educational Opportunity and Social Inequality   226
Dimensions of Educational Inequality   233
Gender   234
Racial and Ethnic Minorities   240
Aboriginal People   247
Social Class   255
Students with Disabilities   266
Regional Inequality   268
Conclusion   273

9   Contemporary Educational Challenges and Reforms   277
Introduction   277
Understanding Conflicting Visions of Educational Reform   278
Rational Planning and Educational Accountability   280
Education and New Technologies   287
Education and Social Diversity   294
Conclusion   297

Websites   303
References   305
Index   333

List of Figures, Tables, and Boxes

FIGURES

1.1 Proportions of Canadian Population, 15 Years and Over, with University Degrees and Less Than Grade 9 Education 3

4.1 The Learning Continuum 80

4.2 Full-time Enrolment in Canada (000s) by Level of Study 82

4.3 Education Expenditures by Level, Canada, Selected Years, 1950–2003 83

4.4 Share of Expenditures on Education in Canada, by Direct Source of Funds, 1950–1 to 2002–3 84

4.5 Net Enrolment Ratio in Primary Education, by Region, 2005 105

4.6 Ratio of Females to Males Enrolled in Primary Education, by Region, 2005 105

4.7 Proportion of Literate Persons Ages 15 and Over, by Region, 1995–2004 106

6.1 Post-Secondary Pyramid: Gender Distribution of Personnel in Key Roles and Positions, Canada (% female) 156

6.2 Aboriginal Child and Youth Population and Educational Services Labour Force, Canada, Provinces, and Territories, 2001 167

7.1 Employment Growth in High- and Low-Skilled Occupations, 1987–2005 185

7.2 Employment Growth by Industry, 1987–2015 185

7.3 Employment Growth by Knowledge Industry, 1991–2003 205

7.4 Diverse Pathways for Youth in School to Labour Market Transitions—Findings from the Youth in Transition Survey, December 2003 207

7.5 Median Earnings ($) for Full-time Full-year Workers, Ages 25–54, by Gender and Highest Level of Education, Canada, 2006 208

8.1 Full-time Enrolment in Selected University Undergraduate Programs by Fields of Study and Gender, 1982–3 235

8.2 Full-time Enrolment in Selected University Undergraduate Programs by Fields of Study and Gender, 2004–5 235

8.3 Female-to-Male Earnings by Highest Level of Education Completed, Selected Years, 1980–2005 238

8.4 Mean Earnings of 1990 Post-Secondary Graduates, Two Years and Five Years after Graduation (1995 constant dollars) 239

8.5 Education by Highest Certificate, Degree, or Diploma, Ages 15 and Over, Aboriginal Identity Categories, Visible Minorities, and Total Canadian Population, 2006 249

8.6 Post-Secondary Participation and High School Dropout Rates for Canadians, Age 19, by Family Income Quartiles, 2003 258

8.7 Post-Secondary Participation Rates (%), Ages 24–6, by Highest Level of Parents' Educational Attainment, December 2005 258

TABLES

4.1   Total and Relative Expenditures ($000s) on Education in Canada, 1950–1
        to 2002–3   83

4.2   Numbers of School Boards, by Province   85

5.1   Young People (13-year-olds) Who Were Bullied or Who Bullied Others in
        the Previous Two Months, and Those Involved in Physical Fighting in the
        Previous 12 Months (%), Selected Nations   141

6.1   Full-time Teachers in Elementary and Secondary Schools, by Gender, Canada,
        Selected Years, 1867–2005   158

6.2   Average Elementary and Secondary Teachers' Incomes in Comparison with
        Average Income in Canada, by Gender, Selected Census Years, 1921–2006   161

7.1   Summary of Major Changes and Additions to Curricula in Canadian
        Elementary Schools   194

7.2   Employment by Industry, Selected Years, Canada, 1946–2006   203

7.3   Percentage Change in the Number of Businesses, by Knowledge Industry,
        Canada, 1991 to 2003   205

7.4   Educational Attainment and Labour Force Participation, Canada, 2006   208

7.5   Employment by Gender, Industry, and Occupation, Canada, 2006   214

7.6   Ten Most Prevalent Occupations for Men and Women, and Fastest-Growing
        Occupational Categories, Canada, 2006   216

8.1   Educational Attainment, by Province and Territory, 2006 (% of Population
        Aged 25–64)   270

8.2   Dimensions of Educational Participation, by Provinces   271

9.1   Girls' and Boys' Self-Ratings of 10 Skills   288

BOXES

1.1   Sociological Interest in the Growth and Social Significance of Education   3

1.2   Research Orientations in the Sociology of Education   13

2.1   A Functionalist Perspective on the Sociology of Education   23

2.2   An Interpretative Perspective on the Sociology of Education   30

2.3   A Neo-Marxist Perspective on the Sociology of Education   37

2.4   A Feminist Perspective on the Sociology of Education   45

2.5   A Critical Pedagogy Perspective on the Sociology of Education   48

3.1   Obstacles and Progress: Two Notable Contributions to Educational
        Reform   56

3.2   Life in a Residential School   59

3.3   Teachers' Duties, 1875   63

3.4   Education Problems in Canada, 1958   71

4.1   Educational Reorganization, School Size, and Student Performance   87

4.2   Funding Cuts, Commercialization, and Educational Inequality   95

4.3   Growing Emphasis on Parent Involvement in Schools   100

4.4   Global Inequalities in Basic Education   104

5.1   Aboriginal Students' Perceptions of a Positive School Climate   113

5.2   Barriers to the Achievement of Anti-Racism in Schools and Universities   123

5.3   A Holistic Framework for Redefining Success for First Nations, Métis,
      and Inuit Learning   128

5.4   Afrocentric Schooling   133

5.5   Bullying and Victimization in Students' Lives   140

6.1   Teaching Consists of a Wide Range of Diverse Activities and Experiences   146

6.2   The Impact of Education Reforms on Teaching and Learning Conditions   150

6.3   Two Views on Teachers' Right to Strike   154

6.4   Serious Issues Affect Teachers in Many Nations   164

6.5   Trends Associated with the Restructuring of Teachers' Work   172

7.1   The Skills Challenge   182

7.2   Education, Skill, and Employment Trends for the New Economy   184

7.3   Comparative School-to-Work Transitions   187

7.4   Credential Inflation and Credential 'Creep'   193

7.5   Employment Prospects in the Knowledge Economy   204

7.6   Youth Employment Trends   218

8.1   Climate Change, Poverty, and Gender: Barriers to Basic Education in
      Developing Nations   229

8.2   Anti-Racism Education   241

8.3   The Educational Attainment of Aboriginal Peoples   253

8.4   Educational Inequalities and Disadvantage in Rich Nations   260

8.5   The Impact of Poverty on Education   262

9.1   Social and Economic Imperatives and School Ratings   285

9.2   Internet Skills among Canadian Youth   288

9.3   Roots of Empathy   295

9.4   Core Educational Challenges in the Twenty-First Century   298

Preface

Education systems and processes have a pervasive impact within contemporary societies. Many of our formative experiences occur in schools, while throughout our life course we are far less likely than previous generations to stray too far from schooling (as learners, parents, or employees). In social contexts heavily shaped by knowledge and information exchange, increasingly more of us are augmenting our initial schooling by taking post-secondary, adult, and continuing education programs and by pursuing a wide range of alternative learning opportunities. Lifelong learning, marked by innovation, adaptability, and the capacity to manage vast amounts of information, is widely touted as the key to success in a globally competitive environment. At the same time, we need to pose questions about which sorts of knowledge and learning systems are most appropriate for the worlds that we encounter and seek to shape. Public scrutiny over education has produced varying answers to questions about what kinds of education we should promote, who should pay for it and who should control it, who should have access to it, and how it should be recognized.

Canadian education has undergone many promising developments, along with some disappointments, in the short period since the first edition of this book appeared. Education is regarded more seriously as the stakes associated with it rise, criticized heavily on some fronts and praised on others. Educational options have expanded dramatically even as some educational alternatives have been cut back. The benefits that can be derived from forms of learning that are inclusive, flexible, fun, and engaging are being rediscovered at the same time that learners are being subjected to more testing, scrutiny, procedures, and expectations that often generate frustration and stress. Patricia Clifford (2008: 76), in a recent commentary in *Education Canada*, alludes to how the contemporary world requires us to seek innovative solutions to problems that may not yet have definitive answers, yet our learning is mostly shaped and evaluated with reference to answers that somebody already knows. There is some hope, nonetheless, that much educational debate is moving from entrenched positions based on uncritical acceptance of presumed truths to serious efforts to understand the strengths and limitations associated with various options and their consequences. There is an emerging impetus to engage in decision-making based on empirical findings from educational research, signified especially in the form of several major collaborative initiatives among researchers, policy bodies, and diverse educational communities. There is also growing emphasis that knowledge and learning are multi-faceted, with mutual benefit derived from sharing and exploring diverse alternatives.

This book argues that debates over educational futures must be informed by both awareness of how institutionalized forms of education have emerged historically and analysis of the practices and experiences that make contemporary education a complex and often contradictory undertaking. The book is written with the recognition that much of my life has revolved around formal education, first as a student at various levels of study, later as a high school and junior high school teacher, and then as a university faculty member. Education and educational change remain challenging focal points for ongoing analysis due to their complexity and their significance for individuals and their societies.

My own observations, insights, and predispositions have been shaped directly and indirectly by many of the educators, students, colleagues, and communities that I have encountered over several years. I acknowledge, in particular, the contributions of several people whose efforts and support have been especially important in the writing and production of this book. My nascent efforts to understand and appreciate the nuances associated with educational matters have been broadened considerably by members of numerous research consortia and educational bodies that I have been fortunate to be associated with in Saskatchewan, across Canada, in China, and elsewhere. My colleagues and students in the Department of Sociology at the University of Saskatchewan have provided a supportive environment to encourage ongoing debate, discussion, and scholarship. Jason Doherty and Beverly LaPointe provided extensive assistance in the preparation of the manuscript and supporting materials. Several other current or recent graduate students, including Trina Evitts, Joanne Butler, Kevin Shearer, and Darlene Lanceley, have provided useful commentary on the manuscript along with fresh insights into educational issues. This edition was nurtured to its final stages by Dina Theleritis, Phyllis Wilson, and Richard Tallman. I appreciate also the efforts of other persons at or associated with Oxford University Press Canada, and the manuscript reviewers, for providing direction and support.

I am especially indebted to Barb for her support in all ways, and to Rachel and Nicole, who are still able to express the joys associated with education in a changing world.

The Sociological Analysis of Education

INTRODUCTION

Education is a vital part of our social existence. Whether it occurs in formal settings or in less formal ways, **education** helps to shape our personalities as well as our life choices and chances. In many respects, all human experiences are educative. We continually engage in processes of self-development, modifying and recreating the world through our everyday activities. Both structured and unstructured forms of education are taking on greater significance in Canada and throughout the world within what is commonly called the information society or knowledge economy in which knowledge and learning occupy centre stage in social relationships and economic activities. The central role education plays in our changing societies challenges us to investigate the implications of educational transformation, including an understanding of how and why education systems have taken their present shape.

This chapter introduces several of the main themes pertinent to a critical examination of education. Its aim is to guide the development of a distinctly sociological understanding, but this is also augmented with insights derived from a variety of academic disciplines and interdisciplinary perspectives. Following a brief introduction to the discipline of sociology and the core questions and frameworks associated with sociological understandings, the chapter identifies four critical approaches to the analysis of education—critical pedagogy, feminist pedagogy, anti-racism education, and political economy—that inform the analysis employed throughout the book.

THE SOCIOLOGICAL UNDERSTANDING OF EDUCATIONAL PROBLEMS

Usually when we think of education, we identify it with formal institutions—schools, colleges, universities, and other structured institutional or learning processes. Viewed in these concrete terms, education tends to be associated with teachers, texts, and tests; knowledge, skills, and values; credentials, opportunities, and rewards; and policy, budget, and public representation. Consider the following questions:

- How and why has formal schooling come to be associated with education?
- Why are children and youth expected to attend schools for at least 10 years—and often much longer?
- Why do some people fail or drop out of school while others achieve success through post-secondary education?
- Why do most school classrooms have a readily identifiable character that distinguishes them from other social settings?

- Which social groups are served by educational institutions, and with what outcomes?
- How does teaching compare with other types of work?
- Why is Canadian education financed mostly by governments, and primarily by local, provincial, and territorial governments?
- What do people really learn at school, and how important is it for jobs and life outside of school?
- What impact do social, economic, and technological changes have on educational processes and achievement levels?
- Who decides what is in the curriculum and how is the curriculum translated into educational practice?

Each of these questions can be answered in many different ways. Canadians hold diverse opinions about many of them, as expressed in the high degree of controversy surrounding contemporary educational issues. Some answers involve historical facts or information that can be gathered through simple observation. Responses to other questions require more detailed data collected statistically, through interviews, or by other methodologies. Nearly all questions are subject to competing interpretations.

Sociology is a discipline or field of inquiry that provides particular frameworks through which we can make sense of questions like those outlined above as well as of the diverse responses that they generate. Sociologists are interested in education because it is so central to human social experience, to our direct and indirect relations with other people. Education, in its various guises, conveys important insights about particular kinds of societies and the people within them. The analysis of educational structures, practices, and outcomes can help us to understand, for example, what kinds of values, beliefs, and ideologies prevail in a given society, how people come to learn about and become organized within particular social structures, and how open and democratic that society is.

The purpose of this book is to analyze Canadian educational practices, structures, and problems from a critical sociological framework. In many cases, international examples are employed to highlight the broader context within which Canadian education is situated. Emphasis is on formal education or **schooling**, as opposed to other types of education, since it is in its institutional forms that education has become most highly integrated into wider social, economic, and political organization. It also explores the changing boundaries between educational institutions and other learning sites. Reference is made to a variety of sociological studies and perspectives developed within and beyond Canada to provide the reader with a sense of how distinct research traditions have been employed to understand schooling. The book adopts a critical orientation, which reveals how education in Canada has been from the outset a complex, contested, and contradictory endeavour. The book is not intended as a manual or an exhaustive history that details all aspects of our education systems. Instead, it employs analytical tools

Box 1.1 Sociological Interest in the Growth and Social Significance of Education

The growing significance of education for Canadians is illustrated in Figure 1.1, below, which demonstrates how, over the past half-century, the share of the population with university degrees has overtaken that portion of the population with less than a Grade 9 education. Sociologists have offered numerous interpretations of this educational growth, and have also examined its significance for society as a whole and for different subgroups within the population.

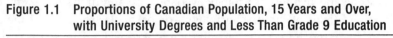

Figure 1.1   Proportions of Canadian Population, 15 Years and Over, with University Degrees and Less Than Grade 9 Education

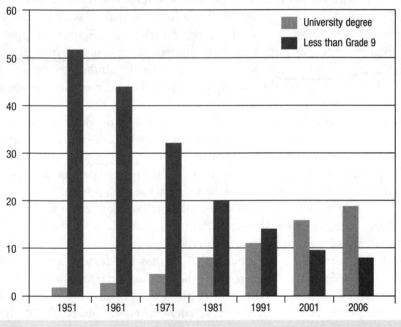

Sources: Data from Guppy and Davies (1998: 19); Statistics Canada, *Census of Canada*, various years; and CANSIM Table 2820004. This is an updated version based on a figure in Clarke (2000: 7).

derived from sociology and related disciplines in an effort to answer questions about why education has developed as it has and how educational issues are interconnected with fundamental characteristics of social organization and social life. The remainder of this chapter examines the issues and approaches central to sociological analysis. The chapter concludes with a brief discussion of how these insights can be applied to educational questions in such a way as to provide a framework for the chapters to follow.

SOCIOLOGY AND ITS RELATION TO OTHER DISCIPLINES

Sociology is the investigation of the relationships between individuals and society. It examines how social structures (relatively enduring patterns of social organization) and social practices (ongoing social activity) both shape and are shaped by human beings. It is a scientific discipline in the sense that it is based on research and theories that attempt, in a systematic and organized manner, to describe and explain important features of social reality. Sociologists analyze such institutions as schools, families, economic and political organizations, religion, the mass media, and the criminal justice system, as well as interpersonal relations, small groups, informal social practices, and much broader and sometimes less visible social forces, such as power and control.

In its scope and methods, sociology overlaps with and draws on several other disciplines and fields of inquiry. Sociology—or particular subfields of the discipline—can share much in common with such other social sciences as economics, political science, psychology, and anthropology, as well as with studies in the humanities such as history and philosophy, and with interdisciplinary approaches in such areas as Native studies, women's studies, environmental studies, cultural studies, and regional studies. Some sociological work is influenced by and influences other fields of inquiry, including geography, biology, medicine, demography, policy studies, and administrative studies.

Despite its complementarity with various academic disciplines, sociology developed from the vision of eighteenth- and nineteenth-century intellectuals, who wanted to construct a distinct science of society modelled after physics, biology, and other natural sciences. In common with closely related social sciences like psychology and economics, many of the tools that sociologists employ to examine the social world involve principles of research methodology and theory construction shared with scientists who study the natural world. However, the studies of the social and natural worlds differ in crucial ways. Social reality, complex and dynamic in nature, is not governed strictly by law-like regularities and it is not readily amenable to definitive statements about cause and effect that are the objective of much scientific inquiry. Social structures and practices are constantly being reshaped and reinterpreted by human activity. Moreover, the sociological investigator, as part of the social world being studied, may have an impact on social actions and how they are understood. Social research involves an ethical dimension that raises questions about what kinds of research activities are socially acceptable and what their consequences are for social life. These problems are shared by other sciences, since all scientific activity involves to some extent human interpretation, phenomena that are subject to change, and ethical questions, but they are much more evident within or central to sociology and other human sciences than in the scientific investigation of non-social phenomena.

With this wide array of influences, it might seem unusual that a discipline like sociology should exist, since most questions like the ones listed earlier can be investigated through one or more of the other disciplines. Two somewhat opposing points can be made in response to this concern. First, it is true that boundaries between disciplines are somewhat flexible, so that it may seem that the only clear distinction between areas is evident in the field by which people identify themselves (e.g., psychologists, educational administrators, and sociologists may all use similar methods to conduct research into the question of why some students drop out of school). The second point, however, involves the recognition that each discipline is constituted around core questions and approaches that can clearly be distinguished from one another. In the example noted above, the psychologist may be most interested in identifying the personality characteristics of school dropouts in comparison with students who stay in school; the researcher in educational administration may be most concerned with identifying ways to keep students in school longer; and the sociologist may be most interested in determining how characteristics of school organization contribute to the dropout phenomenon. The distinguishing characteristics of sociology are discussed below.

The Nature of Sociological Inquiry

Sociology, like most social sciences, emerged relatively recently compared to the humanities and physical sciences. A prolonged period of social, economic, and political upheaval in Europe, particularly during and after the mid-eighteenth century, fostered an interest in sustained inquiry into the nature of society and its relationship to the individual. The rapid advancement of the Industrial Revolution, combined with new social and political arrangements, led to serious questioning about the nature and consequences of social change. People's life experiences were altered amid challenges to existing social conventions and institutions. Among the transformations was a growing emphasis on democracy and individual rights as opposed to more traditional, hierarchical bases of social order. Out of these circumstances emerged both intellectual and pragmatic concerns to understand the conditions that produced social change, to assess the impact of the changes taking place, and to consider the possibilities and prospects for future social transformation. 'Sociology', a term first used by the French writer Auguste Comte in the nineteenth century to signify the need for a scientific study of society, was developed in order to study these issues by examining the relative impact of social stability and social change on people's lives.

Although the thematic focus and methodological substance of sociology have taken on different forms since Comte's time, many of the issues that concerned early sociologists remain at the core of the discipline. Sociology is both a scientific discipline and a moral or human undertaking in which theoretical analysis and empirical research are applied to an understanding of important social problems and issues in order to enhance the world in which we live. The contemporary significance of this historical vision for the discipline has been articulated in the work of recent sociologists. Patricia Hill Collins (2007: 112), for instance, stresses the continuing inspiration offered through the works of such classical social theorists as Karl Marx, Max Weber, Georg Simmel, Émile Durkheim, W.E.B. Dubois, and others whom she characterizes as public sociologists offering a 'commitment to bring the tools of sociology to bear on the important issues of their time. . . . So much of what they did was on behalf of bettering the public.' Similarly, Steve Fuller (2006: 1) contends that, 'The central aspiration of sociology—and the social sciences more generally—has been to make good on the eighteenth-century Enlightenment promise of creating a "heaven on earth" [with an aim] to create a world in which humans exercise dominion over nature without exercising dominion over each other.'

As a discipline concerned to understand and build upon relations between individuals and society, sociology has been guided by several fundamental questions and debates, including the following:

1. At which level—individual or social—should analysis begin?
2. To what extent are individuals the products or the producers of social structures?
3. Is social life characterized more by social stability and consensus or by social conflict?
4. How do we study the social world, and to what ends? Should the study of society be guided by a search for observable facts and laws (positivism) or by human interpretations of the world?

Individual versus Society

All sociological analysis is concerned at some level with relations among individuals and societies. Sociologists do not study individuals in isolation from one another, but focus instead on how people interact with each other either directly (at a face-to-face level) or indirectly (through internalized rules and expectations, the products of human activity, consciousness of others, and institutionalized patterns of behaviour). Different forms of sociological analysis emerge around questions about which factor or set of factors is regarded as most important.

The debate concerning the relations between individuals and society can be illustrated with reference to two key sociological theorists, Émile Durkheim and Max Weber, whose works were instrumental in establishing sociology as a viable academic discipline in the late nineteenth and early twentieth centuries. Durkheim defined sociology as the study of 'social facts', referring to features of society (such as rates of marriage or death, religion, law, and economic systems) that existed in their own right and had an influence on individuals' thoughts and actions. Society, in these terms, can be studied as if it is a real thing because it is present before we are born and after we die, and it affects the lives and character of each human being. Weber, by contrast, defined sociology as the 'interpretive understanding of social action', by which he meant that the discipline should emphasize how people's social decisions and behaviours are guided by interpretation or meaning. Unlike Durkheim, Weber argued that society has no independent existence outside of people's thoughts, motives, and actions (although human actions and creations have a powerful impact on our choices and actions). Posed in simpler terms, Durkheim represents a version of sociology in which the study of relations between individuals and society begins with society, while Weber's analysis begins with individuals and proceeds from there to study social relations. Contemporary sociologists continue to look to these starting points, or some intermediate position, as the basis for analyses.

Human Agency versus Structural Determination

An important question that accompanies the investigation of how individuals are interrelated with society concerns the role that free choice plays in our lives. Although we tend to think of ourselves as unique individuals, we must also recognize that our thoughts, personalities, and actions are heavily influenced by our social background and surroundings. Sociologists do not always agree about the extent to which individuals are shaped by social factors, and vice versa. One view, that of human **agency**, asserts that human beings are active 'agents' whose behaviour and thoughts make society possible. People are seen to be relatively free to make sense of the world in such a way as to make decisions that guide their lives and conduct. The world, according to this approach, is socially constructed—our language, cultures, and institutions are created, maintained, and changed through human activity.

A contrasting, structuralist, view emphasizes that people are social products. **Social structures**, or relatively enduring patterns within society and social life, give rise to our personalities and thoughts, to the choices we face, and to the courses we take in our lives. When we are born, existing social structures determine limitations and opportunities dependent on such factors as gender, race, the wealth and status of our parents, and so on. Our freedom, in other words, tends to be highly constrained by social rules and expectations.

Most sociologists and other social thinkers take a position somewhere between the two extremes of individual agency and structural determination. As Karl Marx (1963: 15) observed, people 'make their own history, but they do not make it just as they please; they do not make it under circumstances chosen by themselves, but under circumstances directly encountered, given and transmitted from the past.' A more contemporary sociologist, Anthony Giddens (1987: 11), has expressed the same point through what he calls 'the "double involvement" of individuals and institutions', in which 'we create society at the same time as we are created by it.' In other words, whatever their starting points, most sociologists agree that society is something more than a collection of individuals such that it must be studied with sensitivity to the reciprocal impact of human beings and social structures on each other.

Stability versus Conflict

As noted earlier, sociology emerged through systematic efforts to understand significant social changes occurring in conjunction with the Industrial Revolution and social upheaval. Some early social commentators feared that the changes were destructive of a social order that could never be retrieved while others welcomed the changes as a mark of progress and hope for the future. These dual concerns, of a search for social stability and a desire for social change and improvement, remain central to the discipline.

Sociologists continue to address these issues from different stances. Some sociologists, following the tradition of Auguste Comte, have attempted to uncover laws governing social order and conditions for social change. Their assumption is that stable social order, supported by consensus about fundamental values, is the normal state of a society. The development of sociology as a science, in these terms, is to identify factors that foster social harmony as opposed to those that are socially harmful or destructive. Excessive conflict and social change that proceeds too rapidly are deemed to threaten the long-term survival of a society. A contrasting approach to social analysis depicts conflict and struggle as normal features of societies. Societies, particularly if they are relatively complex in nature, are likely to contain a diversity of different collectivities and subgroups, each with specific needs and interests. Although overt conflict is not always present or apparent, social change is driven by the demands and actions of social groups to have their interests represented and their needs met. The task of sociology, in this view, is to identify and analyze the social circumstances that give rise to each set of interests.

Positivism versus Interpretative Analysis

There are different ways of looking at the world as well as of determining what should be looked at. The task of social science, for some sociologists, is to replicate, as much as possible, the rigorous approaches associated with physics, chemistry, and other scientific disciplines. The goal of science, understood this way, is to formulate laws and statements about regular patterns of cause and effect in the social world, and to specify the conditions under which these causal relations will occur. This approach, known as **positivism, emphasizes that science must concern itself with phenomena that can be readily identified and measured**. Like many scientists who study the natural world, these sociologists assume that the social world has a definite structure of reality that can be observed, classified, and controlled as we gain objective knowledge about each of its parts.

Other sociologists, by contrast, contend that positivism's claims to uncover objective knowledge about laws that regulate society are false. They argue that all human knowledge, including scientific observation, is based on particular interpretations of reality. Social reality, moreover, is continually being shaped and reshaped because it is based on human actions. For interpretative sociologists, therefore, the proper task of science is to identify the social bases and meanings attached to particular phenomena, and to explore how those meanings are related to people's social actions. This assessment, expressed in its most radical form within some postmodernist orientations, suggests that any scientific quest for universal truths or general laws is necessarily misguided because it does not take into account the diverse meanings and viewpoints that are characteristic of human life.

Other interpretative sociology does not reject the possibility of science, but cautions that we must be aware of the limitations associated with science and the claims or authority that it carries with it.

SOCIOLOGICAL PERSPECTIVES

Sociologists, like anyone else who investigates nature or society, must make decisions about what they study and how they study it. They require guidelines to help them focus their observations and make sense of what they see. In their most general form, these guidelines are provided in the form of what are called sociological perspectives, or ways of looking at the social world. Perspectives point to what is important, based on particular assumptions about social reality and how to study it.

Sociology, it should be emphasized, is not unique in offering perspectives to its practitioners. All sciences rely on specific assumptions that lead to different ways of conducting scientific investigation. In medical research, for example, some researchers emphasize the factors that cause a certain disorder so that appropriate cures or remedies can be prescribed, while others adopt a more holistic orientation that examines health in the context of a wide range of environmental conditions, which themselves must be modified before effective healing can take place. In physics, the study of quantifiable characteristics of matter is contrasted with the analysis of unobservable, changing forces. In all disciplines, perspectives identify ways to address these kinds of issues in a systematic manner.

It should be emphasized that sociologists share some common goals regardless of the perspectives they adopt. All theory is an attempt to enhance our ability to understand aspects of the social and natural worlds, and all research is conducted as part of an effort to provide us with information that tells us something about what those worlds are like. Scientific inquiry is unified by a search for knowledge and understanding, even though there are differences over how that search should be conducted, what the ultimate aim of that search should be, and what should be done with the information generated.

Sociological perspectives are aligned around questions governed by debates outlined in the preceding sections. Although there are different ways of labelling and organizing them, it is generally agreed that the discipline has been shaped by several sociological perspectives, in particular three identified here as structural functionalism, interpretative sociology, and critical orientations.

Structural Functionalism

Structural functionalist analysis examines social institutions and other elements of society in relation to the social system as a whole. It is sometimes known as the order perspective because it is concerned with factors that ensure the maintenance of social stability. As the name suggests, structural functionalism examines phenomena by asking questions about what functions they serve and how they contribute to the orderly operation of the social system. Formal education, for example, serves the social order by transmitting vital knowledge and social aptitudes to successive generations and by sorting and selecting people for entry into roles or positions required by the social system.

Structural functionalist analysis commonly employs an organic analogy in which societies are compared to living organisms. Each part of the social system, like each feature of the organism, has specific roles to play to keep the organism alive and functioning properly. Some functions are more crucial than others to the unit's overall health and existence, but with increasing specialization, as the unit becomes more complex in nature, the system's survival requires each element to be integrated with the others in a unified way. Sociological analysis, as with the analysis of organic structures, proceeds to describe these interrelationships and to identify the conditions required for social stability. The long-term survival of society, according to this analysis, requires that elements (whether individuals or institutional processes) that do not fit with the whole, or are not functioning properly, must be eliminated or modified, analogous to the Western medical treatment of a diseased body.

Although the perspective is highly abstract through its concern with general features of social systems, research conducted by structural functionalists tends to be positivistic in nature. It seeks to outline regular relationships among phenomena through measurement of specific social dimensions, such as degrees of socio-economic inequality, pupil dropout rates, or racial categorizations. In their assumptions that the social world has a definite, observable structure that can be made known through scientific investigation, structural functionalists often attempt to give sociology the status of a more established natural science like physics or biology.

Structural functionalism was highly influential in the development of North American sociological theory and research throughout much of the twentieth century. Its major contributions have been to demonstrate the impact of social structures on social groups and individuals and to point out how various components of societies are interrelated. Nonetheless, the limitations of structural functionalism are evident in a critical examination of many of its central assumptions and procedures.

A first major criticism is most apparent to sociologists who adopt an interpretative orientation to social analysis. Structural functionalism, in its concern to 'map out' the social system and its constituent structures, ignores much of the richness of everyday life. It is frequently open to the charge that it portrays society in such a mechanistic way that it has no place for the activities and realities of living human beings, who in fact are the producers (or agents) of society and social change.

Critical sociologists have pointed to a second main limitation of structural functionalism: its emphasis on social order and consensus tends to undermine or draw attention away from struggles or tensions that operate within society. Many conflicts are more than merely transitional in nature; indeed, significant social divisions may be built into the structure of a given society. Therefore, inequalities and power struggles may be a normal rather than an abnormal occurrence. Social order, when it is evident, may itself be the consequence of political force rather than an indicator of widespread agreement about social goals. The use of coercion to achieve social stability is most obvious in societies ruled by totalitarian regimes, but it is a regular feature of life even in democratic societies. Taken together, these major criticisms sometimes portray structural functionalism as an approach limited by its attempts to impose order and control arbitrarily onto social circumstances rather than to subject them to sustained analytical inquiry.

Interpretative Analysis

Sociologists who work within interpretative traditions portray the social world as produced and interpreted by human activity. As the name of one important branch of interpretative sociology—symbolic interactionism—denotes, the main focal points for social analysis are social interactions and social symbols. People develop and share meanings with one another as they engage in social activity and attempt to make sense of their activity within a social context.

Interpretative sociology, in contrast with structural functionalism, is concerned with the analysis of social processes rather than social structures. Structures serve as guidelines for interaction that comes into being, and can be changed or modified through social activities. Individuals act, comprehend, and have motives; social structures do not. The world, viewed this way, is seen to be 'socially constructed' because the nature and meaning of social reality have no existence independent of our relations with other people, either at a face-to-face level or through the language, beliefs, knowledge, and modes of communication created and shared by people.

Because sociology and other scientific investigations are forms of social activity, scientific data and observations, like other social products, must be understood in terms of how they are processed by the human mind. Science, therefore, is subject to varying interpretations, as are other forms of social interaction. These insights do not mean that it is impossible to conduct scientific inquiry into the social world. Rather, our understanding of science (whether we are studying society or the natural world) must take into account the importance of human values and interpretations in shaping the world and how we see it.

Interpretative analysis is sometimes called microsociology because it is concerned with patterns of interaction at an everyday, interpersonal level, as opposed to the broader, macrosociological orientation of structural functionalism and much critical sociology. While it may seem that the individualistic starting point is not sociological because it does not focus on social structures, it is important to recognize that interpretative analysis studies individuals as participants in social interaction and shared meaning rather than as isolated units. The task of sociology, presented this way, is to help people develop a clear awareness of their own identities and subjectivity, their relations with others, and their place within society.

Interpretative sociology makes a valuable contribution to sociological analysis by showing the importance of our interactions with other people. It highlights the significance of everyday encounters and situations, and emphasizes how meanings are created and shared through social interaction. As opposed to structural forms of analysis that emphasize society at more abstract levels, it places active human beings at the core of sociological inquiry.

Despite its insights, interpretative sociology often fails to provide a comprehensive analysis of social life. The tendency within this approach to focus on immediate social settings is more oriented to description than to explanation. This ahistorical emphasis makes it relatively unable to explain problems such as how it is possible for enduring social inequalities to persist or how broad social positions and expectations may change. In the analysis of education, for example, an emphasis on interactions within the classroom is often unconnected with social structures and practices that shape the organization of the classroom, the curriculum, and the forces that condition the opportunities and experiences of the educational participants. Similarly, an acknowledgement that particular social circumstances and definitions are socially constructed does not necessarily indicate whose definitions are employed or what barriers stand in the way of attempts to introduce new definitions and social constructions.

Critical Sociologies

Various forms of critical analysis have been posed as alternatives to the traditional variants of sociology represented by structural functionalism and interpretative analysis. Critical analysis, as the term suggests, engages in a critique of social structures and practices by probing beyond descriptions of the status quo. The social world, as opposed to something neutral or mutually beneficial to all its members, is characterized by fundamental structural inequalities constituted in part by oppression by dominant groups over subordinate social groups. Critical sociology, in this regard, is committed to social change as well as to social analysis. This does not mean that the approach is unscientific. Instead, in common with interpretative approaches, it argues that science is a necessary human activity uncovering aspects of social reality that tend to be hidden from us in our everyday lives.

These characteristics can be illustrated with reference to two main branches of critical analysis, Marxism and feminism. Marxist analysis emphasizes that class, defined according to ownership and control of productive resources, is the fundamental basis of social inequality and oppression. Feminist analysis sees patriarchy, or male domination of personal and institutional life, as the primary basis of social differentiation. From different starting points, both Marxist and feminist approaches share the view that extensive analysis is required to uncover the dynamics and roots of social oppression and structured inequalities. Both theoretical stances also share a common commitment to changing repressive social conditions, although each contains varying assessments of the nature of, and strategies to advance, social change.

Despite this common ground, there are important differences among particular forms of critical analysis. Even general orientations to analysis such as Marxism and feminism contain sharply divergent approaches. Whereas radical feminism and orthodox Marxism, for example, disagree fundamentally about the origins of social

Box 1.2 Research Orientations in the Sociology of Education

Research, particularly through the systematic collection and analysis of data, is a fundamental part of any scientific discipline. Just as there are differences in how sociologists understand and explain educational problems, researchers in the sociology of education employ a wide range of research approaches and methodologies in their work. This work has produced important new knowledge and provided support or countervailing evidence related to existing theoretical insights. Sociological research on education has also introduced or popularized many significant methodological innovations. Émile Durkheim, whose work provided an explicit empirical and methodological foundation for early social scientific research, explored educational issues throughout his career.

Major studies on the impact that schooling had on social inequality across generations have introduced advanced statistical techniques into social science research in North America, Europe, and other regions since the mid-1950s, while research based at the University of Chicago and other places has provided a long tradition of innovative qualitative analysis of education. Detailed records, reports, and massive statistical databases—collected and maintained by national and provincial governments, international bodies such as UNESCO, and other central agencies involved in education—often serve as rich data sources for educational researchers.

However, these resources can have limited utility for researchers who may not be able to gain access to them and who may require information collected for different purposes and categorized in different ways from those determined by the sponsoring agencies. Recent emphasis in fields like education and health care on the use of empirical research evidence for policy and professional decision-making has provided an impetus for large-scale initiatives to co-ordinate more systematically research initiatives, databases, and findings. In the United States, the implementation of federal legislation designated the 'No Child Left Behind Act' of 2001 represents one of the most visible examples of evidence-based decision-making in education. On a more modest and less controversial scale, initiatives in Canada, such as the creation of the Canadian Council on Learning in 2004, have provided new opportunities for researchers, policymakers, and other partners to co-ordinate research-related activities focused on key dimensions of education and lifelong learning.

Educational researchers typically rely on data collected from a variety of sources. While some specialize in quantitative methodologies and techniques, drawing upon data collected through secondary sources as well as surveys and instruments they have developed through their own research, others employ qualitative methods such as interviews, focus groups, observation, documentary analysis, and narrative accounts. Many combine research methods in order to gain a richer understanding of educational structures, practices, and meanings. Throughout the book, references are made to findings derived from studies and approaches that represent an extensive range of these diverse orientations.

oppression and how best to conduct social research, Marxist feminism and socialist feminism argue that the two approaches can be highly compatible.

Critical educational theories have been subject to recent challenges both internally and externally. Within critical analysis, proponents of various positions have often dismissed or ignored possibilities for shared insights such as an exploration of how factors like class, gender, and race interact with one another or an assessment of strategies for effective educational and social change. Shifting economic, cultural, and political alignments, along with increasing attention to challenges associated with globalization, new technologies, and environmental issues, have also been accompanied by new ways of thinking about the social world and relations between people and nature.

Several researchers, drawing on interpretative analysis, postmodernist critiques, and insights developed within other disciplines, have argued that no single approach is sufficient to provide an adequate understanding either of education or, more broadly, of human life in general (Davies, 1995; Kanpol, 1992). Postmodern thought, in particular, has emerged as a theoretical alternative suggesting that contemporary social life and personal experiences are so multidimensional and fragmented that no unified theory or set of ideas can adequately explain social reality. Despite these challenges, however, critical educational perspectives are able to demonstrate their resiliency when they identify issues and present analytical tools that not only advance our understanding of social problems but also seek to find effective solutions to them.

EMERGING DIRECTIONS IN THE CRITICAL ANALYSIS OF EDUCATION

This book adopts a critical stance towards the analysis of education, in particular drawing on four interrelated forms of critical analysis that have influenced recent thinking about educational matters: critical pedagogy, feminist pedagogy, antiracism education, and political economy. They will be outlined briefly here, discussed more fully in Chapter 2, and integrated into the analysis employed in subsequent chapters.

Critical Pedagogy

Critical pedagogy is influenced by several critical traditions and motivated by the desire to integrate educational theory and educational practice. Like Marxism and feminism, its advocates emphasize the deeply rooted power imbalances and social inequalities that infuse schooling structures and processes. In common with interpretative and postmodern analysis, critical pedagogy also stresses the symbolic

importance of knowledge, language, and social action within educational practices. Education has both cultural and economic significance as a mechanism that
gives shape and meaning to people's life experiences, thereby reinforcing the privileges of advantaged groups relative to powerless segments of society. Educational
practices, according to critical pedagogy, must be restructured to represent the
voices and experiences of all social groups, not just those who have sufficient
resources and power to advance their own interests.

Feminist Pedagogy

Feminist pedagogy, like critical pedagogy, challenges the common view that education is neutral, and commits itself to transform the education system as a consequence of the critique it offers. **Feminist pedagogy** argues that educational
theory and practice must take into account the differential experiences, life
chances, and ways of knowing that prevail for men and women in society. As
teachers, mothers, and students, women tend to be excluded from key roles in educational decision-making and research, which thereby serves both to reflect and to
perpetuate their socio-economic subordination relative to men. As a basis for
achieving the true function of education, which is the empowerment of human
beings, feminist pedagogy seeks to sensitize educators, students, and researchers to
the ways in which gender structures men's and women's lives.

Anti-Racism Education

Educational approaches informed by anti-racism emphasize the powerful social
impact of inequalities and ideologies based on race. **Anti-racism education** aligns
itself with critical and feminist pedagogies in its quest to empower marginalized
persons, while it shares with political economy a critique of material circumstances that produce fundamental social inequalities. Educational institutions and
the knowledge and practices associated with them are implicated in the production and legitimation of racial discrimination and other forms of racism.
However, schooling and post-secondary education can play a crucial role in working to address these problems.

Political Economy

Political economy stresses the interrelationships that prevail among the various
segments of society, including the economic, political, and social realms. Like other
approaches, there are various strands within political economy, ranging from traditional and liberal thought to orthodox Marxist perspectives. This book is
informed by recent developments in critical political economy that examine the
interplay among class, race, gender, and other central factors that shape and are
shaped by people's life experiences. This approach argues that in order to make sense
of social reality, we must examine how people collectively produce and reproduce
both the material and symbolic conditions of their social existence. Education,
viewed this way, has importance as a site in which people's personalities and life
options take shape through interaction among the characteristics and experiences

they bring with them into educational settings, the structures and practices that constitute education on an ongoing basis, and the linkages between education and the socio-economic context within which it operates. More recent political economic analysis, informed by practices associated with globalization, has shifted its focus from education in specific national or regional settings in order to understand linkages with comparative and international dimensions of education.

CONCLUSION

The sociology of education, parallel to the educational realities it seeks to investigate and explain, is a multi-faceted and changing endeavour. It is essential to maintain sufficient scope and diversity in the analysis of education in order to capture the richness of education in its various forms. At the same time, because educational research and theory can be used to guide policy and practice, we must ensure that our understanding of educational matters develops in a comprehensive way, based as much as possible on complete and accurate information that is sensitive to its potential impact on people's lives.

The task to develop a socially meaningful understanding of education is especially daunting at a time when education faces serious challenges often considered to be of crisis proportions. Canada's growing integration into new global economic and political alignments is forcing a reassessment of how education should best be employed for competitive advantage. Significant changes occurring across institutional spheres of contemporary life are accompanied by transformations in how we engage with and make sense of our identities and our relations with social and natural environments. Educational reform and reorganization are further promoted through changing government priorities and operations, important demographic and economic transformations, and strategies developed in response to issues related to regional diversity, national unity, and shifting global relations. Media attention and public outcries periodically focused on real or imagined concerns such as declining educational standards, intolerable illiteracy and school dropout rates, lack of discipline and respect for authority, increasing crime rates among young offenders, and lack of moral guidance and focus among youth have drawn attention to the limitations of existing educational bureaucracies and to desires for accountability and choice in schooling. Changing gender relations, new patterns of immigration, and prospects for self-determination among First Nations have forced educational institutions to be increasingly responsive to issues of representation, cultural diversity, and equity. Shifting arrangements and tensions related to work, income, and family life, and transitions throughout the life course have carried over into schooling, creating pressures for increased flexibility and demands for new educational supports and services at the same time that budgetary needs for public education and social services must be justified in such a way as to ensure they do not fall behind other priorities.

In the chapters that follow, historical and contemporary dimensions of Canadian education, its structure and participants, and the challenges facing it are examined through critical sociological inquiry. Each chapter highlights a theme of particular importance within the sociology of education. Chapter 2 provides an overview of major theoretical approaches and issues, contrasting traditional perspectives with more recent critical analysis. Chapter 3 is concerned with the historical development of formal education in Canada, showing how divergent objectives and contestation have shaped educational policies and practices. Chapter 4 examines the organization and dimensions of contemporary education systems in Canada and other nations. Chapter 5 examines classroom interaction and educational practices, revealing how day-to-day educational activities reflect the tension between the need to produce distinct educational outcomes and less clearly delineated elements of human social development. Chapter 6 explores the nature and development of teaching, analyzing how teachers' work is subject to many of the same forces, such as control by external managers and demands for increased productivity, as other occupations—at the same time as its orientations to educational and social processes lend it a unique professional character. Chapter 7 addresses the relationship between education and work, highlighting in particular the notion that, contrary to persistent demands that schooling and work training should be more closely linked, the nature and purposes of formal education also are determined by other competing priorities. Chapter 8 highlights the ways in which education contributes to both socio-economic opportunity and the reproduction of structured inequalities among various segments of the population. Chapter 9 draws together key themes covered in the previous chapters, focusing in particular on alternative visions of educational reform framed through diverse social and economic vantage points in a context in which the composition of educational participants and expectations about education's social and economic roles are changing rapidly. The discussion links contemporary debates over such issues as educational finance, accountability and choice, technological change, and social inclusion to accommodate diverse educational communities. These related debates reveal the importance of education to fundamental social and political choices and directions.

ANNOTATED FURTHER READINGS

Apple, Michael W. 1999. *Power, Meaning, and Identity: Essays in Critical Educational Studies.* New York: Peter Lang Publishing. This collection of papers by one of the most influential critical analysts of education in North America offers perspectives on issues, practices, and developments central to education systems.

Ballantine, Jeanne H., and Joan Z. Spade, eds. 2008. *Schools and Society: A Sociological Approach to Education,* 3rd edn. Thousand Oaks, Calif.: Pine Forge Press. This collection draws together excerpts from several classic contributions to the sociology of education as well as more recent research contributions, particularly from the United States. Core topics include school organization and relationships, social and political contexts of schooling, equity and inequality, higher education, educational reform, and globalization.

Davies, Scott, and Neil Guppy. 2006. *The Schooled Society: An Introduction to the Sociology of Education.* Toronto: Oxford University Press. The authors offer an introduction to core themes and concepts in the sociological analysis of education that enable us to understand how schools are organized, and how they select and socialize students, in order to fulfill social requirements associated with the emergence of contemporary knowledge-based economies.

Dei, George J. Sefa, Irma Marcia James, Leeno Luke Karumanchery, Sonia James-Wilson, and Jasmin Zine. 2000. *Removing the Margins: The Challenges and Possibilities of Inclusive Schooling.* Toronto: Canadian Scholars' Press. Drawing on varied accounts and experiences with Canadian schooling, the authors outline a framework for the creation of inclusive educational practices that focus on how educational success must be oriented to the needs of students from diverse social and cultural backgrounds.

Jenks, Chris, ed. 1998. *Core Sociological Dichotomies.* London: Sage. The contributors to this edited collection provide an introduction to sociology through an overview of the central debates and themes the discipline is concerned with, including structure/agency, fact/value, local/global, race/ethnicity, and numerous others.

Lauder, Hugh, Phillip Brown, Jo-Anne Dillabough, and A.H. Halsey, eds. 2006. *Education, Globalization, and Social Change.* Oxford: Oxford University Press. This is one of the most comprehensive collections to analyze contemporary education systems from a variety of perspectives, with contributions highlighting theoretical developments, substantive issues, and research findings from leading researchers representing diverse disciplinary and national contexts.

KEY TERMS

Agency Recognition that human beings act on the basis of various degrees of choice and free will.

Anti-racism education An approach to educational theory and practice oriented to identifying and changing attitudes, policies, and practices that discriminate on the basis of race.

Critical pedagogy An approach oriented to progressive educational change by linking educational practices and experiences with social critique and a vision of educational alternatives.

Education The process by which human beings learn and develop capacities through understanding of their social and natural environments, which takes place in both formal and informal settings.

Feminist pedagogy An approach to educational analysis grounded in a critique of gender inequalities in education and the factors that give rise to them, and committed to practices to change those inequalities.

Interpretative analysis An approach to understanding social life that emphasizes the role played by meanings and intersubjective relationships in social activity.

Political economy An approach that emphasizes the interrelationships among social, economic, and political factors in social life; critical political economy examines the causes and consequences of deep-rooted forms of social and economic inequality.

Positivism A philosophic approach that emphasizes sensory experience as the basis for all knowledge, applied as a scientific framework that seeks to derive and test laws based on empirical evidence from systematic observation and measurement.

Schooling Education systems and processes organized through formal educational institutions.

Social structure Elements of social life that are relatively patterned, interconnected, and enduring, often understood with reference to the rules and boundaries associated with different forms of social action.

Sociology An academic discipline concerned with the nature and organization of societies and the relationships that exist among individuals and societies.

Study Questions

1. What is education? How does education differ from schooling and training?
2. Why is it important to examine education from different disciplines and perspectives?
3. Discuss the relationship between sociology and other disciplines with respect to the analysis of educational issues. What distinct contributions can a sociological analysis make to an understanding of education?
4. How important are educational credentials to social participation and advancement in contemporary societies? To what extent can, or should, factors other than formal education be used to assess a person's employment prospects?
5. What major social and economic forces need to be taken into account for an adequate understanding of education?

Chapter 2

Sociological Theories of Education

Introduction

Theories exist to help people explain how and why particular phenomena occur as they do. They are employed as tools that enable us to make sense of the world, and are systematically developed from existing knowledge and tested against empirical evidence.

Sociological theories of education have arisen to explain everything from why some people fail and others succeed to problems of educational finance and everyday classroom interaction. It is sometimes difficult to categorize and assess the importance of sociological theories of education. Because particular groups, including educational administrators, governments, educational participants, and researchers in several academic disciplines, conduct educational research for different reasons, theories of education often are either absent from research or else are highly diversified and scattered in nature. As Parelius and Parelius (1987: 15) warn about the proliferation of educational research findings that are not unified into any theoretical perspectives, 'A glut of discrete findings, with no organizing framework, can be as useless as the untested speculations of the "armchair" theorist.' At the same time, it can be an imposing task to make sense of the sometimes bewildering array of theoretical alternatives in a field like the sociology of education, which is commonly characterized as being in a 'constant state of flux' represented in the '3Ds' of divergence, disagreement, and difference (Levinson and Sadovnik, 2002: 3).

Building on the central sociological questions discussed in Chapter 1, this chapter examines representative theories of education. The discussion starts with a consideration of each of the three main theoretical perspectives, identified as structural functionalism, interpretative sociology, and critical analysis, as a framework to explore debates among proponents of these approaches as well as a foundation out of which have emerged various hybrid theories and critical alternatives. The discussion of sociological theories of education in this chapter illustrates significant issues and models of analysis that characterize each approach, rather than being exhaustive and comprehensive in nature, and culminates by considering guidelines for an adequate understanding of educational problems.

Structural Functionalism and Liberal Theory

The earliest influential sociological theories of education emerged within structural functionalist analysis. In the late nineteenth and early twentieth centuries, French sociologist Émile Durkheim, one of the first writers to develop an explicitly sociological framework, made the examination of education systems a central part of his analysis of society. The crucial problem that guided Durkheim's sociological inquiry is one that lies at the heart of **structural functionalism**—'Why does the individual, while becoming more autonomous, depend more upon society?' (Durkheim, 1933: 37). Durkheim's concern, which remains highly significant today, arose from the observation that it was necessary to discover the bases of cohesion or solidarity that keep societies from disintegrating amid an increase in individualism, individual rights, and self-interest. Durkheim stressed education's importance as an integrative and regulative mechanism that would bind people together and help them develop consciousness of their responsibilities and relationships within the wider society. He emphasized that societies, like individuals, have unique characteristics that set them apart from others. The purpose of formal education is to provide each individual with the knowledge and capabilities that are essential for meaningful participation in particular societal contexts. Education, understood in this way:

> is the influence exercised by adult generations on those that are not yet ready for social life. Its object is to arouse and to develop in the child a certain number of physical, intellectual, and moral states which are demanded of [him or her] by both the political society as a whole and the special milieu for which [he or she] is specifically destined. (Durkheim, 1956: 71)

For Durkheim, the task of sociology with respect to education and other social facts is, therefore, to uncover and specify the 'normal' characteristics for any given society in order to ensure closer integration between the individual and society and among all members of that society. Durkheim's writings on education have received less attention than other aspects of his work among sociologists. Nonetheless, recurrent themes in his work, such as a concern to preserve social solidarity, have gained recent prominence as social policy-makers turn to educational solutions to problems associated with social diversity and cohesion.

Durkheim's assumption—that a core set of social factors is general and shared widely within a society—is a defining feature of structural functionalist and liberal analysis. The work of Talcott Parsons, extending many of Durkheim's insights to the analysis of American social systems, represents the functionalist view that central social institutions like the education system play a key role in maintaining social order. Parsons, like Durkheim, views the task of schools to be more complex than simply to transmit knowledge and values to students. Rather, such knowledge and values are to be internalized by individuals as part of their personalities. The properly 'schooled' person is one who knows intuitively and can act productively on the expectations, rules, and behaviours that accompany and give shape to social life.

Parsons (1959) conveys the most central assumptions and propositions of structural functionalist analysis in his article 'The School Class as a Social System: Some of Its Functions in American Society'. As the article's title suggests, Parsons portrays schools as social systems that reflect and serve in the interests of the wider society. Within industrial democracies, schools exist to channel individuals from the emotional, person-centred demands of home and family life to the more formalized, competitive, and achievement-oriented world of work and public life. In the primary grades, for instance, school subjects are not rigidly divided like they are in high school. Rather, emphasis is on learning fundamental social and intellectual skills without comprehensive testing, and pupils are taught by one teacher (usually a woman, to provide continuity from the mother figure in the home environment). In progressively higher grades, however, there is greater emphasis on competitiveness, merit-based performance, and instruction by several teachers, primarily men, akin to the structure and division of labour that prevail in the workplace (Parsons, 1959: 314–15). Schools, in these regards, have two primary functions—allocation and socialization—that contribute to the maintenance of the social system. First, schooling, through the mechanisms of grading, granting credentials, and more informal selection processes, sorts individuals to fill distinct positions in the social hierarchy. Second, schooling contributes to individual personality formation by inculcating the dispositions necessary for successful participation in general social life as well as those that are suited for the specific social roles and experiences that accompany each person's expected social position.

Structural functionalist analysis, as illustrated clearly in the work of both Durkheim and Parsons, offers a particular perspective on the question of schools' role in social reproduction. Structural functionalists view social reproduction, the process by which social order and continuity are maintained from generation to generation, as consensual and harmonious in nature. Much like in a natural ecosystem, the normal state of society is portrayed as one in which each element (including individuals and institutions) plays a specific part that combines and is interdependent with others in such a way that the vitality of the whole system is maintained. Because all members of an organization or society have a stake in the system, there is an emphasis on mutual respect and common goals. While tensions and conflict may emerge, a successful social organization is seen as one that is able to develop mechanisms to manage conflict and change and reduce the possibility that they may cause damage to the social or institutional system.

Some structural functionalist writers carry these notions further by highlighting what they call the hidden curriculum. Whereas the formal curriculum conveys the social expectations attached to learning and educational outcomes, the hidden curriculum refers to the more informal or less explicitly defined characteristics that, nonetheless, are regular features of the schooling process. School-based learning consists of much more than simply the content of lessons, textbooks, and rules that students are presented with. Important knowledge and skills are also conveyed by daily participation, extended over several years, within the social context of schooling. Students learn values of conformity, competitiveness, deferred gratification, obedience to authority, and adjustment to success and failure through their experiences in classrooms and other school settings (see, especially, Dreeben, 1968; Jackson, 1968).

Box 2.1 A Functionalist Perspective on the Sociology of Education

Talcott Parsons (1959: 277–8) has presented one of the most influential structural functionalist accounts of education in his discussion of the socialization and allocative functions of schooling:

Our main interest, then, is in a dual problem: first of how the school class functions to internalize in its pupils both the commitments and capacities for successful performance of their future adult roles, and second of how it functions to allocate these human resources within the role-structure of the adult society. The primary ways in which these two problems are interrelated will provide our main points of reference.

First, from the functional point of view the school class can be treated as an agency of socialization. That is to say, it is an agency through which individual personalities are trained to be motivationally and technically adequate to the performance of adult roles. It is not the sole such agency; the family, informal 'peer groups', churches, and sundry voluntary organizations all play a part, as does actual on-the-job training. But, in the period extending from entry into first grade until entry into the labor force or marriage, the school class may be regarded as the focal socializing agency.

The socialization function may be summed up as the development in individuals of the commitments and capacities which are essential prerequisites of their future role-performance. Commitments may be broken down in turn into two components: commitment to the implementation of the broad values of society, and commitment to the performance of a specific type of role within the structure of society. Thus a person in a relatively humble occupation may be a 'solid citizen' in the sense of commitment to honest work in that occupation, without an intensive and sophisticated concern with the implementation of society's higher-level values. Or conversely, someone else might object to the anchorage of the feminine role in marriage and the family on the grounds that such anchorage keeps society's total talent resources from being distributed equitably to business, government, and so on. Capacities can also be broken down into two components, the first being competence or the skill to perform the tasks involved in the individual's roles, and the second being 'role-responsibility' or the capacity to live up to other people's expectations of the interpersonal behavior appropriate to these roles. Thus a mechanic as well as a doctor needs to have not only the basic 'skills of his trade', but also the ability to behave responsibly toward those people with whom he is brought into contact in his work.

While on the one hand, the school class may be regarded as a primary agency by which these different components of commitments and capacities are generated, on the other hand, it is, from the point of view of the society, an agency of 'manpower' allocation. It is well known that in American society there is a very high, and probably increasing, correlation between one's status level in the society and one's level of educational attainment. Both social status and educational level are obviously related to the occupational status which is attained. Now, as a result of the general process of both educational and occupational upgrading, completion of high school is increasingly coming to be the norm for minimum satisfactory educational attainment, and the most significant line for future occupational status has come to be drawn between members of an age-cohort who do and do not go to college.

Source: Reprinted by permission of *Harvard Educational Review.*

It is useful to consider here a central assumption of structural functionalist analysis, the presupposition that social stratification and inequality are necessary structural features of advanced societies. The reproduction of society involves an assumed hierarchy of positions that must be filled with suitably qualified and motivated people. This requirement gives rise to the specified functions of schooling, including the tasks of sorting and socializing individuals and contributing to common values. As long as the social system appears to be operating smoothly, with no threats to the system's breakdown, few questions are raised about the kinds of values and inequalities being fostered or about which groups, if any, are their main beneficiaries.

The assumptions about consensus and stratification in structural functionalist theory focus attention on the identification of mechanisms that will assure that the social reproduction process operates effectively and efficiently. In the late 1950s and 1960s, theoretical consideration of the link between schooling and socio-economic needs was enhanced by policy concerns to produce a scientifically and technically sophisticated workforce. Rapid expansion of industrial production and mass-marketed goods and services were stimulated by a combination of factors, including military production in World War II and the subsequent Cold War, the creation of new household consumer products, and relatively high wages and stable labour markets. In North America, the 'space race' between the Soviet Union and the United States served as a symbolic rallying point around which new workforce requirements, driven by science and technological knowledge, were to be implemented. At the same time, the promise of social and economic security fostered growing emphasis on the domestic sphere and the cultivation of closer ties between schools and family life. Schools figured prominently in these transitions, as enrolments were boosted by rising birth rates associated with the post-war 'baby boom' and new educational activities that accompanied expectations about domestic life and leisure-time activities. Educational expansion was further fuelled by demands for a more highly educated labour force and a scientifically grounded curriculum to train experts and service workers required by the new economy. Subsequently, social scientists interested in the prospects education held for wider social and individual advancement extended functionalist orientations through a number of interrelated strands of structural and liberal analysis, including technological functionalism and **human capital theory**, which view education as an investment to stimulate productivity and economic growth.

One variant, status attainment research, emerged as a means to provide empirical evidence that would test the strength of linkages among background characteristics (like gender, race, and socio-economic status), formal education, and other life chances. The research findings, typically drawn from large-scale quantitative data, consistently demonstrate the pervasive nature of social inequality, but are surrounded by conflicting interpretations. Blau and Duncan (1967), for example, suggest that their data offer support for the Parsonian thesis that education has come to replace family background as the primary determinant of occupational placement in the United States. However, other high-profile empirical analyses, notably the Coleman Report (Coleman et al., 1966) and the work of Jencks et al. (1972) in the United States and Floud, Halsey, and Martin (1956) in the UK, attribute the origins of social inequality more to the home and other non-school sites than to schooling. Coleman (1968) emphasizes, as well, that it is crucial to distinguish between equality of results and equality of opportunity. Schools cannot compensate for social disparities on their own, but they can make an impact by providing enriched learning conditions that give all students the chance to compete for access to desired social positions. With respect to Canadian data, Porter (1965) provides a functionalist analysis of education's contribution to social mobility, but adds the important proviso that domination by elites, selected through social factors such as class, ethnicity, and religious affiliation, places limits on the opportunity structure.

It is noteworthy that the studies cited above, conducted primarily between the mid-1950s and the late 1960s, reflect an optimistic faith in education's ability to promote social progress and democratic opportunities. While the optimism is sometimes tempered with warnings that social reforms may be required to fulfill the promise of schooling, very little in these studies challenges the prevailing liberal and functionalist assumptions that inequality is socially necessary. What becomes crucially important is that social stratification must be seen to be based on open and fair selection mechanisms. The major point of debate concerns the degree to which schools could or could not contribute to the equalization of opportunities. It is perhaps not surprising, therefore, that status attainment research, like human capital theory, frequently has been cited to justify social policies and reforms that affect practices both within and outside of education systems. Both the Coleman Report in the United States and the Plowden Report (Central Advisory Council for Education, 1967) in England, for instance, were commissioned by the respective governments as tools to address issues of poverty and provide initiatives to stimulate the social and economic advancement of disadvantaged groups. They drew from structural functionalism the relatively optimistic and unquestioning assumption about the role of education in the service of individual, social, and economic development, although this view was sometimes tempered by research findings and philosophical orientations that gave rise to skepticism about how much difference schooling, at least in its present forms, could make to social change.

Another influential strand of liberal analysis, *educational progressivism*, offers a critique of existing social arrangements, but retains faith in the ability of schools to improve those conditions. Originating within the nineteenth-century progressive movement that promoted a humanistic vision of social change guided by the state, educational progressivism contributed most strongly to a restructuring of educational thought and practice in the early part of the twentieth century. Sociologist Jane Addams (1910) promoted social improvement through co-operation and democratic social ethics, integrating education, social theory, and community-based practice in order to encourage the collective realization of social benefits for all members of society. Interest in this work has been revitalized through recent initiatives to promote lifelong learning, community–school collaboration, and stronger integration of formal education with other social experiences.

John Dewey, probably the best-known advocate of educational progressivism, was influenced by Marx as well as by liberal theory, and also was an associate of Addams, as well as G.H. Mead and other interpretative sociologists at the University of Chicago. Like Marx, Dewey (1966) was critical of a growing uniformity of life within industrial capitalism and advocated the creation of more meaningful connections between school and practical experience. However, reflecting his liberal orientations, Dewey promoted schooling as a mechanism that would ameliorate such pressing social problems as poverty, crime, ethnic antagonism, and social dislocation caused by rapid urbanization, industrialization, and economic change. Dewey sought to replace the adherence to routine and orientation to future rewards in traditional education with child-centred educational practices. He contended that schools should act autonomously from the industrial system and its inherent dangers in order to foster individual growth and social responsibility.

Dewey's progressive, humanistic philosophy seemingly was at odds with some of the major educational reforms derived from industry early in the twentieth century. Influential administrative reformers like Ellwood Cubberly, J.F. Bobbitt, and R.W. Tyler advanced the implementation of rational models of educational management and curriculum construction based on the application of scientific principles to school organization and practice. These approaches, in stark contrast to the liberal emphasis on human development, portrayed education as an endeavour that should be planned and operated as an efficient business enterprise. There was, however, an affinity between the scientific management of schooling and the progressive vision of a better society produced through the intervention of state authorities and scientific expertise. The convergence of these orientations contributed to growing emphasis in the 1920s and 1930s on such innovations as psychological testing of student intelligence and aptitudes, systematic curriculum planning, increased demarcation of school subjects and grade levels, especially at the high school level, bureaucratic school administrative structures, and streaming of pupils by programs and ability.

Progressivism re-emerged as an influential force in educational practice and theory in the 1960s and 1970s. Educational reforms such as 'open' classrooms, curricula and teaching styles that emphasized pupil choice and participation, sensitivity to learners' backgrounds and values, and awareness of the relevance of schooling to everyday life signified a supposed shift from traditional to progressive educational philosophies in an era characterized by widespread challenges to authority and prevailing social structures. Some critics, labelled by Carnoy and Levin (1985: 16–17) as critical progressives, condemned the schools for perpetuating rather than eradicating the problems of mass society, 'arguing that far from being an instrument of social progress, education was actually deadening—much more oriented to producing failure than to developing creative, critical minds that could be the basis for a more humanistic, democratic society.'

The titles of significant studies from this period—*How Children Fail* (Holt, 1964), *Death at an Early Age: The Destruction of the Hearts and Minds of Negro Children in the Boston Public Schools* (Kozol, 1967), and *De-Schooling Society* (Illich, 1970)—convey the message that schools foster, at best, boredom and restricted opportunities for success or, worse, dehumanization and habituation into destructive routines. Unlike the more optimistic assessment of the possibilities that schooling contains for a democratic society, as advanced by educational progressivism, the critical progressive stance contends that schools are not organized and equipped to fulfill their promise and overcome the damaging aspects of the hidden curriculum. These arguments have influenced many proponents of home schooling and other recent movements to adopt alternative forms of educational delivery. Nonetheless, in common with other liberal approaches, these orientations tend to give less prominence to analysis of the root causes of educational problems than to a preoccupation with individual bases of success, failure, and opportunities.

The theories that have been examined in this section have pointed to the real and potential contributions made by formal education to social and economic development. With a few exceptions, they portray education as a progressive force that can expand opportunities for individuals as well as for whole societies. The key to a successful education system is the establishment of mechanisms that will ensure a proper 'fit' between individuals' social background, on the one hand, and the demands of the social system, on the other.

Structural functionalism is rarely employed as an explicit theoretical orientation in current educational research, in part because of some of the problems outlined below, as well as the impact that newer theoretical frameworks have had on the field. However, structural functionalism is highly significant for its formative impact on the development of the sociology of education. It has drawn attention to crucial questions about the relationship between education and other spheres of social life as well as to the role that persistent social inequalities play in advanced societies.

Liberal analyses of education, by contrast, have remained popular among both academic researchers and policy-makers due to their generally optimistic assessment about prospects for expanding individual opportunity and social productivity. Several writers have suggested, as well, that Durkheim's educational analysis warrants rehabilitation as societies look for solutions to challenges posed by social diversity, moral uncertainty, changing relations between individualism and community, and issues of citizenship in a global context (Walford and Pickering, 1998).

Despite their influence, there are several important limitations to structural functionalist and liberal theories of education. In particular, the theoretical model tends to offer a description of an ideal state of affairs rather than an explanation of social reality. As will be documented later, much substantial evidence runs contrary to, or at least makes questionable, the assumption of a meritocratic social structure in which educational achievement and individual effort, and not one's social origins, account for social success or failure. Even when there is a clear relationship between educational achievement and social status or occupational attainment, it is necessary to consider whether schooling reinforces or eradicates social inequalities already in existence. The impact of such factors as wealth, control and restructuring of jobs, and intrinsic rewards such as personal satisfaction with particular jobs or life situations is often not considered in the measuring of social and educational inequality. While inequality is a complex, changing phenomenon, it is also reproduced in both overt and subtle ways. Opportunities for social advancement may be restricted even if we assume that there is an open, fair, and meritorious process by which individuals are allocated to social positions. Functionalist and liberal analyses tend to overestimate the extent to which social reforms can contribute to social change, in the process ignoring or minimizing the significance of more deeply embedded power relations associated with class, gender, race, and related factors. By the late 1960s, the contradiction between promised socio-economic opportunities and people's life experiences resulted in a rethinking of liberal assumptions among many educational participants and analysts. Growing consciousness of the subordination of women and racial minorities, the emergence of the student protest movement, and the persistence of poverty produced a fertile environment in which alternative perspectives in academic research could flourish.

INTERPRETATIVE ANALYSIS OF SCHOOLING

Interpretative analysis has tended to focus on two features of schooling: (1) the meaning and nature of school practices for educational participants; and (2) the importance of language, knowledge, curricula, and other symbolic aspects of schooling. Learning and interaction with others are viewed as social processes, not simply as aspects of social positions and structures as they are portrayed within structural functionalist analysis. Consistent with a broad social constructivist orientation, interpretative sociologists argue that society and social outcomes are not fixed; rather, they are created, recreated, and modified continuously by human activity. Schooling, in this view, is a site of perpetual adjustment as participants attempt to decipher and share meanings with one another and, in the process, shape their personalities and lives. As expressed by Karl Mannheim (1936: 156):

> Modern education from its inception is a living struggle, a replica, on a small scale of the conflicting purposes and tendencies which rage in society at large. Accordingly, the educated [person is] . . . determined in a variety of ways.

In common with other approaches examined in this book, there are diverse roots and strands to the interpretative analysis of schooling.

Max Weber, whose work is at least as influential as that of his contemporary, Émile Durkheim, stressed the importance of education and educational credentials to the rationalization of society. Rationalization, for Weber, is a process that involves science, technical knowledge, and other elements related to systematic planning for the achievement of predetermined objectives. Rationality is perhaps most strongly apparent in bureaucratic organizations governed, at least in a formal sense, by written rules and procedures, a hierarchy of authority, impartial treatment of clients, and hiring and career advancement of officials based on formal credentials. In this context, formal education has special significance as a bureaucratic site in which training is systematically organized to provide individuals with necessary social attributes and legitimate credentials. While this analysis parallels that of functionalism in important respects, Weber is especially concerned with the ways in which credentials are used by officials and other interest groups to advance their own positions (see, e.g., Gerth and Mills, 1946: 240–4, 416ff.). Despite the overwhelming tendency towards control and predictability in modern life, in other words, Weber maintains that the processes by which these outcomes are sought or resisted are of utmost importance. Weber's work has given rise to later studies in both critical analysis and interpretative sociology.

One such approach, known as neo-Weberian analysis, employs Max Weber's theories of bureaucracy and power to analyze contemporary schooling. C. Wright Mills (1951, 1956), who adopts elements of both Marxian and Weberian analysis in his scathing social critique, argues that the process of rationalization has contributed to the rise of a mass society in which our lives are governed by a power elite of business, political, and military leaders. Formal education, particularly within private schools and colleges, is an important mechanism through which access to elite positions can be controlled and elite solidarity fostered. Schooling and training practices facilitate rational processes of planning and management so as to produce a cadre of technical experts.

Neo-Weberian analysis of power relations is often linked with conflict theories as well as with interpretative orientations. These connections are emphasized in the critique of the role of education in advanced industrial society offered by Randall Collins (1971), who disputes liberal functionalist arguments that increased technical requirements for skilled labour are responsible for the expansion of the public education system. Collins argues that the link between schooling and jobs is often marginal, and, in fact, that the skill requirements for many jobs have not increased. Rather, the increase in the levels of formal education required for entry

Box 2.2 An Interpretative Perspective on the Sociology of Education

Interpretative analysis emphasizes the meanings and interactions within schools and other social settings, highlighting their implications for social actors themselves. Ogle and Eckman (2002: 169–70, 184–5), analyzing media coverage of the tragic circumstances surrounding the shooting deaths of 15 persons in Columbine High School (CHS) in Colorado in 1999, illustrate the powerful role that socially constructed images—in this case focusing on dress codes—can play in our orientations to youth, violence, and identity:

> Even in articles published the day of the shootings, media writers invoked appearance as a potential explanation for this act of youth violence. Through this coverage, certain types of appearances were constructed as part of the Columbine problem. These appearances were linked to three different CHS social groups—the Trench Coat Mafia, the Goths, and the jocks—and consequently were imbued with meanings reflective of the values and lifestyles purportedly embraced by members of these groups. The identification of certain appearances as part of the Columbine problem—and thus, as in need of regulation—can be traced to numerous newspaper articles that included descriptions of the gunmen's appearances. . . .
>
> For example, the argument that control of the school environment can be achieved by control of student appearances echoes the premise that by regulating the dress of students, school officials can control the symbolic messages communicated by students' appearances and thereby direct their behaviors, interpersonal interactions, and thus the academic climate. A specific example of such logic can be found in the claim that by prohibiting dress symbols used to express group affiliation, and thereby disallowing the use of dress cues to identify another as a member of a certain peer group, schools could effectively reduce negative feedback exchanged (e.g., taunting) and hostile interactions among rival student groups such as the Trench Coat Mafia and the jocks. Similarly, banning appearances (e.g., black trench coats) that could communicate a message of affiliation with the gunmen or an inclination for violence so as to prevent altercations among individuals who might mistakenly define the situation (i.e., assume another is violent based on his or her dress and behavior, accordingly) also reflects the notion that humans use appearance symbols to assign identities, to formulate behavioral expectations, and to guide their interpersonal interactions.

Source: Paff Ogle, Jennifer, and Molly Eckman, 'Dress-Related Responses to the Columbine Shootings: Other-Imposed and Self-Designed', *Family and Consumer Sciences Research Journal.* © 2002 American Association of Family and Consumer Sciences. Reprinted by permission of SAGE publications.

into particular occupations is a consequence of competition among status groups. The major purpose of schooling, therefore, is to provide credentials and offer legitimacy to particular status cultures within the social and occupational structures. Murphy (1994), employing international and Canadian examples, extends Collins's analysis by showing that Weber's theory enables us to assess how credentials are used in different ways by both dominant and subordinate groups in various struggles over status and **cultural capital** (cultural resources). Teachers' associations, for instance, may rely on the credentials of their members as a way of distinguishing teachers from laypersons wanting to become involved in educational matters, but they may also seek support or alliances with political parties and other organized groups to protect their own interests against more powerful forces.

The interpretative analysis of schooling and other social institutions rose to prominence through a branch of investigation that came to be called the Chicago School of sociology. This approach, which continues to have a strong influence within the discipline, was most active in the 1920s through the work of sociologists at the University of Chicago, who used their dynamic city, with its changing mix of industry, urban development, and social composition, as a living laboratory. The Chicago School stressed the interdependent nature of the personality, or self, and social interaction. W.I. Thomas's notion of 'the **definition of the situation**', which highlights the powerful role that perceptions and shared meanings play in guiding social action, and C.H. Cooley's concept of 'the looking-glass self', which alerts us to the process by which our behaviour and identity are shaped by our awareness of the reactions of others, illustrate the interpretative aspects of this approach. George Herbert Mead's analysis of the dynamic, interactive nature of personality formation contributed to the development of **symbolic interactionism** in sociology and social psychology. For Mead, as recognized by later developmental psychologists, education is part of an ongoing process of human development in which the individual learns and shares social meanings with other people (Ritzer, 2008: 429–30).

One of the earliest, most complete analyses of schooling within the Chicago School tradition is Willard Waller's *The Sociology of Teaching*, originally published in 1932. Waller (1965: 6) examines the school as a 'social organism' constituted through 'a unity of interacting personalities'. His analysis moves directly into the classroom and other school sites, providing rich examples of the complex social relations that link pupils, teachers, administrators, parents, and other educational participants within a distinct school culture. School and social structures are viewed as maps to guide these interactions, but Waller emphasizes that schooling remains a fluid process marked by changing, sometimes conflicting, definitions of the situation. Several writers, informed by Hochschild's (1983) influential analysis of emotional labour, have extended this analysis to explore how gender relations and caring and emotional dimensions intersect in classrooms and other core sites of human interaction (Bellas, 1999).

The interpretative tradition of classroom research was extended by Becker (1952, 1953), who employed detailed interviews to explore how teachers define and act on their roles and circumstances. Becker's analysis points to the process by which teachers' expectations contribute to the social construction of different categories of students, thereby affecting students' educational experiences and chances of school success. A substantial body of later research elaborates how particular definitions of the situation held by educators result in **self-fulfilling prophecies**. Teachers create and apply particular labels to children and their parents (as well as to other individuals, and vice versa), based on common-sense assumptions, background information, and observations from encounters. This labelling influences subsequent educational and social career paths. Rosenthal and Jacobson (1968), in a frequently cited study of children in a San Francisco elementary school, demonstrate that teachers' presuppositions about pupils' learning potentials, even if false, tended to have more impact on student performance than did actual ability. Studies by Cicourel and Kitsuse (1963) and Rist (1970) in the United States, Hargreaves (1967) and Lacey (1970) in the United Kingdom, and Stebbins (1975) in Canada, among many others, support the finding that self-fulfilling prophecies operate as powerful influences on educational outcomes, but this research emphasizes much more fully than do Rosenthal and Jacobson the complex interactions that take place within schools.

Many research findings within the interpretative tradition ultimately support functionalist and critical analyses of social reproduction that show social outcomes of schooling as highly predictable in nature. However, interpretative analysis emphasizes that schooling cannot properly be viewed as a 'black box' that produces preselected results; instead, the most compelling interest lies with what happens inside the school (Karabel and Halsey, 1977: 60). Other classroom studies, including Canadian research by Martin (1976) and Stebbins (1971, 1975), portray schooling as a site within which complex processes of negotiation and decision-making are undertaken by all participants. Albas and Albas (1993), for instance, through observation of students' behaviour in examinations in a western Canadian university, demonstrate that students employ a wide range of actions to avoid being labelled as cheaters. Interpretative analysis, by probing into the sometimes devious ways that people engage with one another and their social surroundings, often conveys a strong sense of cynicism, expressed clearly in a chapter in which Howard Becker (1996) reflects upon many of his earlier influential studies, entitled 'Schooling Is a Lousy Place to Learn Anything In'.

A conscious effort to question both school practices and the structure of knowledge and curricula emerged within what came to be known in the early 1970s as *the 'new' sociology of education*. Critical of previous conventional sociological and educational analysis that took for granted what happens in schools, the new sociology of education sought explicitly to expose the power relations embedded within educational practices (Gorbutt, 1972; Young, 1971). While this approach drew inspiration from emergent critical sociological analyses, its orientation to research problems and methodologies was primarily interpretative. However, as Karabel and Halsey (1977: 47–8) observe, the new sociology of education was predominantly a British phenomenon that paid little heed to previous, mostly North American, classroom research, such as the studies referred to above.

The strength of the new sociology of education is its ability not only to bring the schooling process to the centre of educational research, but also to challenge many of the prevailing assumptions about the content of schooling. Knowledge, and how it is presented in the curriculum and delivered in the classroom, is not an absolute category. Rather, it is socially constructed, given meaning and importance through the social contexts in which it appears. Consequently, much of the research in the new sociology of education, like other forms of interpretative analysis, is devoted to providing detailed descriptions and outlines of the significance of everyday occurrences, such as patterns of joking and teasing in the classroom or the hidden meanings contained within school textbooks. Whereas other forms of analysis tend to overlook or trivialize day-to-day activities, interpretative sociology brings these to the forefront as crucial components of social life.

While offering detailed insight into such crucial features of schooling as classroom processes, interpersonal interactions, and the curriculum, interpretative sociology is often limited by its failure to link what happens in schools with the world beyond schooling. Attention to the intricacies of everyday processes tends to leave unanswered historical questions about change and how things got that way in the first place. Moreover, there is a tendency to ignore the impact of broader social structures, opportunities, and decision-making processes on educational practices and outcomes. Negotiation between teachers and pupils for grades or teachers' contributions to students' self-esteem may influence students' career choices, for instance, but these choices cannot be understood without reference to such factors as labour markets, families, and other socio-economic determinants. Ultimately, like much structural functionalist analysis, interpretative sociology makes its strongest contribution in the description of social life but falls short in its explanatory powers.

CRITICAL ANALYSIS

The various strands in the critical analysis of schooling are unified by their concern to find the underlying causes of educational inequalities and change. Critical analysis, like the other approaches to the sociology of education, has a long history, but in North America, at least, it has really only achieved a position of some prominence since the mid-1970s. Critical analysis stresses that the education system has largely failed in its promise to promote a more egalitarian society. Moreover, this failure is not an accidental by-product that can be corrected by simple reforms. Instead, schooling, in content and process, contributes to the subordination of substantial segments of the population. The meritocratic and democratic visions promoted by liberal and functionalist analysis are criticized as ideologies that serve the interests of dominant social groups. Three distinct orientations to

critical analysis of schooling—political economy influenced by Marxism, feminism, and critical **pedagogy**—are discussed below, with reference to their unique
emphases as well as to recent integrative approaches informed by insights derived
from diverse critical and traditional perspectives.

Marxist educational theory shares with neo-Weberian analysis the assessment
that education systems within capitalist societies are unable to fulfill their democratic potential because of the profound influence of dominant social forces.
Marxism, however, attributes the root causes of social inequality to structures of
class and economic production rather than to competition between status groups.

While Karl Marx wrote very little on formal education, his theories and his
method for analyzing capitalist society offer a foundation for critical analysis,
known as historical materialism, that is absent in other approaches. Marx's analysis begins with the premise that all societies emerge around the ways in which
people meet their basic survival needs. As human beings we develop socially, distinct from other species, by virtue of our ability to labour. Labour, for Marx,
refers in a broad sense to conscious activity devoted to the fulfillment of specific
human needs. Marx's social critique emphasizes how our labour comes to be
alienated through processes by which others gain control over our labouring
activity and the products that we generate through it. Alienation is most extreme
in capitalist society, which is distinguished from other types of societies and
modes of production by the ways that capitalists are able to control and organize
work to maximize profit.

Although most of Marx's analysis focuses on the structural mechanisms that
drive the capitalist system and produce social class antagonisms, Marx also comments on the contradictory nature of schooling. Like other institutions within
capitalism, the education system constrains human potential that is otherwise
necessary for social progress. Schooling, when it is integrated with work and other
crucial social activities, provides opportunities through which people can develop
both critical consciousness and meaningful skills in such areas as literacy and
vocational practice. Organized to serve capitalist priorities of profit and labour
market discipline, however, schools fall far short of their potential, becoming more
like 'sausage factories' than places for human fulfillment. Schooling, under capitalism, is a vehicle for the production of a compliant workforce, providing just
enough knowledge to ensure a supply of workers ready for monotonous jobs while
advancing ideologies that serve capitalist interests (see, e.g., Marx, 1977: 613–15;
Wotherspoon, 1984: 211). Despite the deadening effects of work and other social
practices within capitalism, however, Marx's theory emphasizes possibilities for
the revolutionary transformation of society. Public schooling, Marx contends,
would remain an essential part of communist society, although, by linking work
and education, its aim would be to foster personal and social development rather
than to serve the bourgeois order (Marx and Engels, 1965: 55, 60).

Marx's work, by virtue of its political orientation, has had a major impact on
educational practice. Literacy campaigns and revolutionary movements, inspired

at least in part by Marx and incorporating interpretations of his work adapted to fit particular circumstances, have contributed to various kinds of educational reform in many parts of the world. The student protest movement that emerged in Western Europe and North America in the late 1960s also created a receptive atmosphere for Marxist analysis in the social sciences. Schooling began to be portrayed as an 'ideological state apparatus' (Althusser, 1971) or a form of cultural imperialism (Carnoy, 1974) that contributes ideologically and materially to the perpetuation of fundamentally unequal class relations.

Insights offered by Harry Braverman (1974) exemplify the emergent Marxist critique of work and other social conditions under advanced capitalist society. In common with neo-Weberian analysis advanced by writers like Collins, Braverman challenges the popular liberal assessment that technological change has created enhanced skill requirements and more meaningful white-collar work opportunities. However, Braverman (whose analysis will be elaborated in more detail in subsequent chapters) contends that capitalist control over work involves managerial strategies that produce increasing degradation and deskilling within virtually all occupations. Education, despite its apparent contribution to individual and social development, serves primarily to co-ordinate and prepare students for adjustment to the routines of a world dominated by monopoly capital.

Probably the most influential neo-Marxist study of schooling to appear in the wake of the 1960s challenges to political orthodoxy has been *Schooling in Capitalist America* by Samuel Bowles and Herbert Gintis, published in 1976. Bowles and Gintis make explicit the connections between the capitalist economy and schooling only noted in passing by Braverman, beginning with a critique of the failure of liberal educational reform to deliver on its promise of a more egalitarian and democratic society. They contest, as well, conservative arguments that attribute educational inequality to inherent differences in intelligence and ability. Bowles and Gintis argue, rather, that educational reform can do little in itself to alleviate social inequality insofar as inequality is rooted in the class structure of capitalist society. They identify a **correspondence principle** that operates between educational reform and economic change. They argue that capitalism, in common with totalitarian political systems, restricts democratic participation in order to maintain material and ideological conditions to generate profit and ensure a productive labour force.

According to Bowles and Gintis, formal education in the United States has undergone three major historical changes that correspond to changes in the capitalist economy. Initially, the rise of mass public schooling accompanied the need in the mid- to late nineteenth century for a disciplined wage labour force. During the second transition, between 1890 and 1930, progressive educational reforms converged with the growing concentration of corporate capital and a diversified workforce to produce a bureaucratic education system based on standardization, testing, and systematic control. The third phase involved correspondence between the rapid expansion of post-secondary education and the post-World War II growth of professional and white-collar occupations needed to co-ordinate labour and capital under intensified control by state and corporate agencies. Educational change frequently is marked by struggle because, as Bowles and Gintis (1976: 235) argue, 'Conflicts in the educational sphere often reflect muted or open conflicts in the economic sphere.' However, formal education serves primarily to facilitate the transformation of capitalist development in such a way as to maintain social order.

Bowles and Gintis's analysis has advanced the understanding of educational structures and practices by demonstrating that schooling, at least indirectly, is a central part of the logic that drives capitalist development and reproduces system-atic social inequalities. Their work also provides a historical account, lacking in most previous studies, of forces that have contributed to the formation and growth of contemporary educational institutions.

Despite the acuity of their critique of both traditional educational theories and schooling processes in capitalist societies, the insights offered by Bowles and Gintis have sufficiently strong parallels with structural functionalist analysis that some writers (e.g., Carnoy and Levin, 1985: 21–2) consider their work to be 'critical functionalist' in nature. Among both traditional and critical analyses, in other words, there is general agreement that schools contribute to social, ideological, and labour force reproduction. Yet, there is considerable debate over what kinds of reproduction occur, how fair the system is, and who benefits from it. On either side of the debate, there is a tendency to understate the complexities characteristic of educational realities.

Livingstone (1994: 65–7) summarizes three major problems with the corre-spondence principle advanced by Bowles and Gintis: (1) a failure to recognize that different forms of knowledge, and not exclusively capitalist knowledge, exist and are produced within educational settings; (2) the accumulation of historical evi-dence suggesting that the correspondence between schools and economic change is, at best, incomplete and not necessarily determined by capitalist production relations; and (3) a failure to develop a complete explanation of education that goes beyond relatively simple statements about its functions. Bowles and Gintis, in response to criticisms of their work, have commented that more attention needs to be paid to the contradictions that characterize education and other social rela-tions in advanced capitalism (see, e.g., Gintis and Bowles, 1980). Their work, despite its limitations, has remained a significant reference point for critical analy-sis of schooling because of the crucial questions it raises about how education con-tributes to social reproduction.

Within much subsequent educational analysis informed by Marxism, there has been a tendency either to take for granted the existence of a correspondence prin-ciple or else to elaborate the mechanisms through which schools are linked to state and economic structures. These trends are apparent in critical analysis from a Canadian political economy tradition oriented to explaining the development of Canada's resource-based economy, the Canadian class structure, the social and economic impact of Canada's dependence on European and American capital,

Box 2.3 A Neo-Marxist Perspective on the Sociology of Education

Herbert Gintis and Samuel Bowles (1980: 52–3) outline the correspondence principle that links schooling with the economy:

A main proposition in *Schooling in Capitalist America* held that a major objective of capital, in its interventions into the formation and evolution of the educational system, was precisely the preparation of students to be future workers on the various levels in the hierarchy of capitalist production. Given the quite significant success of capital directly and indirectly structuring schools and in the face of the undemocratic nature of economic life, schools could not fulfill their egalitarian and developmental objectives. We concluded that the only means towards the achievement of progressive educational reform is the democratisation of economic life, allowing for a democratic and emancipatory school system which does not conflict with the formation of adults capable of effective participation in the system of production.

We also argued specifically that the current relationship between education and economy is ensured not through the content of education but its form: the social relations of the educational encounter. Education prepares students to be workers through a correspondence between the social relations of production and the social relations of education. Like the division of labour in the capitalist enterprise, the educational system is a finely graded hierarchy of authority and control in which competition rather than co-operation governs the relations among participants, and an external reward system—wages in the case of the economy and grades in the case of schools—holds sway. This correspondence principle explains why the schools cannot at the same time promote full personal development and social equality, while integrating students into society. The hierarchical order of the school system, admirably geared towards preparing students for their future positions in the hierarchy of production, limits the development of those personal capacities involving the exercise of reciprocal and mutual democratic participation and reinforces social inequality by legitimating the assignment of students to inherently unequal 'slots' in the social hierarchy.

The correspondence principle, we believe, makes four positive contributions to progressive educational strategy. First, its explanatory value is great. Despite the considerable scepticism which greeted publication of our book, critics have made little headway in overturning our major empirical conclusions. Indeed the one major subsequent statistical investigation of sources of educational and economic success—Christopher Jencks et al.'s *Who Gets Ahead?*— dramatically confirms our own findings. Second, in an era where the failures of liberal school reform have become increasingly evident to policy-makers and the public, the correspondence principle shows a positive alternative. Egalitarian and humanistic education are not unattainable due to some inherent defect in human nature or advanced industrial society, but to the undemocratic nature of participation in economic life. Educational reform requires at the same time economic transformation towards democratic socialism. Third, our formulation rectifies an earlier pre-occupation of both liberal and Marxian analysis with the overt content of schooling. By focussing upon the experience of schooling, the correspondence principle provides a consistent analytical framework for understanding the school as an arena of structured social interaction. Fourth, our formulation of the correspondence principle contributes to a more positive understanding of the goals of socialist transition. In older critiques of capitalist society, almost unique stress was laid on the private ownership of means of production. At least as far as educational reform is concerned, we have been able to show that not ownership, but control is central to social inequities. Merely passing from private to social ownership without challenging in any substantial way the social relations of economic life, can have no impact on the egalitarian and humanistic goals of progressive educational reform. The correspondence principle then represents a powerful antidote to the authoritarian tendencies all too often found in an otherwise progressive social movement.

Source: Gintis, Herbert, and Samuel Bowles, 1980. 'Contradiction and Reproduction in Educational Theory', in Barton et al., eds, *Schooling, Ideology and the Curriculum*. Reprinted by permission of Falmer Press.

and subsequent attempts to delineate the emergence of one or more distinct Canadian nations. A preoccupation with historical preconditions and patterns of economic development has often left schooling as an unproblematic or absent force in such literature. In Wallace Clement's (1974) influential analysis of *The Canadian Corporate Elite*, for instance, education is mentioned only in passing as a device for conveying class-based privilege from one generation to the next, while more thorough subsequent reviews of the 'new' political economy literature in Canada (Clement and Williams, 1989; Clement and Vosko, 2003) offer only incidental, if any, allusions to schooling and education despite covering such themes as immigration, gender, labour markets, welfare state policy, media, and youth.

There is, however, a substantial body of political economic analysis of Canadian education. Two important books published in the 1970s focused on a growing literature of critical analysis that emphasized how schooling was integrated with the corporate order under capitalism. *The Politics of the Canadian Public School*, edited by George Martell (1974), documents in a manner that continues to be highly relevant several issues of importance to Canadian education, including the reinforcement of class inequalities, the infusion of corporate values and profit-making strategies into the curriculum, and the political mobilization of teachers' movements. *Reading, Writing, and Riches: Education and the Socio-Economic Order in North America*, edited by Randle Nelsen and David Nock (1978), extends this analysis, detailing such additional issues as corporate control over post-secondary education and the subordination of Native peoples.

These books, along with analyses presented by Lockhart (1979), Schecter (1977), Livingstone (1983, 1985), Wotherspoon (1987), and others, have revealed the extent to which the Canadian education system has been infused with class-based ideologies and practices. Growing concern about the role that corporate interests are playing in aligning education more closely with business and market priorities has stimulated a revival of critical analysis of education (Harrison and Kachur, 1999; Robertson et al., 2003; Taylor, 2001). However, preoccupation with economic reproduction within Marxist and political economy frameworks has often tended to overgeneralize the powers that capitalism, capitalists, and dominant economic forces have in shaping social life, and thereby to undermine education's capacity to change and be changed through interaction among educators, students, community members, and other social forces. Gaskell (1992: 22) observes that 'Critical theory and Marxist theory, despite their impact on scholarship, made few inroads with educational practitioners, who were frequently the targets of the critique, or with policy-makers, who were told there was not much to be done anyway within the framework of a capitalist economy.' Ironically, some Marxist analysis can also be criticized for its commitment to social change, in which the impression is created that, with proper revolutionary consciousness and effective political agents, radical social transformation appears to be inevitable (Davies, 1995: 1465–6).

Growing recognition of the dual nature of education, as a force that can foster critical sensitivity and empower people to take control over aspects of their lives as well as one that contributes to subordination and disempowerment, forced educators and educational researchers to develop more sophisticated educational critiques. Analysis came to focus not only on what is wrong with schooling, which has commonly been the main theme of orthodox Marxism and political economy, but also how education might facilitate individual and social transformation. Political economic analysis is often integrated with insights derived from other critical theories, including feminism and anti-racism, as well as statistical, historical, and comparative research, to produce richer critiques of contemporary educational issues and to suggest alternative visions (Livingstone, 2004; Sears, 2003; Taylor, 2001; Torres and Mitchell, 1998).

Theories of **cultural reproduction** offer possibilities to link detailed examination of specific educational practices, akin to interpretative studies, with processes that contribute to the maintenance of social structures. This approach is heavily influenced by the work of Pierre Bourdieu (1977; 1984) in France, Paul Willis (1977) and Basil Bernstein (1977) in Britain, and Michael Apple (1995, 2004) in the United States.

Bourdieu agrees with the Marxist position that education contributes to the perpetuation of class inequalities and other dimensions of unequal social structures. However, he is more concerned with social practices that affect how these inequalities can be variously reproduced or altered. Capital exists in the form of social, cultural, and symbolic assets as well as being an economic factor. Power and prestige convey definite advantages to members of privileged social groups, which in turn can be transmitted across generations, but these are only effective to the extent that they can be converted from potential to real benefits. For Bourdieu, a person's family background and social circumstances contribute to 'habitus' (dispositions) or deeply ingrained experiential leanings that influence their options and actions in relation to specific types of social situations (which he terms 'fields' of interaction). Schools and other educational institutions are infused with class-based assumptions and expectations related to such things as rules of conduct, manners of expression, and background knowledge, giving some people a competitive advantage over others in their understanding and application. However, education, as it gains significance as a mechanism to grant credentials and provide legitimate access to social and economic opportunities, also becomes a site through which various social groups struggle for position and advantage. Bourdieu and Passeron (1979: 77), echoing neo-Weberian analysis of credential inflation, observe that, 'When class fractions who previously made little use of the school system enter the race for academic qualifications, the effect is to force the groups whose reproduction was mainly or exclusively achieved through education to step up their investments so as to maintain the relative scarcity of their qualifications and, consequently, their position in the class structure.'

The framework introduced by Bourdieu has gained increasing prominence as researchers pay greater attention to the intricate interconnections among schooling, human agency, and structural inequalities (Lareau and Horvat, 1999; Lareau and Weininger, 2003; Sullivan, 2002). In Canada, this approach has been especially useful for offering insights that take us beyond statistical regularities to highlight the ways in which social background and personal circumstances influence choices that have longer-term significance. The analysis of strategies that draw on different forms of capital has been applied, for example, to the exploration of how British Columbia students' social backgrounds and schooling experiences affect the educational and occupational pathways that they subsequently follow (Andres Bellamy, 1993), the economic, cultural, and institutional factors that limit post-secondary educational horizons and access for students from rural areas (Andres and Looker, 2001), the selective mechanisms that contribute to and reinforce gender segmentation in information technology fields (Taylor, 2005), and the intersecting class, social, and cultural factors that have a decisive impact on whether a student continues with or drops out of higher education (Lehmann, 2007).

Willis, through extensive observations and interviews, traced a group of boys in a working-class town in the United Kingdom from their secondary schooling into their early post-school working lives. Willis demonstrates that, while economic reproduction occurs in predictable fashion in the sense that the boys are destined for occupational futures consistent with their class backgrounds, there is a complex interplay among the social and cultural factors that produce those outcomes. Jobs and social positions are not mechanically predetermined but develop through specific choices and experiences that arise, in part, through life in schools. The working-class 'lads' Willis observes engage in forms of resistance and rebellion to schooling that range from mocking school authority to verbal abuse, theft, and vandalism because they see in the middle-class standards of schools little that is of interest or relevance to their lives. By withdrawing from the mainstream of school life, the lads select a path leading to short-term work that at first offers excitement and independence but eventually results in low-paying jobs with few prospects for meaningful working lives. Willis argues that these choices reveal what he calls 'partial penetrations'. In other words, students are able to see through or penetrate weaknesses in the dominant meritocratic ideology because their experience contradicts the official argument that school success and hard work lead to social success. However, their insights are only partial in the sense that the options they choose lead them to a life of deadening routine that reinforces rather than transforms social inequalities.

Michael Apple's analysis of schooling proceeds from the recognition that schools contribute actively to the production, as well as the reproduction, of cultural practices and social structures. Apple, like Willis, accepts the Marxist argument that schools contribute to social control and the maintenance of structured inequalities, but he argues—consistent with the new sociology of education—that schools also create and process knowledge. This work has given rise to a rich tradition of work demonstrating how schools do more than simply transmit knowledge and ascribe places for individuals in society. Within schooling, ideas and understandings about the world and our place in the world are shaped by the actions of educational participants, which in turn are circumscribed by power relations and political economic structures (see especially Weis et al., 2006).

The work of Apple and Willis has helped to advance what has come to be known as **resistance theory**. Resistance theory, unlike the more one-dimensional accounts of social reproduction that tend to be conveyed by structural functionalist and orthodox Marxist analyses, portrays schooling as a venue that is continually subjected to contestation. Students do not blindly and automatically move from schooling into preordained social positions. Rather, their active participation in schooling involves diverse responses that range from enthusiastic acceptance to blatant rejection of the curriculum, of the manner in which it is transmitted, and of other aspects of the schooling process. Moreover, there are significant variations in how curricula and educational practices are presented to and experienced by various categories of students as distinguished by such factors as gender, race, ethnicity, and age. Boys and girls, for instance, are often taught differently and bring with them distinct frames of reference through which they subsequently interpret the curriculum.

Resistance theory, in more general terms, brings to the forefront the dynamic elements of educational practices and cultures without losing sight of the social, economic, and political contexts within which schooling operates. This work is being extended in many important ways to explore the complex ways in which people are coping with uncertainties associated with existence and identity in a world being transformed by global challenges (Dolby and Dimitriadis, 2004). Nayak (2003), for instance, returning attention to the northeast of England where Willis conducted his ethnographic research, explores how diverse youth subcultures are created both within and across boundaries of race, class, and gender as young people attempt to negotiate meaningful places and identities in a world full of risk (a theme also discussed by Nolan and Anyon, 2004). Apple (2006: 681), reviewing notable recent American contributions to the critical analysis of education in the United States, reiterates the vital role that this analysis serves 'to illuminate the ways in which educational policy and practice are connected to the relations of exploitation and domination in the larger society' at the same time as they point to the visions and possibilities for radical change.

Feminist theory has also advanced considerably our ability to understand education, in particular its divergent forms and interests. Feminist analysis has an extensive history that has been reformulated into systematic academic and political discourse over the past four decades. Critiques of schooling that we would now characterize as feminist were prevalent, for instance, in eighteenth-century arguments that access to education was a fundamental right for women as well as for men; in nineteenth-century debates over whether boys and girls should take or be in the same classes as one another, and whether women should be admitted into universities; in nineteenth- and early twentieth-century struggles by women teachers to gain recognition for their work and to improve their working conditions; and in later efforts to incorporate subjects and knowledge pertinent to girls' and women's lives into the curriculum. Despite these historical roots, the emergence of a distinct feminist analysis of schooling can be traced to the rising consciousness in the late 1960s and early 1970s of gender inequalities in education as well as in other spheres of social, economic, and domestic activity (Gaskell et al., 1989).

There are several forms of feminist analysis, unified by recognition of women's disadvantage and lack of privilege relative to men and of the need for social action to redress women's oppression. Most early feminist analyses of schooling focused on questions about sexism in the classroom and curricula and unequal distributions of men and women in different positions within the education system (Kenway and Modra, 1992: 140–8). These concerns are most characteristic of liberal feminism, which proposes reforms to alleviate sex bias and create more equitable gender representation in socially important positions. In schools, for example, employment equity measures are commonly identified as a response needed to compensate for the fact that, while women teachers outnumber men at nearly all levels of schooling up to the senior grades, most educational administrators are male. Liberal feminists advocate change, but argue that gender equity can be attained through modifications within existing social, educational, and economic arrangements.

Other feminists contend that effective change requires a more fundamental restructuring of social practices and structures. It is not sufficient simply to ensure equitable numbers of women and men in socially important positions, or that textbooks contain language and examples that apply to girls' and women's as well as to boys' and men's lives. Radical feminism has pointed out that patriarchy, or the systematic devaluation and oppression of women, is embedded within all forms of social organization. Language, science, politics, the economy, and other spheres of activity are organized around ways of knowing and doing that take male experience as the norm. Women's experience, by contrast, is undermined and relegated to the margins of what is considered to be socially important. Women—and spheres of life such as the domestic and sexual realms that give particular shape and meaning to their lives—are frequently absent as subjects and objects of study. In the sociology of education, for instance, feminist analysts have criticized classroom studies, such as Willis's, for ignoring the central role that gender plays in the construction of student school experience and school outcomes (Weiler, 1988: 41–2). More radical versions of feminism, in the process, have also inspired researchers and educators to take seriously questions about sexuality, body practices, social identity, and related issues that have typically been excluded from education and related discourses.

Socialist feminism, like radical feminism, views liberal reforms as insufficient to overcome gender inequalities, but emphasizes social differences among, as well as between, men and women. Women's subordination must be understood in terms not only of gender but also of class (as well as race and other important aspects of social experience). The way in which gender influences people varies insofar as our lives are shaped by the distinct positions we occupy within society, including the opportunities we have for access to power and other crucial resources.

Feminist pedagogy has emerged as a way to unify women's common concerns, moving beyond specific labels towards clearer articulation of strategies to address practical problems (Luke and Gore, 1992). Feminists argue that the incorporation of women and their experiences into research is an important part of the wider process within which women are to make sense of and reclaim their lives. This involves the recognition of issues that are meaningful in an everyday context but commonly absent from curricula and public discussion, such as domestic violence, public safety concerns, competing family and career demands, and personal encounters with sexism. Women's voices, often emerging through accounts of their own experiences, become an important device to identify, clarify, and seek positive solutions to social problems (Brookes, 1992). In this way, possibilities are created to realize the potential education holds to be truly liberating and progressive. bell hooks (2000: xiii), emphasizing the need for a critical feminism grounded in an understanding of how gender, race, and class intersect, emphasizes that, 'Just as our lives are not fixed or static but always changing, our theory must remain fluid, open, responsive to new information.'

These insights have encouraged recent feminist scholarship, often in conjunction with critical pedagogy, new political economy, and post-structuralist and postmodernist critiques, to develop a vision of social justice that proceeds from an understanding of the multiple causes of oppression (Arnot and Weiler, 1993; Kenway and Willis, 1998). Increasing recognition is also given to analysis that links personal or biographical experiences with wider structures of power and inequality. Gaskell (1992), for example, details how changes in schooling, labour markets, and socialization processes are intertwined with life choices and chances to produce different educational and vocational career patterns for girls and boys and for women and men. Diverse frameworks such as those elaborated by Bourdieu, as well as other critical studies of power, hold considerable potential for advancing feminist engagement with issues associated with hierarchy, domination, and alternative possibilities (Dillabough, 2004).

As with many other theoretical perspectives, feminist analysis has increasingly sought to incorporate a more complex understanding of how personal identities and social opportunities are being reshaped by the complex interplay among shifting political, social, cultural, and economic relationships. The impact of changes associated with globalization and more localized processes tends to be highly uneven. Arnot and Dillabough (1999: 184–5) emphasize a need for struggles for democracy in education to be recast to take into account these changing and contested circumstances, thereby requiring feminist analysis:

> to go beyond a feminist engagement with questions of voice, subjectivity, and difference. It also must remain committed to the idea that women, as agents of knowledge (not foundationalist knowledge!), need to make claims about their identity in order to effect broad social and political change. These agents are not uniform in character; they take multiple, dynamic positions that often are in tension. However, they must be viewed as members of a heterogeneous community who are concerned with how new social and political formations (e.g., neo-liberalism) structure the relationship between gender and democratic education.

There are important gender-based differences in how contemporary social and economic transitions are experienced and understood. These transformations have also forced us to reconsider the meaning of gender and how it intersects with other important social characteristics, including class and race. The expansion of educational opportunities, both in general and in new opportunities in several non-traditional fields, has advanced women's social, economic, and political prospects in numerous ways. At the same time, many women have not had equitable access to or returns from education as a consequence of domestic, occupational, social, and cultural circumstances, as well as institutional and structural factors. Feminist analysis has highlighted, for instance, the disproportionate impact of economic restructuring and state cutbacks that affect employment in government services and non-unionized sectors in which high proportions of women are employed. In the process, women often face further pressures to care for dependants and take on added responsibilities to manage the impact of economic uncertainty in the household and community. Later chapters (particular

Box 2.4 A Feminist Perspective on the Sociology of Education

Feminist analysis has become increasingly concerned not only with questions related to gender-based differences in social positions and identities, but also with a social world that has been transformed, in part, through previous feminist struggles for equity and voice. Johanna Wyn, Sandra Acker, and Elizabeth Richards (2000: 444–6) explore the experiences of women who have moved into managerial positions in universities in Canada and Australia in contexts in which universities themselves are under pressure to adhere to logics based on market forces and new managerial imperatives:

[W]e can conclude that the women in this study have consciously striven to 'make' themselves senior academics and managers, 'differently' from their perceptions of the traditional male academic. As the research reveals, even as relatively powerful players, they are also conscious of the impossibility of being assimilated fully into the taken-for-granted university processes.

Hence, to be a woman manager in a university is indeed to be reminded of an identity one is not, and constantly to have to define the identity one is.

Our study depends on qualitative, narrative techniques to focus on the fine details of everyday experience in the lives of senior women in faculties of education. Their tales of inclusion and exclusion, centrality and marginalisation, innovation and tradition are documented, with attention to the contradictions apparent in the stories of women who find themselves in senior positions in situations where they have few predecessors. Their perspectives support the view that, while we have much to gain from studying women's participation in the management of universities, their contribution cannot be simply characterised as a 'women's way' of leading (Blackmore, 1999, p. 56). The study has provided a perspective on a cohort of women that has engaged in similar struggles in universities across two countries during the 1970s, 1980s and 1990s. Their overwhelming concerns reflect the ideals of this period: those of the improvement of educational opportunity for disadvantaged groups, and the creation of more diverse and inclusive practices within the institution.

In both countries, these senior women saw themselves as being forces for change, with greater or lesser success. Many had feminist commitments (although they might deny feminism in individual ways) and wanted to make the academy a better place for both women and men. Many believed they had something unique to offer as women in leadership roles. Some had instituted specific practices towards that end, for example, making special efforts to mentor and support junior faculty. Both optimism and disappointment framed their accounts. Paradoxically, they were simultaneously central and marginal within their institutions. They might be well placed to innovate and improve aspects of academic work or university practice, but at the same time, they were frequently themselves isolated and acutely conscious of their 'difference' from men senior colleagues and sometimes from other women colleagues as well. . . .

Feminist knowledge production and political work would seem to be at odds with the direction of these changes. Yet, the informal demands on women's emotional labour are likely to increase as women 'struggle to undertake feminist work in conditions which are both increasingly hostile to it and increase the need for it' (Kenway & Langmead, 1998, p. 30). Not all the women interviewed considered themselves feminists, but as we have shown, all were committed to 'making a difference', often along feminist lines. Is the university to which women are making a difference more in tune with the university of the past than that of the future? To the extent that the answer is 'yes', there is a need to develop a new understanding of the role of women in leadership. The women whose perspectives are described in this article have used a range of strategies in 'fortifying the difference', and their views provide a key to understanding what it means to be leaders and managers in these times. We would suggest that the insights gained from their experiences over the last quarter of a century are an important element in the process of developing a new feminist politics of leadership for the twenty-first century.

Source: Wynn, Johanna, et al. 'Making a Difference: Women in Australian and Canadian Faculties of Eduction', *Gender and Education*. Reprinted by permission of the publisher (Taylor & Francis Ltd., http://www.tandf.co.uk/journals).

Chapters 4, 6, and 7) discuss particular barriers that restrict educational advancement, especially for women in non-privileged segments of North American populations and for girls and women in many less-developed nations. Feminism places questions about gender and strategies to foster democratic social change at the heart of our understanding of the social world.

Anti-racism education shares many of the concerns central to feminism and other critical analysis, including a commitment to social change guided by social analysis, with a more explicit focus on differential and unequal treatment based on race. Race, understood in this way, does not exist as a static social category or identity, but is implicated in processes of **racialization** that ascribe to racial characteristics varying forms of significance in the context of power relations. Anti-racism education is not the same as multicultural education, with which it is sometimes confused. Multicultural education shares with liberalism and human capital approaches a focus on rights and cultural differences but gives relatively limited attention to the underlying causes of racial inequalities (Kailin, 2002: 52–4). Racism is perpetuated through social practices and structures that subordinate racial minorities, including the language used to categorize and describe people from various racial and cultural backgrounds. Anti-racism analysis extends beyond the simple categorization of people on the basis of racial characteristics in order to highlight the diverse ways in which people's lives are affected by intersecting forms of oppression based on class, gender, race, and other social characteristics. Racism has played a powerful role in limiting the life chances for specific groups, such as African-American students (Ogbu, 1994) or Aboriginal people in Canada (Monture-Angus, 1995).

An anti-racism education approach has three main concerns—to expose how racism, both in itself and in conjunction with other types of oppression, contributes to the suppression of opportunities for specific racialized groups; to examine the impact of racism; and to develop strategies to counter racially based subordination. Schooling is a primary focal point in anti-racism theory. Educators and the educational contexts that they work in have a significant impact on issues and practices associated with racial difference and inequality. Education contains the potential, alternatively, to critique and modify, or to ignore and reinforce, unequal racial identities and associated practices (Dei, 1996; Dei and Calliste, 2000). Anti-racism education has sensitized educators to the continuing significance of race-related oppression in and beyond schools. It has also posed important questions about how racialized forms of inequality can best be countered. While much anti-racist analysis has focused on 'talk' and awareness related to individual encounters with racism, there is a critical need to embed anti-racism within more systematic practices aimed at fostering effective institutional and organizational change (Srivastava, 2007: 308–9). Part of this analysis has expanded our consideration not only of school practices, but also of the nature of knowledge. Schools historically have severed the links that many minority communities have with traditional forms of knowledge and ways of knowing. However, many racialized populations, including First Nations and African Canadians, have looked towards prospects to reclaim and gain recognition for their indigenous knowledges as part of wider strategies for social and economic empowerment. These challenges have forced educators and educational researchers to reconsider deeply embedded assumptions about what we mean by knowledge, and what the application of these assumptions within schooling practices means for different student bodies. They have also expanded the focus on anti-racism from preoccupation with the racialization of 'visible minority' categories to critical 'whiteness' studies that take into consideration, as well, the practices and discourses around which 'whiteness' has been constructed as an invisible but powerful social entity (Dei et al., 2004).

Critical pedagogy is a related form of analysis that has emerged in an attempt to link educational theory with practice. This is not unique insofar as all critical theory, including Marxism, feminism, and other critical approaches, is unified by the researcher's commitment to try to change the world, rather than to act as an external observer who is studying it in an apparently detached and objective manner. A frequent limitation of the critical theories of education discussed to this point, though, has been their tendency to have little application to real educational settings. Educational participants who have been informed by critical analysis may develop a heightened awareness of their place within schooling as they attempt to rectify problems associated with social and educational disadvantage. However, a

Box 2.5 A Critical Pedagogy Perspective
on the Sociology of Education

Joe L. Kincheloe (2007: 16–17) addresses the role that critical pedagogy must play in a complex world by linking people's lived experiences with an analysis of social structures and power relations in order to work towards social transformation through the empowerment of both teachers and students:

In order to develop a critical pedagogy as a form of cultural politics, it is imperative that proponents of a complex critical pedagogy appreciate the fact that all educational spaces are unique and politically contested. Constructed by history and challenged by a wide variety of interest groups, educational practice is an ambiguous phenomenon as it takes place in numerous settings, is molded by numerous and often invisible forces and structures, and can operate under the flag of democracy and justice in oppressive and totalitarian ways. Practitioners of critical pedagogy report that some teacher education students, educational leaders, parents, and members of the general public often have difficulty appreciating the fact that schooling can be hurtful to particular students from specific backgrounds in unique social, cultural, and economic settings— for example, indigenous and aboriginal students. Many individuals often have trouble empathizing with students harmed by such negative educational dynamics because schooling in their experience has played such a positive role in their own lives.

Thus, a complex critical pedagogy is a domain of research and practice that asks much from those who embrace it. Critical pedagogical teacher education and leadership, for example, involve more than learning pedagogical techniques and the knowledge required by the mandated curriculum. In addition to acquiring teaching methods, teachers and leaders steeped in critical pedagogy also understand the social, economic, psychological, and political dimensions of the schools, districts, and systems in which they operate. They also possess a wide range of knowledge about information systems in the larger culture that serve as pedagogical forces in the lives of students and other members of society: television, radio, popular music, movies, the Internet, podcasts, and youth subcultures; alternative bodies of knowledge produced by indigenous, marginalized, or low-status groups; the ways different forms of power operate to construct identities and empower and oppress particular groups; and the modus operandi of the ways sociocultural regulation operates.

Democracy is a fragile entity, advocates of critical pedagogy maintain, and embedded in educational policy and practice are the very issues that make or break it. Understanding these diverse dimensions and structures that shape schooling and the knowledge it conveys is necessary, critical pedagogues believe, to the very survival of democratic schooling—not to mention the continued existence of democracy itself. The analysis of the ways these complex forces evolve in a globalized, technological, electronic communications-based era marked by grand human migrations is central to the complex critical pedagogy proposed here.

Source: Reprinted by permission of *Harvard Educational Review*.

tendency in much critical analysis to focus on powerful oppressive forces often produces a sense of futility that things cannot be changed. Critical pedagogy aims to overcome the gap between understanding educational reproduction and taking action to provide social and educational transformation.

Education, as presented within critical pedagogy, contributes to the perpetuation of knowledge and power structures that foster the oppression of subordinate groups by dominant groups, but it also contains possibilities to empower persons in subordinated positions to change their lives and the social contexts within which they live. In this sense, while critical pedagogy, as a label, is relatively new, it builds on recognition of numerous historical examples of struggles in which oppressed groups have sought to use education as a means to gain control over their lives—from colonized peoples in Asia, Africa, and Latin America to marginalized inner-city residents and First Nations peoples in North America.

Critical pedagogy begins with a dialectical and dynamic understanding of the relationship between theory and action that locates research, like all human activity, within changing relations of domination, subordination, and resistance (see, e.g., Freire, 1985; Giroux, 1983, 1988; Livingstone, 1987: 7–9; McLaren, 2007: 196ff.; Darder et al., 2003). Giroux and McLaren (1989: xxi) emphasize that critical pedagogy involves a 'language of protest' and a 'critical theory of education' directed towards the task of 'constructing a new vision of the future'. The analysis offsets its portrayals of the despair of everyday life and the social structures that contribute to poverty, dehumanization, and hopelessness with the promise of hope and prospects for meaningful change.

More than most other approaches within the sociology of education, critical pedagogy is grounded in the actions of classroom practitioners. Theory is oriented to address their concerns directly by enabling them to comprehend their own educational realities in relation to wider struggles for liberation. This has sometimes proven to be problematic, in part because the language and philosophical discourse employed within critical pedagogy are posed in terms that have little meaning for all but a few students and educators. While writers like Paulo Freire and Peter McLaren are careful to integrate their analysis with everyday educational experience, there is a tendency in much critical pedagogy to become overly abstract and removed from socio-cultural realities. This is especially true of critical pedagogy that, in its heavy reliance upon postmodernist critiques of conventional theory and practice, often appears to favour the quest for clever turns of phrase while neglecting significant social reference points.

To educators who have become cynical about recurrent waves of fashionable educational ideologies and prescriptions for change, the idealistic and Utopian visions of radical educational reform can be readily dismissed as irrelevant to immediate classroom problems. Nonetheless, critical pedagogy has forced educators and analysts to clarify the nature and significance of educational practices while they maintain awareness of the social contexts that shape educational possibilities and limitations.

GUIDELINES FOR RESEARCH AND ANALYSIS IN THE SOCIOLOGY OF EDUCATION

This chapter has presented an overview of several influential and representative theories within the sociological analysis of education. These theories represent diverse approaches that offer distinct ways of defining research problems, collecting and analyzing data, and explaining educational phenomena. Each of the approaches offers important insights into educational practices and structures. We have observed, as well, that several factors must be taken into consideration to assess the adequacy of any particular theory or approach. What assumptions do we make about the world and how we study it? Does our interest lie, for example, with an explanation of what happens inside classrooms or are we more concerned with social, economic, and political structures (such as questions about educational finance, policy-making, and social inequality) that operate beyond the classroom? Is our focus on:

- current issues or historical developments?
- educational practices or the outcomes of schooling?
- formal or informal aspects of the curriculum?
- factors that give rise to educational stability, or educational change and conflict?

Differing theoretical perspectives and approaches to scientific understanding lend themselves to distinct ways of asking and investigating sociological questions. We must recognize that no single theory can address all of these questions adequately. Increasingly, educational analysis has emphasized the paradox that, while certain problems are more amenable than others to particular theoretical questions and research methods, there is sometimes more common ground between differing perspectives than is often supposed. These considerations do not mean, however, that all theories are equally valid or that we can simply 'pick and choose' an approach in an attempt to investigate social or educational phenomena. Rather, we must be aware of guidelines to ensure that our analysis is systematic and provides an accurate account of the realities we are trying to understand.

It is useful, in this regard, to identify several aspects of educational realities we have considered so far that must be taken into account if we are to develop an adequate sociological understanding of education. These include the following:

- We must recognize education as a broad set of practices that is not restricted to specific institutional forms like schools, colleges, and universities. Education takes place both formally and informally in all aspects of our lives. Educational practices have both intended and unintended consequences.
- Formal education is riddled with contradictions. It can contribute to enhanced social and economic opportunities, individual self-awareness, and greater understanding of our place in the world, but it can also lead to oppression, subordination, and restricted socio-economic opportunities.
- We must be able to understand, and link together, what happens inside schools as well as the organization and operation of the education system as a whole. The analysis of education, in turn, must be integrated with an understanding of wider social processes and structures and strategies for transformation.
- We must be aware of the historical factors that have given rise to educational systems and processes of educational change.
- Formal education involves the production and dissemination of knowledge and skills of various forms. We must be aware of how these processes are contested and often selective in nature, so that we can understand the extent to which they do or do not include and represent diverse social interests.
- We must be sensitive to how the needs and actions of educational practitioners, including students, teachers, administrators, and policy-makers, can both inform and be informed by educational analysis and research. It is important, in this regard, to recognize that none of these groups is homogeneous; rather, they reflect varied experiences characterized by gender, race, ethnicity, class, and other important social characteristics.

CONCLUSION

This chapter has emphasized the importance of theory as a tool to guide our understanding of education and its connections with other social phenomena. Illustrative theories have been presented from three main sociological frameworks—structural functionalism, interpretative analysis, and critical approaches—to highlight the diversity of questions and explanations drawn on by sociologists. The chapter has concluded with a series of issues that need to be taken into account in order to arrive at a comprehensive understanding of education, with the recognition that any single study or theory cannot encompass all of these concerns.

The chapters that follow—informed especially by the insights of critical theories of education—address these issues. Critical analysis enables us to move beyond the surface of educational activities to examine the underlying causes and consequences of educational practice. Through this analysis, ultimately, our aim is not only to understand the contradictory nature of education but to work towards a plan of action that allows us to make progressive changes in educational practices and outcomes.

ANNOTATED FURTHER READINGS

Arnot, Madeleine, and Mairtin Mac An Ghaill, eds. 2006. *The RoutledgeFalmer Reader in Gender and Education*. London: Routledge. This comprehensive reader integrates classic articles on feminist theory with research that explores significant questions concerning relationships between gender and education. Themes include knowledge and pedagogy, gender variations in educational achievement, debates concerning boys' and girls' schooling, curriculum and classroom relationships, and gender, power, and identity.

Bowles, Samuel, and Herbert Gintis. 1976. *Schooling in Capitalist America: Educational Reform and the Contradictions of Economic Life*. New York: Basic Books. This highly influential book emphasizes that, in contrast to prevailing assumptions about education's contributions to social opportunity and equality, educational reform has maintained social inequality by contributing to ideologies and labour market requirements driven by the dynamics of a capitalist economy.

Darder, Antonia, Marta Baltodano, and Rodolfo D. Torres, eds. 2003. *The Critical Pedagogy Reader*. New York: RoutledgeFalmer. This collection integrates core foundational work and more recent theoretical and empirical investigations employing critical pedagogy. Contributions from several authors cited in this chapter, as well as many others, employ various critical perspectives including anti-racism education, feminist pedagogy, and critical pedagogy to investigate classroom practices, globalization and education, teaching, and other important educational issues.

Durkheim, Émile. 1956. *Education and Sociology*. New York: Free Press. This book, bringing together English translations of several of Durkheim's papers, is a classic work that makes the case for, and outlines the foundational elements of, the sociological analysis of education.

Torres, Carlos Alberto, and Theodore R. Mitchell, eds. 1998. *Sociology of Education: Emerging Perspectives*. Albany: State University of New York Press. Contributions to this book examine theoretical developments in the sociology of education and the significance of different forms of educational reform and inequality in comparative perspective.

Waller, Willard. 1965. *The Sociology of Teaching*. New York: John Wiley and Sons. Although originally written and published in the 1930s, this book offers significant insights into school organization and daily interactions that remain fundamental to many educational practices.

Willis, Paul. 1977. *Learning to Labor: How Working Class Kids Get Working Class Jobs*. New York: Columbia University Press. This influential British study examines the complex mechanisms whereby rebellion by working-class youth against school practices and educational authority is channelled into relatively predictable labour market outcomes.

KEY TERMS

Correspondence principle The view that presents educational reforms and outcomes as consequences of economic requirements, labour market needs, and inequalities within a capitalist economy.

Cultural capital The resources that people possess for economic and social success include not only wealth and economic assets, but also knowledge and understandings about social expectations, dominant values, and other pertinent information that institutions use in their ongoing operations.

Cultural reproduction Recognition that, while education contributes to ongoing social inequalities, it does so through cultural and social practices as well as economic requirements.

Definition of the situation The acknowledgement that our perceptions can influence social actions. Interpretative analysis draws attention to the ways in which socially constructed and shared meanings play a crucial role in shaping, reinforcing, or altering social frameworks.

Human capital theory A theoretical approach, with frequent policy applications, that emphasizes education, skill development, and other learning processes as investments that enhance capacities and opportunities among individuals, thereby contributing to general economic growth.

Pedagogy Processes associated with the organization and practice of teaching. The term refers more generally to various kinds of interactions (and how these are understood and organized) in teaching–learning situations.

Racialization Recognition that ways of categorizing and treating people based on racial differences are products of historical and social processes.

Resistance theory Analysis that highlights children, youth, and other students as active participants who can oppose and shape their education and social futures rather than as passive institutional clients.

Self-fulfilling prophecies The notion that the assumptions and expectations that teachers and other service workers hold about students can influence students' lives and futures.

Structural functionalism A theoretical perspective that explains social phenomena with reference to their mutual influence on one another, especially through the social needs they fulfill and the contributions they make to social order.

Symbolic interactionism A theoretical perspective that emphasizes the importance of language, meaning, and use of symbols in our development of self-awareness and, through our relations with others, as the basis of societies.

Study Questions

1. Why are there several distinct theoretical frameworks within the sociological analysis of education, rather than a single approach?
2. Which approach to sociological analysis offers the most comprehensive explanation of educational practices and developments in Canada? Justify your answer.
3. Discuss the relationship between theory and practice in education. To what extent, and with what consequences, can theory and practice exist without informing one another?
4. Discuss which set of factors—those related to what happens inside educational institutions, or those brought in from outside educational institutions—has the strongest impact on educational outcomes. How well are these factors accounted for in the main sociological theories of education?
5. In what ways do educational institutions mirror other major institutions in contemporary societies? How, by contrast, can educational institutions be considered as distinct from other institutions? Discuss the impact of these similarities and differences on the development of a theoretical understanding of education.
6. Discuss the extent to which theory should seek to account for general human experiences as opposed to experiences of specific social categories or groups based on race, gender, sex, or other characteristics.

Chapter 3

Historical Dimensions of Canadian Education

INTRODUCTION

The Canadian education system, as a whole, is one of the largest enterprises in Canadian society. In Canada, over $75 billion annually are spent directly on education, constituting just over 6 per cent of the gross domestic product (the total value of goods and services produced in the nation), while increasing amounts are spent on indirect support for schooling and educational services. Over 6.5 million Canadians are enrolled full-time in elementary, secondary, and post-secondary education programs, and close to 400,000 more are enrolled in part-time programs (AUCC 2007a; Blouin and Courchesne, 2007; Statistics Canada and CMEC, 2007). Education also employs substantial numbers of people in teaching, administrative, and support positions. In 2006, more than 677,000 people in Canada worked either full-time or part-time as teachers and professors, with more than one million persons employed in educational services fields overall, representing 7.5 per cent of the total labour force (Statistics Canada, 2007c).

Canadians, like people in other developed nations, have come to accept formal education as a normal part of their childhood and youth experience. It has become, for many people, a central feature of ongoing development throughout the life course. In many ways, current educational realities stand in marked contrast to the situation a century ago, when most people had very little, if any, formal schooling. Those few individuals who graduated from high school often became teachers or, on rare occasions, continued into post-secondary studies so that they could gain entry into select professional fields or round out their intellectual development for social and political reasons. The dramatic expansion of **public education** in just over a century, from a localized and voluntary pursuit to a highly formalized bureaucracy accompanied by an increasingly large selection of alternatives, is largely taken for granted, as is the fact that almost entire populations participate in schooling and rely on formal educational credentials for career and social advancement. Nonetheless, in common with contemporary public policy discussions about how schooling should be organized and financed, and what kinds of reforms are required to maintain relevant and competitive educational programming, the expansion of public education and efforts to modify or standardize the educational base were topics of heated public debate in the late nineteenth and early twentieth centuries.

This chapter provides an overview of historical factors that have shaped educational growth and transformation in Canada, setting the stage for the next chapter, which outlines the structure, size, and scope of contemporary Canadian education systems. The nation has a rich and highly convoluted educational history that, while unique, is also interwoven with influences, traditions, and developments imported from or occurring in conjunction with events and practices in other nations. The discussion here highlights major dimensions of this development to illuminate issues discussed in other chapters—detailed accounts that offer a more complete understanding of Canada's educational history are widely dispersed in academic and popular written work as well as in diverse oral traditions. Throughout this chapter, particular emphasis is placed on the contested nature of educational reform and on the changing role of state involvement in the organization, financing, and delivery of educational services.

THE HISTORICAL DEVELOPMENT OF EDUCATION IN CANADA

The story of education in Canada, like other institutional histories, involves much more than a straightforward description of key events. Some of the key markers in the development of the education system are associated with significant events and milestones, such as the establishment of schools and universities and the passage of legislation concerning education, as well as with influential individuals. Conventional educational histories have emphasized the prominent role played by influential white men such as Bishop Laval in New France, Egerton Ryerson in Upper Canada, and John Jessop in British Columbia, whose visions and leadership contributed to the advancement of a stable education system in Canada (see, e.g., Johnson, 1968; Wilson et al., 1970; Titley and Miller, 1982). Women's education and the role of women and other minority groups in educational development and reform have been relatively absent in much of the historical analysis of education, reflecting in part a preoccupation with formal political, administrative, and academic matters, which historically excluded from formal education many segments of the population (Fahmy-Eid, 2003: 32–3). Subsequent educational researchers have come to appreciate more fully the significant contributions that women and men representing diverse communities have made to educational development, often in the face of hostile or recalcitrant authorities and complex regulations (see Box 3.1). Education systems are also the product of more mundane events and activities involving countless interactions among students, teachers, parents, and other educational participants (see, e.g., Axelrod, 1997; Houston and Prentice, 1988).

From a critical sociological standpoint, it is important, in acknowledging different ways in which the story can be told, to focus not strictly on what happened but, more crucially, on why things happened as they did, how they are significant for the analysis of social life, and how they can be understood in relation to the social context in which they emerged. Educational practices and changes take shape through the intentions and actions of particular historical actors who, in turn, influence and are influenced by other actors, organizations, and structures. The following brief historical overview outlines some of the most significant features of the education system.

Box 3.1 Obstacles and Progress:
Two Notable Contributions to Educational Reform

We commonly take for granted the existence of educational programs and services that are, in fact, the result of sustained efforts of many committed educators and community leaders, often in the face of sustained resistance or difficult procedural barriers. Helen Raptis (2005: 302–3, 308) details the experiences and strategies of two women, Edith Lucas and Mary Ashworth, whose work with minority students in the mid-twentieth century awakened their awareness of the need for change. Lucas's experience reveals their dedication to new programs, policies, and approaches to language instruction and school–community interactions even when there was no apparent route to advance such change:

Although Lucas, a seasoned teacher and principal, had never before prepared lessons for adult immigrants, she was cognizant that their needs differed from those of children and adolescents. Finding there was 'no book on the market suitable for teaching English to intelligent adults,' Lucas devised her own strategy.[1] On her own time after work Lucas organized a class of newcomers to meet in the evenings in her Victoria office, a stone's throw from the YWCA's quarters. Once she had prepared and 'field tested' a lesson with her own students, she had it 'mimeographed and sent to the YWCA classes for their guidance.'[2]

Lucas eventually compiled her lessons into two books, entitled *English I* and *English II*, each totalling over 300 pages. Upon completing *English II*, students could sit [for] an examination that entitled them to a 'certificate in English and citizenship,' a document they could present as evidence of readiness when applying for Canadian citizenship. By 1954, there were over 115 night schools in BC using Lucas's textbooks, which she described as 'instruction in the rights and responsibilities of Canadian citizenship, teaching at the same time practical English and our customs.'[3] . . .

As a member of the Canadian Citizenship Council and an immigrant to Canada herself, Lucas considered the development of *English I* and *II* to be a 'labour of love,' produced mostly during her own, unpaid time. Lucas preferred to produce her own materials from scratch since she disapproved of many of the available language texts, whose pages were rife with stilted, formulaic phrases such as 'the pen of my aunt is under the lilac bush.' Lucas took pride in her works, which were well illustrated with phrases built around the daily needs of the adult immigrants 'in the sort of sequence in which they are naturally spoken.'[4] . . .

Notes
1. 'Book Enables "New Canucks" To Outshine "Old Canadians"', *Vancouver Sun*, 7 Jan. 1956, 11.

2. Ibid. Each lesson consisted of formal grammar, vocabulary drill, and pages of reading material about a fictitious immigrant family experiencing various aspects of Canadian life, such as government, banking, property insurance, taxation, home decoration, and workmen's compensation.
3. 'Personality of the Week: Dr. Edith E. Lucas', *Colonist*, 3 Feb. 1952, 16.
4. Ibid.

Colonization and Settlement: Education in Canada Prior to the Mid-1800s

The school system as we know it is a relatively recent development, not a natural or inevitable feature of social life. It has been produced and modified within particular social circumstances, often subject to serious contestation over its direction or resistance to its presence and forms. Schooling, by nature, is oriented to change. Implicit within the aims of formal education are the objectives to produce new knowledge, transform individual personalities, and modify or improve social conditions. While there may be little disagreement, at least at a general level, that these are worthy objectives, the demands for educational changes frequently originate within groups or forces that have distinct social agendas or interests, however much these may be challenged and modified by other factors.

Education was a central part of life in what came to be Canada long before there were any formal schools. Early education was distinguished by its incorporation into the daily life practices of First Nations people. Education was crucial for the fulfillment of material needs and cultural survival. According to Kirkness and Bowman (1992: 5), 'It was an education in which the community and the natural environment were the classroom, and the land was seen as the mother of the people. Members of the community were the teachers, and each adult was responsible for ensuring that each child learned how to live a good life.' The integration of education with everyday life suggests a highly informal system of socialization. There is evidence, however, that many First Nations had sophisticated forms of social organization more than 15 centuries ago (Sewid-Smith, 1991: 19–20). While oral traditions such as storytelling were central to learning, complex systems of knowledge were systematically transmitted among generations, sometimes with the aid of visual symbols. First Nations each had their own distinctive bodies of traditional or **indigenous knowledge**, supported by social practices to preserve and transmit core beliefs, values, and competencies. Many of these were endangered through subsequent efforts by European colonizers to undermine or deny such knowledge (Battiste, 2000; Royal Commission on Aboriginal Peoples, 1996a: 526–7).

The First Nations pattern of 'organic' educational practices suited to the practical needs of family, clan, or community has characterized education among many other groups in Canadian society. This has been the case most commonly for children living in regions with no established educational facilities, such as families of early European settlers, Hudson's Bay Company officials, and home-steaders on the Prairies. On some occasions, family or community members attempt to resist, or even assert control over, education despite the ready accessibility of formal educational services. Situations of this kind are most likely to arise when members of minority groups, such as those based on ethnicity or religion, dispute central features of the dominant school system, when parents assert their right to educate the children themselves, or when parents see schooling as interfering with competing demands on their children's time for work, care of family members, or other responsibilities.

The earliest formal schooling in Canada was established by missionaries and religious orders. It was oriented primarily to the replacement of indigenous lifestyles and knowledge with European concepts of morality and consciousness. However benevolent the intentions of religious authorities may have been, denominational education was promoted zealously in the belief that Europeans were morally and intellectually superior to the original inhabitants of North America. Later, myths of the illiterate or noble savage served both to undermine and romanticize Aboriginal life. The representation of Aboriginal peoples as uncivilized or less than full persons enabled colonizing forces to attack traditions they characterized as naive or backward.

These early educational efforts had varying degrees of success. In some cases they were rejected, while in others they were embraced by Aboriginal people. Jaenen (1986), for instance, identifies four distinct phases in the education of Aboriginal people in New France, ranging from missionary education of children and families in the mission field beginning in the seventeenth century to nineteenth-century boarding schools. Changing educational practices reflected colonial desires to devise new strategies to accomplish educational objectives, particularly those oriented to the assimilation of First Nations peoples into European-based life conditions.

Education figured prominently in the fragmentation of First Nations societies. The impact of education was destructive both in content and in form. Not only were Native children taught that their traditional ways were inferior and unacceptable, but the routines and spatial organization of schools often contributed even more strongly to the separation of children from their families and communities. Assimilation was to be accomplished at the cost of breaking down existing social relationships. Schooling was particularly destructive when it attempted to transplant European cultural and educational forms to replace stable indigenous patterns that were attuned to the demands of life in North America. At the same time, Native people were not given opportunities to participate fully and equally in the new social order (Jaenen, 1986: 60). Boarding and residential schools, introduced as official policy by the federal government in the 1870s, acted as 'total institutions' in which children were taken from their parents so as to be removed from 'regressive' influences. Children were subject to harsh disciplinary measures for such offences as speaking in their Native language, and often they were unable to associate with other family members except for brief periods each year.

Box 3.2 Life in a Residential School

Recent stories of separation from family, abuse, destruction of cultural traditions, and social breakdown have highlighted the traumatic effect of residential schools on Aboriginal people and their communities. In these excerpts told by residential school survivors (Jaine, 1993: 83–4, 91–2), the freedom of traditional First Nations education is contrasted with the regimentation that prevailed in residential schools:

Lois Guss

Normally, in a Native family, a child is allowed to learn by trial and error, with love and support being freely given. My experiences in residential school were a sharp contrast to this. There, our natural curiosity was impeded by the outlook of nuns, who had no experience in life and no experience as a parent. Even the natural curiosity of the opposite sex was discouraged and one was made to feel ashamed for even having such curiosities.

There were very few times you could enjoy life as it was so regimented. There was no freedom of thought or expression allowed. Everyone had to conform to a rigid set of standard rules: pray, learn, pray, obey, pray, eat, pray. Up at 6:30 a.m., Mass at 7:00 a.m., breakfast at 8:00 a.m., class at 9:00 a.m., lunch at 12:00 noon, class at 1:00 p.m., sewing and mending at 4:00 p.m., supper at 6:00 p.m., bed at 9:00 p.m. The next day it started again.

Even our bodily functions were regimented; there were certain times to go to the washroom, and castor oil was administered once a year. We had a bath once a week, and laundry duty every Saturday. We attended church once a day and twice on Sunday. On Sundays we had a few hours of free time but we were unaccustomed to such freedom, so we usually looked to an older student to organize our activities.

A Typical Day at St Henri, as told by Alphonse Little Poplar, No. 22

The wake-up bell came early—6 a.m. First we had to go to the chapel for Mass so we could receive Absolution before Communion. Then we had breakfast, watery porridge with sugar already stirred in, no milk, and a slab of bread with no grease. Sometimes they would give us peanut butter for the bread. On those days a nun would go around the table with a pail of peanut butter and give each boy a glob of peanut butter on their bread.

Then we went out to do the chores: milk the cows, feed the pigs, get the firewood.

At 9 a.m. we were off to school for classes. In school we did some reading and things like that. Then we would have recess and then break for noon. Dinner was usually soup and one piece of bread with no grease. Sometimes the soup had a sliver of meat and a potato in it. Those were the good days. We would have berries for dessert when they were in season.

We could never help ourselves to anything when we were eating meals. Everything was served by the nuns. There were no seconds. They fed us the way animals were fed, like slopping the pigs. There was an active blackmarket of stolen food ran by those students lucky enough to work in the kitchen. The students would trade between themselves. Sometimes we would fight over food, we would get so hungry.

After dinner it was classes, recess, and then classes again till 4 p.m. After school we would get a dry bun and any food we could steal, beg, buy, or barter.

Then came chores or play, depending on whose turn it was. If it was chores we had to feed the pigs again, milk the cows, weed the garden, or do the dishes. If it was our turn to play, we did what we could with what we had. We would make our own footballs—a leather bag stuffed with old rags, we made our own sleighs in the winter. We didn't have very much. There was a swing. We didn't have a rink until years later but we could watch the white kids skate.

At 5:30 we had supper which was stew, real thin stew, and bread. Again, everything was served. The slab of bread was put on a plate and then the stew put on it. There were no seconds. Then came clean up, and after clean up there was a short period of play and then we went to bed at seven.

Oh yes, the prayers. There were prayers every time we turned around. We prayed when we got up, when we started a meal, when we finished a meal, when we went to play, when we went to bed. We sure prayed a lot. I guess they must have thought we needed a lot of praying.

We went to bed in the early evening when the sun was still high. I would lie by my window and watch the white children play ball. How I wished I could be there playing with them.

Source: Gus, Lois, and Alphonse Little Poplar from *Residential Schools: The Stolen Years*, ed. by Linda Jaine. Copyright 1993 University Extension Press, University of Saskatchewan. Reprinted by permission of University Extension Press.

Missionaries and other individuals who were privately contracted also provided early schooling for children of British and French origin in Canada. These schools were intended primarily to keep alive connections with established European traditions or to train individuals for specific purposes. Examples of the latter include the provision of training for religious orders, political elites, and teachers. Among the general population, education tended to be sporadic, oriented to the cultivation of loyalty to religious or political orders rather than to anything more than the most basic formal lessons (see, e.g., Titley, 1982).

It is essential to have a sense of the context of the general social structure to understand fully the origins of schooling. The initial development of Canada by European and, subsequently, North American interests was motivated primarily by territorial or commercial concerns. Resource-based industries such as the fur trade, gold extraction, logging, and fishing were highly volatile, and priority was given to measures that would ensure that adequate supplies of labour and access

to resources were available. Moreover, with a few exceptions, such as colonial officials, merchants, and service suppliers who were in a position to settle and raise
families, most of the labour force consisted of men who were single or geograph-
ically mobile. Because many regions had no children other than those who performed domestic chores or engaged in paid labour, and the relatively privileged
groups could arrange to have their children tutored privately or sent to schools
elsewhere, there were few demands for a general system of public schooling until
the late eighteenth and early nineteenth centuries.

The Development of a Public School System
(mid-1800s to the early 1900s)

Increased immigration and settlement of families, the influx of United Empire
Loyalists from the United States, and political and economic threats to Canadian
lands and resources gave rise to new demands for a system of free public schooling. Whereas schooling under denominational and colonial control fostered loyalties to traditional sources (Church, class, and old-country ties), the most ardent
proponents of a common public school system sought the development of distinctly Canadian identities.

Schooling for the general population was to be secular—to overcome the particular intentions of denominational authorities; open to all pupils—to ensure
that the entire population had a common education; and suited to the cultivation
of social and political bonds within Canada. Education was a significant factor in
struggles to break ties with the colonial powers of Britain and France and to preserve Canadian autonomy against American influence. In some instances, such as
among Loyalist emigrants from the United States, parents agitated for schooling in
order to extend opportunities they had previously experienced. In many other
cases, however, the strongest advocates for public schooling were politicians, business people, educated professionals, and educators themselves who sought the
establishment of stable communities (Curtis, 1988; Prentice, 1977). The presence
of a school in a community signified a commitment to future planning and
growth. The **curriculum**, while facilitating basic literacy among the population,
could also be used to cultivate new attitudes and allegiances, along with prospects
for democratic participation, necessary for the growth of a stable social order.

The factors that contributed to the development of public school systems in
Canada reveal the dual objectives of formal education. First, schooling provides
formal learning opportunities through the curriculum. Fundamental skills and
knowledge are made available to all learners, and people are given a chance to
encounter new ideas and challenges. At the same time, however, formal education
also contributes to **moral regulation** and the reshaping of people's identities. In
both structure and content, schooling is centrally involved in the process of disciplining the individual through emphasis on rules and habits rather than on lessons
alone (Corrigan et al., 1987; Curtis, 1988). Political reformers recognized that
schooling could be an important contributing factor to the process of Canadian

nation-building. This process involved, in part, the shaping of individual subjects committed to the Canadian state and its institutions and values. School facilities were among the first and most prominent structures in many communities in recognition of education's importance in state formation and community-building.

Educational promoters faced three main obstacles in their quest to construct a solid educational system as part of the **state apparatus,** or within the framework of the government services and regulations. First, it was necessary to raise money to build schools, hire qualified teachers, and operate school programs. Funds for education had to be raised against competing priorities such as economic development and the construction of roads and other services. Current debates over the extent to which governments should be responsible for educational finance need to be understood in the context of a history of a long, contested, public discourse concerning the proper role of the state in the provision of public services. Second, educational promoters had to mobilize support for public schooling in the face of considerable opposition or indifference from various sources, including religious denominations, supporters of private schools, and community members who saw schooling as an intrusion into private life. Records reveal that just over half of the children in Canada attended schools regularly by the early part of the twentieth century. As late as 1910–11, when over 1.3 million students were enrolled in schools in Canada—which was a substantial proportion of the 1.5 million children in the 5- to 15-year-old age group—the average daily attendance rates remained below two-thirds of those children registered (Dominion Bureau of Statistics, 1924: 157; Leacy, 1983: W67–8). Attendance patterns tended to reflect regional differences in socio-economic circumstances as well as families' material conditions and class backgrounds. There were wide variations in children's school attendance, depending on family means, periodic illness, and local economic conditions such as irregular wages among labourers and shifting labour and employment patterns for children at home, on farms, and in industry (Davey, 1978; Gaffield, 1982). A third problem that plagued early school development was the shortage of a steady supply of trained teachers. Teachers had to have adequate preparation to teach the curriculum, but, more crucially, they had an important role to play in the promotion of schooling. As school employees, they also needed to be loyal to the cause of educational goals as capable representatives in the service of the state (Wotherspoon, 1993).

These problems left many schools in jeopardy, particularly in the poorer and less established regions of the country. Lack of public support and revenue for schooling led to substandard school facilities and low wages for teachers, which in turn made it difficult for some municipalities to attract pupils and suitable teachers. An illustrative case occurred in Victoria when teachers left their jobs for two years, beginning in 1870, after they had not been paid their full wages. The strike action was precipitated by a lack of funds following the refusal of the school board to enforce collection of an educational tax of $2 per resident (Wotherspoon, 1993: 88–9). Until well into the twentieth century, the option of closing down or being left to operate with little or no funding plagued schools across the country.

Box 3.3 Teachers' Duties, 1875

This excerpt from the 1875 rules and regulations for public schools in British Columbia (1875: 47) not only spells out teachers' duties, but, more importantly, it indicates the significance of discipline, habit, morality, cleanliness, and order in the operation of schools:

It shall be the duty of every teacher of a Public School—

1. To teach diligently and faithfully all the branches required to be taught in the school, according to the terms of his engagement with the Trustees, and according to the rules and regulations adopted by the Board of Education:
2. To keep daily, weekly, and monthly registers of the school:
3. To maintain proper order and discipline in his school, according to the authorized forms and regulations:
4. To keep a visitors' book (which the Trustees shall provide) and enter therein the visits made to his school, and to present such book to such visitor, and to request him to make therein any remarks suggested by his visit:
5. At all times when desired by them, to give to Trustees and visitors access to the registers and visitors' book appertaining to the school, and upon his leaving the school to deliver up the same to the order of the Trustees:
6. To have at the end of each half-year public examinations of his school, of which he shall give due notice to the Trustees of the school, and, through his pupils, to their parents and guardians:
7. To furnish to the Superintendent of Education, when desired, any information which it may be in his power to give respecting anything connected with the operation of his school, or in anywise affecting its interests or character:
8. To classify the pupils according to their respective abilities:
9. To observe and impress upon the minds of the pupils, the great rule of regularity and order,—a time and place for everything, and everything in its proper time and place:
10. To promote, both by precept and example, cleanliness, neatness, and decency. To personally inspect the children every morning, to see that they have their hands and faces washed, their hair combed, and clothes clean. The school apartments, too, should be swept and dusted every evening:
11. To pay the strictest attention to the morals and general conduct of the pupils; to omit no opportunity of inculcating the principles of truth and honesty; the duties of respect to superiors, and obedience to all persons placed in authority over them:
12. To evince a regard for the improvement and general welfare of the pupils; to treat them with kindness, combined with firmness; and to aim at governing them by their affections and reason rather than harshness and severity:

13. To cultivate kindly and affectionate feelings among the pupils; to discountenance quarrelling, cruelty to animals, and every approach to vice:

14. To practice such discipline in school as would be exercised by a judicious parent in the family, avoiding corporal punishment, except when it shall appear to him to be imperatively necessary; and then a record of the offence and the punishment shall be made in the school register for the inspection of trustees and visitors:

15. No teacher shall compel the services of pupils for his own private benefit or convenience:

16. For gross misconduct, or a violent or wilful opposition to authority, the teacher may suspend a pupil from attending school, forthwith informing the parent or guardian of the fact, and the reason of it; but no pupil shall be expelled without the authority of the trustees:

17. When the example of any pupil is very hurtful, and reformation appears hopeless, it shall be the duty of the teacher, with the approbation of the trustees, to expel such pupil from the school; but any pupil under public censure, who shall express to the teacher his regret for such a course of conduct, as openly and explicitly as the case may require, shall, with the approbation of the trustees and teacher, be re-admitted to the school.

In the struggle of schooling to survive, educational ideals continually gave way to the demands of harsher realities. While nineteenth-century educational promoters initially sought to advance schooling's status by attracting a corps of male teachers of high moral character and strong educational background, school boards most often had limited resources and hired the cheapest, most readily available teachers, most of whom were young women whose formal qualifications fell far short of desired standards (Prentice, 1977: 108–9; Wotherspoon, 1993: 93). While critics were tempted to blame the worst educational problems on the young women who entered the classroom, it was in fact often the zeal and resourcefulness of these teachers and supportive community members, rather than any higher educational motives, that enabled schooling to flourish (Shack, 1973). Ironically, when schooling became successful in attracting large numbers of students, there was an even greater reliance on hastily prepared teachers to ensure that all schools could be staffed.

In part to compensate, education came to be governed by a growing array of formal regulations. Most jurisdictions, by the late nineteenth century, introduced rules governing everything from textbooks to school behaviour, often in the form of legislation to ensure compulsory attendance, regular taxation, and other matters, as part of an effort to regularize schooling. Strict adherence to daily attendance records and specific classroom routines enabled school authorities to monitor teachers and pupils carefully, while provisions for school finance helped to secure educational stability. Classroom life could be a deadening process of enforced order with rituals of repetition to memorize information (Axelrod, 1997: 57–8). In combination, these measures were important because they represented standards and practices that distinguished schooling from everyday life. Formal education became a central element in the expansion of state rule.

Social reformers promoted schools as critical tools in the state's crusade against the social disorganization that accompanied significant social transformations in the late nineteenth and early twentieth centuries. North American social and institutional life was altered by new industries and technologies, urban growth, the promotion of settlement in the West, and massive immigration. Public optimism about the future was mixed with uncertainty about new challenges. Unemployment, displacement from work, crime, poverty, unwelcome intrusions by 'foreigners', family breakdown, and generally declining moral standards loomed as supposed threats to the social order.

Many diverse reform movements that advocated education and other social intervention into private life grew around and played upon these fears. Government officials, churches and religious orders, employers, workers' associations, community leaders, and numerous other groups (often with different motivations and degrees of success) influenced the shape and direction that formal schooling eventually would take at the centre of public life (Charland, 2000). Some of these interests were driven by concern that rapid changes were undermining the social order and leading to declining standards of living, while others acted out of concern for the welfare of families and individuals disadvantaged by social changes (Moscovitch and Drover, 1987). The state or authorities acting on behalf of the state, representing public as opposed to more particular or parochial interests, gained new powers to act as legal guardians for individuals who were deemed socially unfit or problematic in some way. The Juvenile Delinquents Act, enacted in 1908, enabled the state to provide 'assistance' to young offenders who were portrayed as 'misdirected and misguided'. Similarly, during the 1890s, provincial governments authorized teachers to act *in loco parentis*, effectively granting them parental responsibilities for the time that children were at school. Other reforms, demanded by such groups as charitable and welfare organizations and mental and public health movements, were based on the designation of particular groups as problematic or incapable of supporting themselves, thereby warranting the personal and professional services of official agents.

The arguments employed by social reformers emphasized the need for state intervention in the absence of proper guidance by parents (Sutherland, 1976). A plea written in the late 1860s by school officials in Prince Edward Island for compulsory attendance legislation to counteract the 'evils of irregular attendance' is typical of the justifications of the need for public education and other mechanisms to ensure compliance with state rule: 'If then, from the poverty, the cupidity, or the apathy of parents, the education of their children be neglected, it is surely the duty of the State to interpose its authority in their behalf, by means of a compulsory law' (cited in Prentice and Houston, 1975: 165). This kind of appeal blamed individual children and their parents for ignorance or neglect, leading to social problems that demanded a social solution by the state, which was posed as the protector of the public or common interest. In this case, compulsory schooling was a mechanism to keep children off the streets, teaching them in the process rules of discipline, proper conduct, and perhaps even useful skills and knowledge.

Industry, Science, and the Bureaucratic Organization of Schooling (1910s–1940s)

While the historical evidence indicates that schools were not established simply to meet employers' demands to produce a compliant industrial workforce, industry doubtless affected the rise of public schooling in significant ways. Educational administrators sought to ensure the success of schooling by making the education system relevant—and perceived as useful—to life in industrial societies. They emphasized that students had to be trained to adapt to a changing world and to come out of schools with skills and knowledge that would contribute to their gainful employment. While business and industry officials often had little to do directly with schooling, educational authorities sought to cultivate the support of business leaders, parents, and other public interests in order to stabilize the education system.

Education officials also looked to industry for models to govern curriculum and school organization. The physical arrangement of the classroom, with its rows of desks under the watchful gaze of the teacher, the division of the school day into distinct periods or blocks of time, an early emphasis on memory work and rote exercises, and concern for punctuality, proper manners, and good habits were derived from military and religious training, but they were also highly amenable to a factory system of industrial production. Modern industry, moreover, provided models of organizational and classroom management oriented to educational efficiency. Scientific management, a strategy by which employers could assert control over industrial production processes by dividing tasks into their simplest, cheapest operations, was promoted by many educational administrators as a most effective method of lesson planning. Curricula were to be organized and planned systematically, not left to guesswork and reliance on teaching methods that were used simply because they seemed to work in the classroom (Wotherspoon, 1995a).

Educational reform was also influenced by non-economic factors beyond an industrial logic and work preparation. In the early twentieth century, many educators advocated a philosophy of **educational progressivism**. Educational progressives, combining faith in the twin virtues of science and humanism, viewed schools as institutions that contributed to the realization of social progress by allowing students to develop their full human potentials. They wanted to replace earlier models of child development, which emphasized routine tradition and factory-like regulation, with approaches that provided opportunities to foster interest, creativity, and positive personal growth. Progressivism advocated the incorporation within schooling of subjects that allowed for artistic and interpersonal development rather than strict academic courses. Teachers, in turn, required specialized training, in part to learn the scientific principles on which pedagogy and human development were grounded. In the process, a series of educational reforms emerged. These reforms were driven simultaneously by objectives for a more democratic and humanistic learning environment and by a desire for the creation of 'an educational system which was highly centralized, bureaucratic, autocratic, geared to the development of a meritocracy of intelligence, and designed to lead and direct an adequately socialized majority' (Mann, 1980: 115).

As the school system became governed increasingly by principles of rational organization derived from business and industry, there was a contradictory significance for the development both of schooling and of teaching as a professional occupation. Increasingly specialized training, grounded in science, gave teaching a degree of expertise that could advance its status as a professional occupation. By World War II, schools in most regions of Canada had become centrally organized as bureaucratic structures within larger school units. The average school size in Canada increased from 66 pupils per school in the mid-1920s to 156 in 1960 and 350 in 1970 (Manzer, 1994: 131). There were several advantages to the amalgamation of smaller schools and school districts into larger units. Many smaller schools were not financially viable, and although each school was required to provide a range of basic programs and services, it was often not possible for many schools to offer complete programs or attend to diverse educational needs. Larger schools offered better prospects for stable educational services accompanied by more extensive facilities, more complete educational programs, and a variety of curricular and extracurricular choices. It became possible for school districts to offer teachers better pay and job security and, particularly in the senior grades, to provide conditions in which teachers would be better able to teach in their areas of specialization.

Both community input and teacher professionalism, however, faced direct and indirect constraints that limited their influence on educational practice. Teachers were subordinated within an educational bureaucracy, subject to the supervision of educational administrators and guided by regulations set by officials outside the occupation. Indirect control over teaching was extended by the development of scientific curricula and central planning, which tended to move educational decision-making on many crucial issues, such as selection of textbooks and the organization of curricula, from the classroom to sources outside the school (Popkewitz, 1991). In the process, the treatment of educational matters as technical problems also minimized opportunities for meaningful community involvement in the education system. Experts, claiming legitimacy through training and knowledge related to principles of educational management, child development, curriculum planning, and pedagogy, assumed authority over a growing domain of issues beyond the reach of most public participants.

Educational Expansion in the Post-World War II Period (1940s–1970s)

The role of schooling in society increased in complexity throughout the twentieth century. The dynamic growth of education systems was accompanied by extensive reconsideration and debate concerning the purposes of education in a changing society. Educational practices expanded in two general ways. First, an increasing array of educational institutions, programs, and curricula emerged, incorporating a broad range of courses and subject areas not previously taught. Second, growing numbers of people enrolled in educational programs and remained in them for longer periods of time. The result has been massive increases in enrolments and educational attainments since the end of World War II. At the same time, significant changes occurred in the nature and quality of schooling. For the most part, classrooms were better equipped, teachers were better qualified, and curricular offerings were more diverse than ever before.

Formal education also gained an increasingly central place in social and economic life beyond the schools. Three interrelated developments—the Cold War, scientific and technical advancement, and the growth of the **welfare state**—had a profound impact on schooling after World War II. Canada, to a certain extent echoing concerns expressed in the United States about the growing influence of the Soviet Union and the possible spread of communism, turned to the education system as a mechanism to ensure citizenship, loyalty, and a knowledge base that would ensure the supremacy of North American interests. The war effort had also contributed to highly co-ordinated, productive economic output in many industries, making it possible to invest in new technologies, advanced skills formation, and various forms of state services to stabilize social order and foster social security. By the mid-twentieth century, formal education gained increasing recognition as a credentialling mechanism. The attainment of educational certification became a mark of entry into specific occupations and jobs, in some cases involving requirements for advanced education and training beyond minimal levels previously associated with initial entry into the labour force.

As new employment opportunities were created in a context of rising industrial productivity, mass distribution of consumer goods and services, and the expansion of employment in human services through the growth of the state sector, there was a high correlation between educational achievement and the attainment of stable jobs with good wages and working conditions. Social reformers also looked to schools as sites where people could be taught to develop interests that would enable them to use their leisure time and meet the diverse demands of advanced liberal democracies more fruitfully.

By the 1960s, formal education appeared to be well-positioned to fulfill its promise to contribute to a more equitable social order. Educational expansion, combined with favourable social and economic circumstances, suggested that all persons, regardless of social background, had potential opportunities for social and economic advancement.

Although there was considerable reason to be optimistic, heightened emphasis on the value of schooling prompted a reassessment of educational realities that claimed that education could not always deliver what it promised. Beginning in the late 1950s, as observed in the previous chapter, several studies framed within what came to be known as status attainment research highlighted the continuing association of schooling with substantial socio-economic inequalities. Moreover, people's life experiences did not always accord with emergent expectations. As schooling and the ideologies surrounding its social benefits gained in prominence, it became easy to blame individuals for their failure to take advantage of opportunities for socio-economic advancement.

However, schooling itself also proved to be vulnerable to criticism. On one side critics like Hilda Neatby (1953), in her controversial *So Little for the Mind*, attacked schools for straying from their intellectual roots by catering to an overly broad range of interests. The problem, viewed from this perspective, was that schooling was becoming too diverse, weakening its ability to provide a common core of essential knowledge and values. Other critics, by contrast, maintained that schools were not keeping pace with changing socio-economic realities. They saw it as essential for schools to offer socially relevant knowledge, vocational training, and courses related to new employment requirements. These demands intensified after 1957, when the Soviet Union's launch of the Sputnik satellite prompted fears that North America was losing its technological advantage to new superpowers. Educational institutions came under fire for their failure to produce technically sophisticated and innovative graduates.

Elementary and secondary schools responded by revamping their curricula, giving emphasis to programs in mathematics and the natural sciences. Enhancement of scientific and technical training, prompted by federal funding initiatives, also fuelled post-secondary educational expansion. Nationally, the number of bachelor's degrees awarded in mathematics and the physical sciences increased substantially, from 1,617 in 1960–1 to 7,730 a decade later (Dominion Bureau of Statistics, 1963; Statistics Canada, 1973). Enrolment was encouraged by the addition of programs and research facilities to existing institutions as well as by the creation of several new technical institutes and community colleges throughout the nation. Between 1960 and 1970, education spending increased from 14 per cent of all government expenditures in Canada to 21.6 per cent (Lockhart, 1979: 229), and by 1975 there were 170 public community colleges in Canada compared to just one a decade earlier (Dennison, 1981: 213).

The expansion of the welfare state and focus on scientific training helped fuel the growth of **post-secondary education** in the 1960s and 1970s as demands increased for educated professionals and for workers in the social and human services and in skilled scientific occupations. In Canada, the number of bachelor's degrees awarded in education increased 5.8 times between 1960–1 and 1970–1, while those in law increased by a factor of 5.2 times, those in nursing 4 times, and those in the physical sciences 4.9 times; over the next decade, the number of social work degrees awarded increased by nearly 5 times. Educational and occupational growth in these areas was especially important for providing opportunities for women. The proportion of bachelor's and first professional degrees awarded to women doubled from one-quarter to one-half between 1960–1 and 1980–1. By 1980–1, women received 73.5 per cent of Bachelor of Education degrees (compared to 37.2 per cent in 1960–1), 77.3 per cent of Bachelor of Social Work degrees (44.3 per cent in 1960–1), and nearly all of the degrees awarded in nursing. While only 5 per cent of recipients of Bachelor of Law degrees in 1960–1 were women, that proportion had climbed to over 33 per cent two decades later. By contrast, however, women received only 8.4 per cent of bachelor's degrees awarded in engineering and applied sciences, and 29.6 per cent of first degrees in mathematics and physical sciences in 1980–1 (calculated from Dominion Bureau of Statistics, 1963: 22, 44–9; Statistics Canada, 1973: 456–8; Statistics Canada, 1984: 69–74).

These trends illustrate the strong paradox that characterizes formal education. Expansion of post-secondary education after World War II offered legitimacy to the belief that formal education could provide individuals with meaningful social and economic opportunities. The attainment of higher education credentials not only enabled individuals to gain access to secure and well-paying jobs, but it also opened up possibilities previously unavailable to women and members of other minority groups. At the same time, the issues of who could achieve educational success and what kinds of educational programs were available to different groups remained problematic. As formal education came to be relied on more frequently as a screening mechanism for entry into jobs and other social venues, there was a danger that disadvantaged groups could be left even further behind when socio-economic inequities were reproduced. Social advancement became that much more difficult for people who, for various reasons, were denied educational success. Moreover, as revealed in the distribution of university degrees to men and women, education itself remained highly stratified, producing different opportunities and career prospects for different social groups. While increasing numbers of people were attaining higher levels of formal education, there were considerable discrepancies in the kinds of benefits that people received from their educational credentials.

Educational Crisis and Reassessment since the mid-1970s
Debate and controversy over educational priorities were not restricted to labour markets and credentials. The increasing centrality of education to social life drew attention also to the educational process and to people's experiences within educational institutions. By the end of the 1960s, popular demands for educational reform intensified in an atmosphere characterized by sensitivity to drastic social changes and critical questioning of fundamental social institutions. Technological developments were altering how people lived and worked. Media coverage of international events, particularly United States involvement in the Vietnam War, made startlingly evident the significance of global events for everyday life. University campuses and other educational sites were crucial nurturing grounds

Box 3.4 Education Problems in Canada, 1958

After World War II, educators, policy-makers, and media reports highlighted the need to link education with technological advancement. Following the development of nuclear weapons and the launch of the Sputnik satellite by Russia, educational reformers advocated the adoption of education systems like those in the Soviet Union and other nations, and increased investment in human capital, to encourage the expansion of scientific and technical expertise. In 1958, the Canadian Teachers' Federation, the Canadian Manufacturers' Association, the Canadian Labour Congress, and other organizations sponsored a national Conference on Education, described here by the then-president of the British Columbia Teachers' Federation (Cottingham, 1958: 398–9, 407), to reassess educational practices and establish new educational priorities:

For years people closely connected with education have been increasingly alarmed about the magnitude of the task which we have set ourselves in Canada—to provide the maximum formal education at public expense for every man's child. Perhaps those with most reason to be alarmed at the growing crisis have been the teachers and professors who face their classes every day and know to what extent the time and talents of students and instructors are being wasted or used to best advantage, despite the rising costs of education. Never in the history of our country have so many boys and girls been kept in school and university so long at such great expense as now. Never have teachers and professors been in such short supply. Never have their tasks been so heavy. Never has the supply of well prepared professional, industrial, and technological workers been so far short of the needs of our society.

No matter how critical the problem, in a democratic nation the solution must await the awakening of public opinion and only through the time-consuming democratic process can action be effected. . . .

This conference was planned long before USSR launched its Sputniks into outer space, but these evidences of scientific achievement on the part of our northern neighbor increased the significance of this national discussion on the problems of education in Canada, where our strange scale of values causes us to spend twice as much on liquor and tobacco as we do on formal education and almost four times as much on defense.

Dr Wilder Penfield, distinguished brain specialist and Director of the Conference, gave the keynote address. 'Dissatisfaction with the support of education and the performance of educationists has led to this meeting', he said, 'and the educationists have it in their power to mould our future.' Dr Penfield had visited USSR two years ago. There he found the prestige and the level of pay for teachers and professors considerably higher comparatively than they are in

Canada. Russia had a better system of scholarships for its able students and its training of prospective teachers and university professors was far more rigid and exacting. However, he suspected that in Russia students specialize too early without being grounded in the humanities.

'The specialist who has a broader educational basis leads a better life.' At the same time Dr Penfield felt that more emphasis should be put on trade schools and technical colleges in Canada.

He set the whole problem squarely before the delegates when he said:

'Looking to the future we face two possibilities; the ending of this civilization such as it is, or its final flowering and fulfillment in greater progress. Education is our only hope, our challenge in the peaceful competition of the future. But, if war should come, our wits might well save us. We would be well advised to spend on the cultivation of those wits a sum comparable with what we are spending on explosive defense.' Especially in the field of higher education, Dr Penfield felt that financial support must be doubled, but that support must leave these institutions complete freedom of development. Responsibility for support of teaching at all educational levels rests with the provinces, but industry, labor and the federal government could provide scholarships. . . .

Source: Reprinted with permission from the BC Teachers' Federation.

for the emergence of anti-war protests, radical student movements, and feminism. Many of the concerns were motivated by increasing awareness of the reality that graduates were not getting the kinds of jobs and social opportunities they felt they had been promised through education.

Schooling, in this context, came under attack from nearly all sides. Left-wing and radical movements, while often mobilized and empowered by educational experiences, dismissed schooling as a bastion of bureaucratic traditionalism that stifled, rather than enhanced, creativity and genuine opportunity. The ideas of such writers as Ivan Illich (1970), who advocated alternatives to schooling that required the dismantling of the present education system, gained popularity as well as notoriety both within and beyond educational circles. From the right, critics argued that social radicalism itself both produced and was a product of educational failure. Formal education had strayed from its disciplinary and instrumental purposes, according to this viewpoint, and needed to return to fundamental values, knowledge, and respect for authority in order to prevent social breakdown.

Officially, though, the most successful educational ideology was embodied in liberal and human capital positions. Educators as well as policy-makers revealed renewed interest in issues of equality of opportunity and educational progressivism, modified to meet contemporary demands. Several influential reports presented in the late 1960s and early 1970s, such as those known popularly as the Hall-Dennis Report in Ontario (1968) and the Worth Report in Alberta (1972), stressed that child-centred learning opportunities and educational flexibility were crucial elements in people's ability to adapt to a changing society.

The spirit of change embodied in recommendations contained within the various reports was translated into a flurry of initiatives to restructure schooling and educational practices across Canada. Where resources were sufficient, students were presented with many new options beyond the traditional core curricula in areas such as law, family life, sex education, band and music appreciation, psychology, creative arts, and social studies in order to broaden their development and to better prepare them for the diverse demands of a post-industrial society. Experimental and innovative practices were encouraged in educational circles to overcome what came to be regarded as overly rigid and outmoded pedagogical models based on military and industrial principles. Schools were designed or modified to incorporate open classrooms and learning resource centres to counteract the rigid, box-like structure of existing school spatial organization; boundaries between disciplinary subjects and grade levels were broken down; student evaluation and reporting came to emphasize a wide range of skills, competencies, and subjective observations rather than strictly letter or numerical grades; and teachers were encouraged to draw out the child through critical thinking and social interaction rather than focus strictly on cognitive knowledge and prescribed curricular content.

Some of the changes had immediate impacts on educational practices and outcomes. Curricular revisions and modification of programs and practices to meet local needs or to improve responsiveness to disadvantaged groups, for instance, were long overdue. However, there was considerable resistance to the process of change, and in many cases little evidence to support widespread perceptions that schooling was being transformed in fundamental ways. Many teachers felt that educational reforms had been imposed on them with little consultation and inadequate training and resources to implement them properly. Traditionalists pointed to the chaos, wasted time, and lack of tangible results as evidence that educational liberalization was a drastic failure, which provoked demands for centralized curricula with a 'back to the basics' emphasis. Still other critics pointed out that the changes, as dramatic as they appeared to be, were mostly cosmetic and did not reach the real sources of social and educational problems, thereby perpetuating socio-economic inequalities and failing to acknowledge that the school-age population and their needs were undergoing transitions (Tomkins, 1981: 147–9). 'In short,' as one commentator observed in the early 1970s, 'having failed to satisfy the exaggerated expectations created by its promoters, education is now enjoying an excess of abuse for its considerable shortcomings' (Myers, 1973: 11).

A recurrent problem with educational reform has been that too much attention was focused inside the education system without consideration of crucial social, economic, and political factors that limited what formal schooling could do. Initiatives like the ones outlined above, which were intended to broaden the scope of education, were introduced during a period of fiscal restraint and reorganization of public services. Debate over educational goals and relevance exposed education as a vulnerable target for state measures to control public expenditures (Lockhart, 1979). From the late 1960s into the early 1970s, governments took several steps to contain education that included the introduction of legislation to cut back wages and other resources in the education sector and moves to centralize control over educational decision-making. Teachers' organizations in several provinces, notably British Columbia, Ontario, and Quebec, became increasingly militant in response to the deterioration of teaching and working conditions (LeBlanc, 1974; Repo, 1974). Symptomatic of the position of education generally, teachers felt that they were being made scapegoats for much deeper social and economic problems.

The nature and form of public education remained a core focus of political struggle throughout the 1980s and 1990s. Governments had to contend with significant economic and social transformations, including desires by firms and investors for easy access to the most profitable markets, aging population structures, and competitive pressures from rapidly developing regions of the world. In this context, neo-liberal policy agendas gained ascendancy in many parts of Canada and other nations, frequently targeting education in a series of measures to reduce public expenditures, limit the size of state activity and employment, and expand market-based forms of competition. By the mid-1990s, the volatile atmosphere was captured in a proliferation of media accounts under headlines like 'What's wrong with our schools?' as well as in popular literature that carried such titles as *Class Warfare: The Assault on Canada's Schools* (Barlow and Robertson, 1994), *School's Out: The Catastrophe in Public Education and What We Can Do About It* (Nikiforuk, 1993), and *Busting Bureaucracy to Reclaim Our Schools* (Lawton, 1995). Teachers' fears that their profession and schools were under assault were not assuaged by declining birth rates and public concerns that schools based on models designed several generations previously had become redundant for life in a global age. The next chapter explores how these issues have influenced the reshaping of education into the twenty-first century.

CONCLUSION

This chapter has traced educational development in Canada from an array of practices organized around specific familial, cultural, and local circumstances and requirements to the massive, complex, and often highly contested mélange of public and private enterprises that schooling represented at the end of the twentieth century. The core framework for formal education in Canada, taking shape over several decades, was cemented by the early 1970s when an expanding array of post-secondary institutions and early childhood educational programs augmented the consolidated school systems that delivered compulsory elementary and secondary programs. In the process, formal education systems have grown to encompass a diverse range of participants, curricular programs, and social learning experiences far beyond those that appeared in the earliest schools.

Ongoing economic, labour market, and policy transformations continue to have profound impacts on people's working and private lives (Li, 1996: 136–45; Clement and Vosko, 2003). During the periods highlighted in the last sections of this chapter, demands for both low-skill and highly qualified labour have increased in conjunction with growth in service industries relative to manufacturing and primary industries. Economic and social changes have contributed to shifting social relations and divisions of labour in both the workplace and households. Women's labour force participation rates, now close to two-thirds of all women ages 15 and over, increased steadily, from 20 per cent in 1941 to 40 per cent in 1971 and 60 per cent by 1991. Canada has also imported substantial numbers of workers and family members from other nations, turning since the late 1960s from a focus on Western European and American immigrant sources to Asia, Africa, the Middle East, and the Caribbean to meet demands for highly skilled and professional labour. In the early 1970s, multiculturalism emerged as a new policy emphasis that, along with political demands for recognition of unique rights for francophones and Aboriginal peoples, has been associated with periodic political tensions around race and ethnic relations as well as questions about national unity and relations between individual and collective rights.

Other demographic shifts have affected schooling through changes in the size, concentration, and composition of student populations. The high enrolments that accompanied baby boomers and their children through the education system have given way to declining enrolments in many elementary and secondary school systems and concerns about longer-term prospects for post-secondary enrolments. The increasing urban concentration of the Canadian population, as well as other demographic changes, has had an uneven impact on the ability of school districts to provide adequate and equitable services for all students. The growing concentration of immigrant populations in larger cities, for instance, poses a demand both for increased institutional space and for programming and services that address the needs of diverse student bodies.

The educational changes described in this chapter represent part of a broad reshaping of social, economic, and political landscapes that have affected the character of the nation and the experiences of individuals. These domains and the world they are part of have become simultaneously more specialized and more highly interconnected. The next chapter addresses in more detail some of the core characteristics of education systems in Canada in relation to major transformations occurring in Canada and globally. Public and policy focus on a knowledge society has offered prospects for formal educational institutions and educators to regain much of the respectability and fiscal stability that appeared to be lost at the end of the twentieth century. Nonetheless, this promise is accompanied by significant challenges as educational stakes increase and educational participants and relationships become more diverse.

ANNOTATED FURTHER READINGS

Axelrod, Paul. 1997. *The Promise of Schooling: Education in Canada, 1800–1914*. Toronto: University of Toronto Press. Axelrod provides a concise overview of the early history of education in Canada, emphasizing how education has been shaped by and has affected complex class, gender, racial, ethnic, cultural, and political factors.

Curtis, Bruce. 1988. *Building the Educational State: Canada West, 1836–1871*. London, Ont.: Althouse Press. Focusing on a crucial period of educational history in Canada, the author offers a sociological analysis of the dynamics associated with the establishment of public education within the broader process of state formation.

Lawr, Douglas A., and Robert D. Gidney. 1973. *Educating Canadians: A Documentary History of Public Education*. Toronto: Van Nostrand Reinhold. This rich resource contains policy statements, legislation, administrative documents, and submissions from parents and other community representatives pertinent to key issues and phases in the development of formal education systems in Canada.

Manzer, Ronald A. 1994. *Public Schools and Political Ideas: Canadian Educational Policy in Historical Perspective*. Toronto: University of Toronto Press. The author examines the development of Canadian education through the interaction of political, economic, and ideological forces.

Royal Commission on Aboriginal Peoples in Canada. 1996. 'Residential Schools', in *Volume 1: Looking Forward, Looking Back*, and 'Education' in *Volume 3: Gathering Strength*. Ottawa: Government of Canada, Report of the Royal Commission on Aboriginal Peoples in Canada. These two chapters provide a concise summary of key issues and developments in education emerging through the relationships among Aboriginal people, governments, and other Canadians.

KEY TERMS

Curriculum Programs, courses, and materials arranged and presented formally to meet the objectives of educational institutions.

Educational progressivism An educational movement based on the progressive philosophy that the development of humans, as individuals and societies, advances through the broad cultivation of intellectual, physical, and emotional growth. Popularized in the 'child-centred' orientation of John Dewey early in the twentieth century, the approach has influenced many school reforms since the late 1960s.

Indigenous knowledge Systems of knowledge and ways of knowing, premised on the interrelationships among humans with one another and the environments of which they are part, transmitted among generations through integrated cultural traditions and social systems.

Moral regulation Processes by which notions of right and wrong, and the sense of how to act in manners deemed to be socially appropriate, come to be internalized as part of individual personalities.

Post-secondary education Formal education leading to degrees, certificates, or diplomas beyond high school graduation levels, normally through universities, community colleges, or other accredited institutions.

Public education Educational institutions and programs that are organized, administered, and funded by governments or state agencies.

State apparatus Institutions, agencies, and regulations established, organized, and administered by governments.

Welfare state A policy framework in which governments, rather than individuals, families, or other agencies, are responsible for ensuring the economic security and physical and social well-being of all citizens, including a network of government institutions organized to carry out major social welfare and development functions.

STUDY QUESTIONS

1. How and why did elementary and secondary schooling in Canada and comparable nations come to be organized through the state rather than privately?

2. Which social and economic factors have had the greatest impact on the massive expansion of education systems and educational attainment levels over the past five decades?

3. What factors contributed to increasing stabilization of education systems in Canada over time? What difficulties did these systems and their advocates encounter in the process?

4. What are some of the main visions of schooling advanced by different groups or interests in the development of Canada's education system? Which of these have been most influential in the shape that education has taken, and why?

5. Critically discuss the relationship between public education and minority groups in the development of education in Canada. What have been some of the major issues in these relations, and how, if at all, have they been resolved?

Chapter 4

The Structure of Canadian
Education Systems

Introduction

This chapter examines the nature and organization of contemporary educational activities in Canada, focusing primarily on the structure and core dimensions associated with formal education. In Canada, formal education is a collection of diverse systems rather than a single system. The previous chapter has emphasized how most formal education has come to be regulated and operated through the state, although there is increasing pressure to deregulate and privatize educational services. Here, we consider the arrangements by which education in Canada is regulated and delivered, and summarize key trends associated with educational enrolments, expenditures, and organizational patterns. While much of the focus is descriptive, the discussion in this chapter points to emerging themes and controversies, many of which are addressed in more detail in subsequent chapters. The chapter closes with a brief discussion of comparative educational trends, pointing to debates and issues at the heart of pressures for educational reform in the context of major social and economic transformations.

An Overview of Educational Activities in Canada

Canadians engage in a broad and expanding range of educational activities. The discussion in this chapter and throughout the book emphasizes *formal education*, that is, organized study through state-certified institutions aimed towards the achievement of a degree, diploma, or certificate. Nonetheless, it is important to acknowledge that growing emphasis on lifelong learning, educational choice, and knowledge societies has been accompanied by increased participation in and interaction among diverse forms of educational practices for nearly all members of industrially developed societies. These include *non-formal and adult education*, which refers to courses, educational activities, and training programs organized through clubs, associations, and workplaces to augment formal credentials or to meet selected personal or employment-related needs and interests. Another significant type of educational activity, **informal learning**, generally encompasses all learning activities that occur outside of formally organized educational sites. Informal learning normally focuses on the acquisition of specific knowledge or skills in ways that are more structured than the everyday or incidental learning that occurs through socialization processes (Livingstone, 2004: 14).

In Canada, formal education is a provincial jurisdiction under the terms of the 1867 British North America Act (since renamed the Constitution Act, 1867) and the subsequent Constitution Act of 1982. However, in practice, several agencies and levels of government are involved in the organization and delivery of education. Much of the responsibility for the actual delivery of educational services rests at the local level. School boards, along with recently recognized First Nations educational authorities, generally are accorded the most active role in the day-to-day operations of elementary and secondary schools. Both public and private interests operate post-secondary educational institutions, which are supported by a combination of grants from federal and provincial governments, tuition fees, and funds from corporate and private sources. Increases at all levels in the number of private schools, training institutes, and programs, and the expansion of educational programs outside formal educational institutions, have added to the diversity of educational service providers in Canada.

Figure 4.1 provides a broad overview of the structure of formal education in Canada. The diagram indicates the general transition process followed by individuals through major levels of the education system. The pathways depicted in the figure provide a simple formal description of the general organization of education in relation to labour markets; the boundaries and flows that describe the actual patterns of transitions across different sites of learning, work, and social experience are becoming increasingly more fluid and complex, as will be discussed in Chapter 7.

Elementary and secondary schooling constitutes the largest component of the education system. Most students are introduced to the formal education system at the elementary school level (although an increasing number of children are engaged in preschool programs offered by provincial systems or privately), which normally begins at ages 5 to 7 in kindergarten or Grade 1 and continues to Grades 6, 7, or 8 in most provinces. Curricula at this level tend to focus on a limited number of subjects, where all pupils are exposed to core areas, including language, mathematics, science, social studies, creative arts, physical education, and possibly a few other options. In the early grades, students often receive instruction from only one or two teachers. More distinct boundaries between subjects and exposure to greater numbers of teachers generally prevail by the middle grades. In some provinces, junior high schools serve students between Grades 6 or 7 to Grades 8 or 9 to provide a transition period into high school.

Secondary or senior high school, which normally continues to Grade 12, is organized around more distinct subject areas, providing core courses and electives associated with specific streams tailored to requirements and interests for academic, vocational, career, and other paths. High school graduation is generally required for admission into post-secondary educational programs. In Quebec, however, students proceed from Grade 11 to programs in a CEGEP (collège d'enseignement général et professionnel) that are preparatory for entry to either university education or particular vocations.

Figure 4.1 The Learning Continuum

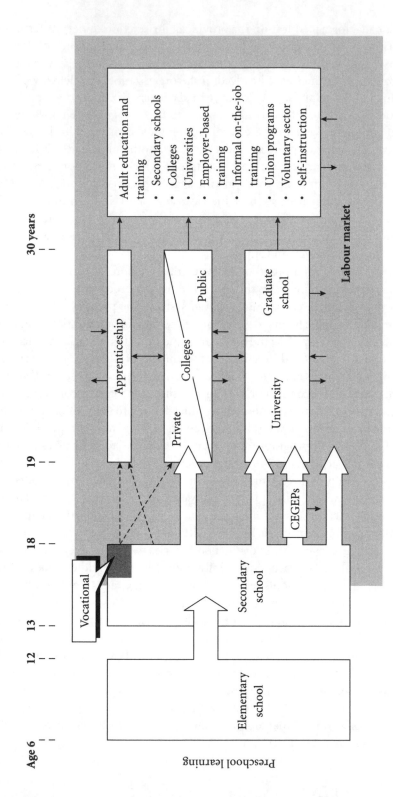

Source: Reprinted from Industry Canada (1992: 17). Reproduced with permission from the Minister of Public Works and Government Services Canada 1997.

Post-secondary education includes universities, which are institutions that grant degrees, and community colleges, which offer diverse programs that may lead to transfer to a university program or to diploma certification. Once they are accredited through provincial legislation, post-secondary institutions usually are granted considerable autonomy to set programs and course requirements, hire faculty or instructors, and establish and enforce academic standards. Trades or vocational training incorporates specific programs, usually of short-term duration, as well as longer apprenticeship programs combining work experience with classroom training, that are oriented to qualification for specific trades or occupations. High school graduation has not always been required as a prerequisite for many of these programs, but this is changing as trades-vocational training encompasses more specialized knowledge and skills and comes to be integrated into the post-secondary level (for details, see Statistics Canada and Council of Ministers of Education Canada, 2007: 146–8).

The trends depicted in Figures 4.2 and 4.3 offer a sense of perspective on changing patterns in educational enrolments and expenditures since the mid-twentieth century. The figures illustrate the significant increases in the size and cost, as well as the shifting composition, of the education system since the early 1950s.

Demographic changes have had a profound impact on educational enrolments and expenditures. Student numbers rose sharply as children born in the post-war baby boom reached school age and progressed through different stages of schooling from the mid-1950s to the early 1970s. Somewhat less markedly, the subsequent progression of baby boomers' children through schooling into the 1980s and 1990s maintained elementary and secondary school enrolment figures close to the historical high point reached in 1970–1. By the early 1970s—the point at which educational expenditures reached their highest levels as a proportion of the gross national product—individuals from the baby-boom cohort were graduating from high school and entering universities, community colleges, and trade programs. Declining birth rates since the mid-1960s have been partly offset by the tendency for more people to stay in school for longer periods of time and by high immigration levels, but total student numbers in elementary and secondary levels have been declining since the late 1990s.

Another striking characteristic of the trends depicted in Figures 4.2 and 4.3 is the growing significance of post-secondary education. Universities and community colleges began to establish a strong presence by the late 1960s, with significant growth since that time, especially at the university level, as enrolments have roughly doubled in each 20-year period since the mid-1960s. While Chapter 7 discusses the implications of post-secondary expansion for different social groups, for now it is important to observe how increasing emphasis on educational priorities is reflected in these patterns of educational growth. One way to understand this is to look at Figure 4.3, which demonstrates, in comparison with Figure 4.2, first, that the amount of money spent by Canadians on education has risen even more dramatically than the number of students and, second, that the funding for post-secondary education has grown even more rapidly over the period under consideration. The disproportionate expenditures reflect, in part, the fact that education at higher levels costs more because post-secondary education typically includes more highly qualified instructors as well as additional costs for infrastructural support, laboratories and research facilities, and other operating costs. These increased expenditures also reveal the growing commitment, especially since the 1960s and 1970s, to investment in higher education associated with an emphasis on human capital development and expansion of a post-industrial or knowledge-based economy in which individuals and governments have been more inclined to promote investment in highly qualified labour. Substantial funding, enhanced by new expenditure programs supported by the federal government, facilitated the introduction of new institutions and programs at the community college and university levels to promote the development of knowledge and workers, particularly in scientific and technical fields. Since the early 1990s, the federal government, in common with most other highly developed nations, has elevated education and learning-related activities to a major priority as part of its innovation strategy to undertake investment for a knowledge-based economy (Wolfe, 2002).

The data in Table 4.1 and Figure 4.4 indicate the changing basis of educational finance in Canada since 1950. The most striking feature is the overwhelming extent to which education is financed by governments rather than private sources.

Figure 4.2   Full-time Enrolment in Canada (000s) by Level of Study

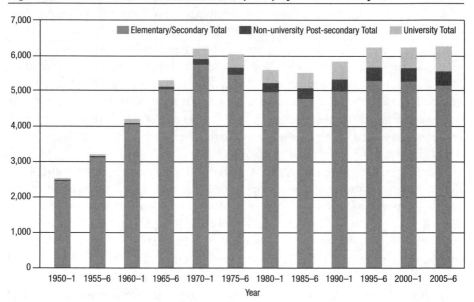

Note: Figures for 2005–6 are estimates.
Sources: 1950–1 to 1970–1 compiled from Statistics Canada, *Historical Compendium of Education Statistics* (Ottawa: Minister of Industry, Trade and Commerce, 1978), Catalogue no. 81–568; 1975–6 to 2000–1 compiled from Statistics Canada, *Education Quarterly Review* (Ottawa: Minister of Industry, Science and Technology, various issues), Catalogue no. 81–003.

Figure 4.3   Education Expenditures by Level, Canada, Selected Years, 1950–2003

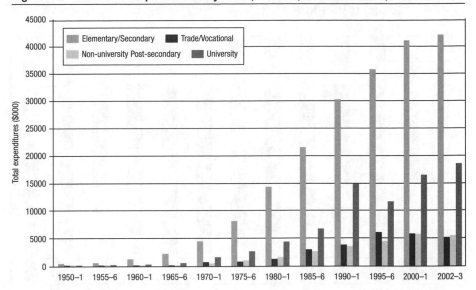

Sources: 1950–1 to 1970–1 compiled from Statistics Canada, *Historical Compendium of Education Statistics* (Ottawa: Minister of Industry, Trade and Commerce, 1978), Catalogue no. 81–568; 1975–6 to 1990–1 compiled from Statistics Canada, *Education in Canada* (Ottawa: Minister of Supply and Services Canada, various years), Catalogue no. 81–229; 1995–6 and 2000–1 compiled from Statistics Canada, *Education Quarterly Review* 9, 1 (Feb. 2003), Catalogue no. 81–003; 2002–3 from CANSIM.

Table 4.1   Total and Relative Expenditures ($000s) on Education in Canada, 1950–1 to 2002–3

	Total Expenditures on Education	Total Education Expenditures as % of GDP*
1950–1	438,751	2.4
1955–6	829,132	2.9
1960–1	1,705,986	4.4
1965–6	3,399,505	5.9
1970–1	7,674,669	8.5
1975–6	12,948,007	7.5
1980–1	22,201,575	7.1
1985–6	34,564,071	7.1
1990–1	48,679,624	7.2
1995–6	58,944,267	7.3
2000–1	66,500,252	6.3
2002–3	75,884,635	6.4

*Figures from 1950–1 to 1960–1 are for gross national product, which results in slightly higher percentages than for gross domestic product.
Sources: 1950–1 to 1960–1: Statistics Canada, *Historical Compendium of Education Statistics: From Confederation to 1975* (Ottawa: Minister of Industry, Trade and Commerce, 1978); 1965–6 to 1995–6: Statistics Canada, CANSIM Tables 3800015 and 4780001; 2000-01 and 2004–5: Statistics Canada and CMEC (2007).

Figure 4.4   Share of Expenditures on Education in Canada, by Direct Source of
             Funds, 1950–1 to 2002–3

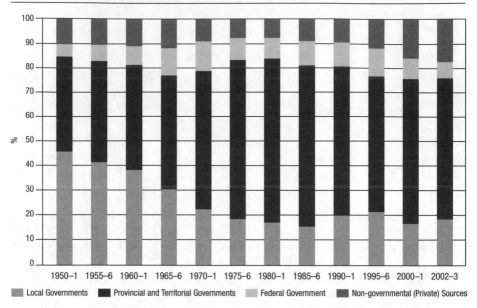

Note: Figures for 2002–3 are estimates.
Sources: 1950–1 to 1970–1: Statistics Canada, *Historical Compendium of Education Statistics: From Confederation to 1975* (Ottawa: Minister of Industry, Trade and Commerce, 1978); 1975–6 to 1990–1: Statistics Canada, *Advance Statistics of Education* (Ottawa: Minister of Industry, Science and Technology, various years); 1995–6: Statistics Canada, *Education Quarterly Review* 5, 3 (Mar. 1999); 2000–1: Statistics Canada, *Education Quarterly Review* 8, 3 (June 2002); 2002–3: Statistics Canada and CMEC (2007).

Consistent with constitutional responsibility for jurisdiction over education, over half of all spending on education is by provincial and territorial governments. Until the 1980s, provincial governments assumed growing fiscal responsibility for education, but since that time there has tended to be increased devolution of costs to local or municipal governments. While several recent government initiatives and fiscal policies seem to indicate the likelihood of a continuing pattern of down-loading of costs for education and other social spending programs to both local and private sources, there is also a counter-tendency towards centralization of educational planning and programming both federally and provincially. It is likely that further variations in these patterns will occur as governments move to streamline expenditures and consolidate their spheres of operations. Since the late 1990s, several provinces have adopted measures to tighten control over educational spending. Most of these reforms have sought to limit discretionary funding by school boards, to cut back on the number of school boards (see Table 4.2), and to ensure that public bodies are more accountable to those who pay for government services (Council of Ministers of Education Canada, 2001: 18–19).

Shifting patterns in educational spending also point to the changing nature of federal government participation in education. Under the Canadian constitutional

Table 4.2   Numbers of School Boards, by Province

Province	Numbers of School Boards	
	Mid-1990s	2006–7
British Columbia	75	60 (59 public, 1 francophone education authority)
Alberta	181	64 (42 public, 17 Catholic, 5 francophone) + 12 charter schools
Saskatchewan	121	28 (18 public, 8 Catholic and 1 Protestant separate, 1 francophone)
Manitoba	57	39 (38 public, 1 francophone)
Ontario	172	72 (32 anglophone and 4 francophone public, 28 anglophone and 8 francophone Catholic) + 33 smaller school authorities
Quebec	158	72 (60 French, 9 English, 3 special status First Nations)
New Brunswick*	18	14 (9 anglophone and 5 francophone)
Nova Scotia	22	8 (7 regional and 1 provincial francophone)
Prince Edward Island	5	3 (2 anglophone and 1 provincial francophone)
Newfoundland and Labrador	27	5 (4 anglophone and 1 provincial francophone)

*School boards were abolished in 1996 and reinstated in 2001.
Sources: Canadian School Boards Association, *Cross-Canada Chart, Education Governance in Canada* (1999), and information from provincial education departments and school board associations.

framework, the federal government's role in education is limited to matters that relate to minority languages, denominational schooling, and the education of designated groups under federal jurisdiction, such as registered Indians, the armed forces, and penitentiary inmates. In some of these areas, federal involvement has diminished through program reductions and jurisdictional transfers, particularly as First Nations and the Yukon, Northwest Territories, and Nunavut have gained responsibilities broadly comparable to provincial powers with respect to education and related areas. In other respects, the federal presence has expanded in education. Arising out of attempts to stimulate the development of various training initiatives and to co-ordinate labour market development strategies, the federal government has initiated several types of funding arrangements and programs, particularly in relation to post-secondary education, vocational training, and research and development initiatives. The federal government has also taken a leading role in promoting educational activities in areas such as multiculturalism, investment in innovation and knowledge-based initiatives, adoption of protocols to ensure comparable standards and transferability of credentials across jurisdictions, and mechanisms to integrate educational planning and policy-making.

The federal government's presence was most evident in its role in promoting educational expansion in the 1960s and 1970s. The federal share of educational funding more than doubled, from just under 5 per cent of total educational expenditures in 1950–1 to over 12 per cent two decades later. While the relative share of federal spending on education has since declined to current levels of less than 9 per cent of all spending on education in Canada, federal involvement in education is likely to remain highly contested and uncertain. Organizations such as the Council of Ministers of Education Canada and the Canadian Council on Learning are advancing a more highly co-ordinated national strategy for education, as global competition and related social and economic transformations have contributed to pressures to reorganize and streamline educational finance and service delivery, demands to co-ordinate educational programming and standards on a national level, and shifting conceptions of federal, provincial, and First Nations constitutional jurisdictions.

Efforts to reappraise and restructure education systems have drawn increased attention to privately funded and operated educational institutions and programs. Traditionally, in Canada, education by or within the private sector has been heavily overshadowed by public education. Governments have been reluctant to extend support and endorsement for private education beyond nominal levels on the grounds that schooling is a public enterprise that provides common learning experiences and opportunities for all segments of the population. The creation of local school boards and implementation of property-based taxation to support schools were designed to ensure that residents could gain input into and have a stake in educational matters. Without these measures, early school reformers feared that private and sectarian interests would dominate and fragment schooling, keeping it out of reach of much of the population.

The development of Canadian education has been heavily influenced by periodic demands by organized religious minorities (usually Roman Catholic and occasionally Protestant denominations) for instruction appropriate to their beliefs. One type of compromise was the establishment in several provinces of provisions to allow for publicly funded and regulated separate or denominational schooling to operate parallel with public school systems (Wilson, 1981). Initially, parents or groups who sought alternative forms of education were forced to finance these themselves with no assurance that programs and credentials would be officially certified or recognized. However, recent trends have seen a blurring of traditional boundaries that once separated public (secular), separate (denominational), and private schooling, sometimes accompanied by an escalation of tensions between advocates of different kinds of schooling. Sustained pressure from religious organizations and other groups resulted in legislative changes in many jurisdictions, beginning with the western provinces and Quebec since the late 1960s, to provide public funding for private schools that meet provincial criteria in prescribed areas like curriculum and teacher certification. Because these issues cut across several deeply embedded and often opposing values and interests, they resurface periodically in the form of intense controversy over different kinds of educational alternatives. The next two sections explore significant aspects of those challenges in relation to issues of market choice and accountability.

Box 4.1 Educational Reorganization, School Size, and Student Performance

The ongoing process of administrative reorganization of schooling gives rise to significant questions about what impact changes are likely to have on student performance and other educational activities. Issues of school and class size are of particular concern among educators and educational researchers. Many of the core issues are addressed in the following account by Pacholik (2007: A1–2) of a study commissioned by one Saskatchewan school board:

A study examining the optimum number of students in a school shows Regina Public Schools are 'definitely in the right direction,' says the board chairman.

'It really validates the process that we're going through with our communities and it lends some validation to the work that our administration has done,' Russ Marchuk said in an interview, adding that most of the city's public schools fall within the study's guidelines.

'All of our schools are good schools . . . the bottom line is as some of the evidence that Dr (Kenneth) Leithwood points out, there are academic parameters that are enhanced when you have schools of certain size,' said Marchuk following Tuesday's board meeting.

'When Dr Leithwood talks about course offerings being equitable, we have to ensure that our schools are of a similar size so that all of our students have access to that teacher expertise that he referred to,' he added.

Marchuk was responding to a report prepared for the board. Leithwood, a professor at the Ontario Institute for Studies in Education at the University of Toronto, conducted a literature review this summer on school size and its effects.

Reviewing 59 studies, Leithwood concluded the optimum school size is approximately 300 elementary students and about 600 students at the secondary level in schools serving a disadvantaged student population.

With schools serving a more diverse student population, Leithwood recommended an elementary school size of approximately 500 students and at the high school level, about 1,000 students.

His numbers correspond closely to those in a report released in the spring by consultant Harvey Linnen on the renewal process underway in Regina public schools. The board had Linnen consult the public on school size options of between 200 and 400 elementary students, and high schools ranging between 600 and 1,200 students.

Leithwood said most of the studies he examined considered a 'small school' somewhere between 200 and 400 pupils.

The school board is grappling with how best to deal with declining enrolment, deteriorating buildings and rising costs.

'At this point in time, we don't have a plan in place,' Marchuk stressed. He added that the public can still give the board input before the administration brings forward a report examining options, likely near the end of November.

In response to a question by board member John Conway, an advocate of small schools, Leithwood said socio-economic status is a big factor. With disadvantaged kids, 'the smaller the better,' he added.

'It's hard to get too small a school for students who really struggle,' Leithwood said during his presentation. Students coming from relatively advantaged backgrounds are better equipped to deal with a larger school environment.

The board asked Leithwood to focus solely on school size and not optimum classroom size. However, in an interview, he said studies show that reducing class size by one or two from a high of 25 to 30 pupils makes little difference. Sizes have to fall significantly below 20 pupils to have a real impact on student outcomes.

Among the 59 studies he reviewed on school size, about 40 originated in the US, while the remainder included Canada, Europe and Australia. Asked about the relevancy to Regina, Leithwood said the effect of size on students is unrelated to country context.

The factors Leithwood was asked to examine were academic achievement, equitable distribution of achievement, attendance and truancy, participation and engagement, course-taking patterns, extracurricular participation, attitudes, behaviour, safety, cost efficiency, teacher retention and attitudes.

Source: Material reprinted with the express permission of Regina Leader Post Group Inc., a CanWest Partnership.

SCHOOL CHOICE AND THE EDUCATIONAL MARKETPLACE

Disparate views of education have been accompanied by various measures in the direction of making individuals and family members, as opposed to governments, more responsible for their own welfare. Volatile social, economic, and political conditions have accompanied globally competitive economic markets, rapid acceleration of new technologies, and significant demographic changes, and these conditions have implicated education in what has been called a 'new politics of the welfare state'. Consequently, social and economic arrangements in advanced industrial democracies have been drastically modified in recent years (Pierson, 2001).

In the realm of education, governments in every major jurisdiction in Canada and other Western nations have adopted numerous measures, including initiatives to modify arrangements for educational finance and governance, regulate teaching and teachers' organizations, reorganize curricula and service delivery, and implement mechanisms to assess performance outcomes and contribute to public accountability in education. There is considerable variation in the kinds of educational reforms instituted within each national, provincial, and territorial setting and in the impact these reforms have had on public schooling and other educational delivery systems. Nonetheless, a remarkable degree of uniformity is evident in the overall direction of change towards stronger emphasis on individual responsibility and a closer match between education and economic imperatives (Portelli and Solomon, 2001; Taylor, 2001; Lauder et al., 2006: 47ff.). The notion of education as a public responsibility, organized and delivered through the state, is being fragmented—by design and by specific events and practices—into multiple educational systems and forms. While numerous competing and contradictory dynamics are at work, educational thinking and decision-making have been influenced in important respects by neo-liberal orientations that characterize schooling and other services as a marketplace subject to the choices of individual consumers.

An expansion of private education and other alternatives to mainstream school systems has been driven by several factors, hastened by government funding constraints in education and interrelated concerns about educational quality, curricular options, and standards, and gaps in the programming options available through public educational institutions (Sweet and Gallagher, 1999). Individuals and parents are also increasingly looking to position children and youth more competitively by pursuing educational options regarded as most beneficial to their interests.

The data in Figure 4.4 illustrate one aspect of these changes in the trend towards growing reliance on private spending in education. For much of the duration represented in Figure 4.4, private sources constituted 10 per cent or less of educational spending, even declining briefly in the 1960s and 1970s when government spending was increased to stimulate massive educational expansion. However, funding from non-government sources, such as tuition fees and private donors, has approached one-fifth of all reported expenditures on education in Canada since 2000. This figure would be even higher if all educational expenses, such as private tutoring or assistance services and family spending on educational materials and aides, were included.

Steady increases also have occurred in the number and proportion of children attending private elementary and high schools in Canada, hastened in part by legislation to allow or provide public funding for alternatives to the public school system. Private schooling now represents about 6 per cent of total school enrolments across Canada, rising from 4.6 per cent two decades ago. These rates are even higher in some regions, notably British Columbia and Quebec, revealing in part a drift of children from public school systems as well as a more general demographic shift that has left many school jurisdictions with fewer school-age children (Canadian Council on Learning, 2006b; Davies et al., 2006). There are several types of **private schools**, including elite or 'preparatory' schools, alternative or 'free' schools, and schools oriented to distinct groups based on racial, ethnic, or cultural traditions, as well as schools operated by religious organizations. A growing array of private institutions provides or sponsors educational services in post-secondary programs, vocational and career training, and adult education. In addition to formal school-based programs, private agencies are increasingly involved in the delivery of educational services such as tutoring, special education programs, preschool and after-school programs, adult education, corporate training, and educational franchises (Davies et al., 2006; Aurini and Davies, 2005).

Parallel growth has occurred in other forms of educational alternatives, including the number of children educated at home. Home-based schooling has expanded significantly as many parents opt to keep children out of public schools. There are different types of home-schooling practices, ranging from philosophies of 'unschooling' to arrangements with school boards for children unable to attend regular classes for particular reasons. Much home schooling is based on religious considerations, but several other factors motivate home-based schooling, such as concerns about academic quality and learning styles, flexibility, or school-based victimization. Most estimates place the number of children of elementary and secondary school age regularly schooled at home in Canada at between 60,000 to 95,000 (about 1.5 per cent of the school-age population)—concentrated most heavily in Alberta, British Columbia, and Ontario—although advocates suggest that at least 100,000 families are engaged in home schooling (Canadian Council on Learning, 2006b; Priesnitz, 2008; Ray, 2001: 28).

The proliferation of private alternatives has been accompanied by an expansion of public educational delivery and program options. Public school systems and post-secondary institutions have modified and diversified their offerings both to attract and maintain enrolment in competition with other agencies and in response to broader educational challenges and needs. School districts have relaxed or removed policies that previously required most students to attend their neighbourhood schools. Many school districts have introduced specialized schools targeted to particular groups, such as immigrant populations, Aboriginal inner-city youth, academically talented students or those with special learning needs, students with specific cultural and arts-oriented interests, adult learners, and students with disabilities. Publicly funded post-secondary institutions have expanded programming and developed alternative modes of course or program delivery, sometimes through contractual arrangements with private agencies. Governments and public school boards have also made arrangements to co-operate in various ways with home-based educators and other agencies, while educational institutions have altered admission policies to acknowledge or give credit for a variety of educational alternatives.

Despite these trends, market-based educational reforms, both as a focus for public debate and in their implementation, appear to be less pervasive in Canada than in many other jurisdictions, including several American states. Advocates of a market or consumer choice model of education claim that educational choice is required to ensure that schools will be more flexible and responsive to community concerns (Easton, 1988: 71–6; Wilkinson, 1994). Chubb and Moe (1990), in their influential argument for school choice, contend that school improvement follows as a logical outcome from the removal of constraints on parents, teachers, and schools, whereby schools (posed as distinct enterprises) would have the autonomy to make changes necessary to attract and retain students and their parents (posed as consumers).

One of the most actively promoted models of educational choice is the establishment of charter schools. Charter schools operate on the basis of a 'charter' or agreement between particular schools and governments that identify specific mandates and features of governance by which each school will operate in conformity with general principles of public education. They are premised on the notion that parents are educational consumers who should be provided with effective input and choices in order to make rational decisions about their children's schooling.

Advocates of charter schools argue that viable alternatives are needed because public schools have become too firmly entrenched in the hands of educational elites and have experienced declining educational standards by attempting to be all things to all people. Some options, such as home schooling and private or independent schooling, are beyond the reach of parents who do not have sufficient time or resources to invest in these alternatives or who do not share the values embodied in these special forms of education. Charter schools, by contrast, are promoted on the basis that they offer the best elements of both public and private schooling. Charter schools, like public schools, are funded by government grants, are ideally open to all pupils, and are subject to provincial curriculum and teacher certification guidelines. Like private schools, however, they have greater autonomy to define their own particular mandates, to make decisions about staffing, resource allocation, and instructional matters, and to ensure that parents' voices are incorporated into educational planning (Lawton, 1995: 68–9; Nikiforuk, 1993: 100–2; Raham, 1996). Others argue that governments should issue educational vouchers that enable parents or students to select their schools (public or private), in lieu of current funding arrangements whereby grants are provided directly to school boards.

Joe Freedman (1995: 40), one of strongest early promoters of charter schooling in Canada, argues that they offer a 'middle ground between choosing schools by voucher and allowing the system to fix itself'. Their success, Freedman claims, is driven by 'the challenge of removing the exclusive franchise from school boards, creating choice for parent clients, providing a focus on outcomes, establishing real autonomy through school status as a legal entity, and creating genuine accountability through the threat of school closure or loss of teaching position.'

One of the most broadly based initiatives to introduce charter-like schooling is in New Zealand, which in 1989 required all school jurisdictions to develop charters as part of a series of initiatives to deregulate and privatize government services. Considerable pressure from interest groups in the United States has led to various forms of charter arrangements in several states, beginning with Minnesota in 1991, which was joined within the next two years by four other states (Lawton, 1995: 70–81). Within the next decade, the number of charter schools had increased to over 1,600, serving close to half a million students in 34 states (Fuller, 2000: 7). There have been several vocal advocates of charter schooling in Canada, notably in Alberta, which has remained the only province to authorize charter schools since the passage of facilitating legislation in 1994 (Bruce and Schwartz, 1997: 408). By 2001, 10 charter schools were in operation out of 12 charters granted, each oriented to particular groups or focuses, including traditional 'back-to-basic' instruction, foreign language instruction, English as a second language, street youth, academically talented learners, fine arts, and science and technology (Bosetti, 2001: 103–8).

Despite the inroads and popular support it has gained in some jurisdictions, charter schooling also faces considerable opposition from educators and educational organizations, as well as from broader community and policy groups. Some opposition arises from concerns that charter schooling is an affront to public education that may undermine established educational structures and bodies. However, serious concerns also arise from prospects that charter schools can be divisive, inequitable, undemocratic, and ineffective in addressing major educational problems (Canadian Teachers' Federation, 1997). Critics argue that educational choice is already provided, or possible, within existing structures of public and private schooling and that charter schooling diverts control and resources from schools that serve the wider community (Crawley, 1995: 168–9; Friesen and Friesen, 2001).

Although charter schools may have some general appeal, advocacy for charter schools and other market models of education is being pursued most actively by individuals supported by or representing groups that have the most economic, political, and cultural capital (Robertson, 1998: 263–6). Critics contend that these advocates stand to gain the most from a bifurcated education system in terms of both individual competitive advantage and the benefits that accrue from the redirection of public funds into private hands. They add, moreover, that while public schools are intended to serve and be responsive to diverse social groups, charter schooling is likely to contribute to the diversion of resources and opportunities away from disadvantaged groups that have the greatest educational needs. There are strong contradictions in both the logic and practice of market-based initiatives in education. Initiatives to regard education as a market governed by consumer choice have simultaneously fostered arrangements in which private firms enter into exclusive contracts with educational institutions to supply particular services or products such as beverages, electronic equipment, or food and cleaning services (Berthelot, 2006: 90–1). Finally, charter schooling and related shifts in the direction of educational accountability and measurement may contribute to the deskilling of teachers' work by setting and controlling performance standards and conduct in such a way as to restrict professional autonomy and increase workloads.

The early evidence from charter schooling and other private alternatives supports many of these contentions, though some evidence is mixed (Bosetti, 2001). Charter schools have drawn students who have been disengaged or dissatisfied with the mainstream education system as well as those from more privileged groups. Similarly, whereas public schools are most likely to enrol students from a diverse mix of backgrounds, children who attend private schools are drawn predominantly from households situated at the top and bottom ends of family income groups (Statistics Canada, 2001b). Private school advocates point to data from comparative student assessment programs that indicate students in private schools achieve higher scores than those in public schools (though this trend is less pronounced in Canada than in many other nations). However, this trend tends to disappear when social class, school diversity, and other background factors are taken into account (Bussière et al., 2001: 38).

Regardless of the impact of particular types of school reform, debates over school choice will continue to be ineffectual as long as they ignore more fundamental issues, including the structural causes of poverty and social and income polarization (Fuller, 2000: 10). Without these factors as a priority, such debates may be more about competitive positioning for corporate resources and family advantage than about meaningful educational reform and improvement. The analysis of alternative forms of educational delivery suggests that no single form of educational governance is likely to address complex questions about educational quality, and that models transferred from other realms, such as business management, are not automatically applicable in an educational context (Fiske and Ladd, 2000: 312–13).

In summary, the various options promoted for educational reform and alternatives to public schooling represent divergent social and ideological interests. It is important not to discount the genuine concerns that all people have to seek changes that will make education more meaningful and rewarding in its varied economic, cultural, social, and moral purposes. The kinds of reform strategies being pursued, however, follow distinctly different courses, leading, in one direction, to a market-driven orientation to the education 'industry', and, in another, to a more person-centred focus on human development, opportunity, and social justice.

The growth of private and home-based schooling and the increased involvement by non-government organizations in education have tremendous significance for educational organizations and practices. As a result, these issues are often fiercely debated. Advocates promote private schooling on the basis that choice is necessary to provide a range of educational options that cannot be accommodated or afforded in a single, public educational system. Private schooling, viewed this way, promotes both human rights and free-market principles by enabling parents and learners to select the kind of learning environment most suited to their beliefs and interests. Critics argue, to the contrary, that the **privatization** of education contributes to fractionalization and reduced opportunities for much of the population. Education is not a commodity meant to be governed by price and market forces but a complex undertaking that contributes to human development and social responsibility as well as to the acquisition of knowledge and skills. Agencies that fund and operate private educational services are often more interested in their own profitability or are governed by specialized interests that run contrary to broader public concerns. As private operations, they are not subject to the same scrutiny and regulations that prevail in state-operated educational institutions to ensure that standards are met and public input is maintained.

The Governance and Financing of Canadian Education

Recent policy and institutional changes and program initiatives make it difficult to provide a comprehensive overview of contemporary educational patterns in Canada. However, several distinctive and competing tendencies are evident. On the one hand, educational restructuring, driven by fiscal rationales and market-based principles or neo-liberal ideologies, has contributed to a number of significant trends. These include:

- institutional downsizing and reorganization;
- **amalgamation** and centralization of educational administration and program delivery;
- the transfer of educational funding and programming from the public to the private sector;
- renewed emphasis on 'basic' or 'core' curriculum areas;
- the definition and measurement of specified learning standards used to determine achievement and placement in and beyond education programs; and
- intensified measures to scrutinize and control the activities of educators and learners (Simon, 2001; Wotherspoon, 1991: 17; Taylor, 2001).

On the other hand, various public, community-based, and private educational initiatives have emerged to serve diverse educational requirements. Programs and services tailored for socially and educationally disadvantaged groups, such as children living in poverty, learners designated 'at risk' or vulnerable to school failure or early school leaving, and cultural minorities, coexist with expensive training programs oriented to narrow, specialized markets. Public educational institutions continue to be governed by principles of effective community participation, relevance to heterogeneous constituencies of learners, and responsiveness to changing social and occupational demands.

It is important to acknowledge that education in Canada continues to be funded predominantly by provincial and territorial governments (supplemented with transfers from the federal government), even with the gradual shift towards heavier reliance on private and local sources of funding. Although its massive size and cost (representing in total between 6 and 8 per cent of Canada's gross domestic product, second only to health as a priority for total government spending) have exposed the education system as a visible target within strategies to reduce government spending or compensate for tax cuts and spending priorities in other areas, public education has also been defended under the guise of human capital approaches as a vital investment in the nation's future.

This double significance is reflected in distinctly different orientations to education spending held by particular social groups. Hart and Livingstone (2007: 10–11; Livingstone and Hart, 2005: 6–7), for instance, report that increasing numbers of people—nearly three-quarters of the Ontario residents they have surveyed since 2000 compared to one-half in the mid-1990s—believe that spending on

Box 4.2 Funding Cuts, Commercialization, and Educational Inequality

Schools and other educational institutions have become more dependent on funding and sponsorships from private sources, including individuals, families, and corporations, as governments have cut or restricted funding. Statistics Canada (2007f) estimates that individuals and households in Canada spend close to $14.5 billion simply to outfit children for the school year, including: clothing and accessories ($249.9 million for girls, $229.2 million for boys, and $106.9 million on unisex clothing); computer hardware and software ($1.1 billion); books, newspapers, and other periodicals ($749.6 million); and stationery, office supplies, and other material ($921.7 million). School fundraising initiatives are also increasingly reliant on families and private sponsors. These trends can have an adverse impact on educational equity and the quality of education, as made clear in the results of a national survey conducted by the Canadian Teachers' Federation, the Canadian Centre for Policy Alternatives, and the Fédération des syndicats de l'enseignement (Canadian Teachers' Federation, 2006):

Beyond the bake sale: Exposing the many faces of commercialism in public schools

How many chocolate almonds does it take to buy an education?

The underfunding of public education has forced schools and school communities to compensate in a variety of ways: door-to-door fundraising campaigns, advertising revenue, exclusive marketing contracts, and seeking donations or handouts from the private sector. Awareness of these activities has been largely anecdotal, up to now.

. . . Among the study's findings (contained in the report *Commercialism in Canadian Schools: Who's Calling the Shots?*) are the following:

- About a third of schools reported the presence of advertising in or on the school, with higher rates in secondary schools than in elementary schools.
- 27 per cent of schools had an exclusive marketing arrangement with Coke or Pepsi.
- The majority of schools reported charging user fees for a variety of services and programs.
- 15 per cent of elementary schools and 21 per cent of secondary schools reported selling services to generate revenue.

Fundraising activities are common in schools, with money being raised for school trips, library books, athletic programs and technology; 60 per cent of elementary schools reported fundraising for library books.

Schools reported raising—through fundraising and other activities including user fees, advertising revenue and partnerships/sponsorships—amounts of money ranging from a few hundred dollars to, in some cases, several hundred thousand dollars.

The study raises some fundamental questions about the implications of commercialism and privatization for students, teachers, schools and public education as a whole.

When schools and communities have varying degrees of capacity to fundraise and attract outside funding, what is the impact on equity? Which students in which communities have access to programs enhanced by private funding, and which do not? As schools compete with each other for external funding (from corporations and individuals), how does education suffer? Do the time and other resources spent on fundraising detract from the quality of education schools can provide? To what extent does an over-reliance on private funding erode the decision-making authority of elected school boards? Are there strings attached to private funding—and with what effects? Who ensures that curriculum and classroom materials provided by private sources are unbiased, complete and accurate? As schools are increasingly dependent on private funding sources, what happens in times of economic instability or dwindling corporate largesse, or when parents are unable to fundraise to the same extent? . . .

The classroom is an environment like no other, a fact not lost on corporate marketers. They openly describe it as an ideal environment in which to reach this increasingly influential consumer group—students—required by law to be in school, five days a week, six hours a day, 10 months of the year, until they reach the age of 16. The school also offers an implicit endorsement of products, organizations and messages associated with it. . . . One has to wonder if comments from governments about our commitment to the 'knowledge economy' are predominantly rhetorical, particularly in light of how dependent schools are becoming—in the absence of adequate public dollars—on private funding sources.

While fundraising is hardly a new activity (ask yourself how many chocolate almonds you've bought to support your community school), the results of this first national survey indicate that school commercialism has clearly moved beyond bake sales and raffles, assuming many forms. They also demonstrate that the goals of these new fundraising campaigns are no longer just for band trips but for books, or desks, or yes, even bathroom facilities. These are hardly 'frills' or 'extras', but rather what most of us would consider part of a basic education.

Source: Material reprinted with the permission of the Canadian Teachers' Federation, The Canadian Centre for Policy Alternatives, and the Fédération des syndicats de l'enseignement.

elementary and secondary education should increase, with the majority of these also supporting higher taxes to fund education. They observe growing support for increased education spending even among groups less inclined in the past to express such a view, including persons aged 65 and over, those self-identifying as Conservative Party supporters, and corporate executives. However, even if public opinion is softening in some respects, the analysis offered by Livingstone and Hart (2005: 5) suggests continuing uneasiness about the future of education, belying in part fundamental differences in orientations to education. While the evidence does not point to a 'crisis of confidence' or tax revolt depicted by the harshest school critics, including neo-liberal advocates of market-based school reforms, it does not fully match the expectations of enhanced commitment to a strong public school system advocated by groups like organized labour, teachers' and parents' organizations, and other community groups (Lewington and Orpwood, 1993: 16–17; Hart and Livingstone, 2007).

Debates over educational funding and organization are often more about priorities than about absolute spending levels. This helps to explain how funding or program cutbacks may be experienced by some educational participants or sectors even as educational expenditures rise or remain relatively constant. While there is general consensus that education is crucial for personal, social, and economic development, there is considerable disagreement about the kinds of education and educational organizations there should be.

It is often difficult to pinpoint the social bases of educational debates because views about education appear in complex and sometimes contradictory ways, expressed by persons who represent diverse social perspectives. People with a broad range of educational experiences and social backgrounds may come together, for instance, to either support or oppose a 'back to the basics' orientation to curricula, culturally sensitive educational practices, or demands for greater discipline and safety in schools.

Apple (2000: 20ff.) analyzes the impact on education of the rise of the New Right in the United States and Britain, and some of his insights apply, to a certain extent, to the politics of education in Canada. The New Right is characterized as a broad movement supporting principles of market-driven free enterprise, opposing state regulation, cynical about state officials, and fearful about loss of authority, tradition, and standards in personal and public life. Rather than operating as a unified group or force, however, the New Right is better understood as an amalgam of disparate forces such as the pro-family movement, business lobbyists, opponents of the welfare state, neo-liberal groups, right-wing organizations, and other populist forces that seek a return to 'traditional' values. Education, because it touches family life, economic futures, and other concerns vital to people's lives, hopes, and aspirations, has been a prime target for reform by the New Right. Apple (2000: 22) argues that:

> The sphere of education has been one of the most successful areas in which the Right has been ascendant. The social democratic goal of expanding equality of opportunity (itself a rather limited reform) has lost much of its political potency and its ability to mobilize people. The 'panic' over falling standards and illiteracy, the fears of violence in schools, the concern with the destruction of family values

and religiosity, all have had an effect. These fears are exacerbated, and used, by dominant groups within politics and the economy who have been able to move the debate on education (and all things social) onto their own terrain, the terrain of 'tradition', standardization, productivity, and industrial needs.

One of the major features that such critics of the education system point to is the size and power of the educational bureaucracy, which is often posed as a monopoly resistant to change. Fears about unchecked growth of the education system are enhanced with depictions of educational administrators, teachers, and other entrenched interest groups who are distant from the real concerns of students, parents, and community members. Journalist Andrew Nikiforuk (1993: 57), for instance, argues in his book *School's Out*:

> Just as the Canadian oil industry did during the boom of the 1970s, educators have spent, built, and added on programs and services without any coherent plan or realistic sense of limits. Unlike the oil patch today, however, educational institutions cannot be effectively regulated or reformed by market forces. As essentially social monopolies, they appear to have become unmanageable because of their autonomous nature.

Similarly, Lawton (1995: 14–15) criticizes the 'bureaucratic bondage' that has removed control over education from parents and other segments of the public into the hands of bureaucrats, professional educators, and administrators. Hepburn (1999: 1), in a report published by the right-wing Fraser Institute to make the case for school choice in Canada, states the apparent problem more bluntly: 'Canadian education is not just inefficient but seriously inadequate. Statistical evidence of poor student performance coupled with the deterioration of public confidence suggests that, if it is not to become obsolete, public education must be redesigned.'

These criticisms have a common-sense appeal because they pose a unifying framework for a series of problems that most people can identify with or have experienced in one form or another. Taken as a whole, the kinds of issues we see or hear about in our educational institutions—rising costs, declining standards, uncaring teachers, lack of accountability to taxpayers and communities, student violence and vandalism, irrelevant curricula, meaningless reporting practices, wasted instructional time—may convey an image of an education system in serious crisis.

There is a danger, however, in adopting an uncritical approach to such a critique. Despite numerous concerns, no consensus necessarily exists over the idea that the education system is failing or in crisis. In fact, as is noted throughout this book, public opinion on most educational issues is divided and highly complex. In a social context within which public and private institutions are regarded with skepticism and declining confidence overall, public schools are rated relatively well, maintaining higher levels of confidence than nearly all other major institutions (Edwards and Mazzuca, 1999; Guppy and Davies, 1999).

Wickstrom (1994: 6–7) identifies seven distinct models to characterize the diverse demands that exist for educational reform:

1. the factory, emphasizing productivity, uniformity, and quality control;
2. the department store or large convention, stressing variety and consumer choice;
3. the family, with a focus on love, compassion, and co-operation;
4. the garden or 'untended meadow', in which growth, interest, and beauty and diversity are crucial;
5. the Olympics, highlighting excellence and competition;
6. the freedom march, oriented according to passion and indoctrination to a specific cause;
7. the clinic, regulated by diagnosis, prescription, precision, and successive stages of sophistication.

While each of these models can be applied to specific groups or philosophies of educational change, most educational practices and opinions encompass a mixture of elements from various models.

One way to gauge the extent to which educational practices and reforms have or have not been able to match the level of expectations surrounding education systems is to examine public attitudes. Major public opinion surveys reveal mixed sentiments about the direction and impact of education change, though levels of confidence in public education systems have remained relatively high throughout the past several decades.

Historical comparisons reveal that public expressions of general concern or dissatisfaction with education have tended to be highest during periods in which education systems have been confronted with expansionary pressures or diminished resources. In response to a Gallup Poll question asking 'Do you think children today are being better educated or worse than you were?', the proportion of those who indicated that they felt children were worse educated rose from 12 per cent in 1948 to 33 per cent in 1976, while the proportion who felt children were better educated declined from 74 per cent to 49 per cent over the same period (Canadian Institute of Public Opinion, 1976: 2). Public concerns over the quality of education also rose during the 1990s, especially in provinces affected most heavily by funding restraints and program disruptions, but these have subsequently abated as funding and service delivery arrangements for schools and other educational institutions have recovered over the past decade. The Canadian Education Association (CEA), for example, has periodically tracked Canadian attitudes since 1979, asking opinion on a variety of matters including requests to assess school performance on the basis of a letter grade. The proportion of those assigning an A grade has declined from 19 per cent in 1979 to 6 per cent in both 1990 and 2007;

Box 4.3 Growing Emphasis on Parent Involvement in Schools

As schools seek to become more accountable and relevant to the interests of the communities they work with, they have placed increased emphasis on issues of community engagement and parent involvement. An extensive body of research evidence shows the benefits of parent involvement of various types. This involvement ranges from volunteer support for classroom and in-school activities, meetings with teachers and school staff, and parent–child co-operation on homework, reading, and other activities outside of the school to more extensive involvement on school councils and other forms of educational governance. In its most positive forms, parental engagement provides opportunities for parents or guardians, children, teaching staff, and administrators to work together to enhance educational experiences and outcomes. Most Canadian educational jurisdictions have created formal mechanisms to institutionalize these relationships, taking various forms, such as parent advisory councils, district education councils, parent–school support committees, and parent involvement committees. These arrangements, unlike more traditional home and school or parent–teacher associations, provide regular opportunities for community members to play a part in decision-making on school policies and other major education-related activities.

Despite the strong advantages these kinds of arrangements can offer through strengthening relationships among homes, communities, and schools, there are several reasons to be cautious. The focus on parental involvement has divergent and sometimes contradictory roots, signifying from various standpoints the expansion of democratic possibilities or the subordination of education to narrow political and economic influences in a context in which public investment in education is falling behind. It represents the growing recognition of education as both an investment and a form of social development for individuals and communities. Educators seek to enhance their legitimacy by drawing community members into schools, but they can also feel threatened by what they see as potential challenges to their expertise and sphere of decision-making. Schools frequently struggle to find truly inclusive and effective forms of involvement. Parental involvement is often defined in unclear terms, is understood in different ways by different participants, and requires adequate bases of agreement and support in order for it to succeed (Stelmack, 2004). Social, economic, and cultural resources also have a strong impact on the extent to which parents are able to participate and feel confident in engaging with educators, especially in a sustained manner. Several factors, including social class, race, and family status, influence the extent to which parents have the cultural and economic resources to meet school expectations or have the time and confidence to participate in a meaningful way

(Lareau and Horvat, 1999; Sweet and Mandel, 2005). Like many educational reforms, the expansion of initiatives to promote parental involvement includes several dimensions that must be understood in relation both to their specific components and to the wider context in which they have emerged.

nonetheless, the proportion assigning failing grades has remained relatively constant, at only 4 per cent, throughout this time period, and close to half assign grades of B or higher (CEA, 2007: 9–10). Attitudes are also mixed on questions relating to the quality of education, with relatively equal proportions of respondents suggesting that the quality of elementary and secondary schooling has improved, remained the same, or worsened, though again the results tend to be slightly more favourable than unfavourable (ibid., 15). Guppy et al. (2005: 15–16) report similar trends in a national survey in which rising proportions—72 per cent of parents and 76 per cent of teachers in 2005—assigned grades of A or B to public schools in their communities.

These findings suggest that the notion that the public is clamouring with one voice for particular kinds of educational reforms is ideologically and socially constructed. Educational reports, policy documents, and anecdotal evidence that highlight educational problems come to be merged into an apparent consensus dominated by business and corporate interests rather than by values and practices emerging from people's real experiences (Delhi, 1993: 116–17). Barlow and Robertson (1994) argue that, akin to the New Right in the United States and Britain, a conservative alliance driven principally by business and religious fundamentalist interests has mobilized public opinion to promote school reforms across Canada that exacerbate class divisions and weaken the schools' ability to respond to the needs of less privileged social groups. Dominant class interests have pressured education further, both directly and indirectly, for neo-liberal reforms and market-based orientations through international and multinational trade agreements (Grieshaber-Otto and Sanger, 2002: 129–30; Robertson, 1998). Within these ideologies and associated reforms, property rights gain ascendancy over personal rights by regarding individuals, variously, as consumers, clients, and products of education. Despite the emphasis on personal choice and freedom, real people and their diverse needs and struggles are regarded as abstractions, like inputs and outputs in an industrial system governed by considerations of cost-effectiveness and competitive advantage.

COMPARATIVE EDUCATIONAL GROWTH

Canada's education systems have their own distinct characteristics, but they are highly influenced by education systems and advancements in other nations. In its earliest stages Canadian schooling drew heavily from European forms of school organization and curricula, particularly from France and the British Isles. The historical development of education more generally is highly diverse and uneven. Collins (2000: 214) observes that education today has not emerged through a linear evolution; rather, the history of education reveals varied fluctuations and interactions among different forms. He outlines at least four main educational models, including age cohort (such as adolescent initiation rites), private apprenticeship, professional licensing and university degrees, and bureaucratic schools derived from imperial and religious practices in China and Japan. Globally based patterns of economic development, colonial systems of rule, and expansion of market forces have created some convergence among education systems, but substantial variations and inequalities in education remain both within and across nations.

Education, both in developing and in highly industrialized nations, is guided by core concerns about how to meet basic skill and citizenship needs particular to local, regional, or national priorities and how to ensure training and skill enhancement for competitive economic growth. Historically, the development and growth of education systems have tended to be marked by a shift in emphasis from the first to the second of these priorities. Many governments, for instance, have adopted policies to ensure that education enhances particular kinds of skill development or channels people directly into the labour market. However, recent educational planning efforts by major international bodies and their participants have tended to pose these objectives as complementary to each other. While the expansion of higher-end skill development and advanced education remain vital priorities within most nations, parallel concern has emerged for the large segments of populations who have limited levels of education, literacy, and other basic skills.

Nations with highly advanced economies, including members of the Organization for Economic Co-operation and Development (OECD), have identified enhanced educational development beyond compulsory schooling, through post-secondary education and **adult education and training,** as a major priority to drive further economic growth and social development (OECD, 2001: 151). Governments and economic agencies across the globe have intensified their demands for educational reforms, motivated by global competition and desires to link growth in knowledge-based industries in conjunction with strategies to create strong public- and private-sector linkages among education, training, and economic growth (Ashton and Sung, 1997). National and international attention has also shifted to the need for educational improvement at the lower end, both to ensure that all persons have basic education and, especially among those who typically are marginalized from education and labour market participation, to foster continuing education (Bowers et al., 1999).

Many nations and regions have modified their educational policies and practices to position their economies for global competitiveness and to demonstrate that the education they offer meets high-quality standards appropriate for an information society. These changes have contributed to growing convergence as education systems adopt similar objectives, organizational patterns, and practices, especially when motivated by targets or structural adjustment policies established by international bodies like the OECD, World Bank, or International Monetary Fund. Nonetheless, because education remains closely tied with questions of national character, cultural significance, and specific economic and political objectives, there continues to be extensive variation across different models and patterns of education and school–work linkages (Brown et al., 2001; Stromquist and Monkman, 2000).

The struggle to reposition education within a changing global order is highly challenging. As with the historical development of education in Canada and other highly developed nations, the expansion of education in less developed regions tends to be accompanied by the promise of enhanced democratic participation and social mobility throughout the population. The dramatic expansion of a highly educated subclass, accompanied by new types of employment in non-traditional fields and high consumption lifestyles in India, China, and many other nations, seems to suggest that some of these prospects are being fulfilled.

It is crucial, in a context in which lifelong learning and higher education are stressed, to recognize nonetheless that significant proportions of the world's population have limited education and face continuing barriers to educational participation. The benefits of educational advancement are not shared equally, and much of the world's population—especially females in the most socio-economically vulnerable groups—is losing ground rather than advancing in educational status. The World Educational Forum, organized in conjunction with the United Nations, in 2000 identified three goals that it sought for all nations by 2015—the achievement of universal primary education; the elimination of gender disparity, first (by 2005) in primary and secondary education and later in other education levels; and the achievement of 50 per cent improvement in adult literacy levels. UNESCO (2007: 91–5) reports that, by 2005, fewer than half of the world's participating nations (51 out of 129) had achieved or were on target to achieve the core targets, while about 60 nations (representing over one-third of the world's population) are likely to fall short in at least one of these areas by the target date; more than 30 nations fall well below the index established to determine overall progress. One of the most serious discrepancies lies in the lack of progress, and in some cases regressive movements, towards achieving gender parity (see Box 4.4).

Education, throughout the world as in Canada, has emerged over the past several decades as a vital tool for social and economic participation, and as a core priority area for public policy. This reality carries mixed significance in that the benefits that accompany education, for societies as well as for individuals, simultaneously expose education as a focus of ongoing political and economic contestation.

Box 4.4 Global Inequalities in Basic Education

Although considerable attention is given to the importance of advanced education and skills in the global economy, prospects to fulfill even fundamental educational objectives remain distant in many regions. UNESCO has observed progress by many nations towards achieving the six basic goals of 'education for all' targeted to be achieved in 2015, but numerous barriers remain to full and equitable educational participation in some parts of the world. The excerpt below, from the mid-term progress report (UNESCO, 2007: 33–4), highlights concerns about continuing educational inequity, including acknowledgement that initial targets to achieve gender parity in basic education have been missed. The following three figures, based on data from the report, summarize regional disparities in progress towards achieving three of these goals:

Goal 5: Eliminating gender disparities in primary and secondary education by 2005, and achieving gender equality in education by 2015, with a focus on ensuring girls' full and equal access to and achievement in basic education of good quality.

- The goal of eliminating gender disparities in both primary *and* secondary education by 2005 was missed in a great majority of countries. Only 59 countries, about one-third of the 181 countries for which data are available, had achieved the gender parity goal, very few of them since 1999. Gender disparities persist in many countries, particularly at the upper levels: while 63 per cent of countries with data had managed to eliminate gender disparities in primary education, only 37 per cent had done so at the secondary level.

- Girls' access to primary and secondary schools, while improving, remains a major issue in countries where overall participation levels are still low. In countries with higher participation levels (developed countries, Latin America and especially the Caribbean, the Pacific), boys' underparticipation in secondary education is a growing problem.

- Gender *equality* has been relatively neglected. Physical violence mainly affects boys; verbal and sexual violence, combined with insecure environments and inadequate sanitation, disproportionately affects girls. Some countries have few female teachers; in many others male and female teachers receive insufficient training in gender issues, which hampers their potential as effective role models. Gender-biased teacher attitudes, perceptions and expectations are common, and boys often dominate classroom time and space. In many instances, textbooks reinforce the gender-specific roles of men and women, and in some cases different subjects are taught to girls and boys. Boys' and girls' levels of achievement are converging, but fields of study and occupational choices continue to be clustered by gender.

Source: © UNESCO, 2008. Used by permission of UNESCO.

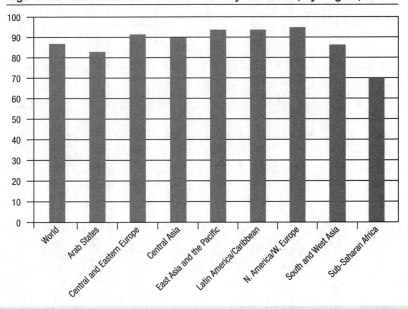

Figure 4.5 Net Enrolment Ratio in Primary Education, by Region, 2005

Note: Percentage of children of official primary school age who are actually enrolled in primary school.
Source: UNESCO 2005. Used by permission of UNESCO.

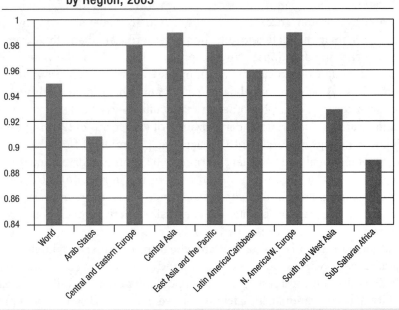

Figure 4.6 Ratio of Females to Males Enrolled in Primary Education, by Region, 2005

Source: UNESCO 2005. Used by permission of UNESCO.

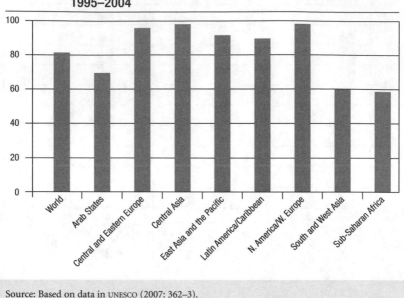

Figure 4.7 Proportion of Literate Persons Ages 15 and Over, by Region, 1995–2004

Source: Based on data in UNESCO (2007: 362–3).

CONCLUSION

As education systems gain prominence in a world where credentials and learning take on central importance, they remain sites of considerable controversy and struggle over their mandate and direction. As more Canadians than ever before come to engage in educational activities, proclamations about the value of education are accompanied by debates concerning the extent to which this value is being realized. Thus, rising educational participation and **educational attainment** levels coexist with concern over phenomena such as illiteracy, school dropouts, uneven educational achievement, and underutilization of vital forms of learning, as depicted vividly in Livingstone's (2004: 13) imagery of 'pyramids' of formal learning and 'icebergs' of informal and voluntary learning. The contradictory character of educational reform is in large part an expression of the intersection of dynamics of global competition and cultural and social change with a contemporary education system that, as the previous chapter has emphasized, derives much of its prevailing structure and orientation from a period of early capitalist development and industrialization. Education is directed towards the transformative potentials in human beings and their societies, but it is organized and structured in such a way that routine, standardization, and restrictions of opportunity often prevail over creativity, flexibility, and innovation. Ultimately, the varied educational systems and practices that have arisen in the midst of recent socio-economic transformations and challenges are not a consequence of any single evolutionary historical process; rather, they represent what education fundamentally is: a somewhat paradoxical and contentious network of social relations and institutional structures.

Issues related to educational reform, relevance, and public confidence in a changing society are revisited in the last chapter, which offers a more thorough examination of the reasons for mixed sentiments expressed in recent debates over educational reform. Formal education is not neutral insofar as it is subject to competing priorities, objectives, and visions about social possibilities. Whether viewed as preparation for work, preparation for life in general, or an essential activity in its own right, education both reflects and influences the social world of which it is a central component. The next chapter explores these complex dynamics further by taking us inside educational processes.

ANNOTATED FURTHER READINGS

Friesen, John W., and Virginia Lyons Friesen. 2001. *In Defense of Public Schools in North America*. Calgary: Detselig. The authors make the case for the benefits of public schooling, presenting a concise summary of the history, purposes, and outcomes of public schooling in Canada, an overview of contemporary educational issues and problems, and a critique of alternatives advocated by critics of public schooling.

Guppy, Neil, and Scott Davies. 1998. *Education in Canada: Recent Trends and Future Challenges*. Ottawa: Minister of Industry. The authors present a detailed picture of historical educational development and recent trends in Canada, drawing from census data covering various dimensions of educational participation, outcomes, finance, and contextual factors.

Robertson, Heather-Jane. 2007. *Great Expectations: Essays on Schools and Society*. Ottawa: Canadian Centre for Policy Alternatives. This volume collects the author's insightful and powerful commentary on contemporary educational matters of key importance.

Sears, Alan. 2003. *Retooling the Mind Factory: Education in a Lean State*. Aurora, Ont.: Garamond. The nature and impact of various dimensions of educational reform are examined critically in the context of political and economic transformations driven by neo-liberal policies and the expansion of market forces.

Young, Jon, Benjamin Levin, and Dawn Wallin. 2007. *Understanding Canadian Schools: An Introduction to Educational Administration*, 4th edn. Scarborough, Ont.: Nelson. This book provides a comprehensive overview of school organization and administration in Canada, addressing issues such as school policy, educational structures, the nature and role of various educational participants, and school reform.

KEY TERMS

Adult education and training Educational and training activities engaged in by persons, normally aged 17 and over, who have completed their basic or initial schooling.

Amalgamation The consolidation of smaller school boards or administrative units into larger units.

Educational attainment The highest level of education that a person has completed, usually expressed in terms of numbers of years of formal schooling or the highest credential achieved by those who are not currently enrolled in an educational program.

Informal learning Learning activities undertaken as part of a conscious or organized effort to gain new knowledge, skills, or competencies outside of programs organized by an institution or agency for specific credit or credentials.

Private schools Educational institutions, which may or may not receive government funding, administered or operated by individuals, associations, or agencies outside the public school system.

Privatization A process in which services or programs operated by the state sector or governments are shifted to private or for-profit firms or agencies.

STUDY QUESTIONS

1. What challenges have education systems been confronted with by periodic growth in the school-age population and the increasing lengths of time that people stay in school?

2. Who makes the major decisions about educational resources, curricula, and program requirements? What are the implications of these decision-making arrangements and power structures for different social groups?

3. Public education in Canada is mostly funded by taxes collected at provincial and local levels, supplemented by contributions from other sources, including the federal government, business firms, and individuals and family members. Discuss how these arrangements affect people's prospects to gain an education in contemporary society. Outline how different social groups would be affected by competing scenarios to modify these funding arrangements.

4. What are the major public expectations for Canada's education systems in the knowledge or information society? How do these expectations compare with educational objectives in less developed nations? Critically discuss the extent to which education systems are meeting these expections.

5. How are educational institutions being influenced by recent emphasis on lifelong learning and global competitiveness? What educational alternatives are viable to meet these challenges?

6. Discuss the impact that social diversity among student populations has had on educational practices and outcomes.

Chapter 5

The Process of Schooling

INTRODUCTION

One of the remarkable features of schooling is its consistency over time. Despite the many changes that have occurred in educational philosophies and practices over several generations, educational institutions and classrooms have retained a distinctive quality that makes it difficult for them to be mistaken for any other setting. Children who are driven to spacious, well-equipped urban composite schools replete with innovative technological devices may not immediately identify with the experiences of ancestors who walked or rode horseback to attend one-room schoolhouses with few books and blackboards made of tarpaper, but people's reminiscences of their school days tend to evoke common themes regardless of when and how they were educated. This commonality is, in part, a consequence of the integral role that schooling has come to play in developmental processes associated with childhood and adolescence and its importance in the transmission of basic knowledge and beliefs from one generation to the next. It is also a product of the massive scale of educational bureaucracies and institutional enterprises. Despite periodic modifications, fundamental patterns of classroom interaction, school organization, and curricula in Canada have remained relatively faithful to nineteenth-century roots. The school system's resistance to particular kinds of change is the focus of extensive discussion and controversy as educators, policy-makers, and various social groups struggle with the issue of what schooling should be like to ensure it remains relevant to the needs of contemporary societies that place a substantial premium on knowledge and its application.

This chapter explores the main patterns of activity that occur within educational processes, examining their significance both for individuals and for more general social relations. Although schools are likely to reveal features that are peculiar to the demographic and social characteristics of the communities they are located in, the school system as a whole is one of the most socially inclusive agencies in contemporary societies. The face of the student body has changed significantly, through patterns of immigration, lengthened periods of education from early childhood to adult education, integration of students with disabilities and others who often were excluded from regular schooling, and shifting cultural practices and expectations. The chapter offers an understanding of how educational institutions variously include and exclude particular individuals and groups throughout the schooling process. It begins with a general discussion of how sociologists analyze the dynamics between human interactions and educational institutions, then examines significant dimensions associated with what might be considered the three Rs of reproduction, regulation, and resistance.

THE MULTI-FACED NATURE OF EDUCATIONAL PRACTICES

A common characteristic in traditional sociological research on education, as observed in Chapter 2, has been a tendency to concentrate either on the details of life within schools or on the expectations placed on schooling through external social pressures and organizations. This dualism of focus is in part an expression of debates over whether human agency or social structures play the greatest role in influencing social life and human behaviour. In practice, internal and external forces, agency, and structure all are important determinants of educational realities. Some aspects of these dynamics, and in particular how they contribute to making educational practice such a varied and often contradictory undertaking are discussed below and expanded on in subsequent sections of this chapter.

Structural analysis stresses the ways in which labelling and hierarchy, as employed both formally and informally within educational settings, contribute to the reproduction of the social order. The standard imagery, from this vantage point, portrays classrooms structured by rows of desks occupied by students facing a teacher or professor at the front of the room. Education is viewed as little else than a form of preparation for work or **socialization** for adult life. Whatever the variations on this theme, the image conveys certain salient features of much educational life—schooling is organized around expectations of conformity, compliance, and standardization, whereby the instructor's position and authority are privileged in comparison with those of the learners. Despite their analytical differences, both structural functionalist and Marxist theorists of education share the position that student classification and streaming are central functions of schooling driven by the requirements of advanced industrial or capitalist social structures. Educational practices are examined not for their intrinsic or unique characteristics, but for their ability to produce individuals who are ready and able to occupy the social positions that await them after they leave the education system.

Interpretative analysis, by contrast, focusing on human agency, portrays labelling, categorization, and social identities within schooling as more fluid and changing processes, often expressed in terms used by educational participants themselves. High school pupils in Newfoundland and Labrador surveyed by Martin (1982), for instance, viewed classroom culture as a series of practices constructed around two main categories of pupils—'teachers' pets' and 'class victims'. Students also categorize themselves and others through various designations, based on factors like academic performance, cultural identification (signifying recreational pursuits, musical or sports-related interests, racial or ethnic identities, drug or alcohol preferences, or gender and sexual identities), or physical characteristics. Teachers also apply labels to pupils as they differentiate among 'good kids', 'troublemakers', 'bullies', 'mean girls', 'yahoos', 'overachievers', 'underachievers', and so on. Many of these labels, and the social interactions they are associated with, reflect or contribute to more enduring patterns of success and failure, but they are also important signifiers of the ways educational settings are constituted as rich and varied sites of social activity.

The failure in many studies of schooling to integrate analysis of activities inside the classroom—and other sites where educational interactions occur—with life beyond the classroom, and to comprehend the relationship between official and unofficial school activities, parallels more general boundaries and distinctions that characterize common perceptions about schooling. People tend to accept formal education as an inevitable part of their lives. When individuals do talk about schooling, it is usually with reference to people they hung around with, interesting or embarrassing moments, successes and failures, and overall impressions rather than about curricula and content that was learned. People are sometimes uneasy because these informal considerations seem to be at odds with the identification of school as the official world of lessons, homework, tests, rules, school-sponsored organizations, and other scheduled activities.

When asked to describe the purpose of schools, for instance, students often revert to language that could almost be quoted from official school documents, even though students rarely pay attention to such statements. A typical conception of schooling, in this case from a Grade 12 female student interviewed in the course of my own research, is that 'School is a place of learning, a place where we learn to interact with people and learn skill[s] that will help us deal with the problems in life with basic reason and understanding.' Whether or not they agree with particular features of schooling, people rarely question the legitimacy of formal education as a mechanism to structure learning, regulate lives, and confer **credentials**. This acceptance is based on distinctions we make that place boundaries between school and other aspects of our lives. As another student, this one a Grade 9 male who generally had a positive orientation to school, observed, 'I dislike the hard work and homework because I like to go home and watch TV and go hang around with my friends.' In other words, for students the official part of schooling is important, but it is not the same as, and sometimes interferes with, 'real life'.

Schooling overlaps substantially with people's social lives to the extent that much school time is occupied by 'joking around', finding ways to pass the time, and discussing parents, relationships, parties, popular culture, or personal issues, yet these events are typically discounted as irrelevant or incidental to education (McLaren, 2007; Contenta, 1993). Students often internalize responsibility for educational success or failure as a personal responsibility, regardless of personal circumstances, as observed in this account from a First Nations student in Grade 12:

> I think if I experienced difficulty [in school] that would be [because of] a low expectation of myself. I have two children, I have a son and a daughter and I have a babysitter, and it takes more responsibility to get them to daycare, to get myself to school and if I can't do that then that's my fault. . . . I can't make excuses, I can't use them as an excuse because it's something I did and it's my responsibility to get my education regardless.

It is crucial to recognize that schooling, in all of its routines as well as its more unique or exciting moments, is an important social activity in its own right even as it serves as a conduit into other spheres of social activity. Life in educational institutions carries its own rhythms and meanings, but it also reveals the pervasive influence of the world beyond the classroom door. The sometimes chaotic experiences of organized schooling leave indelible impressions about what is possible and expected in people's social lives.

Much recent sociological analysis of classroom processes has explored the linkages between social interaction in educational settings and more general historical and structural arrangements. Given the strong correlation that exists between social privilege and success in education and life beyond school, what is it about schooling that preserves this relationship in spite of the supposed role that education plays to provide equal opportunities for all? What are the features of schooling that produce relatively enduring patterns of success and failure? To what extent, and in what ways, does education impose control over people, and how much does it provide opportunities to empower them? Critical inquiry has attempted to address these issues by moving beyond individual determinants of educational attainment and school success to highlight the linkages between human agency and social structure and between formal and informal aspects of educational practices.

THE CONTRIBUTION OF SCHOOLING TO THE DEVELOPMENT OF HUMAN SUBJECTS

The observations made in the previous section suggest that the analysis of schooling, both in itself and through its wider social relations, must recognize formal education as having, in several significant ways, a dual character. Schooling contributes to formal learning and the attainment of knowledge and credentials that can be concretely defined and measured, but it is also characterized by more indefinite tasks associated with its human interactive and social dimensions. As was pointed out in Chapter 2, many important school lessons are derived from a **hidden curriculum** with little apparent connection to formal or overt educational objectives. We learn about such things as competition, success, failure, gender roles, racial identities, cultural understandings, and our place in society through our participation in the daily rituals of schooling. In other words, in addition to its roles of transmitting knowledge and bestowing status, schooling contributes to personality formation. Expressed another way, schooling is involved in the process of **individuation,** which refers to how our identity is constructed through notions of ourselves as distinct subjects.

The idea that our personalities are not fully formed from birth but are shaped as we interact with other people in particular circumstances is a central insight of sociology. Most sociological perspectives, regardless of their specific differences, emphasize the importance of formal education in the process of making us *social* beings. We are expected, through schooling, to develop patterns of co-operation with others and to gain sufficient understanding that we will comply with certain social expectations. Ironically, a fundamental part of our social identities in advanced capitalist societies is oriented towards individualism as a core value. We tend to view successful educational and social outcomes, essentially, as the product of initiative, aptitude, intelligence, and other attributes associated with qualities of the individual, while factors that contribute to failure commonly are given psychological explanations and persistent problems are regarded as ailments in

Box 5.1 Aboriginal Students' Perceptions of a Positive School Climate

Several initiatives have been implemented by school systems to address persistent concerns about the lack of educational success among Aboriginal students in Canada. The experiences described by Aboriginal youth in a Saskatchewan high school that has modified its programming, organizational structure, and social relations to take into account difficulties students often encounter both in and out of school demonstrate how students can benefit from a proactive, positive school climate:

A. When teachers are teaching they always refer to something to do with Aboriginal people, all the time. If it's Psychology, if it's something, because there are always Aboriginal students that go here . . . they use examples or bring up First Nations because everybody gets a little taste of it.
B. [In this school] everybody gets by, everybody has a story, the teacher has a story, they know more about the students than a regular teacher would. . . . The classes are smaller, you get to know everybody real quick. . . . [There is] more of a holistic way of teaching, not just straight out of the textbook, more Native teachers to explain the difference between the traditional and the contemporary.
C. Lots of times [in other schools] the teachers don't understand the situations or they don't understand certain people, they are used to seeing their middle-class kids attending and being good students. I guess if one of those teachers came into this school, their head would spin off their shoulders because there are so many different people with different problems and mostly everybody has some problem because most of the students are young parents. Eighty per cent of the student population here . . . is considered at risk.
D. . . . most of the teachers here will help you out if you have the time to go early . . . it's not just, 'do your work', they take the time to help you.
E. [I can] almost identify the school as a community. . . . The people are really friendly, and I know [it] kinda has a bad reputation . . . but that's always not true, there's a lot of people that have come here and they say it's so mellow and there's like no fighting, you're not really in little groups. Everybody is friends with everybody. There's no prejudice . . . it's small and caring.

need of treatment. The sociological critique of individualist positions emphasizes that individuals are shaped by society not merely because our social lives are conducted in relation to one another, but also in the sense that individualism itself is constructed through social processes.

It is important, in developing a sociological understanding of individual identities and orientations, that we do not dismiss entirely the social role played by individual actors. Fundamental to notions of human agency is the acknowledgement that each person must accept some responsibility for his/her decisions and actions as well as for the consequences that follow from them. At the same time, however, we must be attentive to how schooling and other social circumstances set parameters around which those decisions, actions, and consequences can be meaningful and effective.

Educational practices play a major role in the process by which people's lives and identities are constructed as individual subjects. Most school learning revolves around individual competencies. The individual pupil is monitored, expected to complete assignments, graded, promoted from one grade to the next, and disciplined. Educational credentials are acquired on a competitive basis, separating and distinguishing the identity and performance of each person from all others. We therefore come to identify success and failure, and learn to deal with their consequences, as products of our own efforts. A continual focus within schooling on individual characteristics, efforts, and achievements reinforces similar orientations prevalent within the mass media, workplaces, families, and other social sites, creating an impression that the individual is the natural, inevitable basis of social existence. School knowledge involves the development of an identity based on a modified sense of place or position in society. Education sorts students through continuous assessment and evaluation of pupils within schooling and in the presentation of grades and credentials for the outside world. The operation of the hidden curriculum and the informal interactions among educational participants also serve to construct and reinforce identities both within and beyond schooling.

The processes by which formal education contributes to personality and character formation can be illustrated with reference to the historical example of boarding and residential schools for children of Aboriginal ancestry. Boarding schools, operated by religious denominations, and residential schools, operated by the churches under federal government standards and with government funds after the mid-nineteenth century, were oriented to the assimilation of First Nations children into the dominant social order. Children were separated—sometimes forcibly—from their families for at least 10 months a year. The schools were organized in accordance with the principles of what Goffman (1961) terms **total institutions**, which are isolated from external social settings and governed by strict regimes of administrative scrutiny and control. Authorities in residential and boarding schools had complete control over children's lives for the duration of schooling. In addition to class work, their social lives and labour time (justified as necessary to provide essential job skills) were highly regimented and regulated.

They were treated as inmates, subject to extreme scrutiny and strict disciplinary measures for transgressions such as speaking their indigenous language. The schools were organized to alter the children's identities away from their original cultures to one that was regarded by authorities as appropriate for life in the dominant society. The intended transformation was a radical one, as described by the Royal Commission on Aboriginal Peoples (1996a: 365):

> At the heart of the vision of residential education—a vision of the school as home and sanctuary of motherly care—there was a dark contradiction, an inherent element of savagery in the mechanics of civilizing the children. The very language in which the vision was couched revealed what would have to be the essentially violent nature of the school system in its assault on child and culture. The basic premise of resocialization, of the great transformation from 'savage' to 'civilized', was violent. 'To kill the Indian in the child', the department [of Indian Affairs] aimed at severing the artery of culture that ran between generations and was the profound connection between parent and child sustaining family and community.

'The result', according to Kirkness and Bowman (1992: 12), 'was a tragic interruption of culture' that produced a legacy 'of cultural conflict, alienation, poor self-concept and lack of preparation for independence, for jobs and for life in general.' The residential schooling experience not only affected students directly, but contributed to a legacy of destruction and 'cycle of abuse' whose powerful impact remains deeply embedded in many Aboriginal communities (Royal Commission on Aboriginal Peoples, 1996a: 379; Schissel and Wotherspoon, 2003: 60–3).

Boarding and residential schools are not necessarily representative of schooling in general, given the extreme circumstances in which they functioned as total institutions oriented to the modification of individual personalities, in this case from their grounding in Aboriginal knowledge systems to identities viewed by officials as being more suited for life in Euro-Canadian society. Nonetheless, there are parallels among all types of schooling. Formal education, by its nature, shares the general objective to transform individual character and consciousness. Gracey (1977), in an influential article entitled 'Learning the Student Role: Kindergarten as Academic Boot Camp', shows how formal education is oriented from the outset to establish military-like classroom order and discipline. Various humanistic and progressive reforms, along with recent emphasis on the importance of creativity and innovation to a knowledge-based economy, have softened or concealed much of the disciplinary structure of the classroom. Nonetheless, the rise of a security state that has accompanied military engagement by Canada and the United States in the Middle East and fears about external threats and youth violence have renewed a 'law and order' ethos for many schools (Chomsky, 2003).

The structure of many classrooms continues to resemble late nineteenth-century factory organization, but school regimentation comes from roots that precede mechanized industrial production just as it comes to be transformed by new production and social processes. Nineteenth-century school reformers, in particular, were blunt in their assessment that mass public schooling should involve discipline and habit at least as much as it should be concerned with the acquisition of knowledge and work skills. Schools were consciously constructed to mould the individual and foster new loyalties and allegiances. Educational author-ities devised measures, such as the timetabling of the school day, the physical organization of the classroom, and monitoring and assessment of both pupils and teachers, in such a way to ensure that schooling produced disciplined individual subjects (see, e.g., Corrigan et al., 1987; Curtis, 1988; Wotherspoon, 1993). Today's schools may be less overtly concerned with discipline and personal virtues—in fact, as will be considered later in this chapter, schools are often criticized for being too undisciplined and disorderly—but issues of character, order, and hierarchy remain fundamental to schooling processes.

As these insights demonstrate, it is important to recognize how practices that occur in educational sites both shape and are shaped by what happens outside schooling. The activities we engage in and the identities we develop tend to be mutually reinforcing. Both individually and socially, educational outcomes tend to be affected more deeply by 'things that happened' than by 'what we learned in school'. The extent to which these events may become meaningful depends, in turn, on such factors as our relations with parents and family members, out-of-school interests and obligations, racial and gender characteristics, and the social and economic resources available to us.

REGULATION AND RESISTANCE IN SCHOOLING

One way in which sociologists have attempted to make sense of educational dynamics is to conceptualize schools as sites in which regulation and resistance occur. Schools regulate individuals and social activities as they fulfill tasks associ-ated with their varied expectations, including the dissemination of knowledge, the development of student skills and aptitudes, the production of recognized creden-tials, and the shaping and provision of direction to individuals' lives. In its most extreme and visible forms, such as in the case of residential and boarding schools, regulation is evident through rules, disciplinary procedures, the organization of time and space, and scrutiny by school officials over pupils' activities. Regulation also occurs in subtler forms, such as the recognition of some forms of knowledge and viewpoints as valid and the denial of alternative frameworks and experiences. In schooling, as in any regulative institution, however, official objectives and prac-tices are not always passively accepted by participants. Educators and learners alike use varied strategies and coping mechanisms as they attempt to make their lives alternatively meaningful or simply bearable. Students may mock teachers they dis-like, for instance, overtly flout school rules, or vandalize school property, just as teachers may introduce materials not on the curriculum, refuse to carry out offi-cial regulations, or employ a wide repertoire of other actions in expressing their responses to either specific or general features of schooling. Notions of resistance, whether they reside in disillusionment, optimism, rebellion, or even ridicule and humour, point to the ways in which educational practices can be indeterminate and contested, regardless of the limitations imposed by dominant educational structures and the agents who act on their behalf.

The discussion thus far has portrayed life in educational institutions as a volatile combination of formal and informal, official and unofficial, and determinate and indeterminate features. These educational realities create opportunities for individual and social transformation at the same time as they contribute to the reproduction of existing social circumstances and structures. People carry with them into schooling various background characteristics and predispositions—such as race, gender, income, employment status, parental support, family responsibilities, and emotional states—that both affect and are shaped by their educational experiences in complex ways. One of the most difficult tasks in the analysis of education is to isolate the relative impact of these various influences on people's life conditions, choices, and chances. As noted in Chapter 2 (and elaborated in Chapters 7 and 8), there are strong correlations between educational experiences and outcomes and social characteristics such as class, gender, and race. Social forces interact with unique aspects of our lives to produce distinctly different opportunity structures. As a consequence, regardless of our individual predispositions, our experiences are also strongly affected by whether we are male or female, Aboriginal or non-Aboriginal, poor or wealthy, of urban or rural origin, and so on. Similar interrelationships operate within the education system. Within Canadian education, for example, most senior-level teachers and administrators are men, while women are concentrated in lower-level teaching positions. To understand this reality, it is not sufficient to consider the specific elements that influence day-to-day decision-making within the scope of the classroom or other aspects of individual teachers' lives. We must also know something about how such factors as gender discrimination and differential labour market opportunities for men and women have contributed to the historical development of teaching. While particular career paths are the result of unique experiences, those experiences are preconditioned by strikingly regular patterns defined by social boundaries and expectations.

By recognizing these boundaries and the interactions that take place within them, we can come to an understanding of how relations of regulation and resistance may produce distinct social and educational outcomes. In subsequent sections of this chapter, these dynamics are explored through discussion of four significant types of practice that structure educational experience: (1) *streaming*, whereby students are channelled into distinct learning groups and programs; (2) an emphasis on *official knowledge*, which designates the kinds of topics, information, and content considered to be legitimate or worth knowing within schooling; (3) *hegemony*, through which domination comes to be experienced in people's everyday life experiences; and (4) *silencing*, which refers to processes through which particular kinds of social experience and alternative voices are devalued, marginalized, or denied a place within educational practice.

Streaming

Streaming refers to the placement of students into different programs based on their aptitude, ability, or special interests and needs. Streaming is most visible in situations where learners are differentiated into broad program areas such as vocational or academic streams. Streaming occurs between schools both when the choice of a school is related to the programs it offers and when it is recognized (by teachers, students, and parents) that the nature and quality of education varies from one school to the next. It also takes place within schools and classrooms in the form of various measures such as ability grouping in which pupils are divided into regular, remedial, or advanced streams in basic subject areas.

Streaming tends to be more voluntaristic and less systematically co-ordinated in Canadian schools in comparison with nations such as the United Kingdom, Japan, and Germany, where highly structured educational streams are prevalent, and even the United States, where tracking (grouping within classrooms) and stratified institutional arrangements are widely practised. Pedagogical justifications for streaming are based on arguments that students of similar backgrounds, interests, and abilities can be taught more efficiently and effectively than is possible in mixed classes. According to this justification, pupils receive instruction and assignments appropriate to their levels of interest and understanding, thereby facilitating success and making the educational process more rewarding for the individual. Streaming is also promoted for its potential to make education more relevant to the learner and better oriented to student futures. It is sometimes argued that educational and individual resources are wasted when all students are expected to be taught from the same curriculum at the same pace. This position asserts that people should receive training directly related to the kinds of jobs and futures they can expect.

Critics of streaming contend that these arguments confuse important issues while they hide the damaging realities of streaming. Much of the problem, at least on a day-to-day basis, is associated with the labels and identities that accompany student categorization. Students are highly aware of their status in relation to others and look for cues such as the classroom or work group they are placed in to identify where the system has slotted them. Responses like 'How come I'm with the dummies?' or 'I'm here because I want to go to university' signify pupils' attentiveness to groupings that may not even be officially acknowledged to the students by teachers or administrators. While the occasional placement of students in particular groups may not be highly significant, students' educational careers are given shape by recurrent labels and groupings that affect their self-concepts and educational performance. As noted in Chapter 2, the complex workings of the self-fulfilling prophecy, in which students eventually adopt behaviours consistent with the perceptions and expectations of their ability and roles held by teachers and other officials, have been demonstrated repeatedly through classroom research (Rosenthal and Jacobson, 1968; Stebbins, 1975; Contenta, 1993; Martel et al., 1999).

A regular consequence of streaming is that it does not affect students randomly but, instead, produces results that tend to correspond to existing patterns of social inequality, particularly in terms of race, class, and gender. This operates in several ways.

Gender relations illustrate both how streaming can affect students on a differential basis and how processes related to streaming can change over time. Nearly all school programs are open to males and females alike, but often there are pronounced differences in the kinds of schooling that boys and girls, and men and women, experience. Consequently, as Jane Gaskell (1992: 37) emphasizes, 'Gender itself matters' in the education system:

> At the university level, the small number of women enrolled in engineering and science has frequently been noted. Women are much more likely than men to be enrolled in nursing, education, the fine arts, and most humanities disciplines. At the college level, women are under-represented in trades training and in technologies, but are over-represented in community services and in secretarial and accounting courses. In high schools, the differences occur not so much between academic and non-academic courses, where racial and class differences are found, but within each. Young women are more often in senior French and history courses than in senior physics and computer science courses. They are more often in domestic science and business education than in industrial education.

Gender differentiation is produced by a combination of individual choices and organizational features of the school and wider society. Directions and comments from parents, teachers, guidance counsellors, peers, and others reinforce differential expectations about what kinds of behaviours and choices are appropriate for boys and girls. Many researchers have observed that teachers interact differently with boys and girls. Eyre (1991), observing students in a Grade 8 home economics program, notes that boys tend to dominate discussions, are more likely to be acknowledged by teachers, and are permitted higher levels of boisterousness than girls. In contrast to this situation, in which teachers have modified the curriculum to attract the attention of boys, McLaren and Gaskell (1995: 152) observe in a senior physics class little effort by teachers or students (male and female alike) to empower girls, challenge male authority, or even confront harassment of female students by some of the male students.

Recent research findings and media attention have posed significant challenges to feminist critiques of gender-based differentiation in education. Feminist analysis initially highlighted mechanisms within education and career pathways that undermined girls' educational achievements or diverted women in directions that did not match their aspirations or capabilities. However, a powerful discourse has emerged since the mid-1990s in Canada and many other nations to suggest that boys, not girls, have become educationally disadvantaged. These claims are based on several types of evidence, including standardized test results that repeatedly show girls outperform boys overall on reading and literacy measures, higher school **dropout** rates for boys relative to girls, post-secondary enrolment and graduation trends in which females outnumber males in most programs, and the preponderance of female students as recipients of major academic awards. Schools have come under pressure from media voices, policy-makers, educators, and parent advocacy groups to tailor programs, teaching styles, and curricular activities to boys' interests and needs, reminiscent of efforts in previous decades to make schools more 'girl friendly'. The prominence given to standardized test results led to broader scrutiny about issues such as boys' loss of interest in school matters, lack of reading interest, and stages of developmental progress. In 2001, Durham District School Board in Ontario gained extensive national exposure after it implemented guidelines requiring schools to develop action plans to address systematically the problem of boys' educational difficulties. The board identified several factors, such as the need for 'longer, more complex written assignments from boys; increased use of libraries by boys for recreational reading; more boys in academic after-school programs; more boys being celebrated for reading achievements', which were translated in turn to specific strategies, such as the use of role models to encourage boys, scrutiny of reading materials for gender bias, public acknowledgement of boys' reading achievements, and establishment of after-school programs to attract boys (Fine, 2001: A7; Bauer, 2001).

The introduction of a discourse that has posed boys as educationally disadvantaged has been accompanied by considerable controversy. Many educators are reluctant to embrace strategies to improve boys' educational performance for fear that efforts to target any specific group will reinforce stereotypes about gender and other discriminatory groupings, and undermine efforts to promote education that is inclusive of all students. Some critics link the focus on male disadvantage to a backlash against feminism that blames previous efforts to make schooling more accessible and rewarding to girls for going too far. There are also concerns that the reframing of the positions of boys and girls in schools reinforces a traditional gender duality that identifies the masculine as the rational and the feminine as the irrational. Walkerdine (1998: 168) observes that:

> The ideal child it seems is still a boy, a boy indeed with potential, whose success is being thwarted by women and girls, indeed by the very notion of female success. It is instructive therefore to examine the discourses through which this situation is understood and the way in which what at first appears as a problem with and for boys is too easily translated into a female problem: such a translation certainly accords with educational discourses which target mothers, female teachers, and of course, latterly, feminism.

In practice, the purported reversal of the gender gap can be understood fully only after several key questions are asked about such factors as the basis of comparisons, the processes that contribute to students' selection of particular subject and academic programs, the relative status attached to specific subjects, and the employment and life prospects that follow from specific educational outcomes. Kenway and Willis (1998: 57) illustrate, in part, how these mechanisms may operate:

Although not wanting to draw attention to themselves as high achievers, many students try to avoid being labeled as low achievers by enrolling in higher status subjects. Thus many—predominantly boys—enroll themselves in physics and chemistry with little chance of success. In contrast, a lack of confidence or ambition—or both—are perceived by many teachers to prevent girls from enrolling in physics and chemistry when they *are* able to cope with them. Gender policies and programmes which define able students' choices as acceptable when they are based on physical science and high-level mathematics, and less acceptable when they are not, serve to privilege success in male and academic terms and to devalue success in other areas. Overwhelmingly, this works against girls, who recognise that their futures are not likely to be the same as those of boys. Less obviously, it also works against 'less able' boys, who inappropriately choose subjects which are not likely to match the kinds of post-school options which will be available to them.

While boys and girls alike may be encouraged to aspire to careers in math, science, business, or health care, individual aspirations come to be modified by specific experiences of success or failure in the classroom, cues received from others about the appropriateness of particular goals, and growing sensitivity to categories produced by gender stereotyping. Despite increasing sensitivity to gender variations, it is still true, for example, that men are much more likely to be engineers and computer programmers while women are more likely to be secretaries and nurses.

These trends have reopened many long-standing debates, including questions about the extent to which biological factors influence educational and career pathways. Recent developments in genetic science and brain research have added a degree of sophistication lacking in previous nature–nurture controversies insofar as empirical evidence appears to support claims that boys and girls are fundamentally different with respect to aptitudes, learning styles, and other attributes. While such analysis can be compelling and powerful, it can also lead to conclusions that nothing can be done to change human 'nature', in the process potentially overstating both the veracity of specific findings and the extent to which they can be generalized to apply to wider phenomena while undermining the complex mechanisms through which social practices intertwine with biological factors to produce any given social outcome. The new politics of genetics and renewed nature–nurture controversies, as with previous iterations of debates over whether social or biological factors contribute more to social outcomes, tends to be highly charged and often misguided due to deep political convictions and ideological positions adopted by proponents of differing views. On one side, neo-liberal and socially conservative forces frequently see in genetic research a powerful 'scientific' antidote to feminism and social welfare orientations, often without exploring fully the limitations inherent in this 'science' and the claims associated with it; from an opposing perspective, social constructionists and advocates of state intervention frequently dismiss research findings that in some instances do have to be taken seriously.

These debates often obscure serious examination of how social structures and educational processes interact, in the first instance among themselves, and ultimately with varying biological dimensions, alternatively to restrict or foster educational and social opportunities. It is important to understand the interrelationships among gender-based educational streaming and other significant processes of social differentiation. While much attention has been paid to the differences between boys' and girls' test results in mathematics and literacy, for instance, more substantial variations are produced by social class and inequalities in parental backgrounds (Kenway and Willis, 1998; Bussière et al., 2001: 46–7). Krahn and Taylor (2007), analyzing data on courses selected by 15-year-olds in four Canadian provinces, observe that, 'Young people from more advantaged families were more likely than those from families where neither parent had a postsecondary education and where family incomes tended to be lower to be taking the type of math, science, and English courses that would keep all their postsecondary options open.' Without a clear understanding of how race, gender, and class operate within schooling, the characteristic focus on differences in educational performance can advance a neo-liberal emphasis on the individual at the expense of an awareness of the fundamental social bases of inequality (Burman, 2005).

Class and racial and ethnic relations are reproduced in similar ways, as are discussed in more detail in Chapter 8. Working-class children predominate in lower streams while children of professionals and those from more privileged families tend to be placed in academic streams and schools that are better equipped to produce success (Curtis et al., 1992). Educational experiences and attainments are also highly segmented through similar processes that operate along racial and ethnic lines (Li, 1988; Young, 1987). Henry and Tator (2005: 207–8), in a summary of Canadian research findings, observe that streaming repeatedly works to the detriment of immigrant and visible minority students, often as a consequence of assessment and decision-making processes related to the placement of students in particular streams. They cite as prominent cases the disproportional placement of black students in low-level academic programs and vocational programs, and the concentration of Southeast Asian students in mathematics, science, and computer post-secondary programs. The impact of streaming also extends beyond the allocation of students among distinctive programs or courses. Often, when programs and services such as English/French as a second language or anti-racism programs are created in response to the needs of specific student groups that may otherwise face educational disadvantage or discrimination, they remain vulnerable to cutbacks through resource constraints and educational restructuring decisions (Canadian Race Relations Foundation, 2000: 9).

The contradictory dynamics that operate within formal education are evident within streaming. Practices that are overtly concerned with grouping learners and providing instruction appropriate to their aptitudes and competencies can also operate insidiously to reinforce or produce systematic patterns of inequality. To the educator and educational administrator, grouping and categorization are likely to signify viable practical and pedagogical responses to differences among students that do not necessarily imply any inherent advantage or disadvantage for

Box 5.2 Barriers to the Achievement of Anti-Racism in Schools and Universities

Henry and Tator (2005: 223–5) identify several forms of discourse and coded language that contribute to racism and inequality despite formal commitment to equality of opportunity. These barriers include the following:

The Discourse of Denial

This discourse reflects a refusal to accept the existence of racism in its cultural and institutional forms. 'I am not a racist, and racism is not a problem in this school.' The evidence of racism in the lives and on the life chances of children of colour is indicated by the effort made by the educator and the school to suppress the processes of 'othering'—the marginalizing effects of ignoring the experiences, histories, and cultures of minority students in the classroom, texts, and classroom pedagogy.

The Discourse of Colour Blindness

Educators' attitudes toward racial minorities are expressed in assertive statements about colour-blindness, neutrality, and objectivity. 'I never see a child's colour.' 'I treat all children the same.' The refusal of educators to recognize that racism is part of the 'baggage' that racial-minority children carry with them, and the refusal to recognize racism as part of the daily policies, programs, and practices of the educational system, are part of the psychological and cultural power of racial constructions on the lives of students of colour as well as educators . . . .

The Discourse of Equal Opportunity

A commonly shared assumption among educators is that all students start with the same opportunities, often articulated in the notion that students begin their schooling with a blank slate. However, this negates the fact that by the time a child enters school he/she has accumulated five years of lived experiences that may influence the ways in which learning takes place. . . .

The Discourse of Decontextualization

In this discourse, there is an acknowledgement of the existence of racism, but it is interpreted as an isolated and aberrant phenomenon limited to the beliefs and behaviours of deviant individuals. It is believed that 'students enter the school with "blank slates".' The position of power and privilege that White educators and students enjoy in the classroom is neither acknowledged nor understood. Educators' own racial and cultural identities are generally invisible. Thus racism is decontextualized in terms of what counts as knowledge and how it is taught.

The Discourse of 'Blame the Victim'

This discourse is framed around the notion that equal opportunity is assumed to exist in all areas of the educational system. Thus, the lack of success of Black students, for example, is often attributed to dysfunctional families or culturally deficient or disadvantaged communities . . . . This view is reflected in statements such as: 'Education is not really valued in the Black community as it is in "Canadian" culture.' Or it is attributed to the supposed fact that parents of minority students don't have the same academic aspirations for their children. At the level of the university, this discourse is articulated in relation to questions of representation and meritocracy. . . .

The Discourse of Binary Polarization

This is the discourse of fragmentation into 'we'–'they' groups. 'We' represent the White dominant culture of the school; 'they' are the students, families, and communities who are the 'other', possessing 'different' values, beliefs, and norms. 'The problem with "our" Black/Asian students is that they do not really try to fit in.'

The Discourse of Balkanization

The view underpinning this discourse is that paying too much attention to 'differences' leads to division, disharmony, and disorder in society and in the classroom. 'First they want us to do away with Christmas concerts. Soon we'll be wearing turbans.' 'Before long, we won't know what a Canadian is.' . . .

The Discourse of Tolerance

The emphasis on tolerance suggests that while one should accept the idiosyncrasies of the 'others' (students or faculty who are culturally or racially 'different'), the dominant way is superior. 'We try to accommodate their different norms, but it is not always possible or desirable.'

The Discourse of Tradition and Universalism

This form of resistance is formulated on the premise that the traditional core curriculum should remain unchanged. 'Western civilization represents the best of human knowledge and forms the basis of cultural literacy and educational competence.'

The Discourse of Political Correctness

This discourse is most pervasive in academic culture. Demands for inclusion, representation, and equity are deflected, resisted, and dismissed as authoritarian, repressive, and a threat to academic freedom. 'The standards, values, and intellectual integrity of the university are in danger.'

Source: Frances, Henry and Carol Tator: The Colour of Democracy: Racism in Canadian Society, 3e. © 2006 Nelson Education Ltd. Reprinted by permission. www.cengage.com/permissions.

one category relative to another. At the same time, the direct and indirect messages sent to students, in conjunction with disparate resources and opportunities associated with each stream, have important consequences that contribute to inequalities in educational experiences and outcomes. These dynamics are explored further with respect to the importance of official knowledge and hegemony in schooling and the silencing of particular voices in the educational process.

OFFICIAL KNOWLEDGE

Education is centrally concerned with issues related to knowledge. We commonly view educational institutions as sites in which knowledge is transmitted or disseminated to the learner from teachers, textbooks, and course materials. In fact, knowledge relations in education are much more complex than they appear to be. Knowledge is not simply conveyed from the top down in a strict one-way flow and accumulated through what Freire (1970) calls a 'banking' approach to learning. Instead, it is dialogical and interactive in the sense that all educational participants, whether they acknowledge it or not, share in the ongoing transfer and interpretation of knowledge.

The revitalization of debates over school curricula and standards has opened up important questions about what kinds of knowledge, and whose knowledge, are part of the educational process. Periodic calls for 'back to basics', teaching to a standardized curriculum, or reliance on a selected list of core reading materials are opposed by competing claims that the curriculum is too narrowly framed and unrepresentative of student, community, and cultural diversity.

We must recognize that knowledge is not only disseminated, but also produced, in educational settings. This is most evident in universities and other post-secondary institutes that encompass within their mandates an ongoing involvement in research and scholarly work. However, all participants at every level of the education system contribute to knowledge production in a variety of ways through discussions, problem-solving, and engagement in everyday activities. Knowledge is shaped not only as it is continuously interpreted, processed, and reinterpreted in the interactions among instructors and learners in educational settings, but also through the experiences and understandings brought in from outside of schooling.

The top-down view of knowledge dissemination that dominates conceptions of formal education originates in our relatively unchallenged acceptance of official knowledge. As opposed to recognition of knowledge as something that arises from social interactions in everyday life in and out of school, emphasis on official knowledge gives legitimacy only to those ideas and beliefs that are in some way authorized by designated officials or agencies. What this means is that not all knowledge counts as 'true' or 'real' knowledge. Relations of power and authority act to differentiate between official knowledge, which is regarded as a valued commodity, and knowledge that we use in our everyday experiences, which tends to be devalued or treated as common sense (Apple, 2000: 42–4). The learned or knowledgeable individual, viewed in these terms, is someone who has book learning or formal educational credentials, whereas a person who has considerable expertise in practical matters or know-how is not recognized in the same way if these skills have not been formally acquired or certified (Jackson, 1993: 170–1).

Educational institutions are centrally implicated in the process whereby official knowledge is distinguished from and given privileged status over other forms of knowledge. This occurs in part because of the imperative for formal educational institutions to maintain their own legitimacy so that they are not undermined by other social sites that might wish to disseminate knowledge and bestow educational credentials.

The state plays a central role in granting legitimacy to educational agencies by establishing, co-ordinating, and regulating standards for the recognition of curricula, programs, and instructors. In Canada, provincial education departments are normally responsible for the formal approval of elementary and secondary school curricula and textbooks and, either directly or through bodies they authorize, for the certification of teachers and the establishment of procedures and standards for evaluation, promotion, and graduation. Provincial governments also grant accreditation to universities, colleges, public schools, and some private educational institutions, enabling them to structure their programs, hire qualified instructors, and grant certificates and degrees.

Because the state is expected to act as an arbiter among competing groups and interests, there is a legitimacy to educational practices and forms of knowledge incorporated within these formal structures of governance that is absent in less official social settings. Schools operate within an ideology of value neutrality in the sense that the curriculum is supposed to convey beliefs and knowledge representative of the society as a whole. Education's apparent objectivity is reinforced by the dismissal of ideas that are seen to represent overtly the views of 'special interest groups'. Many school boards have policies that forbid explicit product advertising or the display of corporate logos, for instance, while curriculum materials that depict gay lifestyles or readings produced by groups such as pro-life or pro-choice advocates are commonly protested if not banned from classrooms.

In practice, what comes into the schools is filtered through a selection process influenced by power relations and idea systems that prevail in the wider society. Schooling, like other social sites, conveys particular representations of reality that are not neutral in their origins and impact. This is not always readily apparent, nor is it a simple matter of one group imposing its ideas and values on all others. Several steps within educational and curricular processes allow for input and participation by diverse social agents, contributing to prospects for control by dominant groups as well as to resistance and unanticipated consequences. Apple (2000: 50–9) shows how textbooks can contain ideas that support dominant interests (by presenting one-sided, uncontested views of controversial or complex issues) at the same time as they depict the events and experiences that are meaningful to subordinate groups. Curricula that allow for discussion of issues like working-class history, gay rights, and racial and gender equity can be used in ways that are exploitative as well as progressive. At the same time, not all library books, texts, or curricular materials have an equal chance of making it into schools. Because textbook publishing and production of curricular materials can be a highly lucrative market, some major companies are able to allocate significant resources to promote products to teachers, administrators, and other decision-making bodies. Intensive lobbying efforts by religious organizations and other groups can also affect curricular options both directly, such as by exerting pressures on schools to keep specific resources out of school libraries, and indirectly, by constraining publishers from adopting materials that some groups might deem to be offensive. The curriculum is constructed through selection from a range of material eligible for inclusion into school systems, in conjunction with what is adopted and how that material is used and integrated into other personal and educational experiences.

Considerable flexibility and variation exist in the framing and delivery of school curricula. In Canada, most decisions about curricula and textbooks are made in the first instance by committees in various subject areas composed of administrators, teachers, specialists, government officials, and often representatives from universities, parent groups, and other community organizations. Curriculum-established limits to what is officially considered to be 'school knowledge' will vary from setting to setting, depending on such factors as the range of choices that teachers are given in lesson planning, frameworks established through specific core curriculum requirements, and the presence or absence of standardized or provincial examinations based on prescribed content or learning objectives. Teachers, working within curriculum guidelines, generally have high degrees of discretion to determine what, when, and how particular material will be taught. Curricula and teaching effectiveness are shaped further by informal and unstructured classroom interactions. Classroom practices are marked by a meandering, often indeterminate path that wanders between what is represented as official knowledge and the lessons and understandings that students exhibit after they leave their schools and classrooms.

At the same time, distinctions made between what is and is not considered valid educational content have important implications for different educational participants. Many students, particularly those from white middle-class families, arrive in school with a strong familiarity with the language and operations of the classroom. The greater the correspondence between what schools expect and students' background experiences, the less likely the pupils will be to have difficulties with understanding school rules and course materials. Conversely, students who lack the 'cultural capital' underlying educational practices are likely to be at a relative disadvantage.

Basil Bernstein, a British sociologist of education, offers useful insights into how cultural capital is related to power and control in educational processes. His work, in part, proceeds from a distinction between 'visible' and 'invisible' pedagogies (Bernstein, 1977). Visible pedagogies are educational processes in which there

Box 5.3 A Holistic Framework for Redefining Success for First Nations, Métis, and Inuit Learning

Considerable attention has been given to problems and deficiencies associated with conventional indicators of educational participation, progress, and attainment experienced by Aboriginal people. Recent initiatives to create meaningful options for the kinds of education system that will engage Aboriginal communities and their members more fully have pointed to the need to integrate Western educational values with models of education that provide cultural affirmation of indigenous knowledge, values, and cultural traditions. The Aboriginal Learning Knowledge Centre of the Canadian Council on Learning (2007b: 5–7) is working with a diverse cross-section of Aboriginal communities and educators to develop a framework that seeks to redefine educational success in such a way as to address these issues. The framework builds upon several key dimensions in which learning is:

- holistic, nurturing and developing the individual (emotional, physical, spiritual, and intellectual aspects) and the collective;
- a lifelong process, illustrated in the four quadrants of the medicine wheel, highlighting continuity through individual and generational life cycles;
- experiential in nature, in which observation and participation occur beyond the classroom, in communities and natural environments;
- rooted in Aboriginal languages and cultures;
- spiritually oriented;
- a communal activity, involving family, community, and Elders; and
- an integration of Aboriginal and Western knowledge.

Three models are presented to guide this process (ibid., 18, 20, 22):

First Nations Holistic Lifelong Learning Model
For First Nations people, the purpose of learning is to develop the skills, knowledge, values, and wisdom needed to honour and protect the natural world and ensure the long-term sustainability of life. Learning is portrayed as a holistic, lifelong developmental process that contributes to individual and community well-being. This process is both organic and self-regenerative in nature, and integrates various types of relationships and knowledge within the community.

The First Nations Holistic Lifelong Learning Model uses a stylized graphic of a living tree to depict learning as a cyclical process that occurs throughout the individual's lifespan. This learning tree identifies the conditions that foster cultural continuity and provide the foundation for individual learning and collective well-being.

The model contains four main components. They depict the dynamics that enable First Nations people to experience holistic lifelong learning as a purposeful developmental process. The components include: the sources and domains of knowledge (the roots), the individual's learning cycle (the rings), the individual's personal development (the branches), and the community's well-being (the leaves).

Inuit Holistic Lifelong Learning Model

The Inuit Holistic Lifelong Learning Model presents a stylistic graphic of an Inuit blanket toss (a game often played at Inuit celebrations) and a circular path (the 'Journey of Lifelong Learning') to portray the Inuk's learning journey and its connection to community well-being.

The model contains four main visual components that convey the Inuit approach to holistic lifelong learning. The components include: the determinants of community well-being, Inuit values and beliefs (the 38 community members [each core value and belief is associated with a representative ancestor or family and community member]), sources and domains of knowledge (the learning blanket), and the journey of lifelong learning (the pathway).

Métis Holistic Lifelong Learning Model

For the Métis people, learning is understood as a process of discovering the skills, knowledge, and wisdom needed to live in harmony with the Creator and creation, a way of being that is expressed as the 'Sacred Act of Living a Good Life'. Although learning occurs through concrete experiences that occur in the physical world, this *learning by doing* is grounded in a distinct form of knowledge that comes from the Creator.

This sacred knowledge reveals the laws that govern relationships within the community and the world at large and provides the foundation for all learning. To illustrate the relationships between knowledge and the dynamic processes that comprise the 'sacred act of living a good life', the Métis Holistic Lifelong Learning Model uses a stylized graphic of a living tree.

The tree depicts Métis learning as a holistic, lifelong process, an integral part of a regenerative, living system, as represented by the life cycle of the tree. Like the tree, Métis learning is governed by the Natural Order, an all-encompassing entity that regulates the passage of seasons and the cycles of birth, death, and rebirth. . . . The model contains four main components that represent various aspects of Métis learning. The components are: determinants of community well-being (the roots), the stages of lifelong learning (the learning rings), the sources of knowledge and knowing (the branches), and the domains of knowledge (the leaves).

are obvious hierarchies of authority and knowledge; teachers have explicit control over pupils; the curriculum is organized, directed, and transmitted by teachers; and pupils are monitored and evaluated by teachers in accordance with relatively explicit standards. Invisible pedagogies, by contrast, are characteristic of more open teaching/learning situations in which teacher control over pupils is more implicit; children have greater apparent opportunities to select, arrange, and pace their activities and social interactions; and there is greater concern in teaching and assessment of students with process than with specific measurable outcomes.

Bernstein's analysis focuses on the development of what at the time were newer forms of open preschool classes that came to be based more on activity and play than on work, but it does have relevance for schooling at other levels as well. The open classroom seems progressive because it allows greater flexibility and concern for the learner than is possible under more authoritarian models of schooling. However, Bernstein argues that, under visible pedagogies, students (and parents) recognize explicitly what is expected of them, even if their ability to succeed depends on culturally biased materials and expectations that favour the middle classes. Under invisible pedagogies, by contrast, the standards are much less clear and, moreover, more of the child's activity becomes exposed to the scrutiny of the teacher. Successful performance now requires that students have the know-how or skills to uncover hidden rules and expectations. This educational structure gives a tremendous advantage to children (particularly those whose parents are of professional backgrounds) who have insight and experience to point them in the direction of activities and behaviours that are rewarded rather than penalized.

Hegemony

Critical sociology often makes reference to the concept of hegemony to illustrate how social structures give shape to our daily activity. **Hegemony**, as elaborated in the work of Antonio Gramsci, refers to a process of domination by consent, in which the general population adopts a world view that reflects the interests of the dominant classes (see, e.g., Gramsci, 1971: 12ff.). This analysis allows us to see how our common-sense way of looking at things, which we derive from our traditions and experiences, is constructed so that ruling practices are maintained without usually being evident to us.

Two examples illustrate how educational practices are hegemonic. The first is the way that knowledge is organized and presented in the classroom. The curriculum is usually understood, arranged, and transmitted to pupils, and often even to teachers, in the form of prearranged units of information. Facts, ideas, and subjects are divided and separated from one another in such a way that they sometimes seem to bear no relationship to each other, with little reference to the context within which they emerged and came to be seen as important. Assignments and tests are often based on recall and reference to discrete bits of information. The learning process comes to be narrowly defined around material that can be readily presented and retrieved (Apple, 2004). Schools are hegemonic insofar as they contribute to a taken-for-granted sense of the world by failing to encourage critical thinking and a sense of how various practices and ideas are interconnected.

A second example of how hegemony is produced in the schooling process is the ethic of individualism referred to earlier in this chapter. As we have already observed, we are taught—through schools, the media, and other venues—that our social position and worth are based on individual effort and initiative. This view, for many of us, is beyond question; we accept it because it seems natural to us. In doing so, however, we fail to consider seriously any alternative viewpoints there might be. Individualism is an ideology that draws attention away from the social origin of practices and ideas. In fact, many elements of our realities are socially constructed—they are produced through the interplay among human actors, social forces, and already existing social structures. Viewed in this way, individual ability and initiative count, but they can only be made sense of against a backdrop that places strict limitations on what is possible for any given individual. To ignore these aspects of reality leads to sets of beliefs and circumstances that favour those social interests that are dominant at any given point in time.

Schools are hegemonic institutions to the extent that they do not address or encourage the posing of fundamental questions about the nature of our social reality. They are not necessarily organized to favour explicitly the interests of the wealthy and powerful over the poor and disenfranchised, but when social inequality is not discussed as a central part of curricula and when the world is seen as a collection of individuals rather than as a system based on distinct social positions, one consequence is that prevailing patterns of domination and subordination come to be understood and experienced as natural and inevitable rather than as something to be questioned. As we have acknowledged repeatedly, formal education also affords the possibility for alternative ways of seeing the world and for resistance to official knowledge and hegemony. These will be discussed later in this chapter, following the consideration of another process—silencing—that limits the scope of learning and understanding in educational practices.

SILENCING IN EDUCATIONAL PROCESSES

Silencing operates in two interrelated ways. First, it exists when particular issues are excluded from or discouraged in the classroom. Second, silencing also occurs when the lives, interests, and experiences of particular educational participants are made irrelevant to the schooling process. By dealing with 'the curriculum' or 'the business at hand', schools and other institutions send clear messages about what is and is not important. In the process, some topics and experiences, however central they may be to students' lives, are placed outside the boundaries of what are defined or understood as legitimate areas of classroom discussion.

As we observed with respect to the official knowledge that is central to educational processes, some forms of knowledge and behaviours are rewarded while others are marginalized. Considerable attention has been given in recent years to the cultural bias inherent in standardized curricular material and instruments like aptitude and intelligence tests. Test items, like many classroom activities, often rely on knowledge or experiences that may seem to the teacher or tester to be universal but that in fact reflect a particular orientation to reality not shared by all groups. What occurs is that some world views are given voice, or legitimized, while others are silenced. Many common-sense approaches to problems are dismissed as irrelevant or inappropriate for the classroom. An Aboriginal child from a northern reserve and a black pupil in an inner-city school, for instance, may possess considerable knowledge about complex social activities that they encounter daily outside the school setting, whereas in school their worlds are rarely acknowledged. This is not necessarily a deliberate or calculated attempt to privilege one group over another, yet it has the effect, especially when reinforced over time, of compounding the disadvantage faced by subordinate groups.

Analysis conducted through various critical perspectives demonstrates that silencing operates in numerous ways to control classroom interaction and regulate individual identities. Talking in the classroom is commonly discouraged, unless it is directed by teachers and authorities who are lecturing or giving instructions, or where students are allowed to conduct discussions related to a specific pedagogical task (Shor, 1980: 72). Silencing may operate more symbolically than literally in the sense that students, when they do respond to teachers or professors, may subordinate language or dialect they employ informally in favour of patterns of discourse that are rewarded in educational settings. Remaining silent also functions as a way students may protect themselves from scrutiny by educators or from embarrassment at exposing too much of themselves and their lives (Ellsworth, 1992: 104–5). Bourdieu and Passeron (1977) examine how 'self-silencing' occurs as a result of 'symbolic violence' in the education system. Students who are unfamiliar with or unable to meet the demands that arise from educational standards and expectations are likely to undermine their own capabilities and personalities if they cannot change to achieve conformity. Rather than question how and why such standards reflect social privilege associated with dominant social groups, the individual internalizes educational failure while reinforcing existing power relations. Educational processes can operate in these ways to silence teachers as well as students, depoliticizing participants by undermining their 'authentic voices', thereby reinforcing hierarchies of gender, race, and class (Nugent and Bell, 2006).

Proponents of inclusive education and anti-racism in schooling and other institutional settings point out the deep impact that silencing can have on people's lives. For some persons, challenges to or devaluation of their lived experiences can have damaging psychological consequences. Invisible messages transmitted in the classroom that are based on white, male, middle-class standards, for instance, can lead minority students to see their own identities as undesirable or unacceptable (Ng, 1991). Silencing produces invisibility, which through normal school practices results in negations of self and identity that 'erase the social, cultural, historical, and political realities of marginalized groups in society through the exclusive practices of Eurocentrism' (Dei et al., 2000: 172). Pupils, in response to these processes, may become marginalized and withdraw from participation in school activities, especially if there are conflicting messages between home and school about what is culturally and socially important. Such withdrawal, in turn, can lead to social isolation or to incorporation into alternative groups such as youth gangs or 'counter-school cultures' that define themselves through their defiance against authority (Willis, 1977).

The lack of connection between schooling and student background is a major contributing factor to educational problems experienced by Aboriginal and visible minority children and youth. Schools and other educational sites that fail to do so, or are not able to make a connection between what they do and the lives of the students and communities they work with, increase the likelihood that students will become disengaged from, or disaffected with, their education. Highlighting the gap that Aboriginal youth frequently identify between life in and out of school, the Royal Commission on Aboriginal Peoples (1996b: 482) observes that, 'Education as they experience it is something removed and separate from their everyday world, their hopes and dreams.' Sometimes, even content specific to students' cultural backgrounds can pose confusion or mystification when school representations conflict with what students are told in community contexts. The comments of one Grade 12 First Nations student in a Prairie inner-city school are typical of this concern: 'There is quite a contrast [between what I am told in school and what my people tell me], like the Crazyhorse [the Lakota leader whose legacy is represented in distinctly different ways in Western and indigenous knowledge traditions], the old people know, like my grandpa used to talk about them a lot, and then when you learn about them in school . . . it's a lot different, and I was saying, ok, somebody is lying to me.' Dei et al. (2000: 20–1) contrast educational practices that exclude and marginalize minority students with inclusive schooling; the latter is characterized by an acknowledgement by educational personnel and practices of students' cultural backgrounds in a manner that integrates the community into the school context.

Like other hidden aspects of schooling, therefore, silencing can deeply affect both the schooling experiences and the social futures of students. Beyond the content and

Box 5.4 Afrocentric Schooling

The approval by the Toronto District School Board early in 2008 of a proposal to establish an Afrocentric alternative school has been surrounded by extensive controversy and sometimes highly emotional responses by both critics and defenders of the initiative. The school, guided by principles to integrate the heritage and knowledge of peoples of African descent throughout the entire curriculum and school experience, is intended to address serious deficiencies in educational retention, performance, and attainment among many black students, especially those of Caribbean descent, in the city's schools. Critics attack the initiative as a form of ghettoization, segregation, and regressive policy that could lead to the eventual fragmentation of the entire education system; proponents point to evidence to show that the present system is not working. Often missed in the most extreme debates are the historical roots of the problem and the precedents that exist in other contexts, including a prior trial in Toronto and a Nova School that has operated on Afrocentric principles since the mid-1990s (White, 2008; Dei, 2006). While issues associated with the relationship between racial segregation and schooling are well known, especially in the southern United States, many black communities in Canada have similar experiences of marginalization and social isolation. Black communities established their own schools due to prejudice and barriers that blocked participation in public schools as early as the 1830s in Canada West (Ontario) and the 1840s in Nova Scotia. Subsequent school and human rights legislation formally ended race-based discrimination in the latter parts of the twentieth century, but the exclusion of racial minorities through various socio-economic, geographical, and cultural factors has contributed to the perpetuation of clustering of school populations along racial lines (Kelly, 1998: 30–4). An influential Nova Scotia document, widely known as the BLAC report (Black Learners Advisory Committee, 1994: 35), highlights the numerous systemic barriers encountered by black learners and community members in that province:

> During the BLAC research, we encountered widespread condemnation of the education system as *biased, insensitive* and *racist.* Systemic racism was seen as manifested in student assessment and placement; in labelling of large numbers of Black students as slow learners or having behaviour problems; in streaming; in low teacher expectations; in denigration by and exclusion of Blacks from the curriculum; and in the total lack of responsiveness to the needs of Black learners and concerns of the Black community.

Proponents of Afrocentric or black-focused schooling see the schools as complementing principles of public schooling but offering effective alternatives within systems that continue to fail to deliver on promises to ensure effective educational options for a substantial segment of the population. Sociologist George J. Sefa Dei (2006: 28) contends that,

> If we are to define 'educational success' broadly, then we must recognize that alternative/counter visions of schooling may enhance learning for these young people. While my enthusiasm for Black-focused/African-centred schooling is primarily based on its potential to address issues of Black and other minority youth disengagement and 'push out' from the Canadian school system, the same fundamental principles may help to transform conventional schooling in Euro-Canadian/American contexts, as well.

skills directly transmitted through the curriculum, the knowledge, attitudes, and emotions that are absent from or subordinated within educational practices convey to educational participants critical signals about how the world is organized and should be encountered. Both overt and silent understandings in the classroom contribute to a complex process of manoeuvring and differentiation in which the successful or 'good' students come to be distinguished from those characterized by alternative or deviant labels and identities.

STUDENT RESPONSE AND RESISTANCE

Students must become accomplished actors in a number of ways in the course of their schooling experiences. Their actions contribute to the continuously changing nature of classroom activity. The school day is rarely the smooth-flowing progression of tightly integrated lessons and transitions between classes that appears in official accounts of schooling. Instead, it involves uneven pacing, constant interruptions, and shifting back and forth among planned and unplanned occurrences. Within even just a few moments, students are likely to alternate their behaviour to reflect varying degrees of attentiveness, boredom, overt and covert gestures, dialogue with teachers, and exchanges with other pupils. In contrast with common conceptions of pupils as passive consumers of curricular knowledge, students are continuously engaged in shaping and making sense of the educational process. As Michael Apple (2000: 57) observes, 'students are active constructors of the meanings of the education they encounter.'

Researchers who analyze educational settings frequently employ the concept of 'resistance' to understand how students engage in and respond to their schooling experiences. Most of this research is focused on adolescents at the stage where resistance tends to be most overt. The notion of resistance conveys most immediately a sense of rebellion or rejection of schooling as demonstrated through such acts as vandalism and destruction of school property, overt disregard for school rules, defiance of teachers' authority, refusal to complete assignments, absenteeism, or dropping out. However, students often exercise resistance in subtler ways. Lack of attentiveness to lessons and instructions, whispered comments and notes passed to other pupils, informal mocking of teachers, repeated errands and trips to the washroom, and pressure to discuss issues not on the formal curriculum all can signify reactions against school activities that students consider boring, meaningless, or oppressive.

The concept of resistance adds to our understanding of school processes a sensitivity to the unofficial and interpersonal elements of schooling. Educational dynamics are characterized by continual dialogue and interchange, both verbal and non-verbal. Students, far from being passive recipients of schools' efforts to shape and control the individual, are highly implicated in the directions that their schooling takes and the outcomes to which it contributes.

The presence and significance of resistance should not be exaggerated. Deviant forms of behaviour such as bullying or resentment against authority are often confused with resistance to schooling (Giroux, 1983; Lynch, 1989: 15; McLaren, 2007: 216). Resistance is more appropriately understood as student responses to the dehumanizing and restrictive aspects of schooling that diminish creativity, enlightenment, and self-worth or that devalue meaningful social experiences. Such resistance is usually individual in nature, but it may also be collective. Sometimes, collective resistance is spontaneous, such as when a group of students supports a pupil they feel is being picked on unfairly by a teacher, or when students persuade their teacher that playing ball would be more beneficial than doing a math quiz on a sunny day. Woods (1983: 56–8) emphasizes how both students and teachers employ laughter and other apparent deviations from the formal curriculum as means to negotiate daily classroom interactions. School resistance can also be more organized, as when students engineer a walkout from class or circulate a petition to complain about such issues as overly harsh school regulations or the transfer of a popular teacher to another school. In these kinds of situations, it is noteworthy that student actions generally tend to be accommodative to schooling, with resistance limited to specific instances or features of educational practices.

There is considerable debate about the meaning of different forms of resistance. Kanpol (1992: 57), for instance, distinguishes between institutional political resistance, which is directed against specific features of particular schools or educational environments, and cultural political resistance, which involves movement from critique of education towards the formulation of alternative ideas and practices. Many educators, politicians, and media analysts point to school violence, vandalism, and lack of student respect for authority as alarming indicators of the extent to which educational and social standards have declined in recent years. Other commentators, particularly those who adopt a critical pedagogy orientation, portray student resistance as an outcry against oppression or a noble struggle to preserve their humanity in a dehumanizing world. Schools and school rules, in this view, signify externally imposed authority structures that are threatening to students, particularly those for whom access to meaningful participation in secure jobs and influential social positions seems unattainable. Several researchers have commented on the frequent tensions that arise between teachers and students around issues of physical appearance. Even schools that do not have strict dress codes have unspoken or informal standards regarding appropriate kinds of clothing, hairstyles, and student demeanour. Students, however, often adopt non-traditional styles of dress and attitudes that enable them to express their sexuality and assert a rebellious stance against school authority. A rich tradition of research in Canada and many other nations explores the diverse ways in which students from working-class and minority backgrounds express themselves through particular actions and symbolic representations in order to set themselves apart from dominant values or groups (e.g., McRobbie, 1978; Connell et al., 1982; McLaren, 2007). This literature has broadened to encompass resistance against the regulation of sexuality, ability status, and other characteristics in which schools and youth cultures can work variously to reinforce or undermine dominant normative and behavioural standards.

YOUTH CULTURES AND MORAL PANICS

Schools represent a focal point around which considerable attention has been directed to the contemporary status of children and youth. As gathering places that often crystallize distinct youth cultures built around such designations as punks, metalheads, freaks, skids, skaters, ravers, gangsta' rappers, hackers, and many others commonly drawn from popular entertainment and sports, schools have also been targeted by many critics for their role in fostering some of the more questionable aspects of youth experience. Various youth identities and expressions are typically part of the attachments and insecurities that arise through the developmental process, especially in a context in which roles and expectations for young people are undergoing significant transformations. These identities sometimes encourage a degree of peer acceptance and 'acting out' of tensions and resentment against a social environment that students otherwise perceive as meaningless or actually hostile to them. In the process, many aspects of youth culture have come to be the focus of intense public scrutiny, often accompanied by outrage within mass media and other prominent commentary.

Sociologist Stanley Cohen (1972) introduced the concept of **moral panic** to describe situations in which powerful groups mobilize public opinion against what they portray as threats to dominant values. Socially constructed 'moral panics' framed through discourses that depict contemporary youth as out of control and excessively engaged in deviant and criminal activity have served in particular to stigmatize disadvantaged groups (Schissel, 2006). The extensive media coverage given to incidences of gang-related activities, school shootings, swarmings, physical bullying, violence by girls and boys alike, drug and alcohol abuse, and the use of public websites and electronic technologies to intimidate and embarrass individuals is reinforced by public outcries and pledges by politicians for disciplinary measures. The resulting hysteria often creates a highly skewed image of youth culture, creating a sense that problems exist far in excess of their true scope while neglecting both positive dimensions of youth life and more direct problems that do concern youth.

Prompted by these fears, schools in many parts of North America have asserted their role as disciplining institutions. Some urban high schools have come to resemble prisons with the installation of metal detectors, security cameras, lockdown procedures, locker inspections, and strict monitoring procedures. Governments and schools have also adopted more general measures to address concerns related to public safety and security. Ontario's Safe Schools Act, for instance, implemented in 2000–1, empowers teachers as well as principals to suspend or expel students who are deemed to be engaging in disruptive or violent behaviour. Sometimes called 'zero tolerance' policy by critics and supporters alike, the legislation has been challenged for being applied inappropriately, especially for targeting black students, as well as other visible minority students and students with disabilities (Ontario Human Rights Commission, 2003). The experience related to this legislation, which was amended in early 2008 in response to parental concerns and an investigation by the Ontario Human Rights Commission, exemplifies some of the highly selective and dangerous outcomes that can be produced by moral panics related to children and youth. Many of the groups most negatively affected by security-based measures—including Aboriginal youth, students from low-income families, and those living in domestically fragile situations, as well as inner-city black students and disabled students identified as posing a risk by the Ontario legislation—are those who most require support from schools and other agencies to enable them to benefit from education. Ironically, many of these students otherwise look to schools to provide inclusive, safe environments, in contrast to higher degrees of vulnerability or insecurity that confront them in other domestic, community, or agency environments.

Attention to the most shocking or provocative aspects of youth cultures obscures the more complex and subtle dynamics that characterize the lives and experiences of most young people. Children and youth face a bewildering array of opportunities, challenges, demands, and stimuli. Whereas terms like the 'generation gap' were applied to the social and cultural distance that marked differences in lifestyles, attitudes, and identities between previous cohorts of children and youth and their parents and elders, many social, material, and spatial reference points were shared across these cohorts. Contemporary youth, by contrast, have access to an unprecedented and rapidly changing range of technologies and experiences—both 'real' and 'virtual'—but face at the same time incredible pressures and uncertainty regarding future life plans. Rapid developments and widespread accessibility related to information and communications technologies have expanded exposure to information, forms of social interaction, and stimuli that alter youth's expectations and perceptions of the world, often in ways that parents, teachers, and other non-peers cannot fathom or keep pace with. In the process, their lives are shaped by shifting family and economic dynamics and growing sensitivities to new risks and presumed standards of various kinds, ranging from concern for environmental and climate change, to body image and threats to security and even species survival.

The pervasiveness of market economies and consumer culture, reinforced by and through various communications devices and media, has hastened the extension of what Steinberg and Kincheloe (1997) have designated as 'kinderculture'— a new form of childhood and youth characterized by consumerism, gratification, and identification with disposable objects rather than enduring social and cultural reference points. Leisure time carries many of its own diversions, often leading to the neglect of or opposition to school and what schooling stands for (Nelsen, 2007). In addition, fuelled by a desire for cash (either out of necessity or to support individual consumption) and for recognition that schooling in itself is not enough, many young people are increasingly engaged in paid and volunteer work, which further complicates student life.

Schooling, in the course of these transformations, faces significant challenges. Educators often see themselves competing against media, technology, and consumer culture to capture student interest. Many parents and school critics press for stricter disciplinary measures and educational standards. Others seek educational reforms to ensure greater relevance, incorporating technologies and new methods such as teamwork and problem-solving orientations into the schools.

In the course of these shifts, and despite attention given to the more extreme forms of resistance and deviance, research that has explored in a systematic way what students think of their schooling experiences has shown that they respond to formal education—and other facets of their lives—in mixed and often contradictory ways. A useful categorization of student responses is presented by Connell et al. (1982), who suggest on the basis of their interviews with Australian high school students about 14 years of age that, in addition to resistance, there are at least two other main types of student–teacher relations. The first is compliance, in which students accept school rules and express enthusiasm for their schooling as a way of gaining rewards. The second response is pragmatism, in which students engage in required activities only to the extent that they are seen to be required for achieving objectives, such as passing grades and receiving credentials.

Many other researchers have observed similar processes. McNeil (1986) and Weis (1990), studying American high schools, stress how the ritualistic nature of classroom practices emerges as part of an unspoken agreement between students and teachers. By the time they reach high school, students typically tend to be passive and docile. While the occasional outburst of energetic protest may erupt over particular issues, especially when pupils feel they are being unfairly dealt with by teachers who exercise excessively harsh discipline, double standards, or poor teaching methods (Connell et al., 1982: 84), students rarely challenge either teachers or the school authority structure. Instead, students agree to carry out at least minimal requirements to complete work assignments and keep an orderly classroom—in other words, to do what they think is expected to help the teacher do his or her job properly. In exchange, they expect to get through school with respectable treatment and acceptable grades.

This accord channels potential student dissatisfaction and resistance in such a way that the legitimacy of the education system, and the social system as a whole, is not called into question (see, e.g., Aronowitz and Giroux, 1993; Willis, 1977). Students to a large extent 'buy into' the education system, viewing educational success as desirable for social success and blaming themselves for many of the occasions that they experience failure. Even where more severe problems begin to appear, taking the shape, for instance, of frequent skipping of classes, overt resistance, conflict with teachers, or resignation, students are hesitant to express doubt about the school system except when they are probed or encouraged to speak out. Interviews with early school-leavers, such as those conducted by Crysdale and MacKay (1994) in Toronto, Samuelson (1991) and Tanner et al. (1995) in Edmonton, Randhawa (1991) in Saskatchewan, and Crysdale et al. (1999) in Alberta and Ontario, reveal

Box 5.5 Bullying and Victimization in Students' Lives

As the stakes associated with learning increase, greater concern is directed to the conditions that foster or inhibit learning for various groups of students. These conditions go well beyond classroom relationships and relate to such factors as homework loads, extracurricular activities, work and other commitments out- side school hours, and student safety concerns. Among the most prominent of these factors are problems associated with bullying. A survey conducted on behalf of the Canadian Council on Learning (CCL, 2007e: 33) reveals that four out of five adult Canadian respondents agree or strongly agree that bullying is one of the most serious issues affecting students. While 38 per cent of male respondents and 30 per cent of female respondents indicate that they had been bullied in school, there are strong concerns that bullying has become more seri- ous in nature (ibid., 35). The problem is compounded, in part, by the pervasive impact of new technologies and the broader ways in which we have come to understand bullying and abusive relationships, as illustrated in the summary of four main types of bullying identified by the CCL (ibid., 32):

Types of bullying

1. *Physical bullying*
   - punching
   - kicking
   - pushing
   - tripping
   - pinching
   - pulling hair
   - forced confinement

2. *Relational bullying*
   - social exclusion
   - spreading rumours
   - gossip
   - sending nasty notes

3. *Verbal bullying*
   - name-calling
   - verbal intimidation
   - mocking
   - insulting

4. *Electronic or 'cyber' bullying*
   - similar to relational and verbal bullying but occurs on-line
   - sending false e-mails using the victim's name
   - forwarding private e-mails, pictures, or information

Behaviour related to bullying is a focus of concern in many nations. Incidences of bullying and victimization occur widely among both boys and girls, although boys are typically more likely to bully others and much more likely to engage in physical fighting in school and other settings in which children and youth are concentrated. Several international and comparative studies reveal reported incidences of bullying in Canada to be higher than average, although not as high as in several nations. The table below, constructed from data in a

World Health Organization survey of youth in different age cohorts in 35 nations, illustrates variations in patterns across several nations, placing Canada relatively high in overall incidences of bullying though somewhat below average in instances of physical fighting.

Table 5.1   Young People (13-year-olds) Who Were Bullied or Who Bullied Others in the Previous Two Months, and Those Involved in Physical Fighting in the Previous 12 Months (%), Selected Nations

	Were Bullied		Bullied Others		Were Involved in Physical Fighting	
Nation	Girls	Boys	Girls	Boys	Girls	Boys
Lithuania	69.4	68.2	65.1	76.8	34.5	68.2
Portugal	51.3	55.9	37.8	48.9	24.1	58.4
Ukraine	50.4	53.7	41.5	55.6	16.6	61.3
Austria	48.9	52.4	50.6	64.0	20.4	62.1
Switzerland	42.3	46.9	40.4	59.3	16.1	42.0
Russian Federation	40.0	40.2	33.7	44.3	23.2	66.5
Canada	39.6	39.7	43.9	50.4	26.9	46.7
England	38.2	37.6	26.0	35.5	32.6	58.4
Germany	34.0	42.0	41.6	62.0	18.3	42.6
USA	36.1	39.5	39.5	48.8	28.2	52.6
France	37.6	34.6	36.9	40.1	22.1	55.6
Israel	24.5	48.3	22.7	46.1	19.6	61.3
Wales	32.8	30.6	18.6	31.3	26.2	53.2
Norway	26.3	36.3	21.4	46.0	17.8	57.0
Scotland	31.4	31.0	23.3	32.2	29.2	60.3
Netherlands	28.6	31.6	34.6	46.7	23.7	49.0
Ireland	22.7	32.1	15.7	32.3	26.6	56.9
Finland	25.9	28.3	21.5	38.4	15.0	37.1
Spain	25.3	28.2	26.4	37.9	23.9	57.0
Greece	23.5	28.0	15.3	32.5	32.2	65.2
Sweden	17.9	18.4	11.8	21.0	23.3	52.1
Czech Republic	14.3	20.3	14.1	21.7	29.3	74.2
Average (35 nations)	33.8	37.7	31.0	44.6	24.1	57.3

Source: Compiled with data from Craig and Harel (2004: 135–40).

The extent of concern over bullying is evident in the wide range of anti-bullying programs and strategies that educators, parents, and school administrations in Canada and other OECD nations have introduced to address these problems.

that those who drop out blame the school for producing boredom, alienation, rejection, or lack of preparation for work, but they also express self-doubt and regret over personal factors that contributed to their decision to quit school. The mixture of hope and despair, self-blame and bitterness against the school system expressed by students who fail or drop out before finishing high school is not markedly different from more general student commentaries on their educational experiences.

THE CONCERN FOR SAFE, INCLUSIVE EDUCATIONAL ENVIRONMENTS

Students hold sophisticated and often contradictory attitudes with regard to their schooling experiences. These paradoxical stances reflect students' central but subordinate place within educational structures, their changing roles and expressions as children and adolescents, and their uncertain place in broader social and economic structures. Despite the significant challenges and uncertainties they encounter, children and youth tend to be more optimistic than pessimistic about their futures, hold high educational aspirations, and are generally positive and accepting of their school experiences, even if they are not hesitant to point out numerous issues that concern their lives in and out of schools (Bibby, 2001: 133–56; King et al., 1999: 11–25; Schissel and Wotherspoon, 2003: 82–92). They often identify grievances against outdated pedagogies and curricula, unfair treatement or expectations on the part of teachers, lax standards, or lack of opportunities to pursue information and activities that they prefer, but they tend not to challenge the structures of authority and rewards either within or as represented by schooling. There is a general sense that 'that's just how things are', even when students retain an uneasiness about their lives and futures that transcends anything they can do to make them better.

Student populations are more diverse, sophisticated, and concerned about social, economic, environmental, and political issues than they are commonly portrayed as being. They are highly aware of and engaged with many of the high-profile issues in both popular and alternative media, including bullying and youth violence, substance abuse, matters related to sex and sexuality, labour market options, consumerism, poverty, social disadvantage, and social justice. Their schooling is a crucial but not isolated part of their lives. It is valued for its contributions to knowledge, skills, social connections, and life prospects, but it is also most effective when it is connected with realities outside the classroom. The educational environment, particularly in situations in which schooling is compulsory and there are few alternatives, can be intense, competitive, alienating, and even terrifying for students who are rejected, picked on, or abused by other students and teachers. Alternatively, schools and the students within them are most likely to succeed when schooling becomes a place in which participants find security, acceptance, validation, and encouragement.

CONCLUSION

This chapter has considered how the profusion of incidents and the shifting pace of structured and unstructured activities that constitute the school day are channelled into diverse but relatively predictable social outcomes. Since its inception over a century ago, public schooling has changed substantially in several highly visible ways, including subjects taught, school facilities, classroom resources, background and qualifications of teachers, and dress and demeanour of students. However, basic classroom structures and the aims and orientations of schooling have remained remarkably resistant to change. Schools continue to be regarded as factories for producing products—the schooled individual, credentials, and other end results—just as they are sites for human social development. The varied purposes and practices of schooling are not accidental by-products but direct reflections of the contradictory nature of public education.

ANNOTATED FURTHER READINGS

Contenta, Sandro. 1993. *Rituals of Failure: What Schools Really Teach.* Toronto: Between the Lines. In a highly readable and engaging book, the author discusses how schools' hidden curricula both restrict future prospects for many students and limit the extent to which true education is accomplished through schooling.

Côté, James E., and Anton Allahar. 2006. *Critical Youth Studies: A Canadian Focus.* Toronto: Pearson Prentice-Hall. The authors examine the changes and difficulties youth are experiencing as the transition period between childhood dependency and adult independence is prolonged. Prospects for those aged 15 to 30 are considered with respect to a broad range of social and economic relationships.

McLaren, Peter. 2007. *Life in Schools: An Introduction to Critical Pedagogy in the Foundations of Education,* 5th edn. Boston: Pearson Allyn and Bacon. The author, drawing on his experiences teaching elementary students in a Toronto inner-city school, explores the foundations of a critical pedagogy approach by framing an account of daily school practices within a broader social, economic, and political context, maintaining radical pedagogical reform as a basis for keeping alive prospects for a better future.

Martin, Wilfred. 1976. *The Negotiated Order of the School.* Toronto: Macmillan. The author offers a detailed symbolic interactionist account that understands the schooling process as the outcome of complex layers of interactions and negotiations among various school participants.

Schissel, Bernard, and Terry Wotherspoon. 2003. *The Legacy of School for Aboriginal People: Education, Oppression, and Emancipation.* Toronto: Oxford University Press. The book combines an analysis of how residential schools and other educational developments have contributed to the subjugation of Aboriginal people in Canada with an overview of recent initiatives and commentary from Aboriginal students that highlight how educational promise may be fulfilled in the future.

KEY TERMS

Credentials Qualifications achieved through formal education or training programs and recognized in the form of degrees, diplomas, certificates, or other legitimate awards.

Dropout   A student who leaves school without completing requirements for secondary matriculation or high school graduation. This term is often replaced with 'school-leaver' to take into account the many students who interrupt their schooling and return at one or more later stages to complete further education.

Hegemony   Domination by consent, or ideologies that foster belief in the legitimacy of existing power relations.

Hidden curriculum   The understandings that students develop as a result of the institutional requirements and day-to-day realities they encounter in their schooling. This term typically refers to norms, such as competition, individualism, and obedience, as well as a sense of one's place in school and social hierarchies.

Individuation   The process by which people come to see themselves, and are seen by others, as autonomous individuals rather than with reference to the social relations of which they are part.

Moral panic   The creation of widespread fears built around images of threats to public safety or order, often related to violence, deviant activity, or health concerns, generated especially by exaggerated or erroneous media and political accounts.

Silencing   Mechanisms that restrict student voices or prohibit the inclusion of topics and material that are important to students' lives within the schooling process.

Socialization   The ongoing process of learning and discovery through which people internalize the norms and expectations about cultures and their place within their societies.

Streaming   Formal and informal educational mechanisms that sort students based on ability, social background, or other characteristics into groups, programs, or institutions that have differential status.

Total institutions   Self-contained institutional settings, such as prisons, mental institutions, military sites, and residential schools, separated from the outside world and regulated by formal routines, procedures, and scrutiny with the intent to reshape those who reside, work, or are housed or detained in them.

Study Questions

1. What are the predominant social features of elementary and secondary school classrooms? What explanations can be provided for how these features came about?
2. Critically discuss the nature and impact of residential schooling for Canada's First Nations.
3. Discuss the impact that everyday routines of classroom life have on educational outcomes for different groups of students.
4. What is the hidden curriculum? Discuss its importance, relative to the formal curriculum, for what students learn and retain from their schooling.
5. Which elements of schooling inhibit student participation and engagement? Which ones contribute to greater participation and engagement? Discuss the significance these factors have for students from different social and cultural backgrounds.
6. To what extent are schools self-contained institutions as opposed to sites that are highly influenced by their external environments? Discuss the significance of these circumstances for what students learn in schools.

Chapter 6

Teachers and Teaching

Introduction

Teachers, like students, are central agents in educational processes. Their prominent role in the delivery of educational services makes them nearly synonymous with schooling in the eyes of students, parents, and community members. However, teachers also occupy a somewhat paradoxical position in and out of the classroom. They represent the school and its authority structure to pupils and parents, but they are subordinate to principals and senior administrators in educational hierarchies. They must be highly skilled and competent to gain public confidence to educate and discipline learners behind classroom doors, but they are also subject to public scrutiny with regard to what and how they teach as well as to their overall moral character. They have specialized training and other attributes associated with professionalism, but they do not have the autonomy, authority, or status held by doctors or lawyers. They are advocates for educational causes and learning issues, but they are also waged employees of public or private educational bodies. They are well-placed to be seen as leaders in a knowledge-based economy, but their working lives are replete with tensions and constraints. In short, consistent with the complex nature of the education systems teachers work within, teaching is a highly contradictory occupation.

The paradoxical nature of teachers' roles has long been a predominant theme within the sociological analysis of teaching. Willard Waller (1965: 49), in his classic analysis of schooling, *The Sociology of Teaching*, concisely summarizes the special nature of teaching through his conception of the teacher as 'stranger' in the community:

> The teacher stereotype is a thin but impenetrable veil that comes between the teacher and all other human beings. The teacher can never know what others are really like because they are not like that when the teacher is watching them. The community can never know what the teacher is really like because the community does not offer the teacher opportunities for normal social intercourse.

Waller was writing mostly about teachers in small communities at a time (the book was first published in the early 1930s) when there were likely to be few other relatively highly trained professional workers active in the human services. His observations continue to hold relevance by pointing to the combination of respect and devaluation that today accompanies teachers' work and lives, constituting what Lortie (1975: 10) calls a 'special but shadowed social standing'. Mass media and popular culture, such as movies and television programs, typically portray teachers and the work they do through both positive and negative stereotypes that influence how people think of teaching (Weber and Mitchell, 1999). More crucially, teachers and the work they do are continually shaped and reshaped through their interactions within schooling and broader social and economic transformations (Robertson, 2000; Tardif and Lessard, 1999).

This chapter highlights the diverse and often contested nature of teaching. Following a profile and history of teaching in Canada, consideration will be given to the changing nature of teaching as a particular form of work. While there are some common elements to all forms of teaching, this chapter is most concerned with teachers in public elementary and secondary schools. The vast majority of educators in Canada are public school teachers who, unlike most teachers at other levels, require specialized teacher training and certification. Moreover, public school teachers are primarily concerned with teaching and pedagogy, in contrast with university professors or vocational educators, whose work is defined more in terms of such other responsibilities as research or applied skills.

Box 6.1 Teaching Consists of a Wide Range of Diverse Activities and Experiences

This excerpt from a Saskatchewan teacher's diary of daily activities (Saskatchewan Teachers' Federation, 1995: 34) illustrates the varied nature of teaching:

As I sit here ready to go home, and try to reflect on my day—only fleeting images come to mind:

- several 'broken' zippers that got fixed
- reminders to use a Kleenex
- reminders to get new rulers, erasers, etc. for school
- passing out notes to take home
- secretary telling me to pass out more notes tomorrow because she won't be here
- two children whose homes burnt down a week apart. One happened at 3 am—I could smell the smoke on her when she came to tell me about it
- learning the new library computer prog. during our library period so that I could operate it when the secretary/librarian isn't here
- cramps in my shoulders and neck from too many hours bent over books
- the feeling of a small hand sliding into mine and the upturned face and smile that went with it
- having to 'feel' several sets of cold ears to let me know how 'cold it is out there'
- the cries of 'neat' when new things were heard about penguins

TEACHERS AND TEACHING IN CANADA

Nearly 700,000 persons work as teachers and professors in Canada, with 527,800 reporting full-time employment and another 149,300 working part-time in 2006 (Statistics Canada, 2007c). The full-time teaching ranks include about 310,000 full-time equivalent elementary and secondary school teachers, 40,800 full-time university faculty, and an estimated 30,000 instructors employed full-time in community college, vocational, or trade instructional institutions (AUCC, 2007b: 4; Blouin and Courchesne, 2007: 27). Growth in the total teaching force has been most pronounced at the university level, reflecting the rising importance of post-secondary education, in comparison with the number of elementary and secondary school teachers, which has only recently stabilized after declining during the 1990s. Educational institutions have met changing enrolment patterns in part by increasing reliance on part-time teachers. Part-time teachers represented about 22 per cent of the teaching force at all levels in 2006 (and constituted as much as 23.5 per cent in 2004–5) compared to 14.8 per cent in 1987 (calculated from Statistics Canada, 2007b, 2007c). Some of the growth in part-time teaching can be accounted for by the desire by some to combine teaching with family responsibilities, employment in other fields, or educational upgrading, More significantly, as discussed later in this chapter, the growth in the part-time teaching force represents changes in educational funding, organization, and management orientations that leave a greater share of the workforce in contingent and temporary circumstances.

Teachers are a diverse group, with varying backgrounds, positions, and work experiences. While all teachers may share many common concerns about workloads, student demands, pedagogical techniques, and other aspects of their work, there are significant differences in qualifications and conditions associated with teaching at different levels and institutions and in different subject areas. Teachers at each level and jurisdiction are represented by specific organizations. These are usually called federations or associations, avoiding identification—with the exception of Nova Scotia teachers—as a 'union'. Elementary and secondary teachers are represented by a single organization in most provinces and territories, but there are also distinct organizations for specific groups of teachers in some provinces. Ontario and New Brunswick have separate associations for francophone teachers, while Quebec and Ontario have, in addition to their provincial associations, distinct associations for Protestant and Catholic teachers (as well as an Ontario association for English Catholic teachers). Nationally, the Canadian Teachers' Federation and the Canadian Association of University Teachers bring together affiliate members from particular organizations and institutions (Canadian Teachers' Federation, 2007). Many subject and specialist groups also exist apart from, or in conjunction with, the major educators' organizations. In addition, teachers are often active in the initiation or operation of diverse organizations oriented to educational reform and other matters relevant to education. Post-secondary faculty and instructors are also represented through a variety of occupational and professional organizations. Most Canadian university faculty members are unionized through organizations that, as with teachers, are more typically labelled associations rather than unions. Unionized non-permanent university instructors and college instructors are typically organized through government or public-sector unions or faculty associations.

Teaching is guided by a variety of educational goals and objectives. Three key themes that emerge in the sociological analysis of teaching will be explored in the remainder of this chapter: (1) the development of teaching as a profession; (2) the importance of gender relations in teaching; and (3) the changing nature of teachers' work. Emphasis is given to the ways in which teaching exists as a contradictory form of work organized around competing demands. In some ways these demands are similar to changing patterns of work in general, yet they are uniquely shaped by educational priorities.

Teaching as a Profession

A prevalent theme in the sociological analysis of teaching is an attempt to understand teaching as a profession. The three most common ways of depicting teaching as a profession lie in approaches characterized as *professional trait, historical,* and *pressure group theory* (Ozga and Lawn, 1981). As will be shown below, each of these approaches offers useful insights into the development of teaching as an occupation, but each leaves important questions unanswered.

Teacher professionalism is commonly understood through trait approaches that begin with an assessment of how professional occupations differ from other types of work. Major traits that characterize professions usually include such features as formal credentials based on a body of advanced knowledge, social recognition as high-status work, high degrees of decision-making authority in the workplace, and an altruistic commitment to careers and clients (Carr-Saunders, 1966). Authors who employ this approach tend to use recognized professions like medicine and law as a standard of comparison against which to assess the extent to which teaching is a profession. On this basis, it is commonly concluded that teaching falls short of full professional status because it lacks autonomy and prestige, or that teaching is at best a semi- or quasi-profession that remains constrained by external forces such as other professions and bureaucratic school authority structures (Anderson, 1968; Henchey, 1977).

Teaching is often understood through historical accounts, which are related to trait approaches to professionalism. Studies of this type emphasize the evolutionary strides teachers have made towards professional status. Paton (1962), for instance, outlines four historical phases within which Canadian teachers have organized and sought to achieve professional standing:

1. *1850–1914:* Teachers were brought together principally through meetings conducted by school inspectors and senior educational authorities to inform them of new developments in education and reinforce their loyalties to the school system.

2. *1914–35:* Teachers organized to promote teaching and improve their welfare and working conditions.
3. *1935–55:* Teachers' organizations struggled for official recognition and greater participation in educational policy-making processes.
4. *1955 and beyond:* Teachers sought professional status through improved occupational powers and responsibilities.

Many other studies, such as accounts by Chafe (1969) and Chalmers (1968), respectively, of the development of the Manitoba Teachers' Society and the Alberta Teachers' Association, Skolrood's (1967) study of the British Columbia Teachers' Federation, and Phillips's (1957) overview of the role of teachers in Canadian education, concur with the overall assessment that teachers have progressively gained professional status through better training, improvements in teaching and learning conditions, and greater input into sophisticated educational matters, despite barriers to the fulfillment of some of their aspirations.

A third group of studies related to teacher professionalism concentrates on the dynamics of teachers as organized lobby or interest groups. This approach, like the historical studies, emphasizes how teachers have struggled collectively to better their professional status and occupational welfare (Downie, 1978; Martin and Macdonnell, 1982; Muir, 1968). However, the analysis of teachers' organizations as interest groups highlights two aspects of teaching that indicate there is more to the occupation than simply the desire to be recognized as professionals. First, teachers have often found they can pursue their occupational interests more successfully through **collective bargaining**, labour militancy, or political mobilization than through any kind of acknowledgement that they have achieved professional status (see, e.g., Ungerleider, 1994; CEQ, 1974). Second, because teaching is highly constrained by state regulation, such as provincial legislation that outlines the duties and responsibilities of teachers, the degree to which the occupation can influence educational policy and practice is limited (Lawson and Woock, 1987).

Considerable evidence supports the claims made in the literature that Canadian teachers have made significant progress over the past century towards the achievement of professional status. Whereas most teachers received little formal training at the beginning of the twentieth century, today teachers in nearly all provinces require at least four years of university education to qualify for a teaching certificate, with recent pressures to extend and intensify pre-service training. Teachers' pay scales, which were once set at the discretion of trustees who were often unwilling or unable to secure funds to pay teachers adequately, are now bargained collectively and reflect differences in levels of professional training and experience. Teachers are represented on curriculum committees and other educational bodies that set or influence policies relating to schooling. Their work is informed by critical reflection, collaboration, reliance on specified performance indicators, and extensive in-service and continuing learning. They are recognized, through their professional training and school legislation, as professionals who

Box 6.2 The Impact of Education Reforms on Teaching and Learning Conditions

Successive measures to implement education reforms in Canada and many other nations have created a sometimes overwhelming array of demands that teachers must attend to in their daily work lives. These contribute to new teaching and learning opportunities, but they are also accompanied by extensive tension, stress, and uncertainty. The following summaries, drawn from research conducted with teachers in Newfoundland and Labrador (Younghusband, 2006: 9) and the Prairies (Wotherspoon, 2006: 690–1), highlight these disparate concerns:

Teacher stress and working environments in Newfoundland and Labrador
Teachers talked about being tired, worn out physically and emotionally. As they reflected on a life in the classroom, in a job they loved but found overwhelming, it was clear that the effort to remain effective was taking a toll not only on them, but on their colleagues and, they feared, on their students. 'No time to stop, too many changes . . . some not workable, some have negative effects on students' they said. They described themselves as 'bombarded, overwhelmed, on overload, always on the run'. The word 'impossible' was used over and over to describe their job. Increased demands for accountability from so many levels, each requiring a daunting amount of documentation and paperwork, all added to the hours worked. Recently, a teacher told my education students that he now spends more time on documentation than on lesson preparation. We must ask how that benefits students and how it makes the teacher feel.

Teachers discussed dealing with children who are profoundly needy, not only academically, but also socially and emotionally. They talked about teaching courses for which they had no background or training and how challenging that was, the time it took to prepare, and what it was like to feel that they weren't doing a first rate job.

Then there were the multiple roles expected: guidance counsellor, social worker, caregiver, parent, recess and lunchtime supervisor, fund raiser, extracurricular organizer.

'Just let us teach!' they said.

One participant described it this way: 'Teaching doesn't end at 5 p.m. Calling parents, tracking things down, preparing for the next day—you're trying to juggle and balance the demands. I don't like being set up as a failure. I don't think there is a physical way of accomplishing it' (Younghusband, 2006: 9).

Teachers' work in Aboriginal communities in Manitoba and Saskatchewan
Teachers' circumstances frequently lead to questions about the cumulative impact that various demands associated with teaching have for both teachers and students. A teacher of Aboriginal ancestry working in an elementary school

in a medium-sized city articulates the contradictions associated with her work: 'The school/education systems have been given more and more "parental" responsibilities which take away from teaching time for basic and other skills children need to have to become competitive in or active participants of society. Schools feed, clothe, and try to impress respect upon children—children who go home at 3:30 to not safe surroundings where even the most basic of their needs are not or cannot be met.' . . .

The comments of a teacher working in a remote rural area reveal how the joys of working with the high proportions of Aboriginal students in her district can sometimes be offset by the onus on teachers to take on unrealistic fiscal and professional burdens:

> The classroom has become a safe secure environment for many students. Issues of abuse, incest, depression, and alcoholism come up on a regular basis in my class. I do not feel I am equipped to deal with such issues. There are two school counsellors—who are not trained professionals and are often absent—for 445 students. Therefore, they are extremely busy and overwhelmed. I feel I should receive some training to allow me to better deal with these situations. I have been to one professional development workshop, however, [my school district] would not fund it, nor would the school. Therefore, a one-day workshop cost me half my monthly salary. I am also overworked. I teach [six courses]. I receive one hour for preparation time for every six days of teaching. The school also mandates I coach a sport team, run an after-school club, and supervise detention hall after school for one-half hour. I do not think it is possible for many people to work that many hours under duress.

This combined sense of empathy for colleagues and students, accompanied by a litany of duties and expectations, conveys a near-crisis situation for both the individual teacher (who is 'overworked' and 'overwhelmed') and the education system itself (with a staff 'under duress' unable to attend to students who see schooling as a mechanism to address serious problems in their daily lives) (Wotherspoon, 2006: 690–1).

Source: Wotherspoon, Terry. 2006. 'Teachers' Work in Canadian Aboriginal Communites? *Comparative Education Review* 50, 4:672–94.
Younghusband, Lynda. 2006. 'Teacher Stress and Working Environment: Implications for Teaching and Learning', *Newfoundland Quarterly* 98, 4:8–11.

make decisions regarding such matters as curricular planning, pedagogy, discipline, and evaluation of students. **Teachers' associations** have developed codes of ethics regarding professional conduct and have been actively involved in professional development activities for their members. Teachers have also participated in a wide range of educational decision-making activities that were once left to the discretion of legislators, school trustees, and educational administrators.

Despite marked improvements in the professional status of teachers, factors other than professionalism operate to shape teaching. Legislative and bureaucratic frameworks pose serious limitations to teachers' abilities to act as autonomous professionals. Teachers are the focus of intense scrutiny by parents, politicians, and media commentators who can be quick to dismiss teachers' efforts in the absence of appreciation for the full range of teaching-related activities. However, much of what teachers do is invisible to the casual observer. Ungerleider (2003: 152) highlights how teachers are charged from the outset with managerial responsibilities that few employees in the corporate world are likely to encounter, so that 'Those people who have observed teachers at work are often overwhelmed by the sheer volume of teacher–student interaction, the quantity of paper and material to be managed, the movement of students, and the pacing and sequencing of activity.'

The mixed signals that teachers tend to receive about their work contribute to considerable confusion over the nature and direction of teaching as an occupation. Teachers have not always been successful in developing collective strategies that would enable them to balance professional objectives and concern for students' welfare with campaigns to improve wages and working conditions. They have gained widespread notoriety as powerful lobby groups through their periodic regional or provincial support for selected political parties, their involvement in a number of important social justice initiatives, such as anti-poverty organizations, and their role in Quebec nationalist movements (Lockhart, 1991: 17; Ungerleider, 2003: 161–2). As a result, Canadian teachers' organizations have frequently found themselves in conflict with provincial governments or at the centre of intense media criticism.

By the 1990s, frequent media reports on the theme of 'what's wrong with the schools' had come to reinforce notions that teachers are not doing an adequate job of maintaining order, teaching students proper skills for life in the technological age, or keeping students interested in schooling. Nikiforuk (1993: 112) encapsulates many of these sentiments, observing that 'Self-absorbed, poorly led, and often lacking in self-criticism (criticism now equals self-esteem bashing in some quarters) the profession or trade tends to prize its contributions too smugly.'

These kinds of attacks have become less prevalent in the twenty-first century as public attention has turned more fully to matters related to the impact of government policy and student outcomes. Nonetheless, they continue to have a demoralizing impact on a teaching workforce concerned that it is not receiving the resources and support essential for fulfilling complex educational mandates. The Canadian Teachers' Federation was sufficiently concerned by 2001 to place a full-page advertisement in *The Hill Times*, which reports on the activities of the federal Parliament in Ottawa, to stress the difficulties schools had in recruiting and retaining teachers because of government measures to undermine teaching and public educational quality, educational cutbacks, new societal demands, poor employment conditions, and uncompetitive salaries (Willard, 2001). As large cohorts of experienced teachers approach retirement age, concerns about severe teacher shortages in many parts of Canada are exacerbated by high rates of attrition, especially among beginning teachers, and difficulties in attracting new recruits to the teaching force (Press et al., 2002).

There are signs that teachers are regaining public sympathy through acknowledgement that they cannot be held responsible for setting many of the conditions of their work. Attitudinal surveys suggest that there are now higher levels of public support for teachers than for schools overall (Hart and Livingstone, 2007: 8), with about 70 per cent of Canadians (and over three-quarters of respondents in the Prairie and Atlantic regions) indicating that they are very or somewhat satisfied with the jobs that teachers are doing (Canadian Education Association, 2007: 7). Nonetheless, as highlighted later in the chapter, many teachers continue to experience considerable stress and frustration in their working lives, and are skeptical about the direction of educational policy.

The significance of the challenges that teachers face in their work and in establishing an occupational image suggests that a focus on trying to determine whether or not teaching is a profession is misdirected. What does it mean to acknowledge that any occupation is a profession? Professionalism is not something that is static or absolute. Recent measures to restructure health care, for instance, mean that even established professions like medicine are in danger of losing much of the autonomy and respect they once held. In the continually changing world of education, teachers are subject to similar challenges, with the consequence that they are deprofessionalized in some aspects of their work at the same time as they may gain professional powers in others. Moreover, the nature and organization of teaching are governed by factors that both transcend and shape the nature of professionalism. Two of these are considered below—the importance in teaching of gender relations, and pressures in the direction of what has been conceptualized as the **proletarianization** of teaching.

GENDER AND TEACHING

Much of the discussion so far has presented teachers and teaching at a general or collective level. However, teachers and the conditions in which they work are highly diverse and multi-dimensional. One of the most striking features of the teaching force is its highly segmented gender composition. Women are concentrated in elementary school classrooms while men are concentrated at the post-secondary level and in senior administrative positions. In Canada, overall, over nine out of ten kindergarten teachers, compared with fewer than two out of ten full university professors, are women. More than two out of three full-time teachers in elementary and secondary schools are women; the number and proportion of male teachers is expected to drop further based on demographic trends and enrolment patterns in teacher training programs. The concentrations of women teachers in post-secondary institutions are also increasing, but remain well below those of men, especially in full-time positions and at the highest academic ranks (AUCC, 2007b: 21–2). Within each educational level there are even more substantial differences.

Box 6.3 Two Views on Teachers' Right to Strike

Teaching and teachers' work are given shape through many divergent responsibilities, orientations, and expectations. These elements become especially apparent in periodic debates and controversies over questions of whether, or under what conditions, teachers should have the right to strike. Two opposing viewpoints on this issue are expressed in the following statements by (1) a representative of the Canadian Taxpayers' Federation (Carpay, 2004) and (2) a former president of the British Columbia Teachers' Federation (Sims, 2004):

1. Why teachers should not be allowed to strike

Alberta teachers should not be allowed to go on strike, period. Public education is a vital, essential service on which parents and students depend. Taxpayers pay $3.9 billion per year for Alberta's K-to-12 public system, and are therefore entitled to receive value for that money without disruption by strikes or by threats of strikes. It's not because Alberta's teachers are the best paid in Canada. It's not because their 14 per cent-over-two-years pay increase is much larger than pay increases received by workers in the private sector. It's because the teachers' union enjoys an absolute monopoly over the provision of teaching services and therefore has the ability to hold students and parents hostage to its demands. Premier Klein's government can and should change existing legislation which enables the Alberta Teachers' Association to hold children for ransom through threats of strikes. When teachers strike, parents suddenly have no choice but to seek emergency childcare from 9:00 to 3:00, five days per week. Everyone knows that the number of available daycare spaces is not infinite. And with very few exceptions, parents simply cannot afford to pay for 'reserving' a spot from September to June just in case teachers decide to strike. When teachers strike, students who depended on teachers must suddenly choose between temporarily embarking on a home-schooling program, or learning nothing at all. Home schooling can be a wonderful choice leading to excellent outcomes, but not when it's imposed suddenly and temporarily through a teachers' strike. In short, a teachers' strike is grossly unfair to parents, grossly unfair to students, and grossly unfair to taxpayers. But surely the teachers' union has a right to speak about class size and other education issues? Yes, as do students, parents, grandparents, employers, and all taxpayers. The right to express one's views is not the same as the right to impose one's demands. . . .

Things would be different if the teachers' union did not enjoy an absolute monopoly over education in Alberta. Then parents would have the option of sending their children to other schools, where teachers were not on strike. But a teacher, no matter how well qualified, cannot exercise his or her profession without being a member of the teachers' union. The Alberta Teachers' Association controls education in Alberta, and Premier Klein's government allows it to do so (Carpay, 2004).

Source: Canadian Taxpayers Association.

2. Collective bargaining and the right to strike

Teachers must be able to address their working conditions through collective bargaining—that is the purpose and value of full, free collective bargaining. Our members, 42,000 strong, have repeated over and over the importance of being able to raise these fundamental issues at the table and to bargain clear, firm rules about them. In the wake of the stripping of our rights and our agreement, teacher morale has plummeted and positive school climate has been eroded. Our members will not accept anything less than the right to bargain all terms and conditions of employment.

It is also clear that the public supports our right to bargain class size. Recent polling results show that 78.5 per cent of the public support the right of teachers to negotiate class size and other learning conditions into the collective agreement. . . .

The second element, the right to strike, is inextricably linked to scope. One without the other is meaningless. If the right to strike is taken away or further eroded, teachers' lack of rights will return to pre-1988; perhaps even worsen.

History has proven that it was only when teachers had the right to strike, combined with full scope, that any meaningful bargaining on issues vital to teaching, such as preparation time, school-based teams, and class size, took place. In our view, substantial improvements in education were made as a result of the conclusion of collective agreements under the previous regime of local bargaining. Class sizes were reduced; support for students with special needs was added; preparation time for teachers was ensured; specialist teacher support was provided; and class composition was controlled to ensure quality education for all students (Sims, 2004).

Source: Reprinted with permission from the BC Teachers' Federation.

Data for 2004–5 reveal that within the kindergarten and elementary grades, women constitute 80 per cent of all teachers but just over half of principals and vice-principals in those schools; at the secondary level, 52 per cent of teachers and about one-third of principals and vice-principals are women (Blouin, 2006; O'Haire, 2005: 16). The number and proportion of female senior administrators at school and district levels have been increasing but remain disproportionately low relative to those of men and in comparison with the proportion of female teachers in jurisdictions across Canada (Rees, 1990; Reynolds et al., 2008).

There is an even more sharply defined pyramidal structure in the gender distribution of positions at the post-secondary level (see Figure 6.1). At the university level, nearly three-quarters of tenured faculty, about 60 per cent of faculty in positions leading to tenure, and over 80 per cent of faculty at the highest academic rank of full professor are men (CAUT, 2007: 14). Among full-time university faculty, women are much more likely than men to be concentrated at the lowest academic ranks, although this gap has declined in recent decades (Ornstein et al., 1998: 18; CAUT, 2007: 18). Male and female teachers throughout the education system are also concentrated in particular subject areas in accordance with traditional divisions of labour—for instance, most teachers in mathematics, sciences, and engineering are men while most teachers in general classrooms, health care (other than medicine), business education, and household sciences are women.

Differences in the kinds of teaching positions that men and women occupy have been reflected historically in teachers' salaries. Although the wage gap is diminishing, men continue to earn more, on average, than women at all levels and ranks of teaching. Among full-time university faculty, the average salary for women in 2001–2 was $12,200 (or about 12 per cent) below comparable levels for men, while at the full professor rank, the salary gap was just under half that, at about $5,930 (or about 5.1 per cent) (CAUT, 2007: 6). Much of the disparity can be accounted for by differences in rank, qualifications, age, and experience. Personal factors, such as family commitments, specialized interests, and background in particular subject areas, and age-grade preferences also often contribute to distinct career choices and teaching priorities among men and women. Taken together,

Figure 6.1   Post-Secondary Pyramid: Gender Distribution of Personnel in Key Roles and Positions, Canada (% female)

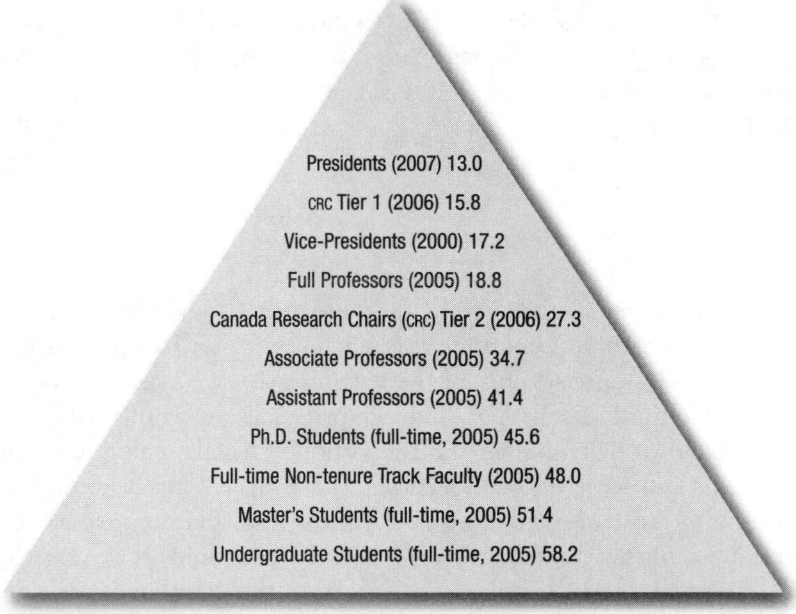

Presidents (2007) 13.0
CRC Tier 1 (2006) 15.8
Vice-Presidents (2000) 17.2
Full Professors (2005) 18.8
Canada Research Chairs (CRC) Tier 2 (2006) 27.3
Associate Professors (2005) 34.7
Assistant Professors (2005) 41.4
Ph.D. Students (full-time, 2005) 45.6
Full-time Non-tenure Track Faculty (2005) 48.0
Master's Students (full-time, 2005) 51.4
Undergraduate Students (full-time, 2005) 58.2

CRC = Canada Research Chairs.
Source: Canadian Federation of Humanities and Social Sciences (2007). Data compiled by Wendy Robbins and Michèle Ollivier, PAR-L, with assistance from the Canadian Association of University Teachers and the Canadian Federation for the Humanities and Social Sciences.

however, these elements are indicative of how individual and structural forces combine to produce unequal opportunities for men and women in teaching, as in many other occupations and spheres of life.

An overview of the historical development of public school teaching in Canada offers some insight into how gender inequities have come to be incorporated into the occupation. Table 6.1 provides an overview of the gender composition of the national schoolteaching force since Confederation. In contrast with recent experience, in which women have constituted between one-half and two-thirds of the teaching force, most teachers until the late 1860s were men. During the first quarter of the twentieth century, fewer than one in five teachers was male, although the relative proportion of male teachers gradually increased from a low of 16.6 per cent in 1920 to nearly 45 per cent in the early 1980s, before dropping to current levels of just over one-third.

The national trends illustrated in the table do not show provincial and regional variations in the **feminization** of teaching. By the time of Confederation, the numbers of male and female teachers were roughly equal in most jurisdictions. In Quebec and many regions of Ontario, however, women teachers outnumbered men by large margins much earlier; in much of western Canada, men predominated until at least the 1880s; and there were more men than women teaching in Prince Edward Island schools until after the turn of the century (see, e.g., Danylewycz et al., 1991; Leacy, 1983: W150–91). Among rural school districts in many provinces, particularly those that employed teachers working in one-room schools, men tended to outnumber women until late in the nineteenth century. In such districts, gender parity often continued for several years after that, although there were variations in the trends from one region or school district to another (Danylewycz et al., 1991).

Danylewycz and Prentice (1986: 60–1) emphasize that many commentators hold mistaken views associated with historical processes through which teaching became feminized. One such myth is that the preponderance of young female teachers at the turn of the century devalued teaching and made it susceptible to extensive regulation by educational authorities, thereby delaying or preventing the occupation from becoming a full profession. While it is true that teachers were frequently subjected to paternalistic control by educational administrators, it is also important to emphasize the strong professional commitment demonstrated by many early women teachers in their efforts to provide effective education despite personal and occupational difficulties (Poelzer, 1990; Prentice and Theobald, 1991; Wilson, 1991). Sometimes, young women entered teaching on a temporary basis until they were married, but many teachers saw the occupation as a lifelong vocation. A spirit of adventure and the ability to innovate were often essential ingredients for the success of those who assumed teaching positions in remote rural areas. Although such teachers initially may have lacked formal training and experience, they played a crucial role in promoting public education and maintaining the school as a vital part of social development in many communities across Canada.

A second misconception related to the feminization of teaching concerns the devaluation or invisibility of teaching as a form of work (Danylewycz and Prentice, 1986: 61). Teaching traditionally has been discounted as something less

Table 6.1   Full-time Teachers in Elementary and Secondary Schools, by Gender, Canada, Selected Years, 1867–2005*

Year**	Male (%)	Female (%)	Total
1867	3,312 (53.8)	2,840 (46.2)	6,152
1870	5,143 (38.6)	8,180 (61.4)	13,323
1875	5,338 (34.1)	10,329 (65.9)	15,667
1880	6,181 (35.1)	11,411 (64.9)	17,592
1885	5,772 (28.2)	14,719 (71.8)	20,491
1890	5,797 (25.7)	16,753 (74.3)	22,550
1895	6,069 (24.5)	18,652 (75.5)	24,721
1900	6,205 (22.7)	21,164 (77.3)	27,369
1905	6,392 (19.8)	25,818 (80.2)	32,210
1910	7,849 (19.4)	32,627 (80.6)	40,476
1915	8,789 (17.5)	41,453 (82.5)	50,242
1920	9,600 (16.6)	48,178 (83.4)	57,778
1925	12,069 (18.9)	51,771 (81.1)	63,840
1930	14,255 (20.3)	55,990 (79.7)	70,245
1935	18,492 (25.3)	54,593 (74.7)	73,085
1940	19,417 (25.8)	55,970 (74.2)	75,387
1945	17,415 (22.5)	60,064 (77.5)	77,479
1950	24,064 (26.8)	65,618 (73.2)	89,682
1955	31,058 (26.8)	84,777 (73.2)	115,835
1960	44,593 (29.1)	108,447 (70.9)	153,040
1965	67,832 (34.4)	129,261 (65.6)	197,093
1970	100,820 (38.4)	161,637 (61.5)	262,457
1975	110,429 (41.8)	153,833 (58.2)	262,262
1980	121,537 (44.4)	152,170 (55.6)	273,707
1985	119,400 (43.9)	152,659 (56.1)	272,059
1990	119,143 (40.1)	177,963 (59.9)	297,106
1995	113,198 (37.9)	185,478 (62.1)	298,676
2000***	108,277 (35.0)	201,085 (65.0)	309,362
2005***	97,954 (31.6)	212,027 (68.4)	309,981

*Data not available for Nova Scotia and Quebec in 1867; Prince Edward Island in 1875 and 1895; Manitoba and British Columbia until 1885; data for Alberta and Saskatchewan not included until 1905, Newfoundland until 1950, and Yukon and Northwest Territories until 1960.
**School year beginning in the year shown.
***Figures are estimates.
Sources: For 1867–1975: F.H. Leacy, ed., *Historical Statistics of Canada*, 2nd edn (Ottawa: Statistics Canada, 1983), W150–2; for 1980–90: Statistics Canada, *Education in Canada* (Ottawa: Minister of Supply and Services Canada, various years); for 1995–2005: Statistics Canada and OECD databases.

than a 'real job' or else has been analyzed separately from other work by virtue of its nature as non-manual labour performed primarily by women. Instead, it is often considered as an extension of unpaid social roles associated with mothering and domestic work (Gaskell and McLaren, 1991). In addition to undermining teaching as work, these views have been used to justify discriminatory practices in teaching, including the maintenance of pay schedules in which female teachers were paid less than men until the mid-twentieth century, as well as the periodic requirement of provincial governments and school boards for women to resign from teaching positions upon marriage. Despite persistent realities to the contrary, female teachers have been depicted by many administrators and policy-making bodies as less dedicated and well-trained than males, and less in need of income and careers to support themselves or their families (Arbus, 1990; Reynolds, 1990).

An analysis of the historical development of teaching in Canada yields important insights about changing gender relations within the occupation. Both men and women have played central, although often distinctive, roles in all phases of Canadian schooling. Gendered divisions of labour were established early. In New France, distinct schools for boys and girls tended to be run, respectively, by parish priests and female teaching orders in the seventeenth century (Johnson, 1968: 8–9). Beyond elementary schooling, at least until the nineteenth century, teaching tended to be conducted by men for men, usually by clergy in colleges or seminaries that offered professional training or by highly educated men who provided elite training to other men of privileged classes.

In general, two kinds of schooling, associated with distinct classes of teachers, prevailed prior to the late nineteenth century. Grammar schools or those established by particular organizations sought teachers who were somewhat qualified and loyal to the goals of the sponsoring authorities. Common schools open to all children in the community were initially established by anyone who claimed to be a teacher or who could hire others to teach. The former tended to be somewhat better paid and more highly regarded than the latter, although there were frequent reports of public disdain for, if not hostility against, teachers in general (Phillips, 1957: 546–7).

One of the main objectives sought by advocates for a system of free public schools in the nineteenth century was the establishment of a stable, highly respected teaching force. This desired form of school organization had contradictory implications for teachers, whose role came to be that of 'subordinate partners' in the education system (Wotherspoon, 1993). Teachers gained some degree of job security and occupational legitimacy through the introduction of measures to ensure that communities had schools operated with public funds and other forms of state support. Teachers also experienced increasing status through the expectation that they would promote public education and be entrusted to supervise and teach children. At the same time, though, teachers were more fully monitored by school inspectors and regulated by state educational administrators. Thus, although they had considerable autonomy and authority in the classroom, teachers became public servants in the sense that their primary obligations and loyalties were to the 'public good' rather than to any specific social interest.

School promoters and educational administrators were interested in developing a teaching force that met their ideals of public education. Repeatedly, in the speeches, reports, and writings of such educational leaders, the ideal teacher was presented as a relatively well-educated and self-disciplined man of high moral quality (Corrigan et al., 1987; Love, 1978). While educational authorities were not opposed to female teachers, they sought males, who they felt would be more committed to public education as a project of state formation. From its beginnings, then, a paternalistic model of authority was incorporated into the public education system so that senior administrators and state officials were almost exclusively men, as were secondary school teachers and senior teachers in larger schools, while women taught in the elementary grades or in ungraded rural schools.

The development of the Canadian teaching force, like many other aspects of education, involved a constant tension between educational ideals and practical considerations. One of the persistent limitations to the fulfillment of educators' visions of the education system was the lack of an adequate supply of suitable, fully qualified teachers. This problem was itself often the consequence of other difficulties within the education system, including negative public images of teachers and low teacher salaries. These factors often reinforced one another. Public schools, by the late nineteenth century, were supported by provincial government grants intended to be supplemented by locally raised funds. The latter, however, were frequently scarce, contributing to inequalities between rural and urban schools and among school districts. Collection of school funds could not always be enforced, especially in poorer regions or districts where the public had little interest in or support for the school system. Therefore, teachers were often paid less than amounts they had been promised, however inadequate those salaries were to begin with (see Wotherspoon, 1993). Teachers' salaries, on average, were lower than the wages of unskilled labourers at the start of the twentieth century (Phillips, 1957: 551–2) and they remained well below average occupational salaries until after World War II, when factors such as the consolidation of school districts, increased allocation of central government funding for education, and aggressive collective bargaining by teachers began to stabilize teacher incomes.

This situation exacerbated gender-based differential pay rates for teachers. Table 6.2 reveals that women have been paid about two-thirds to three-quarters of what men received until relatively recently. However, while teachers experience greater gender parity than other Canadian workers, as a whole, the average income for female teachers remains just over four-fifths of that for male teachers. As the data for 2006 reveal, even for full-time full-year workers in mid-career, female teachers' earnings remain at about 90 per cent of those for male teachers. Altenbaugh (1995: 83–4) indicates that differences in pay among men and women throughout North America stemmed in part from the likelihood that male teachers had more formal training and teaching experience and were concentrated in

Table 6.2   Average Elementary and Secondary School Teachers' Incomes in Comparison with Average Income in Canada, by Gender, Selected Census Years, 1921–2006

	Teachers			All Occupations		
	Male	Female	Total	Male	Female	Total
1921	$1,395	$818	$914	$1,057	$573	$954
1931	1,575	917	1,066	927	559	848
1941	1,416	793	962	993	490	755
1951*	2,673	1,915	2,050	3,468	1,788	2,898
1961	4,712	3,176	3,734	3,679	1,995	3,191
1971	8,420	5,532	6,424	6,574	3,199	5,391
1981	24,039	15,142	18,111	16,988	8,863	13,635
1991	41,266	27,938	31,864	29,847	17,751	24,329
2001	46,356	38,449	40,751	38,347	24,390	31,757
2006**	61,052	55,026	56,920	50,238	38,111	44,435

*For 1951, figures are for median income; for teachers, data for Quebec are not available.
**Data for 2006 refer to median income for full-time full-year workers ages 25–54 and are not directly comparable to earlier years.
Sources: Compiled and calculated from census data; for 1951, data on teachers are from Dominion Bureau of Statistics, *Survey of Elementary and Secondary Education, 1950–54* (Ottawa: Queen's Printer, 1959).

high schools, where salaries tended to reflect higher qualification levels and where teachers were better able to organize to protect their occupational interests. Altenbaugh emphasizes, further, that gender discrimination played a more fundamental role in teaching, as evident in the fact that women were paid less even when they were teaching high school or had more education and experience than men. It has been noted previously, for instance, that gender differences were institutionalized through separate and unequal pay scales for men and women that were systematically maintained by provinces and school districts until the 1960s.

Gender factors also entered into the regulation of teaching by educational administrators and government officials. Public or common schooling, of which teachers were the most visible representatives in local communities, signified the presence of state rule in everyday life. This placed teachers in a position in which their lives and characters were under surveillance away from school as well as at work. The lack of teachers with adequate training and of presumed character to meet the ideal desired by educational authorities posed a dilemma that resulted in new ways of monitoring and managing the teaching workforce.

In the late nineteenth and early twentieth centuries, legislators and educational administrators introduced several measures to regulate teaching. Many of these initiatives were directed in particular towards the preponderance of young women who entered teaching to meet the demands of a growing school system. A system of school inspection was implemented so that state authority would be represented in schools on a periodic basis to compensate for the difficulties involved in monitoring classroom activity on an everyday basis. The school inspector was instructed to assess the character as well as the competency of teachers. The traumatic nature of school inspectors' visits—and the mysterious authority they represented—has become a recurrent theme in Canadian fiction as well as in biographical accounts of students and teachers (see, e.g., Braithwaite, 1979). The system of classroom inspection had the additional effect of reinforcing paternalism and gender-based divisions of labour within educational hierarchies by creating a career path in which it was possible for loyal male teachers to be promoted to the rank of inspector (Fleming, 1986). In the larger urban schools, supervision of teachers was often more directly accomplished through the presence of principals, head teachers, and subject specialists (Danylewycz and Prentice, 1986: 70).

The inspection function was complemented by a second form of control under the guise of legislation and regulations to govern the character and work of teachers. Teachers' duties came to be specified in law and other directives passed down from both the provinces and school boards. Thus, as exemplified in the regulations of British Columbia in 1875 (see Box 3.2), the teacher not only had to teach 'diligently and faithfully' the curriculum set by boards of education, but was also required to promote 'both by precept and example, CLEANLINESS, NEATNESS, AND DECENCY . . . TRUST AND HONESTY' (British Columbia, 1875: 47). Teachers' duties and the demands on their time expanded in conjunction with increases in school size and enrolment, the duration of school attendance, and the scope of the curriculum. In addition to growing class sizes and the requirements to teach new subjects, teachers were faced with paperwork, documenting everything from student attendance and progress to homework and classroom activities (Danylewycz and Prentice, 1986: 66–8).

However, as the quotation above reveals, teachers' personal attributes and lives, more than just their school-related work, were subject to external scrutiny by educational authorities. This applied to both men and women. School officials frequently criticized male teachers for their apparent lack of commitment to teaching or carelessness in their work and personal habits. The lives and habits of female teachers were subjected to even closer scrutiny. Akin to forms of patriarchal regulation of women's sexuality and social activities that prevailed in the family, school board regulations and teachers' contracts stipulated how female teachers should dress, prohibited them from keeping company with men, proscribed the hours they were to be at home, and made them subject to dismissal if they drank, smoked, or married (see, e.g., Apple, 1986: 72–4; British Columbia School Trustees' Association, 1980). The teacher—especially the female teacher—became a public figure who was governed by specified notions of morality as determined by state authorities.

A third form of regulation oriented to the governance of women teachers was the regularization and expansion of teacher training programs. Until the early part of the twentieth century, the qualifications and training required to become a teacher were highly irregular. While many private and secondary schools were able to attract and pay adequate salaries to persons who had undertaken university studies, common schools often hired whomever they could to ensure an adequate supply of teachers. Initially, a person might be considered eligible to teach simply by virtue of having more schooling than the students being taught (or even claiming to have more). State officials, concerned about the quality as well as public perceptions of the school system, promoted the establishment of formal teacher training programs. Teacher training institutions called **normal schools**, which provided prospective teachers with knowledge about curricular subjects and the 'art' and practice of teaching, were introduced as early as 1836 in Montreal and 1847 in Upper Canada and New Brunswick (Johnson, 1968: 156). Over the next several decades, provincial governments and school boards made periods of training in normal schools, usually in conjunction with some high school attainment, a requirement for teacher certification. Nonetheless, as Phillips (1957: 579) observes, 'actually, in all provinces before 1900 a large proportion of elementary school teachers had no more than two years' secondary school education, and either no professional training at all or no such training at the normal school level.'

Normal schools had as their objective the production of a corps of teachers who could at least approximate the ideal advanced by educational authorities. However, these schools also reoriented their focus to the reality that most persons who were entering the teaching force were 'raw, untrained' young women, as they were characterized by at least one school official (British Columbia, 1904: A65). Consequently, normal school training emphasized the cultivation of feminine dedication and loyalty to the public educational enterprise as much as practical classroom knowledge. These paternalistic aims were directed by male administrators in both the school system and the normal schools (Wotherspoon, 1989: 151).

It is necessary to recognize several fallacies in the portrayal by education officials of teachers, and women teachers in particular, as compliant and incompetent novices. First, while there were many 'green' teachers who did enter the classroom with little formal training, most school districts had several examples of teachers who, over the course of extended careers, made significant contributions both to the education of several generations of youth and to the increasing public respect that came to be accorded the school system overall. High teacher attrition rates were at least as likely to be the result of inadequate pay or working conditions, or regulations such as the one to force women to resign their positions upon marriage, as the consequence of individual failings.

Second, teachers were, as they generally continue to be, much more resourceful than they have been given credit for. Teaching, in common with other occupations considered to be 'women's work', such as clerical work, involves highly complex attributes that tend to be discounted as skills (see, e.g., Jackson, 1994). Considerable skill is involved, for instance, in the day-to-day ability to organize and manage classrooms. Most notably in poorly equipped schools or those located at a distance from major towns and cities with libraries and adequate techno-

Box 6.4 Serious Issues Affect Teachers in Many Nations

Teachers in Canada and other highly developed nations have made extensive gains in occupational status and improved working conditions, although their efforts to gain full professional recognition for their work and qualifications are sometimes undermined by educational reforms, funding crises, and other serious issues. In many parts of the world, teachers' work and working conditions have been even more seriously eroded, often to the extent that their livelihoods, schools, and lives can be in jeopardy. Teachers' organizations, educational agencies, and major international bodies, including UNESCO and the International Labour Organization, have drawn attention to these issues in the declaration of 5 October each year as World Teachers' Day. With a focus on serious problems that compound difficult **work conditions** in the best of circumstances, shortages of qualified teachers, and high rates of teacher attrition in many nations, the co-ordinators of the 2007 World Teachers' Day stressed the need to improve teaching conditions: decent working environments for teachers and learners; living wages that are regularly paid; equal pay and equal rights for women; initial and ongoing professional development; involvement in policy-making; and full collective bargaining rights.

Among the numerous problems cited to support these demands, member organizations reported the following (Education International, 2007):

- In parts of Cameroon, teachers (especially those working on contracts or in private schools) are paid wages that do not allow them to support their families, with many having to organize holiday and evening classes, or borrow money at rates of up to 30 per cent interest. Some female teachers have contracted AIDS/HIV, likely a result of engaging in prostitution to maintain a livable income.
- Teachers in Ghana, faced with deteriorating economic and teaching conditions and high fees for professional upgrading, were warned by association officials not to engage in behaviours such as alcoholism, absenteeism, and collecting illegal funds from students that would undermine their professional image.
- Teachers in Manila, the Philippines, marched to protest persistent underfunding of the education system in which they had been 'overworked and underpaid', and to demand immediate release of their insurance benefits.
- Teachers in Sri Lanka declared 5 October a day of mourning to protest inadequate salaries and lack of government action to address key grievances.
- Teachers in several nations, including Colombia, Zimbabwe, and Ethiopia, have been subject to serious human rights violations.
- Severe teacher shortages with the introduction of free public education in some nations, such as Kenya, have resulted in the expansion of school enrolments by over one million students while agreements with the International Monetary Fund prevent the state from hiring sufficient numbers of new teachers to meet prevailing standards.

logical support, teachers have had to develop their own materials and techniques to convey the curriculum and maintain student interest.

Teachers also possess expertise in their ability to facilitate interpersonal relations in and out of the classroom. A fundamental part of teaching is the emotional labour related to teachers' caring and nurturing roles, managing the emotions and feelings of students and other social relationships (Hochschild, 1983; Isenbarger and Zembylos, 2006). As this book has emphasized, the often indeterminate nature of life and social dynamics within schooling is a vital part of educational processes. The teaching relationship includes such things as sensitivity to students' emotional states, informal counselling and advising, mediation between competitive or antagonistic students, and other nurturing activities. These aspects of teaching are often devalued and discredited as real skills because of their parallels with mothering and domestic labour, forms of unpaid labour considered natural. Nonetheless, the 'caring' dimensions of teachers' work remain central to capacities regarded as essential for good teaching. Acker's (1999: 195) observations with respect to one school are applicable to many teaching situations:

> The fact that most of the teachers were women was also one of its strengths. Many of the women had in the past, or were having concurrently, experience in managing homes and families and balancing competing commitments. They seemed well adapted to the flexibility and tolerance for change required for a successful teacher at the school.

A third problem is the image of docility associated with a highly feminized teaching workforce. The fact that educational administrators and teacher-training officials introduced a broad and frequently changing range of regulations to govern teaching signifies that teachers were not readily subordinated. Many teachers demonstrated courage and determination simply to maintain their positions in the face of parents, trustees, and other officials hostile to them or the school. Teachers adopted both formal and informal means to resist measures they felt were extreme or unfair. Women teachers not only advanced struggles for pay equity, improvement of teaching conditions, and curricular change within the school system, but they were also engaged, often in leadership roles, in the suffragist and later feminist movements as well as in other organized groups in pursuit of social justice. Moreover, women did have some formal opportunities to influence the profession more directly. Although women with university degrees and other superior qualifications were more likely to be bypassed for promotion in favour of men, they were not always completely excluded from administrative and senior teaching positions.

These observations are important in helping us to reconceptualize the notion of professionalism. In contrast to approaches concerned with the question of whether or not teaching is a profession, historical evidence suggests that professionalism can more appropriately be understood as a strategy or ideology employed by various forces and agencies, both within and external to teaching, in order to shape the occupation in particular ways (Warburton, 1986). In the same way that school officials continually had to revise how they regulated teaching because it was not possible to construct a workforce of idealized teachers, diverse images and consequences of professionalism have contributed to the development of teaching in Canada.

Some school officials, for instance, were opposed to female teachers because they saw the influx of young women as a deterrent to the achievement of professional status by teachers. Viewed in this context, the introduction of normal schools was a way to upgrade teacher professionalism by providing specialized training and improving teacher qualifications, but it was intended to scrutinize teachers and inculcate in them an appropriate orientation to the school system before they entered the classroom. Similarly, teachers working in different educational settings had unique professional needs. For relatively well-paid, highly qualified secondary school teachers, professionalism was a way to increase their status and power in the education system, while teachers in poorly equipped remote rural schools were more likely to see professionalism as a tool for attaining fundamental improvements in teaching and working conditions. Professionalism, as an ideology, has had a moderating impact by restricting the extent to which teachers have adopted overtly political and militant actions, but it has also been influential in raising teachers' occupational profile, sometimes by their aggressive pursuit of policies and practices that go beyond school-specific issues.

The tendency for many teachers, as well as legislators, administrators, trustees, parents, and the media, to establish boundaries that define legitimate spheres of activity for teachers, and to distinguish these from areas that teachers should not be engaged in, continues to have important consequences for gender relations in teaching. Teachers who have advanced equitable treatment for women in teaching, for instance, have sometimes also been leaders in wider feminist movements. Some have encountered criticism from within and outside teaching for dealing with issues characterized by critics as political rather than educational in nature. Frequently, both educational administrators and leaders of teachers' organizations have dismissed demands by teachers to address issues such as pay inequity, racism, and sexism in the classroom, and to express concern about poverty in the community, as 'unprofessional'. These tendencies have made it difficult for teachers' organizations to take decisive action on such problems as sexual harassment, maternity leave, inequitable assignment of duties, competing demands between home and school, and other concerns that emerge through women's experiences in teaching.

The continuing **division of labour** along gender lines in teaching is clearly illustrated by the data in Tables 6.1 and 6.2 on the positions occupied by men and women in the education system. In general, it remains the case that most teachers in the lower grades and subordinate positions are women, while most teachers in high school and administrative positions are men. Although women today have a much greater impact on educational decision-making than in the past, partly reflected in increased participation rates in senior positions, substantial gender inequality remains within teaching and educational administration with respect to numbers, voice, differential expectations about responsibilities, and role performance (Collard and Reynolds, 2005; Young et al., 2007: 193–5). Employment equity programs, increased recognition of the need for women to take more central roles in educational planning and management as well as delivery, and the leadership that some women have provided to change educational realities and serve as successful role models have had an impact on creating more favourable conditions for gender equity. Various factors, including personal choice, positive and negative attitudes of teachers and administrators, and the ways in which teaching-related activities are differentially recognized in career and promotion decisions within teaching, have contributed to the mixed success in achieving equity objectives (Rees, 1990; Reynolds, 2002).

The teaching profession in Canada faces additional scrutiny and challenges in relation to the increasing ethnic diversity within schools. Teachers are expected to reflect many of the major characteristics of the communities they work in and to play a leadership role by fostering learning environments that are sensitive to the students and communities they work with. With few exceptions (notably visible minorities teaching at the university level), the proportion of teachers and educators at all levels who are visible minorities or Aboriginal has not kept pace with

Figure 6.2 Aboriginal Child and Youth Population and Educational Services Labour Force, Canada, Provinces, and Territories, 2001

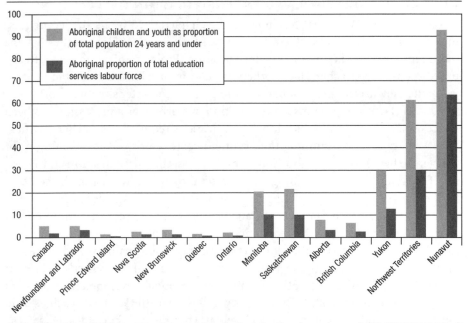

Sources: Data compiled from 2001 *Census of Canada*, Statistics Canada catalogues 97F0011XCB2001040 and 97F0011XCB2002053.

comparable growth in the student body and the general population (Guppy and Davies, 1998: 41–3; Steering Group, 2002). This is clearly shown in Figure 6.2 with regard to the under-representation across Canada of Aboriginal teachers and educational workers relative to the proportions of Aboriginal persons in age cohorts most typically enrolled in formal education programs. While comprehensive current data are not available, the proportions of school-age children of Aboriginal ancestry tend to outnumber the proportion of Aboriginal teachers in elementary and secondary schools by factors of at least 2.5 to three times in jurisdictions in which data are reported, including Manitoba, Saskatchewan, and the Northwest Territories. Racial minority groups, especially within black and Aboriginal communities, frequently cite the lack of representation within the teaching and educational administrative workforce as a serious deficiency in the creation of a racially tolerant and culturally supportive atmosphere (Canadian Race Relations Foundation, 2000: 8–9). Many visible minority and Aboriginal teachers express concern about their work placements, job expectations, and lack of acceptance by other school and community personnel. Broader concerns are also evident as teachers are mandated to implement anti-racist or culturally inclusive program guidelines despite having limited background knowledge, administrative support, resources, and time for preparation. These problems coexist with several promising initiatives in which teachers are strongly supported and committed to develop strong connections and relationships with the communities in which they work (Dei et al., 2000: 141ff.; Schissel and Wotherspoon, 2003: 116–19).

PROLETARIANIZATION AND INTENSIFICATION OF TEACHING

In contrast to the view that teaching can be characterized by its strong progress towards professionalism and gender equity, some commentators argue that the dominant tendency is one of proletarianization. Proletarianization refers to the processes whereby teachers, like workers in many industries, are subject to increasing, externally driven forms of control and pressures to intensify their work.

One of the primary claims for recognition of teaching as a profession has been the continual increase in educational qualifications required for teacher certification. Whereas at the beginning the twentieth century it was not uncommon for teachers to have less than high school completion, secondary education and a period of specialized teacher training were required by the early part of the century; by the mid-1970s, teacher training in most provinces was established in university degree programs, and now most Canadian jurisdictions require a minimum of four to five years of university education, including one or more years of professional studies, prior to certification. Most administrative positions and some secondary teaching positions are restricted to persons with a master's degree or higher in combination with other forms of professional development (Canadian Teachers' Federation, 2007). By the early 1990s, two-thirds of all teachers who taught at the kindergarten to Grade 3 levels and over 70 per cent of teachers in the higher grades (increasing by level) held university degrees (King and Peart, 1992: 22). Despite these improvements in formal educational qualifications, a common complaint of teachers is that there is a disjuncture between their training and the expectations placed on them in the classroom and in other aspects of the job. Those who argue that teaching is becoming proletarianized rather than professionalized emphasize the necessity for examining how teaching is organized and regulated as work, rather than what the formal entry requirements are, in order to assess how 'professional' teaching has become. Moreover, when teaching is analyzed as work, the reasons for teachers' involvement with organized labour and their adoption of trade unionist strategies become more readily apparent.

With respect to teaching, proletarianization can be understood in several different ways. In the most general sense, the concept refers to the attributes that teaching shares with other forms of work that are regulated and controlled by employers or managers outside the occupation. Braverman (1974), in one of the most influential analyses of contemporary labour processes, argues that no occupation is immune from proletarianization and the related process of deskilling, in which workers lose their ability to plan, make decisions, and use a wide range of skills to carry out their work tasks. As was observed in Chapter 2 and will be expanded upon in the next chapter, increases in formal educational credentials and training requirements in many occupations do not necessarily mean that workers use the acquired skills and training on the job. This phenomenon is significant for teachers in two ways: (1) in terms of how teaching is organized as work, and (2) in terms of their responsibilities to educate students whose own work futures are uncertain.

All jobs are organized around the completion of particular tasks. In the case of teaching, the main activities tend to be considered as mental rather than manual labour. Teachers are able to make claims to professionalism in part because many aspects of their work are difficult to codify. This stands in contrast to many other jobs, such as those involved in the making or selling of commercial products, in which employees are expected to follow explicit instructions in accordance with their job descriptions. Teaching, though, is also organized around several technical functions, such as designing lesson plans, grading students, keeping records of student attendance and progress, and following rules and procedures regarding student discipline. For each of these activities, there is likely to be considerable variation from one teaching situation to another with respect to how closely teachers are monitored and expected to perform specified duties or how much leeway teachers have to alter their practices.

Proletarianization occurs as teachers are subject to increasing levels of external control by supervisors or administrators, or when their work is reorganized to minimize the discretion they have over their activities. When standardized curricula or exams are introduced into schooling, for instance, there is potential to assess teachers' performance as much as that of students. Educators' reliance on curricula and lesson plans based on rigidly defined behavioural objectives, or on student workbooks that follow a specified progression of lessons and exercises, requires little input from the teacher in the curricular planning and delivery process. While most teachers are likely to use these materials in conjunction with other resources and to innovate in their lesson planning, the likelihood that they will come to depend on prescribed materials (if, indeed, they are not overtly directed to adopt these materials) increases as class sizes and demands on their time grow. Runté (1998) observes in one Canadian jurisdiction that even when teachers have some discretion over what is taught and how it is taught, the imposition of centralized examinations and standardized tests removes effective education planning and the setting of goals from the school level to more centralized authorities.

Apple refers to the process of **intensification** to demonstrate how important aspects of the work of teachers and other professionals can be proletarianized or deskilled. Intensification occurs when the demands associated with a job are increased. Apple (1986: 41) observes that intensification:

> has many symptoms, from the trivial to the more complex—ranging from being allowed no time at all even to go to the bathroom, have a cup of coffee or relax, to having a total absence of time to keep up with one's field. We can see intensification most visibly in mental labour in the chronic sense of work overload that has escalated over time.

As school districts reduce teaching and support staff and increase class sizes, for instance, teachers are required not only to teach more pupils but also to perform more duties that were once done by other workers. Changes to school budgets and programs mean that many have to teach in areas for which they have little or no training, especially if subjects outside of the core areas or a full range of extracurricular activities are to be retained. New curricula and modified learning objectives require the introduction of new subjects and materials with which teachers have to keep up to date. However, these changes place increased demands on teachers' time in and out of the classroom, especially when there is limited funding and time for in-service training.

These trends are not just hypothetical. Educational researchers and teachers' organizations in many nations have pointed to growing concerns about teacher workload, stress, and other problems associated with new demands imposed on teachers through educational reform and changing school contexts (Hargreaves, 2003; Robertson, 2000; Smyth, 2001; Whitty, 1997). Hall (2004), summarizing research on teachers' work in developed nations, identifies four major transformations that teachers are experiencing across contexts:

1. teachers' diminishing power to determine the curriculum they teach and how they teach it;
2. a new emphasis on teachers' managerial and administrative role with pupils and with other adults working in school;
3. changing pay structures, and a dismantling of union-won agreements;
4. changing conditions of service and new regulatory controls over competence and behaviour.

Similarly, Macdonald (1999: 839–41) observes that teachers in both highly developed and less developed nations are experiencing increased levels of stress, anxiety, and attrition, a result of factors including deteriorating conditions within schools, inadequate resources to keep pace with emerging student numbers and needs, low pay structures especially in relation to other employment options, declines in teachers' status and collective bargaining powers, student misbehaviour, and work overload.

Research tends to contradict common perceptions of teaching as a job conducted in the classroom within the confines of the school day and school year. For Canadian teachers, like people in many other occupations, one of the biggest issues is time—time in the classroom to meet the demands of the curriculum and attend to the diverse needs of students, administration, and other school-related responsibilities; and time outside the classroom to plan lessons, meet with parents, engage in organizational activities, manage extracurricular activities, and upgrade their professional skills and knowledge related to their jobs. Teachers experience intensification of their work both by working longer and by doing more within their working day. Canadian research in many jurisdictions echoes studies from other nations revealing that teachers over the past two decades are typically working longer hours while simultaneously experiencing tremendous pressures associated with rising workloads (Smyth et al., 2000: 171–2). In a survey of Canadian teachers commissioned by the Canadian Teachers' Federation (2005), 83 per cent of respondents indicated that their workloads had increased over the previous four years, over half indicated that they were teaching larger classes, and teachers worked an average of 55.6 hours a week. These results correspond with national labour force data showing that full-time educators at elementary, secondary, and university levels worked an average of more than 50 hours of paid and unpaid labour per week in 2005, about 10 hours more than a decade earlier and about 10 hours per week more than the averages for all combined occupations (Lin, 2006).

Increasing workload pressures have caused additional strains for teachers. A study of Saskatchewan teachers, for instance, emphasizes that 'Teachers describe a relentless pressure to take care of school work even when they are in poor health or experiencing personal difficulties' (Gallen et al., 1995: 56). Similarly, British Columbia teachers report rising stress and health problems related to a number of factors:

- a large volume of work;
- a wide range of workload duties that have changed over time;
- changing class composition;
- seasonal pressures, with intense periods of work in addition to regular loads;
- extensive curriculum changes;
- a wide range of expectations from government, employers, school administrators, and parents (Naylor and Schaefer, 2002: 35).

Box 6.5 Trends Associated with the Restructuring of Teachers' Work

Teachers in Canada and other nations are experiencing significant changes in their work amid global economic restructuring. Smyth (2001: 38–9), writing from an Australian perspective, summarizes many of the prevalent forces and trends:

- [Education] is being constrained by the intrusion of external agencies who require that schools operate in the 'national interest', a claim that is invariably couched in the economic imperative of increased international competitiveness.
- The fiscal crisis of the state is reducing funding to schools, in contexts in which schools are exhorted to 'do more with less'.
- The breakdown of other social institutions is occurring at the same time schools are expected to take on a wider and more complex range of functions.
- Control is being re-centralized, having the effect of conveying the message to teachers that they cannot be trusted and that their work is devalued—this happens in contexts in which it is made to look as if teachers are being given more autonomy, self-control, and decision-making power at school level.
- Schools are expected to operate more like private enterprises, to market themselves, to compete against one another for students and resources— functions that take them increasingly away from the reasons for which they exist, namely, teaching and learning.

All of the matters just alluded to are ripe with implications for teachers' work and have resulted in a number of policy initiatives that:

- require teachers to work within more rigidly defined policy frameworks and guidelines, of one kind or another;
- place greater emphasis on determining the worth of teaching in terms of measurable outcomes;
- supposedly make teachers more accountable by linking outcomes to the actions and activities of individual teachers, classrooms, and schools;
- move teachers and schools in the direction of processes that are more appropriate to those of the corporate and industrial sector—performance appraisal, curriculum audits, quality assurance, and the like;
- preach the virtues of education and schooling as being no different from any other commodity—to be measured and calibrated according to quality standards; packaged and delivered to targeted audiences; and haggled over in the artificially constructed 'user-pays' marketplace of education.

On the other hand, another set of tendencies and trends suggests, erroneously, that the opposite is happening in education. These all have the sound of participation and democracy about them: devolution; competition; choice; autonomy; collegiality; collaboration; self-management; liberation management; teamwork and partnerships; networking and collegiality; flexibility; responsiveness. While these tendencies might look and sound as if they are about giving teachers more control over their work, and in some cases it is true that they do, it is more a matter of appearances in most instances. The work of teaching is increasingly brought under the influence of politicians, policy-makers, and the captains of industry at the same time as claims are made that teachers and schools should take greater control of their own destiny: deciding on local priorities; exercising greater self-management; breaking away from expensive and inefficient bureaucratic forms of organization; and making schools into leaner organizations able to be more responsive.

Although teachers are expected to become more inclusive in their educational orientations to accommodate greater diversity in teaching and learning circumstances, work overload can sometimes limit effective relationships that schools have with students and communities who most need stronger educational outreach (Tardif and Lessard, 2004; Wotherspoon, 2006: 692–3). Changing educational realities and new knowledge requirements have also meant that teachers are spending additional hours engaged in their own formal and informal learning activities (Smaller et al., 2000).

Teachers' experiences of stress and other pressures, as well as their working patterns within teaching and competing commitments outside of their work, are highly influenced by such factors as gender, marital status, teaching level, and career stage (King and Peart, 1992; Canadian Teachers' Federation, 1993). Because of this diversity within the teaching force, research findings on teachers' work are varied and sometimes contradictory. Female teachers, particularly those who teach kindergarten and early elementary grades, for instance, are less likely to report that they have adequate preparation time during the day, but these teachers are also the least likely to report themselves as being in the high-stress group (Canadian Teachers' Federation, 1993: 62, 68–9). However, female teachers tend to be disproportionately affected by the combined impact of shifting forms of workplace control, emerging educational demands, responsibilities associated with caring for children and other dependants, domestic work, and community activity (Naylor, 2002: 140–1). Overall, though, teachers remain highly committed to their work and the students they work with. Despite increased concern about intensification, growing fears about physical safety in schools, legal action for child abuse, and attacks on the teaching profession by politicians and media reports, Canadian literature reveals consistently high levels of overall job satisfaction and pride with respect to teaching.

To understand the apparently paradoxical ways in which teachers describe their work, it is instructive to consider the observations made at the beginning of this chapter. Teaching is shaped by divergent and often contradictory expectations and activities framed through various sites, including the classroom, the school authority structure, the community, and the occupation itself. Consequently, intensification, proletarianization, and **professionalization** are not necessarily mutually exclusive processes. This is why it becomes possible for teachers to view additional demands on their time, involving such tasks as learning techniques to manage larger classes or developing lesson plans around new curricula, as an extension of their professional competencies at the same time as their work is being intensified and deskilled. If teachers feel that their expertise and professional judgement are being used in the process of educational change, they may be more willing to endure increased workloads even when it means they are working harder or putting in longer hours. Apple (1986: 45), describing the situation in a school in which much of teachers' work was reorganized around standardized packages of skill-based worksheets, observes:

> Professionalism and increased responsibility tend to go hand in hand here. The situation is more than a little paradoxical. There is so much responsibility placed on teachers for technical decisions that they actually work harder. They feel that since they constantly make decisions based on the outcomes of these multiple pre- and post-tests, the longer hours are evidence of their enlarged professional status.

These factors become even more significant when we come back to the point that teaching tends to be characterized more by social relationships than by strictly technical operations. The human or interpersonal dimensions of relationships between teachers and students (who most often are children or young adults) are defining features of interaction in classrooms and other educational settings. These social aspects of teachers' work are so obvious that they are easy to take for granted in the analysis of teaching. However, by drawing attention to their importance, we can begin to understand how proletarianization and professionalization interact in teaching.

One of the characteristics that makes it possible for teachers to claim professional status, and thereby to seek improvements in their terms and conditions of work, is the fact that they are working with human beings. From an early point in the establishment of a system of mass public education, teachers had to gain public confidence that they were sufficiently competent, trustworthy, and reliable to manage a classroom of children. Gradually, standards of certification and training, backed by legislation and regulations, ensured that teachers were authorized to conduct classes, evaluate pupils, and perform a wide range of other educational functions.

This legitimacy to work with and assess individuals has had a dual significance for teachers. On the one hand, it has given teachers a privileged status that distinguishes them from laypersons and other workers in the community because it allows them to claim expertise over professional matters such as child development, discipline, pedagogy, and curricular content. As certified representatives of the school system, they have a public responsibility, in contrast to parents and other community members whose interests appear to be more fragmented and private. On the other hand, this responsibility, combined with the fact that they are employees, has meant that teachers are also subject to **moral regulation** and intense administrative and public scrutiny even when they are not directly observed performing classroom duties. Teachers are as likely to be monitored informally, through rumours and conversational accounts of their activities in and out of school, as through more formal kinds of assessment. Thus, while school board regulations concerning teachers' dress and public conduct may not be as stringent as they once were, their moral character, as much as their teaching ability, remains the focus of considerable public interest. Inside the classroom, fears of the school inspectors' visits have been replaced by worries over allegations of sexual abuse, while teachers' social lives continue to be constrained by the dangers of being seen doing the wrong things in the wrong places by students, former students, parents, school officials, and the media.

Recognition of the dual nature of teaching also allows us to understand how technical regulation and intensification occur. Because it is difficult for educational managers and administrators to monitor and assess many of the interpersonal aspects of a teacher's work, demands for increased educational quality and output tend to be met by looking at measurable factors, such as standardized test scores and class sizes. Increases in workloads, however, make it less possible for teachers to attend to the varied needs of all students as well as to other responsibilities. As class sizes go up, for instance, it is tempting, for the sake of both classroom control and pedagogical efficiency, for teachers to rely more heavily on lectures, prepackaged textbooks and assignments, and standardized group activities than on interaction with small groups or individual pupils.

The examples cited above reflect a tendency in which educational productivity is measured in quantitative terms, to favour technical over subjective or interpersonal dimensions of teaching. Chapter 9 considers in more detail how contemporary demands for measurement and accountability in education tend to be framed within limited conceptions of what goes on in schools over approaches that view schooling as a process that contributes to meaningful social participation and opportunities.

CONCLUSION

This chapter has examined teaching as a highly complex occupation characterized by several paradoxes. Teachers are professionals, but they are also workers whose professionalism is highly constrained. Their special status and responsibilities leave them subject to extensive public scrutiny and criticism. They are expected to perform their work with specialized skills and knowledge, but they work under conditions in which they may not be able to put their capabilities and training to use. They are potentially curriculum planners and innovators who at the same time face or succumb to pressures to routinize their activities to the point of monotony and dehumanization. They are in positions in which they are expected to be community leaders and role models for children and other learners, but they also experience restraints and receive criticisms from people who do not fully understand what schooling and teaching are all about.

These contradictions can be understood as inherent characteristics of the teaching occupation rather than as unfortunate or accidental by-products of the school system. Like other workers, teachers are paid employees who are subject to extensive administrative or managerial control governed by demands for efficiency, accountability, and order. Unlike many other workers, though, teachers are entrusted to work intensively in a formative way with other human beings. It is the uncertain nature of these social characteristics that makes teaching both a potentially rewarding and satisfying occupation and one that can often be frustrating and over-regulated.

ANNOTATED FURTHER READINGS

Acker, Sandra. 1999. *The Realities of Teachers' Work: Never a Dull Moment.* London: Cassell. The author provides an in-depth study of the working relationships and lives of teachers at an elementary school, highlighting the complex interactions in and out of the classroom that are vital parts of teaching.

Apple, Michael W. 1986. *Teachers and Texts: A Political Economy of Class and Gender Relations in Education.* New York: Routledge & Kegan Paul. This analysis of economic and cultural pressures to transform education includes a detailed discussion of the changing nature of teaching as a particular, highly feminized, form of work.

Hargreaves, Andy. 2003. *Teaching in the Knowledge Society: Education in the Age of Insecurity.* New York: Teachers' College Press. Building from a critique of the limitations inherent in existing models of schooling and teaching, the author provides a case for remaking schooling to advance teachers' role as knowledge workers dedicated to enhancing human skills and capacities within knowledge societies.

Lockhart, Alexander. 1991. *School Teaching in Canada.* Toronto: University of Toronto Press. This is one of the few studies to examine teaching across Canada, addressing the historical development of teachers' associations, the nature of teachers' work and working conditions, characteristics of the teaching force, and challenges faced by teachers.

Robertson, Susan. 2000. *A Class Act: Changing Teachers' Work, the State, and Globalisation.* London: Falmer Press. The author explores how teachers' work and educational relationships more generally are being transformed amid social, political, and economic restructuring occurring in a globally competitive environment. Detailed analyses of the politics of teaching in England and the United States highlight the many interwoven currents that frame and play out through teachers' professional and class relations.

———— and Harry Smaller, eds. 1996. *Teacher Activisim in the 1990s.* Toronto: James Lorimer. Several contributors demonstrate the impact of educational reform, driven by global economic restructuring, on teachers, teachers' organizations, and schools in Canada and other nations.

Smyth, John, Alastair Dow, Robert Hattam, Alan Reid, and Geoffrey Shacklock. 2000. *Teachers' Work in a Globalizing Economy.* London: Falmer Press. The book addresses the powerful impact of global economic change on teachers' work. Drawing on the analysis of teachers' work and experiences in several developed nations, the authors outline a model for understanding the diverse forces reshaping teaching and teachers' work.

KEY TERMS

Collective bargaining A process by which members of an occupational group, normally represented by a union, enter into agreements with employers on such matters as wages, benefits, and terms and conditions of employment.

Division of labour The differentiation and distribution of jobs and tasks at different levels, which can occur globally or across a society, within a particular form of work or activity, or among social groups.

Feminization The concentration of women within particular occupations or groups, often discussed in conjunction with gender-based forms of discrimination.

Intensification A process through which workers lose privileges and autonomy through rules and procedures intended to increase productivity and tighten control over work outcomes.

Moral regulation Scrutiny of teachers and other workers based on expectations related to their personal characteristics, habits, beliefs, and behaviour.

Normal schools Teacher training institutions that operated from the mid-nineteenth to mid-twentieth centuries to provide beginning teachers who had limited educational qualifications with information, guidance, and practical experience related to the varied dimensions of teaching.

Professionalization A trend in which a particular occupation gains status and recognition through specific credentials, specialized knowledge, or access to specified rights and privileges.

Proletarianization A process in which workers lose control over core aspects of their work, or one in which self-sufficient workers are replaced by employees in subordinate positions.

Teachers' associations Organizations that represent teachers in collective bargaining over salaries and conditions of work and provide teachers with opportunities and resources for professional development, advocacy for public education, and services to support teaching and teachers' well-being.

Work conditions The varied dimensions of schooling and educational organization that affect teachers' work, such as overall workload, class size, preparation time, teaching assignments, supervision of students during the school day, participation in extracurricular activities, and resources to support teaching in particular school contexts.

STUDY QUESTIONS

1. Discuss the extent to which school teaching is or is not a unique occupation in comparison with other forms of work.
2. Critically discuss the question of whether teachers should have the same right as other workers to engage in strikes and other job actions in cases of contract disputes over wages and working conditions.
3. How representative is the teaching workforce in relation to the social composition of Canada's population? What is the significance of this relationship for the education of diverse groups of learners?
4. What factors account for the fact that most Canadian schoolteachers are women? What implications does the gender composition of the teaching workforce have for teaching as an occupation?
5. Many governments and media analysts have blamed teachers for their resistance to change, provision of poor quality education, and other social problems. Critically discuss these arguments, and provide an explanation for negative public perceptions about teaching.
6. Critically discuss the extent to which the promotion of a knowledge economy will benefit educators or detract from their professional interests.

Chapter 7

Schooling and Work

INTRODUCTION

It is widely accepted that a major purpose of schooling is to prepare people for work. This task is carried out both directly, in the provision of skills and knowledge necessary for work, and indirectly, through the development of aptitudes and credentials whose importance is recognized for employment. The rapid pace of technological change combined with economic and social transformations of global significance have given new-found prominence to issues concerning the relationship between schooling and work. In the process, intense debates have raged over the extent to which schooling is, or should become more, relevant to a world that has become so fundamentally transformed. Frequent criticism has been levelled by employers, government agencies, and labour organizations, as well as by parents and students, over the presumed failure of schools and other educational institutions to offer the kinds of preparation that workers require for employment and success in today's globally competitive society. Consequently, the reference points are changing insofar as what happens educationally affects internal as well as global labour markets, economic production, and social relationships.

Education critics contend that schooling is not only contributing to a mismatch between workers and jobs, but that it is also remiss in its efforts to prepare people to adjust to the social realities of a globalizing economy. Chapter 3 examined the expansion of conventional education systems in Canada and other highly industrialized nations in conjunction with the growing complexity of industrial production, scientific advancement, and bureaucratization. Over the past three decades, the subsequent focus of criticism has been the emergence of what is frequently referred to as a **post-industrial society**, in which service-sector work and knowledge are coming to supersede industrial work and manufactured goods as the core foundations of economic development (Bell, 1973; Giddens, 1990). The concepts of brain drain and brain circulation have drawn attention to processes by which people with desirable qualifications and skills are widely sought by governments and industries in several nations. They bring into focus, as well, issues related to investment in specific forms of education, and the degree to which nations may either look to import or risk losing highly qualified workers. These changes have prompted numerous questions concerning how well suited today's schools are for the contemporary world and, more generally, about what these transformations signify for life in that world.

This chapter provides a critical analysis of the relationship between schooling and work. It assesses competing perspectives on these relations, broadly framed around approaches that see in post-industrial or knowledge-based economies unprecedented social and economic horizons and those that take a more cautious stance in observing that capitalist economies are limited in the extent to which rewards can be allocated to those with increased qualifications. The chapter begins with an overview of contemporary demands for educational reform targeted to prepare students for work in a globally competitive environment. Major economic changes are making it imperative that students have access to educational services that provide them with both skills and orientations to learning that will enable them to make successful life decisions under highly uncertain circumstances. At the same time, some of the claims made about the apparent inability of formal educational institutions to adjust to economically driven forces are called into question through an understanding of the complex historical factors that have shaped the relationship between schooling and work. Contemporary critiques of the education system's ability to deliver the kinds of work training sought by many segments of society echo those raised on several occasions for more than a century. Educational planning and practices encompass conflicting priorities that cannot be reduced to a simple economic rationale. It is important, ultimately, to understand the various contributions that schooling makes to labour markets and jobs as phenomena characterized by the competing visions and contradictions inherent within all educational endeavours.

CONTEMPORARY DEMANDS FOR EDUCATIONAL REFORM: THE 'MISMATCH' BETWEEN SCHOOLING AND JOBS

The promotion of educational reform has become an increasingly central component of labour market development strategies in Canada and other advanced industrial nations. The emergence of new forms of work and investment strategy marked by rapid developments in information technology, technological innovation leading to increased productivity, and intense global competition has fostered renewed interest in human capital. Education figures prominently into the equation for its significance in ensuring basic knowledge and social skills for potential workers and consumers, its contributions to advanced levels of training, its integration into a broad array of lifelong learning choices, its value as a commodity within business and other enterprises, and its contributions to innovation. A speech delivered in late 2007 by the Secretary-General of the Organization for Economic Co-operation and Development summarizes the importance that solid educational foundations hold for emerging economic priorities in a competitive environment:

> In the highly competitive globalised economy of today, quality education is one of the most valuable assets that a society and an individual can have. Skills are key factors for productivity, economic growth, and better living standards. Effective and innovative education policies open enormous opportunities for individuals just as faulty educational systems result in declining standards, exclusion, and unemployment. They also underpin healthy and vibrant economies. That is why education plays a central role in OECD's agenda.

Dramatic changes in the global talent pool over recent decades oblige countries to assess the educational progress of their young people in a global context. Today, countries like China or India are delivering high skills at moderate cost and at an ever increasing pace. Other countries—including the developed countries that are members of OECD—cannot ignore these competitive pressures, on pain of harming their own future well-being. (Gurria, 2007)

The central place that education holds in discourses and strategies associated with the knowledge economy carries mixed significance for education, educators, and learners. Therein lies the promise that the promotion of educational priorities will be accompanied by enhanced awareness, resources, and revitalization for educational institutions, mitigating some of the more severe attacks and cutbacks they have endured in previous years. Teachers and other educators may gain some influence and status in the process, while educational programs may benefit from new partnerships with business, governments, and communities. Many proposed educational reforms and calls for enhanced early childhood education and improved support services, including those for disadvantaged groups, echo concerns long held by educators. However, the knowledge or learning agenda also signifies major shifts in existing educational priorities and directions. It increases public expectations about education, posing intense pressure on educators and the institutions they work in to fulfill promises that are not always clearly understood or adequately supported with essential resources. The **new economy** discourse contains both explicit and implicit indictments of educators and the systems in which they work: its implementation involves measures to contain costs, ensure accountability, outline explicit performance indicators, and pose education as a competition aligned more closely with market-based economic activities. Schools are attributed full or partial blame for alienating youth before graduation or for producing graduates with low literacy levels, inability to integrate into labour markets, and limited capacity or aptitude for innovation and entrepreneurship.

A steady flow of reports and position papers distributed by governments, corporate bodies, think-tanks, and lobby groups since the mid-1980s outlines the expectations that the new economy holds for education and training in a context driven by globally competitive economic development. Typically, such reports begin with an overview of the nature and size of the 'education industry', acknowledging that levels of educational expenditure, involvement, attainment, and outcomes in Canada rank at or near the top, relative to other OECD nations. Education is then posed in terms of productivity, quality, and returns on investment, with emphasis on the need to raise the bar in order to retain a competitive advantage. 'Why', it was asked in an influential report by the Economic Council of Canada (1991: 168), did 'Canada, as a nation, not appear to be getting a greater economic return on its substantial investment' in formal education?

More recent policy statements have shifted emphasis from indictments of education's failure to meet its fundamental objectives (which were used in part to

Box 7.1 The Skills Challenge

While Canadians are engaged in unprecedented levels of formal educational activities, governments, businesses, and other agencies are warning that global competition and the rapid advancement of a knowledge-based economy have posed further challenges to improve the pace and level of learning. The federal government (Government of Canada, 2001: 19–20), for example, has identified a 'skills challenge' that warns of the need to increase the long-term supply of highly skilled workers for the knowledge-based society:

> Canada will have great difficulty becoming more competitive without a greater number of highly qualified people to drive the innovation process and apply innovations, including new technologies.
>
> Skill requirements in the labour market will continue to increase at a rapid pace. Firms will be looking for more research personnel—technicians, specialists, managers—to strengthen their innovative capacity and maintain their competitive advantage. Universities, colleges and government laboratories have already begun launching a hiring drive to replace the large number of professors, teachers, researchers and administrators reaching retirement age. This will result in a huge demand in Canada for highly qualified people.
>
> On the supply side, Canada has experienced sluggish growth in higher education participation rates in recent years. In addition, we do not compare well to other countries in terms of upgrading the skills of the existing work force through employee training. While our track record in attracting skilled immigrants is good, we will need to more aggressively seek out highly qualified immigrants in the next decade. If we do not address these issues, Canada will face persistent shortages of the skills required for success in the knowledge-based economy.
>
> Shortages will be exacerbated by international competition for talent as the most advanced economies experience many of the same economic and demographic pressures. If Canada does not take measures now, we will certainly face critical shortages in the talent we need to drive our economy.

These warnings were reiterated more recently in a report by the Canadian Council on Learning (2007d: 5), which cautions against a complacent stance with regard to the state of education in Canada:

> Canadians are becoming increasingly aware of the economic benefits of more education, for individual citizens, and for the competitiveness of our country. We are also coming to appreciate the contributions that learning makes to our health and well-being, and to the strength and cohesion of our communities. Nonetheless, there are serious signs of trouble. We ignore them at our peril.

An astounding number of Canadian adults cannot read, write or do arithmetic at the level required to participate fully in today's globally competitive economy. And literacy and numeracy skills decline with age, indicating that many Canadians are not using these skills.

In addition, the amount of workplace training available in Canada is low compared to many other developed countries. And the workers with the lowest levels of literacy—arguably those who would benefit most from further training—are the least likely to have access to employer-supported training.

Our large and growing immigrant population is also trapped in a paradox: while Canada needs to count on our current citizens and those who will join us from abroad, we must provide immigrants with the language, literacy and skills training they need to flourish within our society and help sustain our economic growth.

Source: ————. *The State of Learning in Canada: No Time for Complacency, Report on Learning in Canada 2007*. Ottawa: Canadian Council on Learning. Reproduced with permission of the Minister of Public Works and Government Services.

justify funding cuts to education or reallocation of resources) to its role as a partner in the pursuit of higher levels of training and excellence. Formal education has been placed along a continuum of lifelong learning, running from early childhood, through schooling, into workplace training, and on to adult education and numerous alternative learning opportunities. A federal government statement on Canada's innovation strategy begins, in part, as follows:

Canada is consistently near the top, and often at the top, of international rankings of the best countries in which to live. We have built a strong and vibrant society with culturally diverse, dynamic communities and enviable education, health, social, and economic systems. . . . Canada is well positioned to enjoy continued social and economic prosperity in the new century. . . . Countries that succeed in the 21st century will be those with citizens who are creative, adaptable and skilled. The so-called 'new' economy is demanding new things from us. The need for ingenuity, creativity and hard work has not changed. How we do our work has. Today's workplace requires higher levels of education and skills. . . . To seize the opportunities before us, learning must be available to all Canadians throughout their lifetime, so that everyone has the opportunity to reach his or her potential. . . . We can and must do more, together. (Government of Canada, 2002: 5–6)

These claims have a simple appeal. Widespread acceptance of the view that education is positively associated with socio-economic success is borne out by statistical evidence that, in general, the more education one has the greater the likelihood of labour force participation, the lower the rates of unemployment, and the higher the average incomes. In 2007, for instance, the overall unemployment rate for labour market participants aged 15 and over in Canada was 6 per cent, ranging from 4 per cent for graduates from post-secondary programs to over 12 per cent for

Box 7.2   Education, Skill, and Employment Trends for the New Economy

The introduction of new technologies, movement towards a knowledge-based economy, and shifts in the nature and scale of production and consumption have contributed to substantial changes in recent and projected future employment prospects. A report by Lapointe et al. (2006: 15, 19–20, 39–42) for Human Resources and Social Development Canada highlights the relationship among education, skill level, and job prospects:

Employment Growth by Industry

Since 1987, the total number of jobs in Canada increased at an average annual rate of 1.5 per cent. Employment in the service-producing sector grew at a slightly above-average rate of 1.9 per cent, while the rate in goods-producing industries was well below the average at 0.5 per cent.

Employment Growth by Occupation

In 2005, more than 8.7 million non-student workers were employed in highly skilled occupations and 5.8 million in low-skilled jobs. The distinction between high- and low-skilled occupations is based on the 2001 National Occupational Classification (NOC). The NOC classifies occupations according to the education level or training usually required to work in a given occupation. High-skilled occupations include occupations usually requiring university education (skill level A), college education or apprenticeship training (level B) and management occupations, while low-skilled occupations usually require secondary school or occupation-specific training (level C) or only on-the-job training (level D).

The Canadian economy has undergone structural changes generated by rapid technological advancement and expanding trade liberalization. These two factors have intensified worker specialization in highly skilled tasks. Since 1987, highly skilled occupations have grown at an annual average rate of 1.7 per cent, compared to the economy-wide average of 1.4 per cent. Six out of 10 jobs created during that period were in highly skilled occupations.

Among high-skilled occupations, two sub-categories—occupations usually requiring a university education (3.1 per cent) and management occupations (1.7 per cent)—have recorded particularly strong employment growth since 1987. This is reflected in the employment share of occupations usually requiring a university education, which climbed from 13.1 per cent in 1987 to 17.3 per cent in 2005. More specifically, the major contributors to growth in highly skilled jobs have been computer and information systems occupations, engineers, human resource management professionals, policy and program officers, researchers and consultants, and psychologists. Occupations requiring a college education or apprenticeship training recorded the lowest employment growth (1.1 per cent) among high-skilled occupations.

Figure 7.1 Employment Growth in High- and Low-Skilled Occupations, 1987–2005 (index: 100 = 1987)

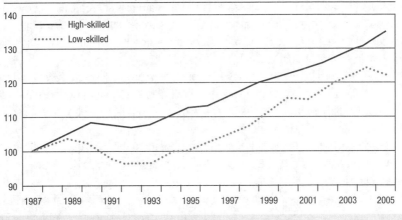

Source: Statistics Canada, Labour Force Survey

Non-student employment in low-skilled occupations has increased at a slower than average pace (1.1 per cent) since 1987.

Demographic and macroeconomic developments will lead to changes in Canada's industrial structure. First, slower population growth is expected to reduce output and employment growth for most industries, while changes in the age structure of the population will have an impact on the industrial structure by favouring service-providing industries, particularly in the health sector.

Figure 7.2 Employment Growth by Industry, 1987–2015 (index: 100 = 1987)

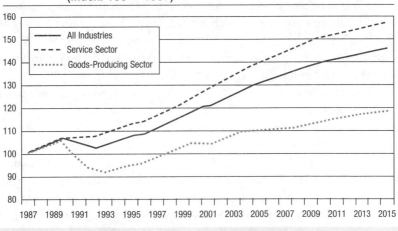

Source: (1987–2005) Statistics Canada, Labour Force Survey
(2006–2015) HRSDC - SPRD, Labour Market and Skills Forecasting and Analysis Unit, 2006
Reference Scenario

Other structural trends will have an impact on Canada's industrial mix, including the continuing shift towards a more knowledge-based economy, globalization and reduced accessibility to some natural resources. Finally, cyclical events such as the pick-up in demand for aeronautical equipment, higher oil prices and the improved fiscal outlook of governments will significantly impact growth in several industries.

Over the next 10 years, employment growth in the service sector will outpace that in the goods-producing industries, continuing a trend that began in the late 1980s. Employment in the service sector is expected to rise at an annual average rate of 1.2 per cent (an increase of nearly 1.6 million jobs during the 2006–15 period). In the goods-producing industries, the average annual rate of new job creation, at only 0.8 per cent (slightly more than 0.3 million jobs), will be less than the average of 1.1 per cent.

Over the next 10 years, more than two-thirds of the 1.7 million new non-student jobs created (69.2 per cent) are expected to be in occupations usually requiring postsecondary education (university or college) or in management. In 2005, approximately 60 per cent of all non-student workers had jobs in these categories.

persons who did not have a high school diploma (Statistics Canada, 2007d). Moreover, there is a general sense that the importance of education and technical training for jobs and work is growing. In a report pointing to evidence that Canada's post-secondary educational expansion is not keeping pace with growth occurring in many other nations, the Canadian Council on Learning (2007c: 31) stresses that '[t]he majority of the occupations that are forecast to experience excess demand are those requiring post-secondary education. As a consequence, the linkages between the educational institutions and the labour market will be even more critical than in the past.' There is increasing consensus around the assessment that job-relevant education and training are critical components of both personal and national success in a global economy.

It is sometimes difficult to gain a clear sense of shifting relations between schooling and work because assertions that schools are failing to provide the kinds of training necessary for today's job market are often embedded within broader ideologies that call for fundamental transformation of the education system. These results suggest that, while there may be some general public uneasiness about the quality and job-specific relevance of education, there is nowhere near consensus surrounding the view that schools are failing in their central missions that is assumed in the rhetoric to promote economically driven educational reform.

The vigorous emphasis on the significance of education for economic development strategies highlights an exchange among educators, business leaders, and government officials that has often been uneasy and uncertain. There are numer-

Box 7.3 Comparative School-to-Work Transitions

Education systems and their role in the transition to work differ across nations. Kerckhoff (2000: 472) examined the educational systems of Germany, France, the United States, and Great Britain and concluded that 'the transition process varies greatly among those four societies.' Here he summarizes the two different models he found:

From the review presented, it is possible to construct two ideal types of educational systems. Type One systems are highly standardized and stratified, and their educational credentials recognize vocational specialization. Type Two systems are relatively unstandardized and unstratified and their credentials have little vocational relevance. It appears that Type One societies have a stronger education–occupation association, lower rates of return to full-time school, fewer increases in educational credentials, fewer job changes, and lower rates of early occupational mobility. In effect, the transition from school to work is more orderly and stable in Type One societies.

Germany comes closest to having a Type One educational system, and the United States comes closest to having a Type Two educational system. France and Great Britain have mixtures of the characteristics used in this typology.

Difficult problems in studying the transition from school to work still remain. One is finding a definition of the first job that is wholly adequate for comparisons across societies. A related problem is the societal variation in the opportunities for increasing one's level of educational credentials while in the labour force rather than only while outside the labour force.

ous visions of the appropriate linkages between schooling and work, just as there are different models in which those relationships are applied. In North America, unlike nations such as Germany or Japan, little direct relationship exists between schooling and employment. Employers and educators often regard one another with skepticism or distrust, with the former assailing schools for their inability to produce the kinds of workers and skills they demand while the latter condemn business for its skewed sense of education and its failure to see that schooling is concerned with much more than simply training for employment and profit. The absence of dialogue and engagement among employers and educators is often posed as an obstacle to effective educational reform. However, this has begun to change through several new partnerships and growing integration of schooling and work innovations such as co-operative learning and internship. The consequences for education and students are mixed, as will be observed later in this and subsequent chapters.

The Relationship between Schooling and Work

The expectation that schools should be evaluated in terms of how well they are preparing youth for work appeals to the logic that schools exist primarily to channel people into the world of work. This assessment, though, ignores the reality that formal education is about much more than job training, and is oriented also to education in a broad sense. Schooling is emphasized throughout this book as a complex, often contradictory set of arrangements that encompass personal development and moral and aesthetic capacities that are not necessarily governed by labour markets and workplaces. It is important, in these respects, to consider as problematic the extent to which, as well as how, schools contribute to work preparation, and how these forms of preparation are related to competing educational objectives.

It is important to acknowledge as well that significant social and economic transformations are changing how we understand, talk about, and experience these relationships. Three interrelated discourses that appear prominently in contemporary accounts of school–work interconnections—as represented in the concepts of lifelong learning, life transitions, and employability—draw attention to the magnitude of these changes. **Lifelong learning** highlights the extension of education and learning activities beyond the basic or conventional school years to encompass formal, informal, and continuing learning activities in various sites from early childhood throughout the life course. The related concept of **transitions** points to the increased likelihood for people to combine work and learning or to move across different education, training, and work situations over the course of their lives, as opposed to making a linear shift from initial education to a long-term career. **Employability** also signifies the dynamic conditions produced by the rapid pace of change in jobs, technologies, and knowledge production and application. In contrast with an understanding of the contributions of schooling to 'employment' (with regard to linkages between specific educational requirements and specific jobs or careers), the notion of 'employability' (understood as the capacity to maintain attachment to the labour market) highlights the mix of core and specialized skills and aptitudes that people will require in order to adapt to rapidly changing social and economic environments.

The following discussion addresses these issues by examining, initially, the kinds of contributions schools do make to work preparation, including (1) the granting of credentials; (2) curricular knowledge relevant to participation in the labour force; (3) the relationship between work and organizational features of schooling that are part of the hidden curriculum; (4) social features of the hidden curriculum related to individual characteristics and interpersonal relationships; and (5) general contributions that schools make to the economy as mass markets and workplaces. It will be seen that a substantial degree of correspondence exists between educational structures and processes, on the one hand, and economic productivity and work training, on the other.

However, there are at least three important limitations to the view that schools should be more responsive to requirements for work preparation. (1) Historical evidence demonstrates that mass public schooling, from its inception, was not intended to be governed narrowly by jobs or economic considerations. (2) Continuing debate and alternative views identify schooling as an undertaking that must be responsive to diverse educational objectives beyond training for work. (3) There are barriers to the extent to which schooling can and should be the most effective institution for labour market preparation. The next two sections discuss each of these dimensions in turn, before attention is directed to more detailed consideration of how relationships between schooling and work are changing in Canada and in other countries.

THE CONTRIBUTIONS OF SCHOOLING TO WORK AND THE ECONOMY

Formal educational institutions make several direct and indirect contributions to labour markets and wider economic processes. Among these are: credentialling; explicit employment preparation through the teaching of knowledge and skills; implicit employment preparation through the establishment of the structure and discipline of work; the channelling of students into social and work roles; and the role of education itself as both workplace and market.

Credentials

One of the central functions of schooling is to bestow diplomas, certificates, degrees, and other credentials upon successful completion of particular educational programs and levels of study. Many hiring and promotion decisions, as well as eligibility requirements for certain jobs, are based on specified types of educational achievement or credentials earned through education and training programs. Educational credentials become relevant to employment decisions in different ways. In some instances, possession of a credential implies that the individual has acquired particular kinds of knowledge or met standards of rigour deemed to be essential for a job. In many other cases, educational achievement is used as a screening mechanism to limit the number of qualified applicants seeking particular jobs, regardless of whether the education or training is directly relevant to the work positions. These issues are discussed below, briefly, and developed more fully later in this chapter in the context of debates about work skills.

Workplace Skills and Knowledge

Another important function of education and training programs is to transmit knowledge and skills related to employment situations and the workplace. This knowledge includes information that may be necessary for specific occupations, as well as general know-how considered valuable by employers and that therefore makes a person employable. The role and outcomes of educational institutions have gained increasing prominence in conjunction with the attention given to the rise of post-industrial society or knowledge-based economies for their contributions both to the production of new knowledge and to the cultivation of knowledge workers.

The most direct and apparent relationship between formal schooling and jobs tends to be in vocational training, certification, and professional degree programs required for entry into specific occupations such as welding, hairdressing, law, and medicine. These kinds of programs are organized in accordance with technical specifications and requirements for licensing or certification deemed critical for practice in the specified field. Outside of these areas, other courses, subjects, and programs are usually seen to have a looser connection with jobs, providing either a general background in an area or offering fundamental knowledge desired by employers, beginning with basic competencies like the ability to read, write, and compute through to more advanced, abstract, or specialized types of knowledge and skills.

The connections among technological development, societal advancement, and educational expansion have been articulated most powerfully through *human capital theory* and related strands of sociological and economic analysis focused on understanding the rise of post-industrial societies. Human capital theory regards education as an investment in human resources that offers potentially valuable returns for individuals and society as a whole. Economic development in advanced industrial and post-industrial societies requires not only highly developed material resources, but also sufficiently skilled and motivated individuals. A society's ability to compete successfully in a highly advanced economic environment depends on the extent to which it is able to produce trained, innovative personnel who can contribute to scientific and technological development.

Within sociology, **technological functionalism** influenced the logic of human capital orientations by emphasizing the impact of changing technologies on educational requirements. Social progress, defined in terms of the advancement of technical and scientific expertise, demands an increasingly qualified and specialized population. Consistent with liberal and functionalist theories of stratification outlined in Chapter 2, technological functionalism views formal educational requirements, first, as a means to disseminate socially important knowledge and skills and, second, as a mechanism to ensure the social placement of individuals on the basis of merit. The theory attributes the massive expansion of public education in the twentieth century primarily to technological change, so that increasing numbers of people are achieving higher levels of education while curricula are becoming increasingly more sophisticated and demanding (Clark, 1962). Educational advancement, from this perspective, is necessary to keep pace with and advance technological change as a stimulus for further economic development (Bell, 1973).

Human capital theory and its variants have drawn attention to the expansion of formal opportunities for social advancement, especially those determined by credentials accomplished through schooling, as opposed to more informal mechanisms of sponsorship and restricted mobility that supposedly prevail in non-industrialized nations. A stratified but meritocratic social order, in which individuals achieve jobs and rewards on the basis of merit or competence, is deemed essential for a society whose welfare and progress depend on the skills, technical expertise, and commitment of its members. While these theories were fashioned primarily in North America to highlight the emerging economic competition from highly developed nations in Europe, they have gained subsequent impetus in conjunction with the advancement of technologies in Japan and other Asian nations. They have been applied more recently to the analysis of economic expansion, high-skilled labour, and the growth of a middle class in less developed parts of the world, in part to justify investment in these regions and in part to highlight new competitors seen as potential threats to North American domination.

As these observations suggest, there is much more than theoretical significance to human capital theory. Governments and employers in Canada and other advanced industrial nations and rapidly developing nations have drawn upon concepts and research influenced by human capital approaches as part of the rhetoric and as an active component in labour market development strategies, including massive programs to develop scientific innovation and knowledge transfer. In the latter part of the twentieth century, curricula were reorganized to emphasize mathematics and sciences in elementary and secondary schools, new community colleges and technical institutes were built across Canada and the United States, and government expenditures on post-secondary education increased substantially. The influence of human capital theory remains very much alive through contemporary reforms and ideologies that emphasize competitiveness, human resource development, and the need to match skills with jobs. Business and government leaders draw on such arguments to promote programs to retrain workers, for example, or initiatives to increase productivity in the workplace.

Human capital and technological functionalist arguments underlie many discussions of the emergence of a 'new economy' based on learning and knowledge related to rapid developments in information and communications technology (Drucker, 1993). These discussions emphasize the imperative for all people to further their education in order to adjust to and work in post-industrial societies. However, they are most focused on high-level knowledge, sometimes termed the 'Triple Helix' of university–industry–government synthesis to signify the revolutionary nature of such developments (Leydesdorff and Etkowitz, 1997). While such collaborations are not new, their scale and scope have accelerated dramatically as government agencies and industries, along with participants in various other community groups, engage in strategic partnerships with educational workers and institutions. Education institutions at all levels are involved in these kinds of initiatives, but such activity is concentrated most intensively at the post-secondary level, particularly as university-based researchers are teamed with partners from other sectors in various ways, including major collaborative research projects, centres of excellence, high-tech parks, and innovation clusters (such as California's Silicon Valley or Canada's Ottawa Valley) devoted to develop new technologies, applications, products, patents, and ideas.

These arrangements have produced several exciting innovations and prospects, but they are not without their difficulties. Many analysts dispute the relatively optimistic assessments of relations between schooling and work advanced by proponents of human capital theory and post-industrial society, while other criticism is directed to several dangers inherent in trends that subordinate education to economic priorities. The first issue—challenges to the assertion that increasing education necessarily contributes to improved job prospects—is discussed briefly here and explored in more detail later in this chapter; the second point, which addresses the limitations of reducing educational practices to economic factors, is the focus of the next section and is revisited in Chapter 8.

Among the more problematic aspects of human capital theories are claims about the levels of education actually required for work and the specific connections between attributes and skills developed through education and those performed on the job. Several factors other than required skill levels or technical requirements can account for levels of education or training associated with particular jobs. Education often serves as a screening mechanism to narrow large pools of potential job prospects or to 'signal' to employers those candidates who are likely to have particular attributes and characteristics regardless of forms of training actually needed for the job.

Collins (1971, 2000) offers one of the most pointed critiques of technical and human capital explanations of educational expansion, positing an alternative account that highlights the persistence of *credential inflation*. The dramatic rise in educational attainment throughout the population of highly developed nations can be understood in terms of competition for desired positions as people seek ever greater levels of formal education for entry into job markets in which there is no clear logic between what they learn and the knowledge they need to perform on the job. Despite progressive increases in both the overall levels of education throughout the population and those required for entry into many occupations or jobs, there is often a relatively loose connection between technical requirements associated with particular credentials and skills or tasks performed in the workplace. Consequently, while much recent attention has been focused on the need for workers to gain higher levels of skills and education for work in a knowledge-based economy, many labour force participants reveal that they possess more knowledge and skills than they need for the jobs available to them (Livingstone, 2004).

Before examining empirical evidence pertinent to these contending visions of the relationships among education, skill, and work requirements, and considering the implications these trends have for different groups of learners and workers, it is instructive to acknowledge that the rhetoric to reform education and training in Canada to meet employers' demands for certain kinds of labour is not new. The following passage calling for the introduction of technical and industrial training in the schools was issued 120 years ago in the *Report of the Royal Commission on the Relations of Capital and Labour in Canada* (1889: 119), but it bears a striking similarity to contemporary demands for educational reform in the face of global competitiveness:

> To be successful competitors with foreign manufacturers we must have workmen as
> highly skilled in their respective callings as those with whom they have to compete.
> To do so, the same facilities must be provided to give the cultivation and training
> necessary to acquire skill and knowledge as the workmen of other countries have.

Box 7.4 Credential Inflation and Credential 'Creep'

The rising number of students pursuing post-secondary credentials and the uncertain job market are contributing to desires and pressures for many students to extend their educations even further, as Bourgon (2008: A4) reports:

MAs Are Becoming the New BA

Enrolment in master's and graduate programs is increasing across the country, leaving many to wonder if their meagre undergraduate degree will be enough to land them the perfect job. According to Statistics Canada, in 2001 over 31,000 students earned their master's degree, up 9 per cent from 2000. It was the seventh year in a row that the number had risen. . . .

There was a time when earning your undergrad put you ahead of those with just a high school diploma.

With the rise of those who graduate with an undergrad, many students see the master's as a way of making themselves more employable upon graduation. 'There was no great yearning for me', said [Andrea] Warren [who is now studying for her master's in Ethnomusicology at the University of Toronto] of her decision to go to grad school. 'It was more of a "Well, what am I going to do now?"' Warren said that she doesn't have a clear vision of what she wants to do with her life, but she knows that to go further in the realm of music she'll need a master's degree.

'Thirty is the new twenty', said Christine Moore, a career counsellor at Dalhousie University in Halifax. She added that there's no pressure for young people to settle down with a job while in their twenties. 'Grad school is the new phenomenon.'

'Credential creep . . .'

Credential creep is the phenomenon that puts the MA in the same position the undergrad was in [during] the 1980s. It also means that one day the Ph.D. might turn into the undergrad degree and MA of today. . . .

'You have to connect the dots between the value of the degree and your future', said Moore, noting that undergraduate students learn skills in their undergrad, like research and organization, that are transferable and that make them employable.

The Almighty Job

Getting a job after graduation is easier said than done. Many employers need to weed out the good applicants from the dozens of students that all apply for the same job. Distinguishing by degree is a quick and simple way of doing that.

Similar statements have been made repeatedly over the years, perhaps an indication that schools have not responded well to demands that they become more relevant to employers' needs. Despite this impression, though, periodic curricular reforms have been justified by their contributions to changing job markets. Sutherland (1976: 155ff.) documents how schools introduced subjects such as agriculture, industrial arts, domestic science, bookkeeping, and other forms of **vocational and technical education** following vigorous pressure for change from various lobby groups in the nineteenth and early twentieth centuries. More recently, courses in computers and natural sciences have been introduced or modified to keep pace with technological developments and demands for highly skilled scientific workers. Table 7.1, which outlines some of the most important subjects introduced into school curricula over the past two centuries, demonstrates the periodic introduction of vocational subjects into programs initially dominated by academic subjects.

Despite periodic curricular modifications and innovations designed to reflect vocational and employment concerns, educators have tended to oppose the idea of turning schools into training factories. In some cases, vocational and career-oriented courses were introduced more for the pragmatic consideration of gaining employers' support for the school system than for enthusiasm over the academic or curricular merits of the subjects. Vocational and technical subjects continue to remain distinct from core areas of the curriculum in schools with academic programs. Moreover, there are often considerable discrepancies between the formal listing or presentation of a subject in a curriculum description and the actual teaching of that subject in the classroom. These issues, as will be discussed later in the chapter, make the relationship between schooling and work preparation more problematic than it might otherwise appear to be.

Table 7.1   Summary of Major Changes and Additions to Curricula in Canadian Elementary Schools

1825–50:	reading, writing, arithmetic, religion (Bible reading), needlework, cooking
1850–75:	grammar, geography
1875–1900:	kindergarten classes, literature, history, music, drawing
1900–25:	nature study, art, manual training, physical training, hygiene, household science
1925–50:	social studies, science, industrial arts, home economics, health, physical education, enterprise, languages, phonics
1950–75:	French and French immersion, business and commercial education
1975–2000:	whole language instruction, language arts, computer studies, technological education, Native studies, technical vocational education, hospitality and tourism, life transitions
2000–current:	wellness, co-op learning and work experience, literacy and new technology education, media literacy; discovering the workplace; skills for success in high school; environment and resource management

Sources: Phillips (1957: 433); Katz (1969: 67); various provincial curriculum guides.

The Discipline and Structure of Work

Beyond the teaching of vocational and career-oriented knowledge or subjects, formal education contributes to labour force participation in many indirect ways. Previous chapters have shown that student school experience is shaped at least as much by everyday practices, unwritten rules, and informal expectations as by the overt transmission of knowledge and skills. This hidden curriculum is defined by Apple (2004: 13) as 'the tacit teaching to students of norms, values, and dispositions that goes on simply by their living and coping with the institutional expectations and routines of schools day in and day out for a number of years.'

The 'expectations and routines' that constitute the hidden curriculum—in terms of both the organizational and social characteristics of schooling—are heavily influenced by work. The spatial and temporal structure within most educational institutions has a great deal in common with nineteenth-century factory organization. Physically, schools tend to be arranged as a series of box-like classrooms or special-function areas (gyms, libraries, art rooms, resource centres) oriented to regimentation and control. There are also strong parallels between schooling and industrial work organization in terms of models of supervision and assessment, the division of classes by grade and subject, streaming within grades or subject areas, and the hierarchy of authority that prevails both administratively and in the conduct of classes.

Workplace discipline also is reflected in the regulation of school time. The day is broken into distinct periods, usually signified by the ringing of bells. Students' bodily functions, including eating, are directed by timetables and school rules, and pupils frequently are required to seek permission to use the washroom or get a drink of water. These arrangements are structured in such a way that students come to internalize routines associated with the day-to-day patterns of life in many workplaces.

Channelling Students into Social and Work Roles

The hidden curriculum is oriented to individual as well as organizational characteristics. Writers working within both traditional (e.g., Jackson, 1968; Dreeben, 1968) and critical (e.g., Bowles and Gintis, 1976; Willis, 1977) perspectives agree that much of the social reproduction accomplished within schooling occurs through the cultivation of dispositions and attributes necessary to function in contemporary society (Lynch, 1989). This analysis stresses that what is important is not so much the specific knowledge required for any particular job or social position as the general preparedness and ability to meet expectations that are attached to out-of-school roles. Through their schooling, students encounter circumstances such as competition, success and failure, deference to authority, deferral of gratification, and other situations that prepare them for later social experiences. They must also develop an awareness of how the world is structured and how it operates in order to ease their transition into work and other social settings.

Researchers have become increasingly concerned to adopt approaches that can help to make sense of these complex relationships. As observed in Chapter 2, the framework developed by Pierre Bourdieu (1977, 1984) to integrate interactions among individuals, social backgrounds, and social structures through the analysis of concepts like 'habitus', 'cultural capital', and other forms of inequality has been especially influential. Lesley Andres Bellamy (1993, 1994) adopts Bourdieu's framework to analyze how Canadian students make choices about their post-high school futures. *Cultural capital*, understood in conjunction with economic capital and other social resources, refers to the attitudes, behaviours, preferences, and general sense of how things operate that individuals must possess to be socially successful. Constituted in this way, cultural capital is neither neutral nor equally accessible to all social groups. Andres Bellamy (1994: 122) observes that, for Bourdieu, 'the culture that is transmitted and rewarded by the educational system reflects the culture of the dominant class.' This places students who possess the prior knowledge or sensitivity to the qualities that enable them to meet educational expectations in an advantaged position in comparison with students who lack cultural capital. The related concept of **habitus** refers to a 'system of dispositions' produced by our past experiences, which are embedded in our perceptions and interact with new social circumstances. It operates as a kind of internal code that affects how we approach and understand everyday practices.

Using data from interviews and surveys involving educational participants in diverse Canadian contexts, several researchers (e.g., Andres Bellamy, 1993; Andres and Looker, 2001; Taylor, 2005; Lehmann, 2007) demonstrate how educational institutions are implicated in complex processes of decision-making, actions, and organizational characteristics in such a way that students view their choices about work and post-secondary studies as an unproblematic part of their normal progression from family life. Schools, in this way, contribute to labour force reproduction by fostering dispositions regarding success, failure, and future plans even if they are not directly involved in job training and employment selection. This insight complements the findings of other influential studies, such as those of Willis (1977), Anisef et al. (2000), and Lareau and Horvat (1999), which demonstrate that school organization, social background, and students' lived circumstances affect one another in such a way that students often 'choose' predictable futures without being directly pushed into those positions.

Education as Workplace and Market

Schools and other educational settings serve a purpose beyond preparing students for work in that substantial economic activity takes place within them and through them—educational institutions themselves are workplaces as well as markets in which billions of dollars are spent annually on goods and services.

Large numbers of teachers, administrators, maintenance and support staff, purchasing agents, and other personnel are employed in the education business. As the previous chapter on teachers has emphasized, education workers are subject to many of the same dynamics that operate within wage employment in general, even though educational work also contains unique characteristics related to educational processes. Besides their work with students or educational clients, educational workers engage in economic production insofar as they develop products, knowledge, and skills that may be of benefit to particular employers, corporations, or social interests. While this activity is most evident at the post-secondary level, where faculty members and other researchers are expected to cultivate and disseminate knowledge, classrooms and education systems at all levels are open to experimentation and innovation, the benefits of which may extend beyond the education system.

Education also has economic significance as a site responsible for the purchase of massive quantities of goods and services. Given its size and, in some instances, centralized decision-making, which leads to the adoption and purchase of textbooks, course materials, technologies, and supplies for entire school districts, post-secondary institutions, or even provinces, the educational market is a highly lucrative one. Educational institutions also stimulate economic activities in other ways, beyond their importance for the consumption of instructional resources. The construction of educational facilities, especially during peak growth periods such as the 1960s and 1970s, has had a significant economic impact on communities. Even when few new schools or universities are being built, employment is created through the maintenance and repair of educational facilities, as well as in their day-to-day operation. The food and beverage industry is supported directly by school cafeterias, while there tends to be a concentration of restaurants, bars, bookstores, and entertainment and service operations around universities and community colleges. Large corporations have found schools and universities such lucrative markets that they have entered into sometimes controversial agreements to provide funding for scholarships, sports, and other programs in exchange for exclusive agreements to sell their products. The economic spinoff from education is also important in other respects. The computer industry, for instance, has pursued the educational market aggressively in part because it recognized that many students and parents will purchase hardware or software packages compatible with new technologies employed in the classroom.

The role of business and industry in the classroom has long been debated by educators. As education systems are confronted with declining levels of government funding, prospects for reliance on materials and services that are donated, purchased in bulk, or provided at low cost from corporations and other external agencies are likely to increase. Many corporations introduce curricular materials or sponsor school teams and events, such as essay-writing competitions, that may produce a favourable climate or corporate image at the same time as potential recruits or ideas are being harnessed for corporate objectives (Apple, 2004: 143–4; Regnier and MacLean, 1987). While corporate partnerships have promoted some areas of innovation and access to resources that would not otherwise be available to support students, programs, and research in public educational institutions, many educators and observers point to the growing danger that reliance on corporate bodies and fiscally driven planning are skewing educational priorities.

Thus, some have argued, basic educational services directed towards a wide range of learning needs and community interests will be sacrificed to more glamorous initiatives based on narrow and unrepresentative agendas (Axelrod, 2002; Currie and Newson, 1998; Robertson, 1998).

Clearly, in a growing number of dimensions, education is highly integrated with economic activity. Through direct labour force preparation and participation, as well as through more general involvement in the production and consumption of particular commodities, education can be considered an industry essential for economic advancement of both individuals and societies. Nonetheless, considerable tension exists between the view that schooling should become guided more fully by economic considerations and the position that education must remain oriented to other principles than commercial ones.

DISCONTINUITIES IN RELATIONSHIPS AMONG SCHOOLING, WORK, AND ECONOMIC ACTIVITY

While the evidence presented so far suggests that there is considerable merit to the idea that schooling has a central role to play in the reproduction of the labour force and in the stimulation of economic activity in general, it is necessary to address some of the limitations to this relationship. In particular, schooling has been responsive to competing priorities that place emphasis on personal and social development as well as economic factors.

Education and Morality

Mass public schooling, from its inception, was not strictly concerned with labour force preparation. Early education officials cautioned against the dangers of reducing schooling to its economic functions. Writing in the early 1880s, for instance, New Brunswick's chief superintendent of education contended that 'The primary function of the public school should not be subverted to provide technical instruction'; rather, 'the public school is primarily an agency for the general education of all classes of youth', where such basic training consists of the elements of physical health, intelligence, and character (cited in Lawr and Gidney, 1973: 93–4). As Table 7.1 indicates, the core areas of the curriculum have been concentrated in academic areas (such as reading, writing, mathematics, languages, sciences, history, and geography) or subjects oriented to personal development (health, physical education, drawing, and music) rather than workforce training. Certainly, each of these areas contributes in a general way to labour force development, particularly through the provision of basic skills, discipline, and orientations to work required for the performance of wage labour. However, social and political objectives, at least as much as economic ones, figured prominently in the origins and rise of mass public schooling.

In many ways, the Church rather than the factory provided the inspiration for a formal system of public education, although not in a direct way. Order, discipline, and habit may have been amenable to industrial work, but they were more explicitly promoted as essential attributes for individuals attuned to life in a new social and political order. Corrigan, Curtis, and Lanning (1987: 21, 24) argue, for instance, that early school reformers were concerned with 'the creation of particular kinds of political selves' in the form of individuals who would engage in social relations through 'willing' or 'cheerful obedience'. The school's mission, like that of the Church in this regard, was to produce morally regulated individuals. Such morality, however, was to be produced in the public realm, with adherence to the bourgeois state rather than to any particular religious denomination. Across Canada, legislation concerning the establishment and maintenance of public schools addressed this objective by the creation of highly centralized provincial educational administrations, although room was allowed for diverse community input through delegation of many responsibilities to local and district school boards (Tomkins, 1977: 11–14).

The location of educational authority within the state was intended to counter the overt influence of groups considered to have narrowly defined interests, including religious denominations as well as business and industry. Industrial leaders were often indifferent to or had little regard for public schooling. During the rise of the factory system, especially into the late 1860s in the more industrialized areas of central and Atlantic Canada, schools were perceived as intrusive to employers who relied on children as a low-cost labour force. The main value of schooling, from this point of view, was as a vehicle for social control to keep idle children from engaging in crime or other mischief on the streets when they were not working. Ironically, much of this 'idleness' was a consequence of children's decision to leave schools that did not provide them with sufficient job-specific skills (Houston, 1982: 139–40). Education authorities were sensitive to these trends, sometimes seeking reforms intended to win the support of employers for educational causes, but they continued to ensure that schooling could not be reduced to any kind of crude vocational training.

The Right to Learn

Public education, since its origins, has continued to be driven by competing forces that are not restricted to training for work or other economic purposes. Carnoy and Levin (1985: 14) point out that schools are driven by the contradictory dynamics of what they call a **capitalist imperative** and a **democratic imperative**. They contend that, 'On the one hand, schools have traditionally reproduced the unequal, hierarchical relations of the nuclear family and capitalist workplace; on the other, they have represented the expansion of economic opportunity for subordinate groups and the extension of basic human rights.'

These dynamics themselves are subject to debate and contestation. Included within the capitalist imperative, for instance, are employers' demands for appropriately disciplined and skilled workers and working-class demands for education and training that will result in meaningful, well-paid employment (Livingstone, 1987: 62–3). The issue of who benefits from education extends beyond class lines, encompassing demands for opportunity and representation from various groups, including women, racial and ethnic minorities, residents of rural areas and remote communities, and many others. Competing interests are reflected in debates over major issues, including what is taught in schools and how extensive the provision of public education should be, as well as more specific concerns such as the length and timing of the school year or what kinds of reading materials are included in school libraries.

A brief look at the major objectives of schools and education systems reveals how diverse educational aims are. The *Report of the Royal Commission on Education* for British Columbia (1988: 68) observes that, for more than a century, extending their central mandates as 'agencies of learning':

> schools have been viewed as multi-purpose institutions whose endeavours go far beyond educational functions—various public elements at various times have seen schools as agencies for civic development, as laboratories for democratic practice, as institutions to sustain a common culture and common values, as places to remediate the behaviour of wayward youngsters, and as centres for community life. Within the public imagination, the potential of schools has sometimes seemed boundless; we have turned to schools to reduce crime, improve public health, inspire patriotism, minimize civil strife, eradicate prejudice, promote social justice, set children on the 'right road', and, in the long run, even contribute to international understanding.

The degree to which these varied objectives are given priority varies over time and place as well as among social groups. Coulter (1993: 71, 81) reports that Canadian youth in the 1930s expressed serious concern about unemployment and skill development, but by the mid-1940s a national survey of youth revealed that job preparation was ranked below both 'helping to think clearly on the problems of life' and 'helping to understand modern society and the responsibilities of a citizen' as key purposes of schooling. Nearly three decades later, a national survey conducted by the Canadian Education Association indicated that the top two reasons for schooling were the attainment of self-satisfaction and the goal 'to get along better with people at all levels of society', while only 18 per cent of respondents suggested that the primary reason for schooling was 'to get better jobs' (Lauwerys, 1973: 14). In 1999, over half of respondents to a national survey indicated that schools needed to devote greater attention to 'the basics' such as reading and writing skills rather than computer skills, whereas a slight majority felt that youth should be encouraged to learn specific trades or skills in community colleges instead of pursuing a general university education (Angus Reid Group, 1999: 5, 17). Results of more recent polls have echoed public concern that universities are not fully equipped to meet labour market needs in particular industries or regions despite the general contributions made by post-secondary education to employability (Strategic Council, 2007: 5).

One pattern that emerges in surveys of this nature is that job preparation and training gain force as priorities in times of high unemployment and uncertainty or transitions in labour markets. This helps to explain why these issues have once again moved to the forefront in recent debates over educational reform. Employers' interest in having a supply of adequately qualified labour converges with individuals' expectations that education will lead them to a stable employment future at a time when most people have been exposed to harsh realities associated with occupational restructuring and the threat or experience of joblessness.

Job Training in the Schools

Despite the force of recent arguments that schooling should be doing more to help prepare individuals for the labour market, the question remains as to how effective schools could be even if job training were to become their primary orientation. As currently structured, formal education faces several impediments to directing and placing students into jobs. Considerable changes occur in personal aptitudes, labour markets, employment needs, and technologies over the normal period of 12–13 years that it takes an individual to proceed from kindergarten to high school graduation. Even if it could be assumed that schools were vocational in nature (thereby ignoring the varied purposes of public education), it is doubtful whether they would have the resources and ability to meet labour market requirements, particularly in a context in which jobs, technologies, and skills are continually being redefined and reorganized. Several critical questions would need to be addressed:

- Should people be educated for self-employment or wage labour and, if the latter, would major corporations or small businesses prevail?
- Which skills would be common to all pupils and which would be developed within particular educational streams and at what levels?
- Would individual or community interests be outweighed by employers' interests?
- What kinds of credentials and expectations would mesh with prospects for employment after the completion of formal education?

Many of these issues are currently at the centre of both public policy discussions and academic analysis of work–school linkages. The notion of 'transitions' has replaced a long-standing sense of a linear transition process as people move through their life courses from family to school to work to retirement (Ashton and Lowe, 1991: 1–2). The rethinking of school–work linkages is given focus by emphasis on lifelong learning, innovations in areas such as adult and continuing education, and the rapid expansion of alternative forms and sites of educational delivery. European research draws attention to a 'new life course' dynamic in which individuals are required to become increasingly more self-reflexive and strategically adaptive as conventional social roles and expectations are destabilized by constant social, cultural, and economic changes (Vinken, 2007). Given these concerns, discussion turns in the next section to contemporary changes in work as they pertain to education.

EDUCATION AND WORK IN CANADA

The Canadian labour force and the kinds of jobs that workers have been engaged in have changed significantly over the past few decades. As shown in Table 7.2, shortly after the end of World War II, one-quarter of all workers were involved in agricultural work and nearly one-third were blue-collar workers (secondary sector), while fewer than two out of five were classified as white-collar workers (what is now called the tertiary or service sector). By 2006, however, only about 2.1 per cent of workers remained as part of the agricultural labour force and the proportion of blue-collar workers was less than one in five, but over three out of every four workers were employed in the service sector. The single largest industry category, identified as 'service', encompasses seven major subcategories—education, health care, social services, information, culture and recreation, accommodation, and food services—each of which is larger than the total number of workers in primary-sector industries. This has meant, at least in a general way, that types of work that typically require formal educational credentials have become increasingly central to the labour force as a whole.

In the same way that the occupational classifications of workers have changed, the nature of work and the composition of the labour force have become much more diverse. New technologies, services, product lines, and forms of work organization have altered the jobs we do and the way we work. The transformation of working arrangements, in turn, affects and is shaped by shifting patterns of employment and demands for distinct kinds of workers. Canada's paid labour force, which at the time of Confederation consisted predominantly of men of British and French origin, has become increasingly feminized as well as more racially and ethnically heterogeneous. Today, most men and women, regardless of age, marital status, and social origin, are labour force participants. At the same time, the changing occupational structure has meant that the prospects for and future of work are highly uncertain for substantial proportions of the population. This is particularly true for youth who are about to enter into the workforce as well as for persons with disabilities or of minority group status who have historically experienced marginalized labour force participation.

Important social and economic transformations have been mirrored in the changing relationship between schooling and work. In the nineteenth century, schooling had little importance for the majority of the population except as a brief point of contact to gain basic reading, writing, and social skills. Other than for the select few persons who entered professions, such as medicine, law, teaching, and the clergy, education bore little formal relation to the kinds of jobs most people worked at, such as farming, fishing, mining, manufacturing, and commercial work. The primary importance of schooling was in its service as a socially stabilizing force, keeping young people occupied, off the streets, and under public surveillance. As we have seen, however, the importance of formal education increased through the twentieth century to become a major conduit for entry into the labour market.

Table 7.2 Employment by Industry, Selected Years, Canada, 1946–2006 (% of total)

Industry, by Sector	1946	1951	1956	1961	1966	1971	1976	1981	1986	1991	1996	2001	2006
Primary													
Agriculture	25.4	18.4	13.9	11.2	7.4	6.2	4.9	4.4	3.9	3.5	3.1	2.2	2.1
Forestry	1.8	2.3	2.1	1.4	1.1	0.9	0.7	0.7	0.6	0.5	0.6	0.5	0.4
Fishing, trapping	0.6	0.6	0.4	0.3	0.4	0.3	0.2	0.3	0.3	0.4	0.2	0.2	0.2
Mining, oil/gas extraction	1.6	1.5	2.1	1.3	1.7	1.6	1.5	1.9	1.6	1.4	1.3	1.2	1.5
Primary Total	29.4	22.8	18.5	14.2	10.5	9.0	7.4	7.3	6.4	5.8	5.3	4.1	4.1
Secondary													
Manufacturing	26.0	26.5	25.7	24.0	24.4	22.2	20.3	19.3	17.3	15.1	14.3	14.9	12.8
Construction	4.8	6.8	7.4	6.2	7.0	6.1	6.7	5.9	5.4	5.7	5.3	5.5	6.5
Secondary Total	30.8	33.3	33.1	30.2	31.4	28.3	27.0	25.3	22.7	20.8	19.6	20.4	19.3
Tertiary													
Transportation, communications	7.4	7.8	7.8	8.1	7.6	7.7	7.5	7.1	6.7	6.3	5.0	5.2	4.9
Public utilities	0.7	1.0	1.2	1.2	1.1	1.1	1.2	1.2	1.0	1.1	0.9	0.8	0.7
Trade	12.3	14.1	15.8	16.9	16.5	16.5	17.3	17.1	18.0	17.6	15.6	15.8	16.0
Finance, real estate	2.7	3.0	3.5	3.9	4.3	4.8	5.3	5.5	5.7	6.1	6.4	5.9	6.3
Service*	16.8	18.0	20.3	19.5	22.7	26.2	27.1	29.6	32.6	35.4	41.1	42.6	43.6
Public administration	—	—	—	5.9	5.9	6.5	7.2	7.0	6.9	6.8	6.0	5.3	5.1
Tertiary Total	39.8	43.9	48.5	55.5	58.0	62.7	65.6	67.5	70.9	73.3	75.0	75.5	76.6
Total (%)	100	100	100.1	99.9	99.9	100	100	100.1	100	99.9	99.9	99.9	100
Total number (000s)	4,666	5,097	5,585	6,055	7,121	7,958	9,776	11,398	12,095	12,916	13,421	14,946	16,484

*Includes public administration until 1961.

Sources: For 1946–91: Bernier (1996); data for 1996–2002: *Labour Force Historical Review* (2006), Statistics Canada CS71-0004/2006-MRC.

Box 7.5 Employment Prospects in the Knowledge Economy

Increased competitive pressures and rapid development of new technologies have created a volatile economic climate for many sectors. As new job categories and businesses are created or expand, others have disappeared, fuelling demands for higher education while creating considerable uncertainty with respect to employment prospects. These trends are illustrated in the analysis, by Kanagarajah (2006: 7–9), of employment by firms in high-, medium-, and low-knowledge sectors (defined with reference to ratios that take into account proportions of research and development personnel, workers with post-secondary education, and positions in natural sciences, engineering and mathematics, and professional and technology-related fields):

Of all firms that were created during the 1990s, roughly one-quarter ceased to operate within the first two years. . . . Just over one-third survived 5 years or more and only one-fifth were still in operation after 10 years. The survival rates of firms improved tremendously after the mid-1990s. Those that were created during the second half of the decade were more likely to keep operating than their counterparts born in the early 1990s. This was due partly to the economic recovery that followed the 1990–1992 recession.

On average, the number of businesses grew by about 9,300 each year during the 1990s. This was the difference between the average of 138,100 firms that began operations each year and the average of about 128,800 a year that went out of business. Businesses employing 100 to 499 workers experienced the strongest growth.

In 2003, just over one million businesses were operating in Canada, up 12 per cent from a decade earlier. . . . In 2003, only 0.2 per cent of firms employed 500 or more employees, but they represented 43 per cent of total employment. The vast majority (92 per cent) of companies employed fewer than 20 workers, and they accounted for 21 per cent of total employment.

Strongest Growth in High-Knowledge Sector

Most of the growth in firms between 1991 and 2003 occurred in the services-producing sector. During this time, the number of businesses in this sector increased 15 per cent, while it stagnated in the goods-producing sector, increasing by only 1 per cent. Within the services-producing sector, the number of firms in high-knowledge industries nearly doubled (+96 per cent) from 32,000 to 62,000 firms, while the number in medium-knowledge industries rose 18 per cent from 283,000 to 334,000 firms. The number of firms did not change in low-knowledge industries within the services-producing sector. Examples of industries in the high-knowledge category include high technology and bio-technology industries.

Table 7.3 Percentage Change in the Number of Businesses, by Knowledge Industry, Canada, 1991 to 2003

Knowledge-based Industries	Goods	Services	All
Low knowledge	−10	0	−3
Medium knowledge	6	18	14
High knowledge	25	96	78
All	1	15	12

Source: Statistics Canada, 'Business Dynamics in Canada', 2003. Catalogue no. 61-534, released 10 March 2006, p. 7. Available at: http://www.statcan.gc.ca/pub/61-534-x/61-534-x2006001-eng.pdf.

In the goods-producing sector, the number of firms in high-knowledge industries also grew at a much faster pace than in other industries. As a result, high-knowledge industries experienced by far the fastest growth between 1991 and 2003. Overall, their number rose a solid 78 per cent, more than five times the rate of 14 per cent among medium-knowledge industries.

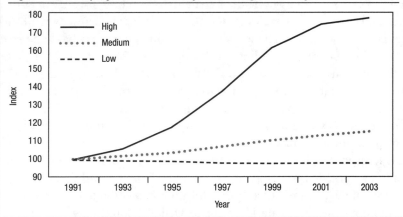

Figure 7.3 Employment Growth by Knowledge Industry, 1991–2003

Source: Statistics Canada, 'Business Dynamics in Canada', 2003. Catalogue no. 61-534, released 10 March 2006, p. 8. Available at: http://www.statcan.gc.ca/pub/61-534-x/61-534-x2006001-eng.pdf.

Overall, low-knowledge firms fared even worse, as their number fell 3 per cent during the 12-year period. Even though business growth was very strong in the high-knowledge industry, this sector actually accounted for only 30 per cent of the net increase of 112,000 firms between 1991 and 2003. The reason is that relatively few firms were operating in this sector at the beginning of the 1990s. In fact, almost half (53 per cent) of the net increase in the number of businesses originated in the medium-knowledge industry. This occurred mainly among small firms . . . .

Just under one-half of firms in the high-knowledge industries survived five years or more.
Chances of survival for firms varied by industry; it was the highest for those that started operating in the high-knowledge industries. Between 1992 and 1997, 46 per cent of these companies survived five years or more. In contrast, 39 per cent of medium-knowledge firms lasted for five years or more, as did 33 per cent of low-knowledge industries.

Source: Statistics Canada, 'Business Dynamics in Canada', 2003, Catalogue no. 61-534, released 10 March 2006. Available at: http://www.statcan.gc.ca/pub/61-534-x/61-534-x2006001-eng.pdf.

In recent years, the social and economic purposes of schooling have been reassessed. What had come to be regarded as a relatively fixed pattern of progression through the major individual life roles has been redefined as a process of multiple transitions in the context of global economic changes (see, e.g., Anisef and Axelrod, 1993; Hango and de Broucker, 2007). There is not so much a single point of entry into labour markets as a persistent shifting across educational and work settings. Just as increasing numbers of students seek part-time employment to gain experience and support themselves during the time they are engaged in formal studies, they are also more likely to return to educational programs after they have started work in order to upgrade their credentials or retrain for new lines of work. Movement between part-time work and studies, periodic unemployment, changes in the nature of work, and changing educational requirements have altered traditional relations between schooling and work. We are being told more frequently that 'lifelong learning' has become the norm that will govern our educational futures and that adaptability is the key to success (Livingstone, 2004: 14–15).

In general, evidence points to the likelihood that people with higher levels of education and diverse educational backgrounds will be more successful in job markets than those who have more limited educational credentials. Education is positively associated, for instance, with the chances of finding a job, having more meaningful work, and securing better incomes. Table 7.4 and Figure 7.5 provide indications of the relative return from education in relation to labour force participation and income. The data illustrate, as well, the continuing presence of substantial gender inequities within labour markets. Similar trends also hold true for minority groups, including immigrants and Aboriginal peoples (Li, 2003: 110–12; Schissel and Wotherspoon, 2003: 111–14).

The importance of education for job prospects takes on greater significance in light of recent evidence that it has become increasingly difficult for young adults to achieve a secure position in the labour market. Recent labour market entrants, in sharp contrast to their predecessors in the late twentieth century, have an abundance of job options in many regions of Canada. Nonetheless, many of these jobs are insecure, contingent on the shaky fortunes of resource industries, or, with the exception of positions requiring highly specialized skills or extensive experience, concentrated in low-paying services and related areas. Bowers, Sonnet, and Bardone (1999: 39)

Figure 7.4   Diverse Pathways for Youth in School to Labour Market Transitions—Findings from the Youth in Transition Survey, December 2003

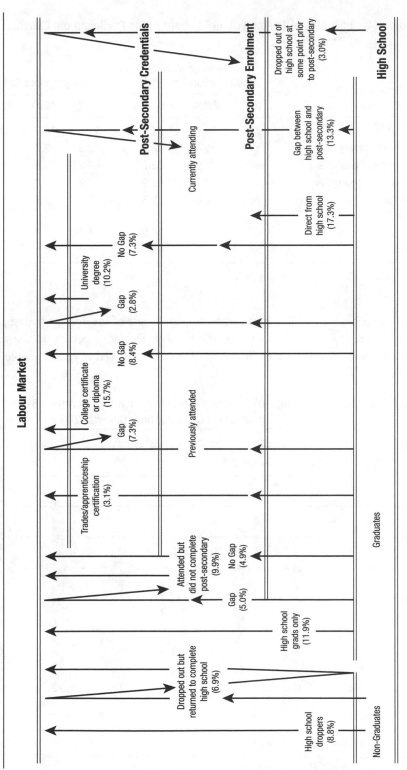

Note: Gap refers to a break of four months or more between high school and post-secondary studies.
Source: Adapted from Figure 1.2 and data in Appendix 1 in Hango and de Broucker (2007: 19, 66)

Table 7.4   Educational Attainment and Labour Force Participation, Canada, 2006

Highest Level of Educational Attainment	Labour Force Participation Rate (%)			Unemployment Rate (%)		
	Total	Males	Females	Total	Males	Females
0–8 years	24.5	33.3	17.0	12.5	11.2	14.7
Some secondary	51.2	58.4	43.7	12.3	12.2	12.4
High school graduate	69.5	76.9	62.7	6.2	6.5	5.9
Some post-secondary	69.0	72.1	65.9	7.3	7.7	6.8
Post-secondary certificate or diploma	76.6	80.8	72.5	5.1	5.4	4.8
University degree	80.1	82.2	78.0	4.0	3.8	4.1
Totals	67.2	72.5	62.1	6.3	6.5	6.1

Source: Statistics Canada, CANSIM Table 2820004.

observe a general trend in which '[t]he economic state of the average young person in OECD countries falls short of what is desirable. Despite a decline in the relative numbers of youths and the proliferation of programs aimed at young people in the

Figure 7.5   Median Earnings ($) for Full-time Full-year Workers, Ages 25–54, by Gender and Highest Level of Education, Canada, 2006

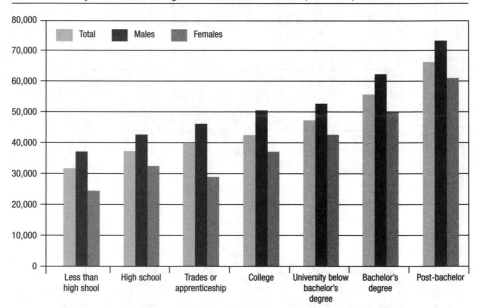

Source: Compiled from data in Statistics Canada, 'Income and Earnings Highlight Tables, 2006 Census: Table 2—Median 2005 earnings for full-year, full-time workers by education', Catalogue no. 97-563-XWE2006002, at: <www12.statcan.ca/english/census06/data/highlights/income/index.cfm?Lang=E>.

past two decades, their employment and earnings position has worsened, in some countries substantially.' Beaujot and Kerr (2007: 15) summarize data from Canada revealing that '[t]he relative economic position of youth, particularly young men, declined throughout the 1980s and 1990s, despite the fact that they had higher credentials in terms of education.' Governments and other agencies in Canada have recently turned to other countries, with stronger linkages between initial education and workforce entry that provide some protection both for young workers and for employers, for examples in beginning a systematic search to develop strategies that would more closely integrate schooling and employment (Taylor, 2007).

As labour markets become more volatile and competitive, there is additional pressure to achieve greater levels of education and training. Just as workers who enter job markets with strong educational credentials have greater employment and career opportunities than those with less education, a growing body of evidence points towards the importance of both formal and informal job-related education and training in maintaining employment success. While individuals with a broad range of educational backgrounds are engaging in such training, the benefits are not equally shared among all labour market participants. Livingstone (2004: 26, 27, 30) reports significant increases in adult and continuing education among virtually all social groups, particularly among young adults or those who had previously dropped out of school, but cautions that '[t]hose who have higher levels of formal schooling are more likely to participate in most forms of further education.' A report on adult learning in Canada and other OECD nations echoes this theme, concluding from the literature not only that 'well-educated adults benefit the most from organized forms of learning' but that 'a similar pattern [exists] between educational attainment and participation in active modes of informal learning' (Statistics Canada and OECD, 2005: 88).

This evidence seems to reinforce the general argument that individuals, even if they are already highly educated, require extensive educational credentials and continual upgrading to remain competitive in today's job market. By implication, those who fail to achieve high levels of education and up-to-date training are relegated to the growing pool of marginal or long-term unemployed workers. These factors point to two common claims regarding educational restructuring: (1) that efforts to improve credentials are an individual responsibility, and (2) that governments and employers must work more actively to overcome the mismatch between workers and jobs.

Unfortunately, the description of the trends outlined above does not offer any indication of the extent to which education and training are actually required on the job. We need to consider, in other words, whether the increase in educational credentials is a function of the growth of more sophisticated jobs or whether it is, instead, a consequence of credential inflation and other factors beyond work-related skills and training.

Proponents of the first thesis point to the impact of information technology on the creation of jobs that require a more highly educated and trained labour force. The expansion of jobs that require high qualifications occurs in three ways—

through demands created by the emergence of new industries or enterprises in creative, scientific, and technical fields; through the creation of new jobs in high-level professional, technical, and service work; and through upgrading and new skill demands in already existing jobs. Advanced education is required as work-related tasks become more specialized and sophisticated. Since the mid-1980s, job growth in Canada, the United States, and other highly developed nations has been clustered in industries that possess high concentrations of **knowledge workers**, i.e., professionals, engineers, scientific and technical workers, computer special-ists, senior managers, and the self-employed who possess high levels of training, specialized skill, and/or decision-making authority. The trends presented earlier (Box 7.2) are reinforced in the observation concerning data from the 2006 census reported by Statistics Canada (2008b: 15): 'The Canadian economy . . . still places a premium on workers with higher levels of education.'

The growth of highly skilled jobs and knowledge work is necessary, advocates claim, to drive productivity for both large and small firms in a highly competitive economy. Education and training can increase the degree of complementarity between the interests of workers and employers because they not only assist indi-viduals in their ability to secure employment but also to influence the wages, per-sonal benefits, and working conditions of employees. Bowlby (1996: 35) indicates that, in addition to receiving higher wages, 'Graduates with a direct education–job relationship are the most likely to be satisfied or very satisfied at work, much more than graduates in unrelated jobs.'

A less optimistic view, however, is taken by those who emphasize that the cate-gorization of jobs or industries by job titles and education levels is highly mislead-ing if we do not examine how work is actually changing. Recent economic restructuring has been characterized by the disappearance of stable, better-paying work and the proliferation of low-end jobs as businesses pursue strategies to reduce labour costs. In traditional industries and businesses, existing jobs often are phased out or deskilled while newer jobs, particularly in the service sector, are con-centrated in low-skill, low-paying occupations. Education serves as a screening device independent from competencies required on the job. As general education levels rise and job descriptions change, employers are able to keep wages low through competition generated by labour surpluses, claims that available workers do not have suitable skills to match the available work, new labour-saving tech-nologies, and the transfer of production from regions or nations with high-cost labour to those with lower labour costs and living standards. Much recent employ-ment growth has been in service industries characterized by part-time, temporary, or insecure work, low wages, few benefits, and often poor working conditions. Increasingly, the absence of secure, high-status jobs drives workers into jobs and fields where they are unable to use their capacities and skills. The problem of lack of credential recognition has gained widespread attention due to publicity sur-rounding experiences by highly qualified immigrants who are often frustrated by their inability to gain appropriate jobs or official credit for their foreign training and skills. While significant, this issue is related to a more general job deficit.

Analysis of the Canadian workforce reveals that one-third of Canadian workers aged 20–9 with post-secondary educational credentials indicated that they were overqualified for their jobs, with as many as one in five workers with university degrees holding jobs that required no more than high school (Crompton, 2002: 23; Lowe, 2002; Li et al., 2006: 3).

Recent evidence on the changing nature of employment has pointed to a much more complex picture than that revealed in the two arguments outlined above. Much attention has been focused on the tendency towards polarization of job growth distributed among high-end and low-end jobs, with a corresponding decline in the share of employment and protections for workers in mid-level jobs over the past two to three decades (Economic Council of Canada, 1991; Heisz, 2007; Osberg, 2006). This analysis highlights the decline of employment in goods-producing industries relative to substantial increases in service-sector employment. Both sectors, in turn, are characterized by diverse clusters of internal characteristics. Demand for highly educated, skilled, well-paid employees in many industries has increased as a consequence of new production and information technologies. However, increased productivity, workplace restructuring, and corporate and public-sector downsizing have also contributed to large-scale layoffs, intensification of work, and **deskilling**. In the process, several prevalent trends emerge, most notably including the expansion of white-collar work (in managerial, administrative, professional, clerical, sales, and service occupations), the growth of part-time and self-employment relative to full-time paid employment, and deepening problems for the most vulnerable segments of the labour force (Heisz et al., 2002; Kerr, 1997).

It is often tempting, in the analysis of labour force trends, to look at these patterns in an abstract way as if they affected all workers equally. In fact, however, labour market changes have very different implications for distinct categories of workers. Employment-related polarization encompasses several dimensions, as highly divergent work environments affect different sectors of the workforce in a highly uneven manner—as the workweek has declined for some workers, others are working well beyond standard working hours while increased earnings at the top are offset by lower overall wage and benefit packages across much of the workforce (Lowe, 2007). Since the mid-1980s, the degree of labour market polarization, or the gap between the highest- and lowest-paying jobs, generally has dropped for women, grown for men, increased substantially for workers less than 35 years of age, and remained high for visible minority groups and Aboriginal people (Human Resources Development Canada, 1996: 6; Canadian Council on Social Development, 2003). Hughes and Lowe (2000) conclude that such factors as the gender and age of workers and occupational conditions are more likely than computer technology to contribute to polarization within the labour market. Occupations associated with high job vacancies also tend to be polarized among those with relatively high skill requirements and those that are not unionized and have low wages. Galarneau et al. (2001: 33) observe that, 'Even in periods of strong economic growth, a substantial share of job vacancies are outside the high technology sectors. In 1999, more than 40 per cent of job vacancies and 50 per cent of long-term job vacancies of profit-oriented establishments were in the retail trade and consumer services industries.'

The high profile given to the growth of knowledge work also obscures the fact that more than three-quarters of Canadian workers occupy jobs that are classified as non-knowledge occupations (Baldwin and Beckstead, 2003: 5). While the global reach of technologies and markets has made it possible for enterprises and employment to transcend location, this has had mixed implications for workers. The most highly qualified workers who possess specialized skills for which there is considerable demand may be able to pursue rewarding work in any number of locations, but employment prospects are also affected by outsourcing of jobs to locales in other nations and reliance in many industries on immigrant and temporary labour sources. Knowledge-sector jobs with the best working conditions tend to be clustered in major metropolitan centres and regions with a highly developed infrastructure, including proximity and ready access to core services, transportation and communications links, and universities and major research facilities. While considerable investment along with media and policy attention are concentrated on innovation and high-level employment options, many of the most innovative firms associated with the new economy have relatively few employees while others rely on large numbers of relatively low-skilled, low-waged production and service workers (Brown and Lauder, 2006; Strathdee, 2005).

Some commentators, therefore, have argued that the structure of work is best characterized in the form of a segmented or dual, rather than a unified, labour market (Piore, 1979; Clairmont and Apostle, 1997). This kind of analysis seeks to explain how members of subordinate social groups, notably visible minorities as well as female workers, are concentrated in lower-paying, more insecure jobs in contrast to white men, who tend to be concentrated in the better jobs. A primary labour market, in which relatively highly qualified and unionized workers are able to demand better wages and working conditions from larger employers, is distinguished from a secondary market in which smaller, more competitive businesses seeking cheaper labour costs require a more unstable labour force. Segmented or dual labour market models are useful in demonstrating that not all workers are competing for the same jobs, and also offer some insight into how educational qualifications can be used to differentiate distinct pools of workers. The practice of streaming in Canadian schools, for instance, operates to select students for particular positions within segmented labour markets (Curtis et al., 1992).

Despite the insights they offer, segmented labour market theories do not provide a complete explanation of inequalities within labour markets. Labour markets are both more diverse and less static than depicted by this approach. The face of work been altered in many ways by changes in the organization of work, new technologies, demographic shifts, and labour market dynamics. The demise of jobs in traditional labour markets such as manufacturing, combined with the growth of small business and increasing employment in non-traditional occupations, has also blurred the boundaries between primary and secondary segments of the labour force. Immigrant selection criteria increasingly have emphasized skills, qualifications, and other human capital attributes even though many immigrants continue to face specific social or race-based barriers (Li, 2003: 122–3).

Significant continuity and changes in gender segmentation also are evident. Whereas fewer than 20 per cent of women aged 25 and over participated in the paid labour force in 1946 and only about one-third did in the late 1960s, nearly two-thirds (62 per cent) of women were labour force participants in 2006. Men's participation rates have declined somewhat over the same time period but still remain relatively high, at about 90 per cent in 1946, 85 per cent in the late 1960s, and just under three-quarters (73.8 per cent) in 2006 (Bernier, 1996: A48–9; Statistics Canada, 2007c).

Table 7.5 presents two ways of looking at overall employment distribution, comparing permanent versus temporary work by major industrial categories, and full-time versus part-time status by occupational categories. The data show that women are represented in substantial numbers and proportions in a wide range of occupational groups. Women's participation in many higher-paying fields, such as managerial, administrative, and professional occupations, has increased in conjunction with more open access to advanced levels of education. However, the data also show that women are most highly concentrated in only a few areas. They are highly concentrated in areas like health care and education, as well as trades sectors and industries related to business and finance, but their work in these fields, as well as in food and accommodation services, tends to be in clerical, sales, and service positions characterized by low wages and benefits, poor working conditions, and relatively little autonomy. Women are slightly more likely than men to be employed in positions classified as temporary, but about one-third (35.4 per cent) of women compared to 12.2 per cent of men are in occupations classified as part-time.

While some of these differences can be accounted for in terms of personal preference and differences in qualifications, experience, and other characteristics, the patterns depicted in Table 7.5 provide a glimpse of a more general tendency for precarious and non-standard employment forms of employment to grow relative to more traditional full-time permanent employment (Vosko, 2007). Trends revealed in census data suggest that, other than nursing and teaching for women, managerial positions in the sales and services sectors for men, and information systems analyst, very few of either the largest occupational categories or those which have demonstrated the highest growth since 2001 require specialized credentials beyond high school or specific occupational training (Table 7.6). Comparisons among persons who work full-time on a full-year basis show that women earn on average only two-thirds of the wages earned by men, with the lowest ratios of women's to men's earnings tending to be in sales, services, and other occupations in which there are high concentrations of female workers. The segmentation of the labour force along gender lines is even more pronounced when part-time and temporary workers are taken into consideration, given that much of this labour is performed by women working for relatively low wages and benefits. Vosko (2003: 27) observes that, despite significant shifts in the nature of work that have created some advances for female workers, women remain highly vulnerable because 'the erosion of minimum standards legislation, the deterioration of collective bargaining, unemployment insurance reforms, and cutbacks in the federal public service are fuelling new patterns of gendered labour market inequality.' Armstrong and Armstrong (2001: 66) emphasize that, despite improved educational and employment opportunities, women continue to be segregated in jobs that parallel the kinds of personal service and domestic labour they carry out in the household. Educational participation has created new social and employment opportunities for women, but traditional gender roles are also reproduced through demands and responsibilities that occur through the intersection of household, schooling, and workplace (Gaskell, 1992). Moreover, especially for women and those in the most precarious labour market situations, the amount of labour and related tensions involved in finding jobs, getting to work, caring or arranging care for children and other household members, managing household and leisure activities, and attending to other dimensions of work–family arrangements, is substantial and can pose further vulnerabilities (Corman and Luxton, 2007).

Table 7.5   Employment by Gender, Industry, and Occupation, Canada, 2006

	Female 000s	(%)	Male 000s	(%)	Total
Industry, permanent employment					
Agriculture	34	36.6	59	63.4	93
Other primary industries	45	19.1	191	80.9	236
Utilities	26	23.2	86	76.8	112
Construction	80	13.3	523	86.7	603
Manufacturing	532	28.0	1,369	72.0	1,901
Trade	1,053	50.3	1,040	49.7	2,093
Transportation and warehousing	154	25.4	454	74.8	607
Finance, insurance, real estate, and leasing	504	62.4	304	37.6	808
Professional, scientific, and technical services	313	48.0	339	52.0	652
Business, building, and other support services	208	48.0	226	52.2	433
Educational services	543	64.2	302	35.7	846
Health care and social assistance	1,173	84.9	209	15.1	1,381
Information, culture, and recreation	235	48.1	254	51.9	489
Accommodation and food services	471	61.7	293	38.4	763
Other services	227	52.4	206	47.6	433
Public administration	339	47.5	375	52.5	714
Total, all industries	*5,935*	*48.8*	*6,228*	*51.2*	*12,163*
Industry, temporary employment					
Agriculture	17	36.2	29	61.7	47
Other primary industries	6	15.4	33	84.6	39
Utilities	3	30.0	7	70.0	10
Construction	10	7.5	125	92.6	134

continued

Table 7.5   Employment by Gender, Industry, and Occupation, Canada, 2006
(continued)

	Female 000s	(%)	Male 000s	(%)	Total
Manufacturing	47	37.6	78	62.4	125
Trade	128	53.8	110	46.2	238
Transportation and warehousing	17	28.8	42	71.2	59
Finance, insurance, real estate, and leasing	31	56.4	23	41.8	55
Professional, scientific, and technical services	32	46.4	37	53.6	69
Business, building, and other support services	45	42.9	60	57.1	105
Educational services	173	65.8	91	34.6	263
Health care and social assistance	158	83.6	31	16.4	189
Information, culture, and recreation	73	49.0	76	51.0	149
Accommodation and food services	101	62.3	61	37.7	162
Other services	36	63.2	21	36.8	57
Public administration	70	56.9	53	43.1	123
Total, all industries	*946*	*51.9*	*877*	*48.1*	*1,823*
Occupation, full-time					
Management	499	35.2	917	64.8	1,416
Business, finance, and administrative	1,723	69.0	774	31.0	2,497
Natural and applied sciences	232	21.4	851	78.6	1,083
Health	582	78.0	164	22.0	746
Social science, education, government service, and religion	738	65.8	384	34.2	1,122
Art, culture, recreation, and sport	171	50.4	168	49.6	339
Sales and service	1,277	50.6	1,250	49.5	2,526
Trades, transport and equipment operators	122	5.3	2,174	94.6	2,297
Primary industry	89	17.6	418	82.4	507
Processing, manufacturing, and utilities	297	30.4	680	69.6	977
Total full-time	*5,729*	*42.4*	*7,781*	*57.6*	*13,510*
Occupation, part-time					
Management	49	52.7	44	47.3	93
Business, finance, and administrative	402	81.9	90	18.3	491
Natural and applied sciences	18	34.0	35	66.0	53
Health	219	90.1	24	9.9	243
Social science, education, government service, and religion	213	75.5	69	24.5	282
Art, culture, recreation, and sport	94	62.3	57	37.7	151
Sales and service	945	68.3	438	31.7	1,383
Trades, transport and equipment operators	38	24.2	119	75.8	157
Primary industry	31	40.3	46	59.7	77
Processing, manufacturing, and utilities	22	48.9	24	53.3	45
Total full-time	*2,029*	*68.2*	*946*	*31.8*	*2,975*

Note: Numbers are rounded.
Source: Statistics Canada, CANSIM Tables 2820010 and 2820080.

Table 7.6   Ten Most Prevalent Occupations for Men and Women, and Fastest-Growing Occupational Categories, Canada, 2006

Top 10 Occupations, by employment numbers	Skill Level*	Total Employment 2006	Percentage of Total Employment	Change 2001–6 (%)
Men				
Retail salespersons and sales clerks	C	285,800	3.2	28.6
Truck drivers	C	276,200	3.1	17.4
Retail trade managers	0	192,200	2.2	–4.0
Janitors, caretakers, and building superintendents	D	154,100	1.7	13.9
Farmers and farm managers	B/C	147,800	1.7	–12.5
Material handlers	C	147,000	1.7	10.4
Automotive service technicians, truck and bus mechanics, and mechanical repairers	B	143,000	1.6	16.6
Carpenters	B	142,400	1.6	30.0
Construction trades helpers and labourers	D	133,600	1.5	55.2
Sales, marketing, and advertising managers	0	102,600	1.2	11.0
Total, top 10 male occupations		*1,724,700*	*19.4*	*14.5*
Total, all occupations (men)		*8,884,805*	*100.0*	*6.9*
Women				
Retail salespersons and sales clerks	C	400,000	5.0	20.7
Cashiers	D	255,500	3.2	16.1
Registered nurses	A	249,400	3.1	15.7
General office clerks	C	244,200	3.1	10.4
Secretaries (except legal and medical)	B	237,300	3.0	–6.5
Elementary school and kindergarten teachers	A	214,600	2.7	10.2
Food counter attendants, kitchen helpers, and related occupations	D	194,800	2.4	13.5
Early childhood educators and assistants	B	157,700	2.0	25.2
Food and beverage servers	D	152,000	1.9	–1.9
Light duty cleaners	D	147,400	1.8	19.8
Total, top 10 female occupations		*2,252,900*	*28.2*	*12.0*
Total, all occupations (women)		*7,976,375*	*100.0*	*9.8*
Occupations with largest increases, 2001–6, by total number of employees				
Retail salespersons and sales clerks	C	685,800	4.1	23.9
Construction trades helpers and labourers	D	143,900	0.9	57.1
Truck drivers	C	286,100	1.7	18.2
Cashiers	D	299,200	1.8	16.9
Nurse aides, orderlies, and patient service associates	C	169,700	1.0	28.0
Registered nurses	A	265,900	1.6	16.2
Customer service, information, and related clerks	C	191,600	1.1	23.4

continued

Table 7.6   Ten Most Prevalent Occupations for Men and Women, and
Fastest-Growing Occupational Categories, Canada, 2006 (continued)

Top 10 Occupations, by employment numbers	Skill Level*	Total Employment 2006	Percentage of Total Employment	Change 2001–6 (%)
Administrative clerks	C	101,700	0.6	53.9
Information systems analysts and consultants	A/B	138,400	0.8	34.2
Carpenters	B	145,000	0.9	30.3
Total men and women, all occupations		*16,861,180*	*100.0*	

*Skill levels and occupational categories are based on National Occupational Classification. Skill level refers to credentials or levels of education and training typically required as qualifications for a job.
Skill Level:
O = Management.
A = Occupations usually require university education.
B = Occupations usually require college education or apprenticeship training.
C = Occupations usually require secondary school and/or occupation-specific training.
D = On-the-job training is usually provided for occupations.
Source: Statistics Canada, 'Canada's Changing Labour Force, 2006 Census'. Catalogue no. 97-559-XWE2006001, released 11 March 2008, pp. 13–14. Available at: http://www12.statcan.gc.ca/english/census06/analysis/labour/pdf/97-559-XIE2006001.pdf.

As the evidence and trends outlined in the preceding paragraphs suggest, labour markets are highly complex and changing entities. The possibility that a person will find relatively secure employment with limited education or can follow an educational track that leads to clearly definable, rewarding career opportunities is becoming increasingly remote for labour force entrants. The highly mixed signals that arise from these circumstances contribute to heightened uncertainty and stress for individuals who are considering or reassessing their employment prospects. The most optimistic assessments suggest that we have moved well beyond a situation described by Osberg et al. (1995: 182–3) in the 1990s as one dominated by problems of 'increasing unemployment, the polarization of incomes, rising poverty, and greater dependence on transfer payments—all have their special complexities, but there is a root problem, a lack of jobs.' Young workers, recent immigrants, and others who are especially vulnerable to economic shifts must rely on part-time work, periodic retraining, or jobs that do not match their qualifications in order to break into the labour market (Beaujot and Kerr, 2007; Human Resources Development Canada, 2000). However, labour market instability and uncertainty are not isolated to these groups. Since the late 1980s, periods of economic restructuring and recession made it increasingly difficult for graduates of trades and vocational programs, who might be expected to have work directly linked to their training, to find and keep such jobs (Bowlby, 1996: 38; Myles and Fawcett 1990: 16). Subsequent labour market developments have been marked by notable increases in reliance on shifting and temporary work forms as employers seek to maximize flexibility and competitive positioning.

One of the major contradictions evident in these trends is the coexistence of large numbers of workers who are undereducated and underqualified for available

Box 7.6 Youth Employment Trends

Young Canadians are experiencing an increasingly more complex and uncertain set of options and circumstances as they navigate their way between schooling and work. Analyzing data for youth aged 22–4 in 2004 drawn from the Youth in Transition Survey, Hango and de Broucker (2007: 11–13) summarize a number of key dimensions of these transitions:

Important background factors associated with education-to-labour-market pathways
- Females are less likely to follow the pathway of dropping out of high school and are more likely to go on to some type of post-secondary program prior to entering the labour force. They are also less likely to delay the start of a post-secondary program than are males.
- In terms of ethnic background, the most salient finding is that Aboriginal youth are more likely than non-Aboriginal youth to leave the educational system with a much lower level of attainment.
- The presence of a long-term limiting condition is a hindrance to further education; these individuals are much less likely to follow pathways leading to the completion of a post-secondary degree or diploma.
- Youth who attended high school in Quebec were more likely than youth from Ontario to drop out of high school; yet if they did graduate from high school and attend a post-secondary program, they were more likely than their counterparts from Ontario to go directly following high school.
- A greater number of siblings led to a greater risk of not finishing high school prior to entering the labour market, as does not living in an intact family (two-parent, non-step family) during high school. As well, the typical universally positive relationship between educational attainment levels across generations was found: youth with parents who had a high level of education were more likely to go to a post-secondary program prior to entering the labour market.

Linking intervening factors to educational pathways
- Marks matter. A very strong relationship was found between grade-point average and dropping out of high school: youth with very low marks in high school were much more likely than those with mid to high marks to drop out and not return. For youth who had attended post-secondary programs, very high marks predicted that the teen would go directly to a post-secondary program after high school rather than delaying.
- Working some hours in high school can be beneficial, while working a great number of hours (over 20) can be detrimental, leading to a greater risk of dropping out of high school. Working over 20 hours a week in high school was also associated with teens delaying their attendance at a post-secondary institution following high school.

- Individuals who had a child or who entered a conjugal union during their teenage years are disproportionately represented among those who dropped out of high school, as well as among those who dropped out but later returned (second-chancers); they were less represented among the paths leading to post-secondary attendance.
- Parental expectations regarding their child's education are generally high, and higher expectations are associated with higher educational attainment.

Linking educational paths to labour market outcomes
- Almost 80 per cent of youth who were not in school in December 2003 were employed. The likelihood of employment is highest for individuals who had delayed post-secondary attendance after high school, but then either graduated from college or university, and for college graduates who had not delayed their post-secondary attendance after high school graduation. . . .
- The odds of employment also increased as the number of months spent out of full-time school increased, for males, for individuals who had no children, and for those who had worked more hours in high school.
- . . . On average, post-secondary graduates (regardless of whether they delayed post-secondary attendance following high school graduation) earned more than the median. High school dropouts (whether or not they returned to school) and those who entered but did not complete a post-secondary program earned less. However, some university graduates were earning less than high school dropouts, though this is at least partly attributable to the university grads having had less opportunity for work experience. . . .
- In addition to the effects of school pathway, several additional interesting results were found for other indicators. For example, women have lower earnings than men, earning almost 28 per cent less than their working male counterparts. Meanwhile, working a greater number of hours in high school had a positive effect on earnings: working on average 20 hours per week increased earnings by about 20 per cent, as compared to not working at all. However, it adversely affected educational attainment. . . .
- The most common occupations were in sales and service, while the least common were in management or business-related. Young adults with post-secondary degrees or diplomas were more represented among management and business-related jobs, as well as professional, scientific, education and government jobs. Meanwhile, young adults with a high school diploma or less were more represented among the goods-producing and primary sectors and those who entered but did not complete a post-secondary program were more represented among the lowest-paying sales and service occupations, likely leading to their low earnings observed earlier.

Source: Statistics Canada, 'Education-to-Labour Market Pathways of Canadian Youth: Findings from the Youth in Transition Survey'. Catalogue no. 81–595-MIE2007054. Available at: http://www.statcan.gc.ca/pub/81-595-m/81-595-m2007054-eng.pdf.

jobs along with a substantial pool of labour market participants who are overqualified and underemployed. Statistics Canada data concerning employment experiences of graduates of post-secondary programs reveal, in general, that those with the highest levels of formal education tend to show the strongest match between job skills and education, with a slightly higher degree of fit for women than for men (Finnie, 2001: 14). Livingstone (2004), through his own research and in summaries of other findings, demonstrates the simultaneous existence of two large groups of workers—those whose formal educational credentials exceed their job requirements and those who feel they do not have sufficient skills or training to carry out all their job tasks. More specifically, he shows that **underemployment** and subemployment are themselves subdivided among distinct categories of labour force participants, depending on such factors as the levels of qualifications workers have, the credentials required for entry into certain occupations, the knowledge and skills employed on the job and those that workers have but cannot use in their work, and workers' perceptions about the relationships among these factors. Between one and three out of five workers in North America—and more in working-class positions—are likely to be underemployed according to various dimensions based on the reality or perception that they have recognized skills and credentials they are not able to employ in their jobs, at the same time as these workers are engaging in more formal and informal training on and off the job (Livingstone, 2004: 94–5; Livingstone and Scholtz, 2007: 153–4).

In summary, it is difficult to make comprehensive judgements about the degree of match or fit between education and jobs because of the highly complex and changing nature of work and labour markets. Jobs and labour markets, and the manner in which they intersect with education and training, are undergoing massive transformations, but there are highly divergent ways of understanding the dimensions and implications of those changes. The escalation of a long-term shift from jobs related to physical resources and material goods production towards work concentrated in services and knowledge sectors is accompanied by changes in the kinds of competencies and relationships people need in order to prepare for and conduct their working lives. The present educational situation in post-secondary institutions can be explained by a combination of factors, including intense competition for many jobs, powerful ideological and rhetorical linkages between social advancement and educational advancement (sometimes supported by general empirical evidence), and anxiety induced by labour market change and uncertainty. These social pressures have fuelled an escalation in levels of educational attainment, and these educational levels exceed what is required across much of the current job market. Even those individuals in a position to make long-term plans for their career futures are subject to the possibility that credential requirements may change or that certain jobs may be substantially reorganized or could disappear altogether before their formal education is complete. The discourse of lifelong learning, acknowledging ongoing transformations in the nature of work and periodic transitions among diverse employment circumstances and learning sites, has replaced conventional notions of a pathway that leads from schooling into a clearly defined career. In general terms, individuals with the highest levels of formal education clearly are in the best position to benefit in terms of finding stable, well-paying, meaningful work. However, even among highly educated workers there is a strong possibility of no available work relevant to their training, while pressures mount for continuous retraining and upgrading. By contrast, those with limited amounts of formal education are more likely to have difficulty finding and keeping work, but when they do, in many cases even they may be overqualified for their jobs. For youth faced with the prospect of seeking work, regardless of their levels of educational attainment, the pressing question of what kinds of job options they should pursue is becoming increasingly uncertain.

CONCLUSION

This chapter has addressed issues related to the relationship between schooling and work. While the goal of preparing youth for entry into the labour force has long been a central concern of educators, just as it has been a recurrent matter for public debate, the chapter has emphasized that there has never been a strict correspondence between formal education and work training. Labour market preparation has been only one of several objectives of education systems. This, combined with the varied demands of employers, the changing nature of most occupations, and the complexity of transition processes between schooling and work, means that there are limits to the responsiveness that formal education can maintain to labour market demands.

While considerable attention in policy discussions and the media has focused recently on the apparent failure of formal education to produce the kind of workforce required in a competitive global economy, much of that emphasis has offered a relatively uncritical analysis of the kinds of job choices and school–work connections that labour market entrants are confronted with. Clearly, many improvements are needed in the ways that schools approach labour market preparation. It is not sufficient, however, to lay blame with schools or individuals for the mismatch between workers and jobs. A combination of factors that links individual life circumstances and choices with structural characteristics of education and work opportunities contributes to the kinds of life courses that people follow. This chapter has focused mostly on general trends, but the evidence has pointed to the highly uneven and unequal structures of opportunity and reward associated with access to education, labour market options, and socio-economic outcomes. Chapter 8 examines these phenomena in more detail.

ANNOTATED FURTHER READINGS

Anisef, Paul, Paul Axelrod, Etta Baichman-Anisef, Carl James, and Anton Turrittin. 2000. *Opportunity and Uncertainty: Life Course Experiences of the Class of '73*. Toronto: University of Toronto Press. This book offers one of the few systematic long-term studies of the educational, occupational, and life pathways followed by students as they complete their schooling and move through adolescence into adulthood.

Bills, David B. 2004. *The Sociology of Education and Work.* Malden, Mass.: Blackwell. Drawing on data on and examples of the changing relations between education and work in the United States, the author provides a clear introduction to major issues associated with the sociological analysis of these relationships focused around competing perspectives that highlight, respectively, meritocracy and credentialism.

Brown, Phillip, Andy Green, and Hugh Lauder. 2001. *High Skills: Globalization, Competitiveness, and Skill Formation.* Oxford: Oxford University Press. The authors assess critically conventional assessments of the importance of highly skilled knowledge work in the global economy. They demonstrate, through case studies drawn from the United States, the United Kingdom, Japan, Germany, South Korea, and Singapore, that the most optimistic accounts overstate the extent to which highly skilled work pervades developed economies, and outline alternative models of high skills that accompany diverse political economies and policy strategies.

Crysdale, Stewart, Alan J. King, and Nancy Mandell. 1999. *On Their Own: Making the Transition from School to Work in the Information Age.* Montreal and Kingston: McGill-Queen's University Press. The authors report on a study based on youth accounts of their varied schooling and labour market experiences, highlighting social background and educational factors that make for successful integration as well as issues that mark uneven transitions.

Livingstone, D.W. 2004. *The Education–Jobs Gap: Underemployment or Economic Democracy.* Aurora, Ont.: Garamond Press. Offering a comprehensive analysis of the relationship between education and work in contemporary economic contexts, this book demonstrates how the broad range of educational experiences and capacities is not given sufficient recognition and scope in many jobs and labour market situations.

Lowe, Graham. 2000. *The Quality of Work: A People-Centred Agenda.* Toronto: Oxford University Press, 2000. The author examines contemporary trends and attitudes regarding the changing nature of work, building from critique towards a framework for the creation of meaningful work opportunities that address people's concerns for greater personal development and fulfillment.

KEY TERMS

Capitalist imperative Pressures to reproduce hierarchy and inequality through schooling and other institutions in order to ensure profitable production and other needs associated with capitalist economies.

Democratic imperative Pressures to ensure that schools and other agencies are governed by priorities for widespread participation, expanded socio-economic opportunities, and social justice for all groups.

Deskilling A process in which workers lose control and autonomy over their work, either through the centralization of decision-making in management and new technologies, or the fragmentation of jobs into more simplified and directed tasks.

Employability The possession of skills and attributes considered essential for individuals to remain part of the labour market and adapt to changing economic conditions.

Habitus Relatively stable systems of dispositions, habits, or tastes that constitute the basis for how we understand the world.

Knowledge workers Workers, generally with high levels of skills and qualifications, who are engaged in the production, manipulation, and dissemination of knowledge, often involving extensive use of information and communication technologies.

Lifelong learning The notion that learning extends on a continuum from early childhood through adulthood, occurring in a variety of institutional and informal settings rather than being confined to formal learning within selected programs, institutions, and age cohorts.

New economy A term used to highlight the shift in emphasis from industrial production within specific industries, firms, and nations to economic activities driven by information and high-level technologies, global competition and international networks, and knowledge-based advancement.

Post-industrial society A form of social and economic organization based on rapid developments related to knowledge, information, advanced technology, and service-sector work. It is made possible by, but does not eradicate the need for, sophisticated advances in the production of raw materials and manufactured goods.

Technological functionalism A perspective that emphasizes industrial and technological development as the basis for educational expansion and emerging knowledge requirements.

Transitions The pathways that people follow from family life, into and out of education, and into various jobs or other social situations throughout their life course.

Underemployment A situation in which a person has educational credentials, skills, or other capacities that are not required for or used in her/his jobs.

Vocational and technical education Education and training programs that lead to certificates or other credentials oriented to specific occupational requirements.

Study Questions

1. Critically discuss the argument that education is failing in its primary purpose to provide the skills and training that individuals require for competitive performance in the new economy.

2. Outline and explain the impact that changing job structures and labour market requirements have had on educational practices over the past century.

3. Discuss the extent to which education systems across Canada and other nations should or should not be harmonized with one another in order to provide job skills that are transferable from one setting to another.

4. What is post-industrial society? Discuss the extent to which Canada has become a post-industrial society and how accompanying changes have affected education and employment prospects for men and women in different circumstances, including those entering the job market and those with extensive work experience.

5. Critics from various perspectives have suggested there is a strong mismatch between education and jobs. Critically compare and contrast the main competing orientations to this mismatch, indicating the extent to which each is supported by available evidence.

6. Outline and explain the degree of correlation between levels of education and levels of employment, income, and labour market success.

7. Debate exists over the question of whether work is becoming more highly skilled or workers are increasingly deskilled. Compare and contrast these positions with reference to research findings and recent trends related to work in Canada.

Chapter 8

Educational Opportunity and Social Reproduction

INTRODUCTION

One of the primary themes in the sociological analysis of education is the assessment of contributions made by formal education both to social equality and to socio-economic opportunity. This interest runs parallel to high social expectations about the value of schooling as a vehicle for social mobility. There is widespread faith in the ability of education to elevate living conditions and advance individual opportunities for all participants. International comparisons of social and economic development among nations, for instance, regard the general levels of education attained by a population as one of the most common indicators of the advancement of a society (UNESCO, 2007) in the same way that learners, their parents, and prospective employers tend to regard schooling as a key determinant of an individual's future success.

While there is little question, in general terms, about the importance of the connection between education and socio-economic opportunity, the degree to which education has been able to contribute effectively to greater social equality has been subject to repeated challenge from different ends of the political spectrum. Compulsory education, along with social welfare, income and tax transfer programs, and other state policies devoted to minimize the impact of poverty and reduce social inequality in Canada, the United States, and other highly developed democratic societies, has not eliminated pronounced gaps that separate the advantaged from the disadvantaged segments of the population. Empirical evidence demonstrates that education on a global scale has had an uneven or ambiguous impact on development, although there continues to be high public confidence in education's ability to drive economic, political, and cultural development (Chabbott and Ramirez, 2000). A summary report from UNESCO (2007: 2), cited earlier in this book, emphasizes that, 'Despite overall enrolment increases, subnational disparities in school participation persist between regions, provinces or states and between urban and rural areas. Children from poor, indigenous, and disabled populations are also at a systematic disadvantage, as are those living in slums.' The persistence of educational inequality has been accompanied by recurrent debates over the causes of general social inequality and related demands for reforms in education and other social programs.

This chapter focuses on central debates and issues related to the relationship between formal education and social inequality. It addresses questions such as the following:

- What is meant by social inequality and educational opportunity, and how are they related?
- Who benefits from education and what kinds of return do individuals and groups receive from their formal schooling?
- How much does formal education contribute to the reproduction or the eradication of social inequality?
- What are the limitations on education being able to fulfill its promise of better social futures for individuals and social groups?
- What are the prospects that social and educational reform can overcome these limitations?

The Nature and Causes of Social Inequality in Canada

Canadians often pride themselves on the observation that their country ranks ahead of most other nations on indicators related to standard of living, quality of life, and relative equity among groups. Extreme gaps between the haves and have-nots are not nearly as visible as they are in most parts of the world, whether in developing or developed regions. Nonetheless, social inequality in Canada is prevalent along several dimensions. These include disparities in the possession of or access to income and wealth, political power, and ideological power (see, e.g., Clement and Vosko, 2003).

Regardless of which measure is considered, Canadian society is highly stratified according to inequalities of gender, race and ethnicity, class, region, age, and many other social factors (Bolaria, 2000; Curtis et al., 2003). Women, who earn on average less than three-quarters of the average incomes of men, continue to be concentrated in subordinate roles in both the household and workplace (Armstrong and Armstrong, 2001: 66; Vosko, 2007). People of Aboriginal ancestry and members of groups considered visible minorities frequently are marginalized and limited in their ability to gain access to important economic and political positions. While wealth is concentrated among a small core of individuals and firms, large disparities between the privileged and underprivileged are growing. Rice (2002: 117) observes that the new economy, in addition to perpetuating earlier divisions between 'good jobs and bad jobs', is also blocking social mobility, with the consequence 'that Canada will continue to develop two economies, one for the haves and one for the have-nots. Opportunities will flow to those who have the advantage of educated or well-off parents, while those with poor parents will have limited opportunities.' Households headed by young adults, lone parents, seniors, and Aboriginal peoples (especially among women in each of these groups) are much more likely than other households to be living in poverty, often for extended durations (Canadian Council on Social Development, 2007).

The chances of finding secure employment, decent wages, and access to adequate living conditions and social support also vary according to where people live. Regional inequalities are acknowledged in government policies that distinguish between the 'have-not' provinces—notably in Atlantic Canada—that receive equalization payments from the federal government and the 'have' provinces (most typically Ontario, Alberta, and British Columbia). There are also significant inequalities within regions, frequently though not exclusively on a rural/urban and north/south basis. Historically, for instance, the sovereignist movement in Quebec originated out of contradictions, most evident in terms of disparities among anglophones and francophones, both within the province and between Quebec and the rest of Canada (Denis, 1995).

EDUCATIONAL OPPORTUNITY AND SOCIAL INEQUALITY

Formal education is highly implicated in considerations of social inequality because of its importance as a state-managed mechanism to transmit values and regulate credentials and access to highly valued social and economic positions. Educational opportunity is widely accepted as a key mechanism for expanding the distribution of social and economic positions and rewards. Nonetheless, differing claims are made about the meaning and nature of educational opportunity. Lessard (1995: 178–9), citing Lévesque (1979), outlines three distinct meanings of the concept of educational opportunity—equality of access, equality of treatment, and equality of results, each of which corresponds to different political philosophies.

The first meaning, equality of access, refers to the notion that all individuals should be guaranteed little more than the opportunity to attend schools or other formal educational institutions. This view is associated with a conservative or a laissez-faire approach that emphasizes individual responsibility. The state's role is limited to assurances that schools and other vital public services are available to all citizens and that the rules governing these services are fairly applied. Beyond that, people should be expected to look out for their own welfare and be held accountable for their own success or failure. This ideological position, especially when it is combined with concern about government debt, has driven recent reforms to downsize the welfare state through funding and program cuts in education as well as in related areas such as social welfare, health care, and unemployment insurance.

The second concept, equality of treatment, corresponds to a liberal philosophical orientation that stresses that the state must take a more proactive role with respect to education and other social services. Consistent with cultural explanations of inequality, this view argues that persons from varying social backgrounds have distinct needs, interests, and characteristics that have to be taken into account in the planning, delivery, and evaluation of educational programs and services. It is not sufficient simply to 'bring people to the classroom door'; instead, the opportunities presented can only be taken advantage of when there are assurances that they are meaningful and relevant to the needs of learners and other clients.

The third approach to educational opportunity, which emphasizes **equality of results**, emerges from a critical or social democratic philosophy grounded in a structural explanation of inequality. In contrast to the first two orientations, this position demands an even greater sense of social responsibility on the part of both the state and the more privileged groups within society. People tend to be poor, unemployed, or **socially disadvantaged** not through any fault of their own but rather because the social system produces poverty, unemployment, and structural inequality as conditions of its ongoing existence. Individuals should not be blamed, for instance, for being born into poor families or for living in communities in which factories close down or fisheries are jeopardized. Therefore, a proactive approach is required to ensure that all members of a population have access to a wide range of educational and social services and programs to guarantee them at least minimum standards of living and opportunities for success.

Individual and Structural Explanations of Social Inequalities

The diverse conceptions of educational opportunity draw attention to competing explanations for the persistence of inequalities both within and outside of schooling. Different theories and public policy perspectives related to social inequality are not only linked with particular assumptions about how the world is organized; they also carry distinct implications regarding prospects for social change. If we assume, for instance, that inequality is a necessary feature of human societies or that it is the product of innate individual characteristics, we may be inclined to believe that little can be done to alter existing social arrangements. By contrast, if we view inequality as the product of social factors, we are more likely to support social policies or government actions such as proposals for affirmative action or tax benefits for the poor. In fact, while various and wide-ranging theories attempt to explain inequality, the most common variants in these debates are positions that, on the one hand, emphasize individual or cultural factors and, on the other hand, stress social structural factors (Bolaria, 2000).

Individual explanations of inequality regard each person as responsible for his or her own success or failure. Disadvantage and poverty are viewed as consequences of low ambition, inadequate skills or abilities, or some other faulty personal characteristics, while those who succeed are considered more capable or talented, exercise personal drive and good judgement, and demonstrate good work habits. These capacities are seen to reside in either the biological or personality structures of individuals.

Social Darwinism, which was popular in the late nineteenth century, for example, promoted the view that individuals were sorted according to their abilities or 'fitness' to succeed. The notion of 'survival of the fittest' was introduced by sociologist Herbert Spencer (not Charles Darwin, as is often supposed) to indicate how social progress required a naturally competitive selection process to enable the strongest (i.e., those who could contribute the most to socially desirable outcomes) to succeed while the poor and weak should be left to fend for themselves (Ritzer, 2008: 33).

Although this view is highly controversial and has lost favour among most social analysts, it continues to appear in various guises, particularly among the political right. Neo-liberal perspectives, which prioritize individual rights over collective interests, and advanced genetic research, which seeks to map the biological foundations of life forms, emerge as threats to more sociological understandings of human relations (Fuller, 2006). In recent decades, widespread attention has been given to the view that intelligence is distributed and inherited unequally among the population, thereby accounting for higher rates of educational and socio-economic failure among **visible minority** populations such as blacks in the United States (Jensen, 1973; Herrnstein, 1973; Rushton and Bogaert, 1987). Herrnstein and Murray (1994) reignited controversy in the 1990s by arguing in *The Bell Curve* that because of a 'cognitive partitioning', through which the population comes to be subdivided into distinct intellectual categories, often on racial lines, it is not possible for everyone to benefit from education. They contend that only select groups should have access to higher education, while those with low IQs should not be expected to graduate from high school.

These views are among the most extreme examples of the individualist orientations to social inequality. They have been widely criticized on several accounts, including their failure to question faulty assumptions about how social characteristics like race, gender, and intelligence are defined and measured, problems with their methodologies and use of data, and their lack of attention to such structural factors as social policy and legislation that restrict opportunities for particular groups (see, e.g., Fraser, 1995). Fischer et al. (1996: 18), observing the impact of social policies and other factors that perpetuate social inequality, state emphatically that 'It is not that low intelligence leads to inferior status; it is that inferior status leads to low intelligence test scores.' Nonetheless, this approach shares much in common with the widely held liberal assessment that social rewards are allocated on the basis of merit through competition among individuals. The relative success people have in attaining particular social or economic positions is therefore seen to be determined by ability, effort, and personal achievement. This analysis presupposes that social structures and institutions such as education are relatively open, accessible, and fair to all persons.

A variant of the individualist position is found in cultural theories of inequality, which argue that some cultures are more oriented than others to traits that are rewarded in advanced societies. According to this view, persons from modern cultures are better situated than those with a traditional value orientation to identify with goals and adopt characteristics that lead to social and economic success. Traditionalism, 'cultures of poverty', and lack of an achievement orientation are presented from this viewpoint as impediments to progress, thereby contributing to the subordination of the culture as a whole as well as to the limitation of opportunities for individuals within those cultures (Hurst, 1992: 229–30).

Structural orientations to social inequality do not share the assumptions made by individual and cultural theories. A structural approach does not 'blame' individuals or their cultures for possessing deficits or failing to live up to the standards and expectations by which success is determined. Instead, inequality is regarded as a phenomenon that is socially produced and reproduced on at least two levels. First, structured inequalities permeate social systems and institutional processes.

Box 8.1 Climate Change, Poverty, and Gender: Barriers to Basic Education in Developing Nations

Schooling in many nations is constrained by significant barriers to participation, programming, and advancement, revealing the combined impact of schooling and the environments in which schools operate. A report from the United Nations (United Nations Development Program, 2007: 45, 86–7) highlights how the requirements to attend to basic daily needs are intensified by climate change, making it difficult for persons, especially girls, in many developing nations to attend school:

Women and young girls have to allocate large amounts of time to the collection of firewood, compounding gender inequalities in livelihood opportunities and education. Collecting fuelwood and animal dung is a time-consuming and exhausting task, with average loads often in excess of 20 kg. Research in rural Tanzania has found that women in some areas walk 5–10 kilometres a day collecting and carrying firewood, with loads averaging 20 kg to 38 kg. In rural India, average collection times can amount to over 3 hours a day. Beyond the immediate burden on time and body, fuelwood collection often results in young girls being kept out of school. . . .

For the poorest households, increasing labour supply can mean transferring children from classrooms into the labour market. Even in 'normal' years, poor households are often forced to resort to child labour, for example during the lean season before harvests. Droughts and floods intensify these pressures. In Ethiopia and Malawi, children are routinely taken out of school to engage in income-generating activities. In Bangladesh and India, children in poor households work on farms, tend cattle or engage in other tasks in exchange for food during periods of stress. In Nicaragua in the aftermath of Hurricane Mitch, the proportion of children working rather than attending school increased from 7.5 to 15.6 per cent in affected households (Baez and Santos, 2007; de Janvry et al., 2006).

Source: Macmillan, Palgrave. Excerpt from UN Development Programme, *Human Development Report 2007/2008.* Reproduced with permission of Palgrave Macmillan.

Second, social groups do not share equal access to opportunities, positions, and rewards that accompany those systems and processes. Success and failure, in these regards, are determined by factors other than individual characteristics and efforts. The social system is organized in such a way as to define and produce failure in particular ways, which in turn creates advantages or disadvantages for some groups relative to others.

In Canada, numerous discriminatory policies at the federal, provincial, and municipal levels have restricted opportunities or prohibited access to services on the basis of race, gender, and other social characteristics. Historically, for instance, there have been policies to prohibit women and people of Asian ancestry from attending universities or registering in specific programs and to limit the length of time that registered Indians could attend public schools. Similarly, lack of access to material resources has restricted the ability of members of socially disadvantaged groups to achieve success in important political, economic, and social spheres of activity.

Competing individual and structural explanations of inequality extend beyond academic analysis into social policy considerations. Various policy alternatives are organized around issues such as what role the state should play in regulating people's lives, providing human services, promoting personal incentive, and recognizing individual or collective rights. Over the past century, intense contestation over these questions frequently has accompanied the rise of—and subsequent efforts to reshape or dismantle—the welfare state.

The Politics of Educational Opportunity

The politics of education in Canada, often parallel to the development of the welfare state, make evident the extent to which alternative understandings of social inequality and educational opportunities play a role in educational practice and decision-making. The history of Canadian education reveals periodic tensions and struggles over the extent to which educational opportunity should be guaranteed and extended by the state. The introduction of mass public schooling in the nineteenth century was itself supported by arguments that all children, regardless of class or social background, should have access to common educational experiences. State-supported schooling ensured that children would be able to attend school even if their parents could not afford to pay tuition costs. Compulsory attendance legislation from the late nineteenth and early twentieth centuries, and later enforcement of truancy regulations to ensure that children were actually in the classroom, expanded the state's role beyond simple assurances that all children had access to schooling. Opposition to these initiatives was countered by arguments that schooling was necessary for the public good and that its domain superseded the interests of any particular individuals or groups. Until recently, the status of education—as one of a limited number of universal social programs available on an open, affordable, and accessible basis to all eligible Canadian residents—has been relatively unchallenged (Rice and Prince, 2000: 169).

The justification of schooling as a resource for the common good has been the basis of repeated attempts (not all of which have been successful) to introduce, modify, or delete particular curricula, programs, and services because they were targeted at other than the general clientele of the public school system. Previous chapters have revealed how, over the years, courses in areas such as physical education, family life, citizenship education, multicultural studies, Aboriginal studies, computer and technological education, and anti-racism education have been added to curricula. Schools have come to take on diverse new roles, including counselling, public health, and other social services. At the same time, education systems remain vulnerable to lobbying to remove curricula, programs, personnel, or materials deemed too costly, unnecessary, or offensive to certain groups.

Debates over the ability of formal schooling to provide conditions for **equality of opportunity** must take into consideration the ideological nature of claims about the 'common good'. Such claims typically are made on the basis of interests expressed in accordance with the requirements or demands of particular social constituencies, posed in such a way as to represent the general interest. In the most general terms, for instance, there is likely to be widespread agreement with the idea that schools should teach literacy and mathematical and social skills, among other things. However, the kinds of curricula, teaching approaches, learning materials, and modes of evaluation used in the teaching of these areas, and how these are combined with other aspects of the schooling process, involve choices to be made from a range of alternatives. In this way, what is taught, how it is transmitted, and what is conveyed to the learner are rarely universally representative but, instead, are reflections of inequalities and power arrangements that operate both within the education system and through the wider society.

The issue of educational equality also raises questions about the extent to which all students should be subjected to identical educational experiences. The argument that it is sufficient for schools to present a common curriculum to all students places the onus on students, regardless of their social backgrounds, to compete with one another on the basis of universal standards. School programs that provide for integration or mainstreaming of children who come from families that do not speak the language of instruction or of physically or mentally disabled students, for instance, are founded on notions that equate equality with 'sameness' of treatment. An alternative position recognizes that different groups have distinct needs to which education must respond. Curricula and teaching methods that fail to take social differences into account are disadvantageous to minority students. 'Anti-racism education' is based on the view that educators must incorporate into educational processes both acceptance and understanding of racial diversity and pedagogical strategies to combat systemic oppression (Dei, 1996). Similarly, feminist pedagogy emphasizes that gender disparities are reinforced when educators fail to recognize how male and female students have different social experiences that translate into different learning styles.

Current debates over social and educational inequality are shaped by conflicting demands from various interests and perspectives. Governments in several nations, including Canada and its provinces and territories, have been increasingly responsive to neo-liberal and individualist arguments that the state should not, and cannot afford to, offer too broad a range of programs and services in public enterprises like education when these are targeted to the needs of what have come to be defined as 'special interests'. Affirmative action, education equity, inclusive curricula, multicultural education, English as a second language (ESL), sexuality, and arts and music programs are some of the areas singled out by such critics as 'frills' or private issues that are costly, socially divisive, and counterproductive to educational needs in a highly competitive economic environment. Members of minority groups and other people most affected by lack of access to meaningful social and economic opportunity, by contrast, have become increasingly more vocal about their rights and entitlements. These concerns are frequently raised as a consequence of experiences of continuing discrimination and obstacles to the fulfillment of equity objectives. Cutbacks in programs and state services designed to enhance educational and economic opportunities have placed the least privileged segments of the population in an even more vulnerable position when they cannot gain access to the programs and resources required for competitive success.

Differing interpretations of the meaning of educational opportunity and inequality are also associated with differences in how educational opportunity is assessed or measured. The remainder of this chapter will focus on the most common determinants of inequality, addressing such factors as educational attainment, participation rates of different social groups, and relationships among education and income, labour force participation, and other relevant measures.

Before these indicators are examined, however, it is important to emphasize that educational success or failure cannot be understood only in quantitative terms. Acknowledgement must be given to the human and social dimensions that contribute to differing educational experiences and outcomes. Education is not an abstract process but a composite of lived practices that have real consequences for people's lives and futures. As emphasized throughout this book, schooling is characterized by a complex array of day-to-day occurrences in educational settings that intersect with external demands and structures. Success and failure take on differing interpretations just as they are produced through the interaction between personal experiences and social structural forces. For instance, we tend to place the greatest social and economic value on the attainment of a university degree, yet the completion of a high school diploma may be a major accomplishment for a person who has returned to school much later in life after being forced in youth to work to support a family following an interruption such as the death of a parent or an unplanned teen pregnancy. Similarly, a mid-range grade may be viewed as a failure by a student whose parents expect nothing less than performance that will lead to admission to an elite university, but the same grade may be a triumph for a student designated by school officials as 'at risk' or who is experiencing life difficulties or struggling to maintain an interest in school.

The Assembly of First Nations (1988: 72) points out that notions of educational quality from which measures of success and failure are derived are culturally laden, and emphasizes that educational success from a First Nations perspective should be based on the following goals: '(1) education should prepare children to gain the necessary skills for successful living and to contribute to community and (2) education should reinforce the student's cultural identity.' The Canadian Council on Learning (2007b) has reiterated the need to understand educational opportunity and performance by situating educational practices and student experience in an overall social context; they are not merely objects to be measured

in quantitative terms (see Box 5.3). Regardless of how opportunity and performance are defined or interpreted, they have important consequences for people's
lives and well-being.

DIMENSIONS OF EDUCATIONAL INEQUALITY

The following sections examine the most prevalent indicators associated with educational inequality, taking into account that schooling and its outcomes cannot
fully be understood in isolation from the social practices that constitute or contribute to school life. The discussion highlights questions about who is enrolled in
educational programs, what the characteristics are of students who enrol in and
graduate from particular programs, and what the benefits of formal education are
for people from particular social backgrounds.

The question of who goes to school can be answered simply, at least in general
terms. Almost every Canadian, with the exception of the very youngest and most
elderly, is engaged in some educational activity on a regular basis. Nearly one-fifth
of the total population is enrolled in full-time formal educational programs.
Nearly all children (about 19 out of 20) aged 6 to 16 attend school on a full-time
basis. Among young adults in the 20–4 age group about 35 per cent were enrolled
in full-time educational programs and an additional 6 per cent were engaged in
part-time studies in 2007. In addition, about half of the adult population participate in organized forms of adult learning and at least four out of five Canadians
regularly engage in informal learning activities in any given year (Statistics Canada
and CMEC, 2007; Statistics Canada, 2007b; Rubenson et al., 2007: 14; Livingstone
and Scholtz, 2007).

The composition of school-age populations and student bodies has undergone
significant transformations. Immigration has contributed significantly to the linguistic, racial, and cultural mix in Canadian schools, especially in the largest metropolitan centres. In 2006, about one in five school-age children in Vancouver and
one in seven in Toronto were born outside Canada, with recent immigrants (those
arriving between 2001 and 2006) representing up to half of the non-Canadian-
born cohort. Immigrants arrive from diverse places and backgrounds; about 60
per cent of recent arrivals were born in Asia and the Middle East, and over half of
recent school-age immigrants in Vancouver and Toronto speak languages other
than English or French at home (Statistics Canada, 2007a). Aboriginal people are
also becoming more concentrated among school-age populations, especially in the
Prairie provinces and northern regions. Aboriginal people represent about 3.8 per
cent of the Canadian population, but the proportion rises to 6.3 per cent among
children aged 14 and under, including one-third of children in Manitoba and over
one-quarter in Saskatchewan (Statistics Canada, 2008a). In addition to racial, cultural, and linguistic diversity, schooling incorporates large proportions of students
who encounter various social, economic, and physical challenges. At least one in
seven Canadian children, and one-quarter of those living with a lone parent , lives
in a low-income household (Statistics Canada and CMEC, 2007: 185). An estimated

4 per cent of Canadian children of ages 5–14 have physical disabilities or chronic conditions that limit their daily activities, while at least one in four children under the age of 11 exhibits one or more learning or behavioural problems (Kohen et al., 2007; Willms, 2002: 54). Whereas children with special needs were previously segregated into special classrooms or excluded from schools, about 60 per cent of students who receive special education for learning disabilities, emotional and behavioural problems, speech impairment, intellectual or physical disabilities, or other problems are now integrated into regular classrooms for most of their instruction and school-related activities (Bohatyretz and Lipps, 1999: 9; Kohen et al., 2007). Parallel trends in the growth of student diversity are exhibited, in many cases, within post-secondary and adult training institutions.

Educators and educational institutions face a significant challenge to balance student diversity, through strategies that promote integration and inclusion, with external demands for differentiated social and economic outcomes. The sections below highlight the persistence of major discrepancies in educational participation, performance, and outcomes, concentrating on dimensions of educational inequality associated with gender, racial and ethnic minorities, Aboriginal peoples, social class, and region.

GENDER

Gender-based inequalities are less evident within enrolment patterns than in terms of what happens within educational processes. Because almost all children attend school, there are no significant gender differentiations in enrolments at the elementary and secondary levels. Long-standing gender inequities in post-secondary enrolments have shifted over the past two decades. Overall, proportionately more men than women were enrolled in post-secondary programs until the mid-1980s, after which time the number of women has exceeded the number of men. For example, the ratio of female to male full-time undergraduate university students was 0.8 to 1 in the mid-1970s, but this ratio approached current levels of 1.3 to 1 by the late 1990s. Women's participation rates are even higher when part-time students are taken into account. There are marginally more male than female students in graduate-level studies, with women outnumbering men in master's programs and men constituting about 55 per cent of students in doctoral programs (Statistics Canada and CMEC, 2007: 273–4; AUCC, 2007a: 10–15). Some critics, such as Hoff Summers (2000), view these kinds of trends as evidence that schools, influenced by feminism, have contributed to ideologies and practices that produce disadvantage for males. The evidence, however, points to a much more complex picture.

Gender emerges as a significant factor when areas or programs of study are examined. Women's increased overall educational participation has been characterized by growing proportions of women in nearly every field of study. Nonetheless, as illustrated in Figures 8.1 and 8.2, the gender-based distribution of university students remains highly uneven. Since the early 1980s, approximate gender parity has been reached in such traditionally male-dominated fields as

Figure 8.1   Full-time Enrolment in Selected University Undergraduate Programs by Fields of Study and Gender, 1982–3

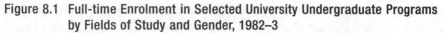
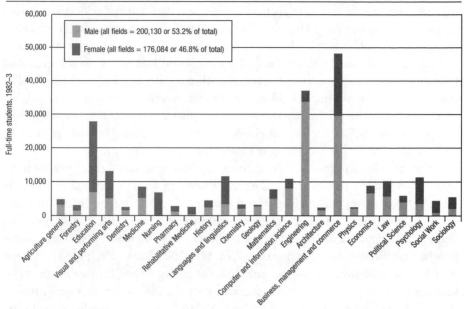

Source: Statistics Canada, *Education in Canada 1985–86* (Ottawa: Minister of Supply and Services Canada, 1987), 86–9.

Figure 8.2   Full-time Enrolment in Selected University Undergraduate Programs by Fields of Study and Gender, 2004–5

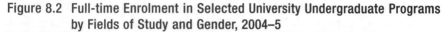
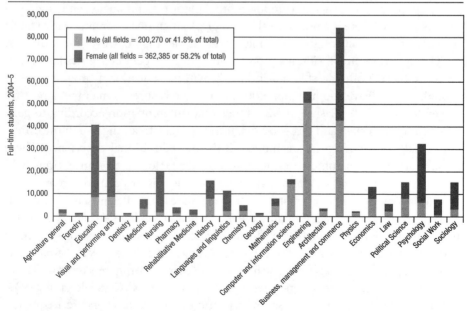

Source: Canadian Association of University Teachers (CAUT) 2007a: 25–31. CAUT *Almanac of Post-Secondary Education in Canada, 2007*. Ottawa: CAUT.

agriculture, law, medicine, history, political science, and large, high-growth business-related fields. Women also have had an increased presence, in both numerical and proportional terms, in economics, mathematics, natural sciences, and, to a lesser extent, engineering. The main focus of women's increased university participation remains, however, in fields already dominated by women, notably education, nursing, arts and cultural fields, languages and linguistics, sociology, social work, and psychology. Although current national data are not available, similar trends pertain for community college enrolment as well, where women are highly concentrated in clerical, human services, or support-related career programs while men dominate in fields related to physical sciences, engineering and applied sciences, and information technologies (Statistics Canada, 2001a).

These trends carry through to graduation, which provides a more precise indicator of specified fields of study. Consistent with enrolment trends, substantially more women than men receive undergraduate university degrees in all but a few major disciplinary areas—architecture, engineering and related technologies, mathematics, and computer and information sciences—in which cases men constituted about three-quarters of degree recipients in 2004 (CAUT, 2007: 33–4). There is only limited evidence, in these patterns, that the emergence of the new economy or knowledge society discussed in the previous chapter, with its emphasis on innovation, changing business opportunities, and information technology, is contributing to some convergence in fields of study. While degrees and diplomas in fields associated with business, management, and commerce demonstrate some of the highest growth among areas of post-secondary studies for both men and women, growth rates tend to be much higher for men than for women in the main fields related to innovation, such as computers, information technologies, and engineering. As a result, there are prospects that too great an emphasis on innovative fields of study, at least as currently posed, may widen rather than narrow gender divides.

The literature on educational processes reveals how **gender segmentation** can be reproduced both directly and indirectly within educational programs, even though schools have adopted numerous proactive measures to maintain a posture of gender neutrality. Gaskell (1992) argues that differentiation according to gender—along with class and race—occurs both through streaming and in the different signals and messages transmitted within the educational experience. These signals, operating in conjunction with such other factors as preconceptions held by parents and peers, gender-specific role models, distorted media representations, inadequate curricular materials, teacher biases, insufficient school support, and classroom practices that reinforce stereotypical or segmented gender expectations, influence the production of distinct educational paths or careers for male and female students (Bernhard and Nyhof-Young, 1994; Eyre, 1991). Female students also perceive signals from teachers, in the form of comments or attitudes, to channel them into gender-segregated occupational tracks (Crysdale et al., 1999: 33). In senior grades and post-secondary studies, female teachers are frequently absent or clustered in selected fields, contributing to a lack of role models in the classroom and a potentially limited capacity for consideration of issues of critical importance to female learners. Sometimes, even efforts meant to alleviate gender inequity can have the opposite impact. Kenway and Willis (1998: 208–9) point to a 'gender/generation gap' through which some teachers maintain outdated notions of gender that do not take into account significant changes in students' lives and identities. Relatively systematic messages can be conveyed as a student's social experiences come to be shaped through interactions with parents, peers, teachers, and other people in such a way as to produce distinctive trends and patterns based on gender (Mandell and Crysdale, 1993).

The messages that students receive about gender and gender roles within schools and through popular media and other relations outside of school can often offset or contradict one another (Moss and Attar, 1999: 143). Despite the availability of an array of educational, career, and personal options that exceeds opportunities open to previous generations, adolescent girls are also under considerable pressure to present themselves in a manner that is at once assertive and modest, assessed against physical and behavioural standards that may be incompatible with one another and difficult to achieve. Consequently, adolescent girls are considerably more likely than their male counterparts to hold negative views about themselves and to express lack of confidence about their appearance and capabilities, which often manifest themselves in serious eating disorders and other problems associated with low self-esteem (Bibby, 2001: 40; Canadian Women's Foundation, 2005: 18–20). Paradoxically, while many of the tensions and insecurities are directed inwardly for many girls and young women, media and public scrutiny point in another direction, towards phenomena like aggression, bullying, and violence expressed in terms of the problem of 'mean girls'. Such concerns, though typically overstating the actual occurrence of problem behaviours, draw attention to the complex relationships that adolescent girls and boys must negotiate within contemporary circumstances that pose numerous challenges and uncertainties for them. Concerns about female aggression, for instance, are often motivated by a backlash against feminism and other supposed threats to a social order governed by norms that privilege patriarchal, masculinist, and heterosexual standards. However, while these may divert attention away from issues that are far more pressing for youth, they also highlight both the risks that youth often face and the shifting expectations about gender, sexuality, identity, marginality, and overall social positioning that make it difficult for youth to find their way in a changing world.

The differential educational experiences of males and females contribute to the **social reproduction** of important inequalities beyond the classroom. Figures 8.3 and 8.4 offer two perspectives on intersections among gender inequalities, education, and income. Consistent with patterns observed in the previous chapter, Figure 8.4 demonstrates that average earnings increase for each subsequent level of educational attainment for both men and women. Nonetheless, both figures reveal the persistence of a gender-based wage gap, with women's earnings lower than those of men at every level. The gender gap in earnings generally decreases as education increases, with women periodically having the advantage at the doctoral level. However, relatively few women possess doctoral degrees, in part as a consequence of gender-biased channelling in earlier years of education. As the number of persons with higher levels of credentials has increased over the past two decades, the overall impact on earnings has been different for men and women. Men have generally increased their earnings with each subsequent level of education, while the returns to education for women are less pronounced. Analyzing trends in census data between 1985 and 2000, for instance, Boothby and Drewes (2006: 11) contrast women's earnings relative to those for men, observing that, for women, 'Trades certification appears to have had little to no impact on earnings over high-school completers . . . the earnings benefits of continuing on to a college diploma have increased for women, but by a smaller margin than is the case for men . . . [and] earnings for university-educated women have increased very little in relation to high-school completers.' As policy and investment decisions come to highlight high-tech and knowledge-sector work, there are dangers that patterns in labour market supply and selectivity (such as women's increased overall post-secondary participation concentration in areas like education, health, and general fields of study, in comparison with men's over-representation in engineering, technology, and related fields), combined with more diffuse forms of labour market discrimination, will perpetuate or widen the observed gender gaps (Frenette and Coulombe, 2007: 22, 24). These trends point to the importance of understanding the intersection of family, labour market, and educational factors.

Figure 8.3 Female-to-Male Earnings by Highest Level of Education Completed, Selected Years, 1980–2005

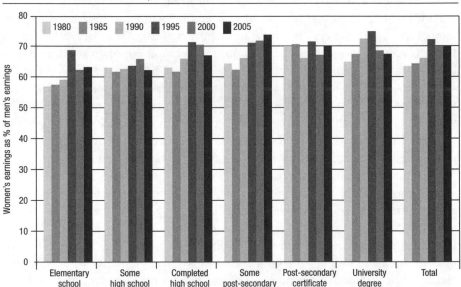

Source: Compiled from data in Statistics Canada, CANSIM Table 2020104.

Figure 8.4   Mean Earnings of 1990 Post-Secondary Graduates, Two Years and Five Years after Graduation (1995 constant dollars)

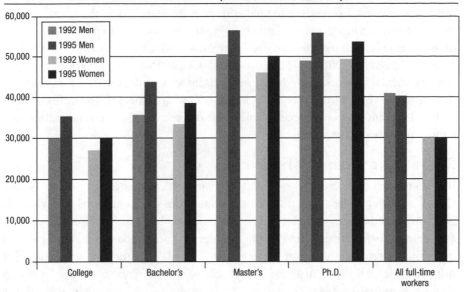

Source: Compiled from data in Finnie (2000: 29, 34).

Processes that contribute to gender segregation in education also operate in a similar manner, and reinforce one another, in the spheres of work and family life. Domestic responsibilities, orientations to marriage and family, and personal experiences, among other factors, affect educational attainment and employment and career prospects (Hamilton, 2005). The actual or projected interruption of an education program or career due to pregnancy or family considerations, for instance, normally affects women's lives and opportunities more than it does those of men. As many women have experienced benefits through access to education, both personally and in terms of their ability to acquire better-paying, more secure jobs, there has been some broadening of social opportunities and sharing of tasks in the household and other spheres of life. Nonetheless, especially in working-class families, women continue to bear the highest degree of responsibility for domestic work, caring, and maintenance of activities within communities and non-profit sectors (Pupo and Duffy, 2007). Women in both managerial and professional occupations and in lower-paying and less secure jobs—especially those jobs that entail caring responsibilities—experience substantially higher degrees of work overload and work–life stress than men (Duxbury and Higgins, 2003: 12–13). The enrolment and graduation trends outlined earlier suggest that education will continue to be an important basis through which women can gain entry into non-traditional positions and occupations that will contribute to greater gender parity in terms of labour force participation, wages, and other benefits.

Nonetheless, potential advances in these areas are limited by internal labour market dynamics and persistent gender discrimination, as well as by more general economic restructuring of the kind discussed in Chapter 7 that creates pressure to downsize the labour force, change skill requirements for workers, and minimize labour costs. Even when formal education has worked to the initial advantage of women who obtain relatively high-status jobs, women continue to be disadvantaged compared to men over the course of their entire careers (Canadian Labour Congress, 2008: 6–7; Frenette and Coulombe, 2007). Overall, despite improvements in women's educational attainment and benefits, the evidence demonstrates that gender inequalities still exist with respect to the kinds of educational credentials people receive and in the connections between education and subsequent life circumstances.

RACIAL AND ETHNIC MINORITIES

Increasing racial diversity is one of the major characteristics of contemporary Canadian society. The rising number of people from different social backgrounds is accompanied by growing heterogeneity and complexity in relationships within and among social groups in relation to different social, economic, cultural, and individual circumstances and experiences. Canada's history of education for minority populations is mixed, although schooling has frequently played a strong role in marginalizing and suppressing the interests of large segments of the Aboriginal population as well as black populations and other visible minority groups in some regions. In general terms, evidence suggests that increased educational opportunities, especially since World War II, have been beneficial for racial and ethnic minorities. Nonetheless, several important, and sometimes shifting, differences exist in the educational experiences and achievements among various racial and ethnic groups. In his landmark study of social stratification in Canada, Porter (1965) stressed that barriers to equitable educational participation have contributed to the inability of minority ethnic groups to attain proportional representation in positions of power and privilege, thereby undermining the claim that our social system is fully **meritocratic** and democratic. Today, although Porter's argument has been challenged and reassessed by many researchers, some of those inequalities remain in place or have been subsumed by new forms of inequality. While Canada's schools include numerous exemplary cases of progressive multicultural and multiracial relationships, the presence of serious problems—racial profiling, race-based violence and harassment, and differential educational treatment and pathways for particular minority groups—reveal the pervasive impact of both overt racism and more covert forms of discrimination in many aspects of Canadian life.

In terms of overall or average educational achievement, persons of Aboriginal ancestry (discussed more fully in the next section) have significantly lower overall rates of educational attainment and are much less likely to attend and complete post-secondary studies than other Canadians. Among other people within the adult population and in the labour force, those of Jewish and Chinese origin have the highest average years of schooling and are most likely to have a university

Box 8.2 Anti-Racism Education

Anti-racism education builds from an acknowledgement of the diffuse impact of race and racial inequalities, working towards understandings and practices that transcend race-based power relations and other forms of inequality. This process includes not only sensitization to personal identities, stereotypes, and discriminatory actions, but also recognition of the need to address long-lasting legacies of historical and structural injustices. Several community and educational groups, as well as national organizations like the Canadian Race Relations Foundation, have developed programs and materials to promote anti-racism education. The excerpt below is an exercise developed by youth for the United Nations Association in Canada to stimulate critical reflection and action through anti-racism initiatives, and asks the reader to identify various ways in which white skin affects daily life (Abboud et al., 2002: 51).

Read over these examples, and identify those which apply to you because of your skin colour.

1. I can turn on the television or open the front page of the paper and see people of my race widely represented.
2. I can, if I wish, arrange to be in the company of people of my own race most of the time.
3. I can say something positive about my own race without feeling that I'm saying something racist.
4. When I am told about our Canadian heritage, or 'civilization', I am shown that people of my colour made it what it is.
5. I can go into an art gallery and find the work of artists of my race hanging on the walls.
6. I can go into a university/high school and find professors of my race in all the departments.
7. I can go into a hairdresser's shop and find someone who knows how to cut my hair.
8. I can be at any cultural gathering or event and feel completely comfortable.
9. I can swear, or not answer letters, without having people attribute these choices to the bad morals or the illiteracy of my race.
10. I can do well in a challenging situation without being called a credit to my race.
11. I can criticize our government and talk about how much I disagree with its policies without being told to go back where I came from if I don't like it here.
12. I can be pretty sure that if I ask to talk to 'the person in charge', I will be facing a person of my skin colour.
13. If a traffic cop pulls me over, I can be sure I haven't been singled out because of my race.

14. I can talk about my ancestors without feeling guilty about what people of my race may have done in the past.
15. I can take a job with an equal opportunity employer without having my co-workers on the job suspect that I got it because of my race.
16. If my day, or week, or year is going badly, I wonder if each negative situation has racial overtones.
17. I can walk onto a bus [or] train [or into a] cafeteria or school room and find it easy to sit next to someone of my race.
18. I can choose blemish cover (cover-up) or bandages in 'flesh' colour and have them more or less match my skin.

degree. Particularly among the foreign-born, those from Southern European origins tend to have the lowest levels of formal education (Li, 1988: 79–81). These patterns endured throughout much of the twentieth century, but there is evidence that visible minorities—especially Asian men—as well as Southern and Eastern European groups, have experienced considerable gains in their average educational attainment over the last four decades (Forcese, 1997: 116; Guppy and Davies, 1998: 23; Finnie et al., 2005: 19–20).

To a certain extent, the modified reproduction of racial and ethnic inequality can be explained by immigration policies and practices that since the late 1960s have placed increasing emphasis on the selective recruitment of highly qualified labour. Until the post-World War II period, the nation's labour market needs were met predominantly by Canadian-born workers augmented periodically by immigrant labour, mostly from Europe or other industrially developed English- or French-speaking nations, to fill low-wage or semi-skilled positions in agriculture and manufacturing sectors. By the late 1960s, the gradual emergence of what is referred to in the previous chapter as the post-industrial or service economy created conditions in which Canada had to look to additional sources to secure qualified workers, especially in many occupations that required professional credentials or specialized skills and training. The aging of the post-war baby-boom generation and their impending retirement, combined with relatively low domestic birth rates, have fuelled further demands for immigrants to sustain the workforce and population base through the twenty-first century. Beginning in 1967, immigration policy and selection criteria were amended to apply a point system recognizing factors like age, credentials, language proficiency, and demand for job skills rather than country and race of origin. These transitions have had significant consequences for the relations between education and minority populations. In particular, recent immigrants represent considerable social and cultural diversity, they are now predominantly from visible minority populations originating in nations throughout Asia and other non-Western regions, they are increasingly well-educated but not always fluent in English or French, and they tend to place a high value on the education of their children.

The impact of these policy changes is evident in comparisons of educational attainments by immigrants and Canadian-born populations. In the years immediately following implementation of the points system (during the 1970s and 1980s), slightly more than half (52 per cent) of immigrants aged 25–64 who arrived in Canada had high school or less (compared to between 55 and 75 per cent of the general population in these age cohorts over the same period). Recent immigrants in general are even more highly educated than the Canadian population. In 2006, just under one in six of Canadian-born labour force participants aged 25–54 had a university degree and about one-third had no more than high school credentials, whereas among landed immigrants within these age cohorts who had immigrated during the previous 10 years, over half had a university degree and about one-quarter had high school or less (Zietsma, 2007: 21).

The relationship among race and ethnicity, immigration, and education and the economic benefits associated with education are considerably more complex than these general trends reveal, indicating substantial variations according to class, gender, race, and other significant characteristics. Various immigrant and visible minority groups are clustered at both professional, high-skill, and (especially among visible minority women) lower-status occupational positions (Pendakur, 2000: 151–6; Guppy and Davies, 1998: 122–3). Immigrants, in part due to the credentials and capacities that they bring with them, perform relatively well overall on many economic criteria. Intensified global demand for knowledge-sector workers with specialized skills and advanced credentials elevates the importance of immigration for securing workers to fill positions in many professional occupations and scientific and technical fields. Nonetheless, as the previous chapter has revealed, these sectors constitute relatively limited proportions of the total labour force. Immigrant and migrant labour has been an important source to fill positions in manufacturing and construction industries, as well as in food, accommodation, and other service areas frequently characterized by low wages, poor working conditions, and limited job security. Recent immigrants, in particular, have encountered particular difficulties, relative to persons born in Canada and even compared to previous cohorts of immigrants, in finding secure employment, especially in fields for which they are qualified (Zietsma, 2007: 21–4). Whereas such problems typically diminish over time as immigrants settle into the host society, improve their English or French language competency, and gain Canadian contacts and work experience, this process of labour market integration has slowed down or even ceased for some cohorts of recent immigrants. Many immigrants, especially women and visible minorities, encounter selective barriers that have long-term implications for career options, occupational mobility, and life prospects. Reitz (2001) observes considerable variations both between immigrants and non-immigrants and among different immigrant groups, but finds overall that immigrants receive lower returns on both education and work experience than do persons born in Canada. These findings are reinforced by data from the 2006 census revealing that the earnings gap between immigrants and Canadian-born workers has increased, even among the highly educated. In 1980, immigrant men and women who had arrived in the five previous years earned on average 85 per cent of what Canadian-born earners received, whereas by 2005, the earnings ratio had widened, with recent immigrants making only 63 per cent and 56 per cent of Canadian-born counterparts for men and women, respectively (Statistics Canada, 2008c: 21).

Several proactive measures have been adopted to counter discriminatory practices, policies, and attitudes and to remove barriers that restrict full participation by racial minorities in all spheres of social life. However, overt discrimination, structural barriers, and complex practices such as limited or non-recognition for foreign credentials and work experience continue to have a differential impact on segments of visible minority and immigrant populations. Some immigrant groups—such as those of Chinese, South Asian, Filipino, West Asian, and Arab origins—are more likely than other Canadians to hold a university degree, while others, including black and Latin American men, are less likely to have a degree, and higher than average proportions of women from Southeast Asia and South Asia have less than high school. In contrast to the small pool of highly qualified immigrants who find ready work in their fields, sizable proportions of the immigrant population (especially among women) begin in a relatively strong employment position yet have almost no career mobility (Creese et al., 1991: 72–3; Li, 2003: 122–3). Similarly, Kazemipur and Halli (2001: 234) find that while education had an impact on alleviating poverty within the general population from 1991 to 1996, that relationship did not hold for immigrants, especially those in visible minority groups. Tran (2004: 11), summarizing trends since the mid-1980s, observes: 'Foreign-born visible minority men, especially recent immigrants, saw their labour market outcomes deteriorate faster than Canadian-born non-visible minority men', while among women, 'employment rates increased for all except foreign-born visible minorities although foreign-born visible minority women were more highly educated than most other women.' In addition, immigrant children and their families, depending on their circumstances and previous experiences, have varying capacities to negotiate the demands associated with new school and community environments. In addition to the process of transition itself, immigrants often are confronted with unfamiliar school rules and procedures, cultural and linguistic barriers, uncertain access to support and resources, economic vulnerability, and sometimes trauma and victimization during or prior to leaving their home countries (Ngo and Schleifer, 2004: 30).

Two prevalent themes emerge in the literature on race, ethnicity, and Canadian schooling. (1) Race—and, to a certain extent, ethnicity—does have an impact on people's educational experiences and social opportunities. (2) Ethnicity and race cannot be understood in isolation from social class, gender, and other important social characteristics. The increasing number and diversity of immigrants, and especially the high concentrations of immigrant populations in larger metropolitan areas, have elevated the profile of race relations and multicultural issues in Canada. These changes have been accompanied by new challenges and opportunities, but they have also raised awareness and frustration over long-standing problems. Recent initiatives to establish Afrocentric schools in Nova Scotia and Ontario, for example (discussed previously in Box 5.4), have drawn criticism based on claims that minority rights and segregation are undermining public school values, on the one hand, while highlighting for proponents the historical failure of mainstream education systems to provide adequate cultural validation and educational integration for black students. Similarly, the profusion of media depictions of threats posed by a proliferation of youth gangs, organized in many cases around visible minority or Aboriginal membership, illustrates both the public fears generated over racial diversity and the attraction for some minority group members to be drawn into alternative lifestyles that promise an escape from the hostility and marginalization they encounter in schools and other social settings.

Several researchers have emphasized the changing and complex nature of race and ethnic relations in Canada, documenting the ways in which family, work, schooling, and other institutional environments interact to produce continual modifications and tensions among ethnic identity, ethnic group cohesion, and diverse cultural adaptations (Fleras and Elliott, 2003). McLaren (2007: 226–7), observing children of West Indian origin in a North York school, notes that underprivileged black students engage in forms of resistance in opposition to dominant school and social expectations if they see that they must attempt to deny their 'blackness' to succeed. James (1993), examining the school-to-work transition process for black youth in Toronto, stresses that, while respondents he interviewed tended to assume individual responsibility for their own success or failure, their lives and self-concepts were continually affected by racist stereotypes and structures prevalent both within and beyond schooling. Visible minority and Aboriginal students, though receptive to the substantial opportunities for equity and participation afforded by schooling, remain keenly aware of the many manifestations that they and other students encounter of racism and discrimination (Bibby, 2001: 42–3; James, 2003: 131–64; Schissel and Wotherspoon, 2003: 82–3).

Much as with gender and class, with which they interact, racial and ethnic factors enter into the complex web of social arrangements in such a way as to produce differential experiences and career and educational futures for students of distinct social origins. Jackson (1987: 181) refers to these school practices, as they come into existence through the choices and actions of students and teachers, as 'differentiating practices' that emerge:

> as practical organizational solutions to the conflicts and contradictions which both school life and the labour market pose for ethnic minority students. Both the student and the educator may feel justified with their choice of practical solutions, particularly if the student experiences success in his/her courses in the short run. However, this is to disregard the 'hidden injury' of long-term educational disadvantage.

The federal government's policy of multiculturalism, in effect since the early 1970s, stands as an important institutional response to the reality of and problems associated with racial and ethnic diversity in Canada. Multiculturalism provides a good example of how state policy has shifted over time in conjunction with differing social realities and conceptions of equality. McAndrew (1995: 165) points out that multiculturalism signifies the state's response to the 'pluralist dilemma in education' whereby divergent social interests express 'conflicting visions of the role that school plays in either reproducing or transforming ethnic/religious/racial inequalities'.

Multiculturalism is intended to foster tolerance and understanding for the broad mosaic of cultural groups within Canadian society. At the same time, it represents the state's interest in perpetuating a common national purpose. In the area of education, in particular, as Fleras and Elliott (1992: 183–5) emphasize, multiculturalism signifies a pronounced change, in jurisdictions outside Quebec, from a preoccupation with integration and assimilation in compliance with English-speaking, white standards of conformity to official recognition of pluralism and diversity, encompassing among its objectives the desire:

(a) to diminish the ethnic 'problem'; (b) to eliminate discrimination and promote intergroup harmony; (c) to foster genuine equality and justice for ethnic minorities; and (d) to improve intercultural sharing, understanding, and communication.

In education, multiculturalism has been implemented in various ways across Canada, including such measures as heritage language instruction, the development of curricula to represent diverse cultural traditions, cross-cultural training for educational workers and administrators, and the provision of specific services or opportunities for minority students. The uniqueness of multicultural educational policy and initiatives in each province or region reflects both the fact that education is a provincial responsibility and the reality whereby each jurisdiction has its own distinctive cultural composition and political climate (McAndrew, 1995: 170–4). In general terms, multicultural policy has changed in emphasis since the mid-1980s from an initial concern with cultural understanding and tolerance of racial or ethnic differences towards a more active orientation on race relations, equity issues, and institutional change (Fleras and Elliott, 1992: 68–9). Canadian schools in general have clearly become more sensitive to issues involving cultural diversity and minority learners, although it is difficult to determine how much of this, rather than being the result of the impact of multicultural policies and practices, is due to the reality that many communities are much more racially heterogeneous than they were two or three decades ago.

With respect to anti-racism education, Henry and Tator (2005: 212–14) note that, despite several prominent policy statements and initiatives concerned with the eradication of racial bias and discrimination through education, racism continues to be a problem both within schools and in the communities in which they operate. Even programs like ESL, for instance, which are intended to provide training directed to the special needs of students who lack language or social skills essential for success in mainstream classrooms, can marginalize and stigmatize minority children. Rockhill and Tomic (1995: 222) observe that 'The segregation of children into special classes for ESL instruction further marks their difference from the other students. When this is coupled with being seen as having a problem, a deficiency or lack, feelings of deviance and shame are reinforced.' Multicultural and related programs, in these regards, act in a contradictory way, fostering tolerance of diversity and generating opportunities for minority groups, yet at the same time representing state efforts to manage race and ethnic relations as ongoing problems without providing assurances of full equality for all groups (Wotherspoon, 1995b).

ABORIGINAL PEOPLE

Aboriginal people have had a long and often devastating relationship with schooling in Canada. Residential schooling and subsequent encounters with provincial and territorial education systems have contributed to a legacy in which both personal and community experiences of failure, marginalization, and disillusionment are widespread. The Assembly of First Nations (2005: 2), expressing a sentiment echoed by many communities and observers, has declared with reference to both reserve-based and provincial school systems that 'The current state of First Nations education is unacceptable.' Nonetheless, as signified in the title of a recent book, education is also envisioned as 'the new buffalo' that will serve as the foundation for cultural survival and empowerment among First Nations and other Aboriginal people (Stonechild, 2006). Aboriginal peoples represent relatively small proportions of the total Canadian population, but the Aboriginal population is young, expanding more rapidly than the general population, and highly concentrated in specific regions, including the Prairies and northern territories (Canadian Council on Learning, 2007b: 4).

Before the significance of these factors is discussed in more depth, it is important to acknowledge two general observations. First, despite substantial improvements that have been achieved through many promising recent initiatives, Aboriginal people fare considerably less well than other Canadians with respect to educational attainment. Prospects for educational success, in turn, are highly associated with such critical aspects of social and economic well-being or problems as poverty, housing, crime and victimization, health status, employment, and income. Second, the Aboriginal population is highly differentiated, representing diverse cultural, legal, social, and economic groupings, identities, and positions (Wotherspoon, 2003).

These discrepancies tend to be most evident for First Nations students living on reserves. Between the mid-1990s and 2003–4, for instance, the proportion of registered Indians aged 6–16 living on-reserve who were enrolled in full-time schooling declined from 87 per cent to 80 per cent, compared to over 95 per cent of persons of comparable ages in the general population (Indian and Northern

Affairs Canada, 2005: 45, 46). Disparities in educational participation rates are even more pronounced at the post-secondary level. The latest available data, from the late 1990s, show that only 6.6 per cent of the registered Indian population aged 17–34, compared to 11.4 per cent of the general population in the same age cohort, were enrolled in full-time university studies. Similar inequalities are evident in patterns of educational attainment. The Saskatchewan Association of University Teachers (2006: 4) observes that in 2003, in a province with one of the highest Aboriginal populations, First Nations represented 13.2 per cent of the population but only 2 per cent of students who graduated from post-secondary programs.

Data from the 2006 census reveal that, among those aged 25–64, over half of persons of Aboriginal identity (53.5 per cent), compared with fewer than two out of five in the general population (39.4 per cent), had high school equivalency or less, while only 7.5 per cent of the Aboriginal population as opposed to 22.9 per cent of the general population had a university degree (calculated from Statistics Canada, 2008e). Figure 8.5 provides a more detailed look at the distribution of educational credentials across population groups for the population aged 15 and over. The data reveal important differences in educational patterns both within Aboriginal populations and among Aboriginal people, visible minorities, and the population as a whole, suggesting that we must be cautious not to overgeneralize the circumstances that pertain for any social group. Educational attainment is lowest among the Inuit and among registered Indians living on-reserve (close to three-quarters have not yet completed credentials beyond high school and only about 3 per cent have a university degree), while slightly less than two-thirds of those with North American Indian identity living off-reserve have Grade 12 or less and about 7 per cent of Métis and off-reserve Indians have university degrees.

Several factors have contributed to the under-representation and under-achievement of Aboriginal peoples in Canadian schooling. As noted earlier, schooling was an important instrument both in the early colonization of indigenous peoples by Europeans and in subsequent efforts by the Canadian state to assimilate or acculturate indigenous populations within a dominant framework often marked by racism and hostility towards Aboriginal peoples and their cultures. As was the case for other visible minorities until well after World War II, First Nations have rarely been given opportunities to represent themselves and their interests in educational decision-making and curricular materials because of the dominant educational orientation towards Anglo-conformity.

In addition, for most Canadians education is a provincial responsibility, whereas education for persons defined by the Indian Act as registered Indians is under federal jurisdiction. One consequence of this divergence has been separate and distinct institutional structures for Aboriginal children, including boarding and residential schools, whose legacy of destruction and pain continues to resonate throughout Aboriginal communities (Schissel and Wotherspoon, 2003; Miller, 1996). This constitutional framework has also contributed to jurisdictional dis-

Figure 8.5 Education by Highest Certificate, Degree, or Diploma, Ages 15 and Over, Aboriginal Identity Categories, Visible Minorities, and Total Canadian Population, 2006

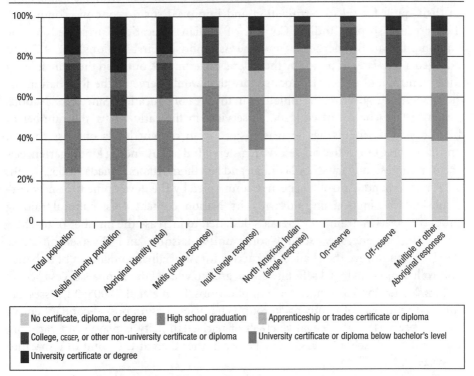

Legend:
- No certificate, diploma, or degree
- High school graduation
- Apprenticeship or trades certificate or diploma
- College, CEGEP, or other non-university certificate or diploma
- University certificate or diploma below bachelor's level
- University certificate or degree

Note: On-reserve and off-reserve figures are for those identifying North American Indian single response identities only.
Source: Compiled from data in Statistics Canada publications 97-562-X2006017 and 97-560-X2006028.

putes that have restricted educational funding and services for First Nations people and produced considerable variations in the nature and quality of educational services provided to different segments of the Aboriginal population.

These factors have contributed to the variations in educational attainment among on- and off-reserve registered Indians, non-status Indians, Métis, and Inuit, as shown in Figure 8.5. Compounding these legal and historical circumstances, Aboriginal students have experienced discrimination, lack of culturally sensitive curricula and learning materials, an absence of teachers trained to work with Aboriginal learners and communities, and other problems that have restricted their educational opportunities and success (Satzewich and Wotherspoon, 2000: 126–38).

Recent struggles on the part of Aboriginal peoples to gain input into and control over crucial aspects of their education illustrate the contradictory nature of the relationship between education and socio-economic opportunity. Persistent barriers to educational access and experiences of educational failure have contributed to higher than average rates of unemployment, poverty, and other types of social and economic marginalization among Native peoples. At the same time, education has been regarded by First Nations as a sphere of strategic importance in their quest for self-determination and improved socio-economic conditions. The position paper, 'Indian Control of Indian Education', presented by the National Indian Brotherhood (now the Assembly of First Nations) in 1972 and adopted a year later as policy by the federal government, outlined the principles of local control and parental responsibility that would serve as the foundation for subsequent self-government initiatives in the area of education. Since First Nations began to take control of educational services in the early 1970s, the number of band-operated schools has increased steadily to current levels of close to 500, enrolling three out of five on-reserve registered Indians attending kindergarten, elementary, and secondary school (Indian and Northern Affairs Canada, 2005: 37, 49). The shift to band control has been accompanied by the development of new curricula and teaching/learning aids with First Nations content, cross-cultural training programs, teacher-training programs designed to increase the number of teachers of Aboriginal ancestry, school–community liaisons, and diverse initiatives designed to improve the chances of success for Aboriginal students in both band-controlled and provincial schools. The degree to which educational success occurs in basic education has longer-term implications. Finnie et al. (2005: 22), assessing the relative impact of family background characteristics on post-secondary enrolment, observe that the 'negative effect of native ethnicity is played out early on, during the high school years . . . or before, rather than at the point of entry into post-secondary schooling.'

The impact of these developments has been mixed (Assembly of First Nations, 1988; Castellano et al., 2000; Kirkness and Bowman, 1992; Schissel and Wotherspoon, 2003). Growing sensitivity to the need for educational improvement among Aboriginal communities, combined with appropriate programming, services, and personnel, has contributed to increasing educational participation and attainment rates among Aboriginal populations at almost all levels. About 23,000 status Indian and Inuit students annually are now enrolled in post-secondary education programs with funding support delivered through bands from the Indian Affairs branch of the federal government, and about 3,500 funded students graduate each year. While these numbers represent dramatic increases over the past three to four decades (just over 800 First Nations students were funded to attend post-secondary programs in 1969–70 and about 8,600 were enrolled by the mid-1980s), there have been declines since the 1990s, when as many as 27,000 students and 4,000 graduates a year were supported by federal funding (Indian and Northern Affairs Canada, 2005: 53, 57; Standing Committee on Aboriginal Affairs and Northern Development, 2007). The actual number of Aboriginal students and graduates is higher than these figures indicate, since many First Nations students and other Aboriginal groups do not qualify for or receive federal funding, but the trends nonetheless point to the more general difficulties many Aboriginal students are confronted with in being able to continue into and finance post-secondary programs. The Assembly of First Nations suggests apart from the small number of students who are funded annually, at least two to three times that number are prevented from pursuing post-secondary studies because of lack of funding (Standing Committee on Public Accounts, 2005: 10).

Despite these barriers, significant numbers of Aboriginal people return to school later in life to upgrade basic education or to achieve higher credentials. More than half of university and college students of Aboriginal ancestry, compared to just over one-third of the general post-secondary student body, are aged 22 years and over (Canadian Millennium Scholarship Foundation, 2005: 5). Census data reveal that for those aged 20–4, the non-Aboriginal population has close to double the participation rate of the Aboriginal population (40.5 per cent to 24.1 per cent, respectively), but Aboriginal people have higher participation rates, by factors of two to four times for each age cohort from 30 to 64 (Statistics Canada, 2003: 47). Despite the persistence of numerous obstacles and resistance to change, some elementary and secondary schools have made significant progress to accommodate Aboriginal learners and communities, with demonstrated improvements in student attendance, academic achievement, student motivation and work habits, staff awareness, and the incorporation of positive role models.

Several jurisdictions have begun to incorporate a comprehensive, integrated approach into their educational planning and delivery, recognizing that the most severe problems faced by learners cannot be resolved through schooling alone. Saskatchewan, for instance, has adopted a community schools policy built on a vision to provide:

> a comprehensive range of best educational practices for meeting the diverse learning needs of at-risk and Indian and Métis students. They provide a responsive, inclusive, culturally affirming and academically challenging learning program and environment and are effective in addressing the challenges of the communities they serve. As hubs for a network of community organizations and activities, they use collaborative approaches to foster the development and well-being of the entire community. (Saskatchewan Education, 1996: 6)

More recently, this vision was augmented and broadened to the entire provincial school system through the adoption of a model called 'School Plus' intended to 'describe a new conceptualization of schools as centres of learning, support and community for the children and families they serve', building on partnerships with diverse communities and human service agencies (Government of Saskatchewan, 2003: 1). The Royal Commission on Aboriginal Peoples, in placing education at the core of its far-reaching aim to achieve full participation in the economy and self-sufficiency of Aboriginal people, has stimulated several innovative educational developments (Castellano et al., 2000). Insofar as there is an impetus within all levels of governance, including First Nations as well as federal and provincial authorities, to foster such an integrated approach to social and educational development, it is possible that more meaningful opportunities can be provided to large segments of the Aboriginal population.

Nonetheless, several problems remain. The gradual path towards progress in meeting many of the needs of First Nations students and communities remains hindered by lack of resolution of the kinds of critical problems that Kirkness and Bowman (1992: 52–3) reported on several years ago, including poor attendance and motivation, high dropout rates, poverty and racism, tensions between schools and families, high mobility, and language difficulties. Many of these concerns, along with frustration over the slow pace of efforts by Aboriginal Elders, parents, and other community members to gain effective input into and control over their education, have been repeatedly expressed to various educational and policy-making bodies, but they have met with little productive response (Royal Commission on Aboriginal Peoples, 1996a, 1996b). Aboriginal students generally express highly positive assessments of schools, teachers, and the importance of education for life success, but they also encounter racism, institutional barriers, and cultural divisions that can significantly impede their educational progress (Assembly of First Nations, 2005; Silver and Mallett, 2002: 29–30; Schissel and Wotherspoon, 2003: 82–92). At the post-secondary level, Aboriginal students are most likely to suggest that financial barriers and poor grades are deterrents to higher education, but high proportions also attribute a lack of welcoming environment as a barrier to continuing their studies (CMSA, 2005: 4).

Aboriginal people have had some success in converting educational credentials, particularly in professional fields, administration, and business and commerce, into labour market and economic advances. There is some evidence that, for Aboriginal people living off-reserve, high levels of credentials tend to offer relatively high returns on employment and income prospects (Luffman and Sussman, 2007). However, the Aboriginal population, both overall and with respect to those with higher credentials, remains highly segmented, often concentrated within specific areas. Aboriginal people pursuing post-secondary studies remain relatively under-represented in the most prestigious or highly skilled fields, focusing instead in such areas as human services, trades and construction, and technologies for men and commercial and human services and clerical programs for women (Statistics Canada, 2003: 46; Luffman and Sussman, 2007). Hull (2000: 108) observes that educational pathways and returns are highly mediated by class, gender, Aboriginal status, and region for Aboriginal people, concluding:

It is clear that, by and large, registered Indian women continue to have weaker labour market participation and success than registered Indian men and that there continue to be high concentrations of men and women in particular occupations. It also appears that within urban areas registered Indians experience greater extremes of occupational success on the one hand, and government dependency on the other. These extremes are closely related to educational attainment.

Box 8.3 The Educational Attainment of Aboriginal Peoples

The Royal Commission on Aboriginal Peoples (1996b: 433–4, 440, 476–7) offers a concise summary of the factors that have contributed to the restriction of opportunities for educational success and limited integration into the labour force among Aboriginal youth:

In Aboriginal societies, as in many societies, children are regarded as a precious gift. Control over the education of their children has been a pressing priority of Aboriginal peoples for decades. This is not surprising. The destiny of a people is intricately bound to the way its children are educated. Education is the transmission of cultural DNA from one generation to the next. It shapes the language and pathways of thinking, the contours of character and values, the social skills and creative potential of the individual. It determines the productive skills of a people.

Aboriginal peoples are diverse in their histories, environments and cultures, but their deep commitment to education cuts across all boundaries. In our public hearings, Aboriginal parents, elders, youth and leaders came forward to tell us of the vital importance of education in achieving their vision of a prosperous future. Education is seen as the vehicle for both enhancing the life of the individual and reaching collective goals.

For more than 25 years, Aboriginal peoples have been articulating their goals for Aboriginal education. They want education to prepare them to participate fully in the economic life of their communities and in Canadian society. But this is only part of their vision. Presenters told us that education must develop children and youth as Aboriginal citizens, linguistically and culturally competent to assume the responsibilities of their nations. Youth that emerge from school must be grounded in a strong, positive Aboriginal identity. Consistent with Aboriginal traditions, education must develop the whole child, intellectually, spiritually, emotionally and physically.

Current education policies fail to realize these goals. The majority of Aboriginal youth do not complete high school. They leave the school system without the requisite skills for employment, and without the language and cultural knowledge of their people. Rather than nurturing the individual, the schooling experience typically erodes identity and self-worth. Those who continue in Canada's formal education systems told us of regular encounters with racism, racism expressed not only in interpersonal exchanges but also through the denial of Aboriginal values, perspectives and cultures in the curriculum and the life of the institution.

The human costs of this failure are immense. It saps the creative potential of individuals, communities, and nations. Yet, despite the painful experiences

Aboriginal people carry with them from formal education systems, they still see education as the hope for the future, and they are determined to see education fulfil its promise. . . .

By the time they enter high school, many Aboriginal youth have spent eight years or more in an education system from which they and their parents feel alienated. In public schools, the absence of support for Aboriginal identities is overwhelming: no Aboriginal high school teachers; only a limited curriculum dealing with contemporary Aboriginal languages, cultures, history, and political issues; an emphasis on intellectual cognitive achievement at the expense of spiritual, social, and physical development; and the marginalization of youth in decision-making about their education.

At the high school level, most parents are even less involved in their children's education than at elementary school levels. Their exclusion from decision-making is intensified where there are no local high schools, where teachers and administrators are non-Aboriginal, and where Aboriginal parents are in a minority. Issues of culturally appropriate curriculum, language education, parental involvement, and funding for curriculum development and culture programs are all present in the education of youth, as in the education of the child. Additional challenges encountered in the education of youth are the need for youth empowerment; the need for local high schools; the opportunity to return to high school; and the transition from high school to economic activity and careers.

Source: *Report of the Royal Commission on Aboriginal Peoples, Vol. 3, Gathering Strength,* 1996. Pages 433–4, 440, 476–7. Reproduced with the permission of the Minister of Public Works and Government Services, 2008, and courtesy of the Privy Council Office.

In many cases, however, educational improvements have not been sufficient to overcome deeper problems like absence of sufficient jobs and discrimination. In addition to limited employment opportunities in many communities in which Aboriginal people are concentrated, or lack of available jobs to match education or work experience, many Aboriginal people indicate that 'being Aboriginal' can produce difficulties in their search for jobs (Statistics Canada, 1993). Indian and Northern Affairs Canada (2004) acknowledges that systemic factors such as human resources practices that are not culturally sensitive, as well as attitudinal factors such as stereotyping, discrimination, and racism, compound the barriers that restrict equitable employment options for Aboriginal people. Aboriginal people with the highest educational credentials tend to receive significant returns for their education, but considerable evidence points to the reality that Aboriginal people in general are more likely than other Canadians to experience a diminished relationship between education and social and economic opportunities (Canadian Race Relations Foundation, 2000: 24–6).

SOCIAL CLASS

Despite a long tradition of analysis of the relationship between social class and other dimensions of social inequality, until recently a surprisingly small body of systematic data has been available to document those relations with respect to Canadian education. This problem, in large part, is a consequence of differences in the definition and measurement of class inequality. The most common conceptions of **class**, derived from structural functionalist analysis, emphasize social stratification, relying on such indicators as income, occupation, parental education, and other variables that can be empirically measured and compared (Forcese, 1997: 22–8). These kinds of indicators can be readily identified, but require considerable resources and massive databases, such as census sources, if they are to be analyzed in a comprehensive way.

Alternative conceptions, including those derived from Marxist analysis or others following the critical analysis of contemporary European researchers such as Pierre Bourdieu, emphasize class as a relational concept that requires much more intensive scrutiny of what people do and how they do it in relation to other people, productive property, and labour processes (Nakhaie, 1996; Veltmeyer, 1986). This kind of analysis has rarely been applied to a consideration of educational inequality because of the detailed information required to place people in class relations and to assess their educational backgrounds, not to mention the inclination among many researchers and agencies that compile large quantities of data to disregard this conception of class. Regardless of how class is defined and operationalized, however, the interaction between social class and educational inequality is a persistent, and potentially growing, phenomenon.

The strong two-way association between social background and education exists because social privilege increases the chances of gaining higher educational credentials, which in turn increase the likelihood of subsequent socio-economic success. As we have already observed with respect to gender, race, and ethnic inequality, nearly all groups have experienced some benefits from the expansion of Canada's education system in the latter part of the twentieth century. Porter et al. (1982: 313), in an analysis of students' educational plans and paths in Ontario, concluded that the education system is somewhat meritocratic in that, regardless of social background, students tend to have high aspirations and access to educational opportunities, and that factors like mental ability and self-concept do count. About two-thirds of all Canadians have more education than their parents, while only 7 per cent have less formal education than their parents; in 1993, 'just over half the population had attended a post-secondary institution, compared with a little over 10 per cent of their parents ... while 70 per cent of the parents had not graduated from high school, only 30 per cent of their children had failed to do so' (Fournier et al., 1995: 24, 26).

However, these opportunities are not distributed equally. The rapid expansion of post-secondary education in the late 1960s and early 1970s produced some relative gains in educational opportunities for women and some ethnic minorities, but overall patterns of class inequality have remained relatively stable (Anisef and Okihiro, 1982: 131). Class plays a strong role in influencing students' aspirations, usually indirectly through its impact on the programs students entered into, their parents' expectations, and the self-concepts of the learners (Porter et al., 1982: 313). Forcese (1997: 133) argues that educational institutions tend to serve as 'gatekeepers to "success"' rather than as facilitators for upward social mobility because they restrict the numbers of students from lower-class backgrounds who benefit from formal education:

> Education was to have been the means of overcoming the inheritance of social class. However, as presently constituted, the educational system favours the already priv-ileged, and screens out the already disadvantaged. Rather than defeating stratifica-tion, formal education is a cause of persisting and increasingly rigid stratification.

More recent research confirms the tendency for educational inequality to be reproduced across generations. Class-related factors, including parental income, wealth, occupation, and education, recur prominently in both Canadian and com-parative studies that examine indicators associated with education. Ornstein (2007: 150), examining historical relationships between education and class in the United States, cautions that globalization is likely to restrict opportunities for class mobility that were limited in the first place: 'Only if inequalities of income and wealth are kept within a limited range can education be used as an equalizer . . . Because . . . measures [to address these issues] are not being implemented, we are witnessing a rise of a new aristocratic class, based on wealth and power.' Expressed in less dramatic terms, Guppy and Davies (1998: 123) conclude from a compre-hensive overview of education trends in Canada that, in comparison with gender and ethnicity, 'class background seems to be the far more enduring source of edu-cational inequality' once general educational improvements are taken into account. Family income affects not only educational directions, but also the abili-ty graduates have to secure jobs and higher incomes (Grayson, 1997).

The likelihood that a young Canadian will engage in post-secondary studies, especially at a university level, increases with each successive level of parental edu-cation and household income (Knighton and Mirza, 2002). Even though more Canadians, regardless of background, are participating in higher education, rela-tively enduring patterns of inequality persist. Persons from high-income families are about twice as likely to attend university, and slightly more likely to attend col-lege, than persons from low-income families (Drolet, 2005: 12, 16). Siedule (1992: 19), comparing the impact of various socio-economic factors including family income, family structure, province of residence, and ethnic background, demon-strates that the difference between favourable and unfavourable conditions can make a difference of up to five years in the amount of education a person attains. Over a decade later, Finnie et al. (2005: 22) observe that the likelihood of university attendance increases by as much as 5 per cent for each additional year of parental education, with an overall result that, when other factors are held constant, 'the relative university attendance rates for those whose parents have a high school diploma and those with at least some university education are 29 versus 53 per cent in the case of men, and 37 versus 65 per cent for women.' Class background intersects with other crucial factors to influence prospects for educational success, as demonstrated in the analysis by Curtis et al. (1992: 10) of the Ontario 25–34-year-old population:

> More than a third of the people whose fathers were industrial workers, or were self-employed, dropped out of high school. Nearly half of those whose fathers were unskilled workers dropped out. Those people from single-mother and poor visible-minority households probably fared even worse. On the other hand, less than 10 per cent of the people whose fathers were company managers or professionals dropped out of high school. . . . Employers' and professional-class kids are much more likely to go to university than are working-class kids—somewhere between two-and-a-half to four times as likely.

These findings indicate that there is some educational mobility—people from diverse backgrounds are represented at all levels—but they also reveal that the chances for educational opportunity are greater for those who are already relatively well situated. The data in Figures 8.6 and 8.7 demonstrate that the likelihood of post-secondary attendance increases in conjunction with parental income and education levels. Family background has an impact on the level of post-secondary studies as well as overall participation rates. Whereas community college programs draw students from all socio-economic backgrounds, university enrolment patterns are more strongly associated with family income (shown in the top chart) and parental education. The strong association between parental education and university participation is more pronounced than illustrated in Figure 8.7; the fourth column from the left represents parents with any post-secondary certification, whereas within this category, students whose parents have university credentials are nearly twice as likely as those with non-university post-secondary credentials to attend university.

The mechanisms by which class inequalities are reproduced are highly complex, consistent with the analysis offered by such writers as Bernstein, Bourdieu, Gramsci, Apple, and others discussed in previous chapters. Researchers have begun to analyze in greater empirical detail the mechanisms that contribute to selectivity and inequality in educational pathways. Individual predispositions and experiences combine with signals from peers, family members, and educators in such a way as to lead into certain pathways or trajectories, as opposed to others, regarding such matters as how long to stay in school, what subjects to study, what careers to seek, and how much effort to apply to particular courses (Andres Bellamy, 1993). Class-related elements enter into the degree of influence that

Figure 8.6   Post-Secondary Participation and High School Dropout Rates for Canadians, Age 19, by Family Income Quartiles, 2003

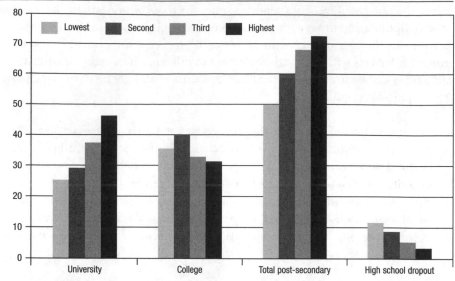

Source: Compiled from data in Zeman (2007) and Frenette (2005a: 18).

Figure 8.7   Post-Secondary Participation Rates (%), Ages 24–6, by Highest Level of Parents' Educational Attainment, December 2005

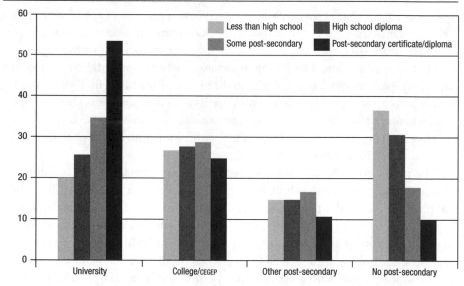

Source: Compiled from data in Shaienks and Gluszynski (2007: 10).

parents can have on their children's education, for instance, through the extent to which family members can provide time and money to support educational studies, and involvement in networks where interaction with other parents, teachers, and employers provides advantageous feedback and direction (Lareau, 1989: 116–19). While often posed in terms of distinctions between high status and less socially valued attributes or forms of cultural capital, class differences can both be transmitted and potentially reduced by regular behaviours such as parental reading with children (de Graaf et al., 2000: 107–8).

Previous chapters have cited literature that points to the strong association between parental income and other markers of advantage on the selection of high school courses required for admission to university and post-secondary studies (Krahn and Taylor, 2007). Many other considerations, including individual self-confidence, ability to read and perform well in test situations, selective use of information from teachers and career counsellors, and job interview skills, are also likely to be associated with class (Grayson, 1997; Tanner et al., 1995: 52–4). Differentials in family background offer varying capacities to provide resources and experiences that, in turn, contribute to substantial variations in reading ability, school grades, and school quality that influence subsequent educational and career options. Frenette (2007: 23) highlights the importance of understanding the interplay among these factors, observing that 'differences in academic performance across the income distribution may themselves be the result of differences in family income. Families with more financial resources may spend more money on books for children, take their children to museums, spend more on daycare in the early years, locate in neighbourhoods with better schools, etc. These actions may result in higher performance on standardized and scholastic tests, and thus, in a higher probability of attending university in the future.' The Program of International Student Assessment, based on reading, science, and mathematics skills tests administered to youth in more than 30 nations in selected years, demonstrates that socio-economic differences tend to be less pronounced in Canada than in most other OECD nations, and that a variety of factors, including parental interest in their children's education, reading at home, and numerous aspects of school climate, influenced student outcomes. Nonetheless, the survey also demonstrates that **socio-economic status**, whether determined by parental background or school composition, continues to be one of the strongest determinants of student performance in all Canadian provinces and participating nations (Bussière et al., 2001: 47; Bussière et al., 2007: 41–2).

Public concern about access to higher education has increased with the prominence accorded to notions of the emergence of a knowledge or information society. There is both widespread faith and a sense of urgency across social groups in which educational attainment is perceived to be a fundamental tool for social and economic participation and an avenue for advancement. Educational success remains tied to notions of individualism and competitiveness, which may serve an ideological purpose that acts in the interests of those who benefit most from existing social arrangements. However, there is also pragmatic acceptance of the reality that education, whether directly or indirectly, is critical for engagement in

Box 8.4 Educational Inequalities and Disadvantage in Rich Nations

Results from comparative tests of educational achievement indicate the varied roles that schools play, in conjunction with social, demographic, economic, and policy factors, in the reproduction of educational inequality, as illustrated in this summary of findings by the UNICEF Innocenti Research Centre (2002: 2):

- Educational performance in some OECD countries is consistently better than in others—whether measured by the percentage of students reaching fixed benchmarks of achievement or by the size of the gap between low-achieving and average students.
- A child at school in Finland, Canada, or the Republic of Korea has a higher chance of being educated to a reasonable standard, and a lower chance of falling a long way behind the average, than a child born in Hungary, Denmark, Greece, the United States, or Germany.
- The percentage of 15-year-olds judged 'unable to solve basic reading tasks' varies from under 7 per cent in the Republic of Korea and Finland to more than 20 per cent in Switzerland, Germany, Hungary, Greece, and Portugal.
- High absolute standards of educational achievement (measured by the percentage of students achieving a given benchmark) are not incompatible with low levels of relative disadvantage (measured by how far low-achieving pupils are allowed to fall behind the average).
- For the OECD as a whole, the average gap between high and low math scores in the same year is approximately nine times the average progression between one year and the next (Grade 7 to Grade 8).
- Between-school variance in educational performance is very much higher in some countries than in others.
- There is no simple relationship between the level of educational disadvantage in a country and educational spending per pupil, pupil–teacher ratios, or the degree of income inequality.
- In all OECD countries, educational achievement remains strongly related to the occupations, education, and economic status of the student's parents, though the strength of that relationship varies from country to country.
- Inequality in learning achievement begins at an early age and attempts to mitigate educational disadvantage need to begin even before a child starts school through good quality early childhood care and education.

Source: United Nations Children's Fund Innocenti Research Centre, 'A League Table of Educational Disadvantage in Rich Nations', *Innocenti Report Card* No. 4, UNICEF IRC, Florence, 2002, p. 2.

contemporary social life. Research on youth who have left school before high school graduation, for example, shows that those who do not continue tend to blame themselves, at least in part, for their actions, while the majority of dropouts now return later in life to complete their basic credentials and proceed to post-secondary studies (Tanner et al., 1995; Hango and de Broucker, 2007: 23). Nonetheless, there is also growing public awareness that many Canadians encounter barriers that restrict access to higher education. Recent national and Ontario surveys report that between two-thirds to three-quarters of respondents consider students from low-income families to have below-average opportunities to attend post-secondary programs; qualified Aboriginal students and students with disabilities are also perceived by between one-third and one-half of respondents to have limited opportunities (Livingstone and Hart, 2005: 13; Canadian Council on Learning, 2006a: 33–4).

Continued belief in the legitimacy of schooling to facilitate individual access to jobs and other social rewards is based, in part, on the kinds of evidence outlined above, which show that many people do benefit from converting their educational achievements into social mobility and success. Hunter and Leiper (1993), for instance, suggest that factors like human capital theory and 'market signalling', in which employers rely on educational credentials as an indication of future employee productivity, interact to produce a strong relationship between formal education and earnings. Even when the evidence is contradictory and individuals are aware that significant barriers to social mobility exist, the stakes are sufficiently high to ensure that most of us play by the rules—i.e., while not all of us can achieve educational success, and educational success does not in itself guarantee a good job, the consequences of not having an education are severe enough to motivate people to get as much education as they can. There has been a persistent, even growing, gap, for instance, in average family wealth between families whose major income recipient was a university graduate and those who are not university graduates (Morissette et al., 2002: 18).

Poverty is one of the more widely recognized costs of low educational achievement. There is a strong two-way relationship in that poverty rates are highest among those with the lowest levels of education and educational problems are often most severe among those living in poverty. Persons living in poverty are most highly concentrated among those with the least education—over one in five persons with high school or less spent at least one year between 1999 and 2004 living below the after-tax low-income cut-off line, compared to just over one in 10 persons with a university degree (including those whose incomes were low while they were studying), and 4.8 per cent of those with less than high school, compared to 0.6 per cent of those with a university degree were poor for the entire six-year period (National Council of Welfare, 2007: 2).

Being poor also increases the risk of further educational difficulties. The likelihood that a student will drop out before completing high school (a trend that also holds for those who do not return for additional education) is substantially higher

Box 8.5 The Impact of Poverty on Education

Amid general economic prosperity, poverty prevails within many segments of the Canadian population. Poverty influences educational experiences and outcomes, and it is associated with educational attainment. Low income is linked with many factors that have a detrimental impact on educational success, including nutritional and health problems and living conditions that may not be conducive to full educational participation. Campaign 2000 (2007: 2–3), a national network of groups dedicated to education and action to end child poverty, reports on major dimensions, causes, and consequences of child poverty:

Child poverty is family poverty. And some families are more vulnerable than others.

Persistent social and economic inequality in Canada based on gender, race, length of time in Canada, and ability is reflected in disproportionately high child poverty rates among families that face barriers of systemic discrimination. Lone mothers and their children continue to be one of the most economically vulnerable groups with almost 1 in every 2 female lone parent families (47 per cent before tax) living in poverty. Women earn approximately 71 per cent of what men earn for full-time, year-round work, and are more likely to be found in low-wage work.[1] New immigrants are key to our continued economic and labour force growth, yet low income rates among this group are more than three times higher than for people born in Canada.[2] One in every two children in recent immigrant families (49 per cent) lives below the poverty line according to the 2001 Census. Despite the highest educational credentials and skills of arrivals to Canada, current newcomers experience a sharp decline in living standards when compared with immigrants from past decades. Valuable skills are squandered and wealth creation is foregone when Canadian employers fail to recognize international work experience and credentials.

Child Poverty Rates among Selected Social Groups
- 1 in 2 for children in recent immigrant families (49 per cent)
- 1 in 2.5 for First Nations children living outside First Nations communities (40 per cent)
- 1 in 3 for children in racialized families (34 per cent)
- 1 in 4 for children with disabilities (28 per cent)
- 1 in 4 for children living in First Nations communities (28 per cent)

For immigrants of colour, barriers to employment are compounded by discrimination faced by racialized communities.[3] One in every three children in racialized families (34 per cent) lived in poverty in 2001. When compared to people of European background, racialized people experience higher unemployment rates and are more likely to be in low-paying occupations.[4] The poverty rate for children with disabilities is 28 per cent.

Families with a parent or child with a disability are more likely to rely on social assistance as a primary source of income. They face barriers to full inclusion and encounter immense financial, social and emotional stresses. For adults with disabilities, employment rates are low, with 51 per cent of working age adults with disabilities employed.[5] . . .

Families are still living in deep poverty.

The average low-income family is living on an annual income that is $9,000 to $11,000 below Statistics Canada's before-tax, Low-Income Cut-off. The average low-income, two-parent family would need an additional $11,100 a year to bring them up to the poverty line, and the average female lone-parent, low-income family would need $9,200 per year.

Why do families continue to live in deep poverty in Canada during great prosperity? Many are stuck in a poverty trap where parents cycle between social assistance and low-wage work. People most often rely on welfare due to unemployment and underemployment, separation from a spouse and poor health or disability. Welfare rates in all provinces and territories remain far below the poverty line. Adjusted for inflation, many provincial welfare rates are lower now than they were in 1986.[6]

More parents are working, but they're still poor. Full-time work at minimum wage is not an escape from poverty.

A growing Canadian economy has led to more access to the workforce for low-income parents, but they're not finding jobs with sufficient pay, hours and benefits to lift their families out of poverty. Government welfare programs aim to move people off social assistance and into jobs, but with low wages and poor working conditions, social assistance poverty is often replaced by labour market poverty. No matter where you live in Canada, the minimum wage does not bring a full-time, year-round minimum wage worker up to the poverty line.

Notes

1. Canadian Research Institute for the Advancement of Women. (2005). *'Women and Poverty'*. Ottawa: CRIAW. After-tax data indicates 33 per cent of female lone-parent families live in poverty.
2. Picot, G., Hou, F., Coulombe, S. (Jan. 2007). *Chronic Low Income and Low Income Dynamics Among Recent Immigrants.* Ottawa: Statistics Canada.
3. 'Racialized persons' refers to people who face systemic discrimination based on socially constructed concepts of race and includes those born in Canada as well as newcomers.
4. Teelucksingh, Cheryl and Grace Edward Galabuzi. (May 2005). *Working Precariously: the impact of race and immigrant status on employment opportunities and outcomes in Canada.* Toronto: Canadian Race Relations Foundation.
5. Human Resources Development Canada. (2003). *Disability in Canada: A 2001 Profile.* Ottawa: Human Resources Development Canada.
6. National Council of Welfare. (August 2006). *Welfare Incomes* 2005. Ottawa: NCW.

Source: From Campaign 2000, a cross-Canada network of over 120 organizations working to end child and family poverty. www.campaign2000.ca.

than average among those in lower socio-economic groups and those whose parents had little formal education (Gilbert and Frank, 1998: 15–17; Zeman, 2007). These trends reflect, in part, class-based differences both in dispositions towards education transmitted from parents to children and in the cultural and economic resources that students are able to draw upon in the classroom (Andres Bellamy, 1993).

There is growing awareness of the impact that poverty and associated 'risk factors' have both during early childhood and throughout the life course. Low income and poverty are associated with nutritional deficiencies, ill health, emotional and behavioural disorders, and social disruptions that produce frequent absences from school, attention deficits, engagement in risky behaviours, and other factors that have an adverse effect on school performance (Lee, 2004; Statistics Canada and CMEC, 2007: 15; Health Canada, 1999: 46–7). These problems accumulate over time, so that health risks are greatest among adults who have the lowest levels of educational attainment (Roberge et al., 1995: 17). Particularly for older students, economic pressures sometimes force youth to combine schooling and work. Although some students who combine schooling with moderate hours of work may have increased chances for high school success, those who are forced to work longer hours, thereby reducing the time available to attend class, complete assignments, or meet other school-related demands are more likely to encounter educational difficulties (Bernier, 1995: 19–20; Bushnik, 2003).

Schools themselves, as well as the circumstances of those living in poverty, can also contribute to lower educational achievement among the poor. Olson (1995: 205) argues that children from working-class and poorer families are penalized in part because schooling, teaching, and the curriculum are organized and oriented in such a way as to be irrelevant to the needs and interests of those children. Curtis et al. (1992: 66) argue that, in addition to strong class differences (along with racial, ethnic, and gender ones) in the distribution of students into higher and lower educational streams, resources are diverted from programs in vocational and general education, where the less privileged are likely to be found, into special programs like French immersion, classes for 'gifted' students, and private schools that typically serve students from more privileged backgrounds. Educational outcomes are highly affected by the complex mix of educational practices, the culture of school organizations, the extent and use of school resources, students' socioeconomic backgrounds, and the mix of students within specific schools and classrooms (Frempong and Willms, 2002).

Recent trends suggest that class and educational inequalities are likely to compound one another further. With about 13 per cent of Canadian children living in poverty (Canadian Council on Social Development, 2007), youth from disadvantaged backgrounds, as well as those with disabilities, are less likely than other youth to complete high school and more likely to experience difficulties in labour market participation (Hango and de Broucker, 2007: 26). Despite consistent evidence, there has been an absence of comprehensive policy to address problems for low-income households, whose family members endure heavier responsibilities for financing their own education and securing social support as educational costs rise and government services and financial support erode.

This problem has implications for students at all levels of schooling, given the importance of fiscal and cultural capital for educational success, but it may be most visible among those who proceed to post-secondary studies. The issue of access to higher education has gained prominence in the face of concerns by student organizations, educators, and other groups about the impact of increasing tuition fees. There is some evidence that the gap in university participation rates widened initially, as students from families with the lowest socio-economic status had an increasing disadvantage relative to those from higher SES family backgrounds during the period after 1989–90 in which tuition fees first began to rise significantly (Bouchard and Zhao, 2000: 28). Although this gap appears to have levelled off somewhat over time (Drolet, 2005), the preceding discussion has revealed an ongoing association between post-secondary participation and both household income and parents' education.

Tuition fees are increasing in an environment in which there are high degrees of uncertainty and fluctuation in employment opportunities for young people. Moreover, changes to sources of financial assistance, such as the Canada Student Loan Program, have altered the nature and amounts of funding available to students. Tuition increases do not in themselves account for reduced accessibility to university since students have generally tended to be drawn from relatively privileged backgrounds, and other barriers, such as lack of services for non-traditional groups and those most in need of assistance, do restrict access (Levin, 1990: 52–6). In addition to financial concerns, several factors, such as school grades, cultural resources, and motivation, pose barriers to post-secondary studies, but Berger, Motte, and Parkin (2007: 54) emphasize that low-income youth are most likely to experience problems in all of these regards and therefore are most apt to defer or steer away from post-secondary studies. The impact of tuition increases has also been mitigated somewhat by special assistance or tuition support programs for students from low-income families and designated groups, but these programs tend to have restricted terms of reference and capacity to support only a small proportion of eligible students.

Further differentiation or selectivity in access to post-secondary studies occurs as some students combine school and work, others rely on family sources or borrowed funds to cover their educational costs, and still others opt to enter the labour market directly. Income inequality is evident in the tendency for students to look increasingly to support from parents or other friends and family members to finance at least part of their studies. Close to three-quarters of post-secondary students report that they rely on some form of financial assistance from parents. This ranged among Canadian post-secondary students surveyed in 2003–4 from about two-thirds (64 per cent) of students whose family incomes were $30,000 or less to 89 per cent of those with family incomes of over $100,000, with students from the highest income group reporting nearly twice as much total funding from parents, on average, as those in the lowest income group (Berger et al., 2007: 84). Students are also burdened with increasingly higher debt loads through borrowing from private sources and government student loan programs. Nearly half of graduates receiving college certificates or diplomas since the early 1990s and just over half of those receiving university degrees owed debt from student loans programs at the time of graduation (Dubois, 2006: 5). The average levels of indebtedness for undergraduate university students has more than doubled to $24,047 in 2006 from $11,636 (in 2006 dollars) in 1990 (Berger et al., 2007: 129).

These trends make it more difficult for students from less privileged backgrounds to attend the post-secondary programs of their choice, or worse, they may restrict access altogether (Ouellette, 2006; Finnie and Garneau, 1996: 28). In cases in which tuition fees have been unregulated and escalated most dramatically, particularly in some professional degree programs such as medicine, law, and dentistry, over-representation of students from upper-income groups has increased relative to those from middle- and lower-income groups (Frenette, 2005b; Ouellette, 2006). Evidence also indicates that accumulated debt and other fiscal barriers are affecting students' ability to enter or complete college programs that have typically offered greater post-secondary options for students from diverse social and economic backgrounds (Berger et al., 2007: 130–1). Given these concerns, attention to issues of access to post-secondary studies is being extended to questions about student retention and completion. For various reasons, many post-secondary students interrupt their studies periodically, sometimes for substantial lengths of time and in other cases without returning to complete their programs. Determining factors include inadequate financial resources, isolation and lack of support networks, personal and family commitments, work opportunities, and limited commitment to or interest in their studies. Available data suggest that between one-fifth and one-quarter of students who enter post-secondary programs in Canada leave prior to completion. While students do not complete their post-secondary studies for a variety of reasons, a striking correspondence exists between the factors associated with post-secondary attendance and those related to post-secondary completion (Lambert et al., 2004; Butlin, 2000: 15, 20). These factors often interact strongly with one another, as illustrated by the case of First Nations students who are alienated by educational institutions that do not take into account personal, cultural, and economic factors (Monture-Angus, 1995: 81–4). In short, class inequalities continue to shape and are reinforced by the education system.

STUDENTS WITH DISABILITIES

People with disabilities have been one of the least well-served groups in the long-term quest for equitable educational and social participation. Misunderstanding, discrimination, and exclusion from school, work, and other core spheres of social life are common experiences among persons with disabilities.

Changes in the way that students with a disability are treated by education systems have broadly corresponded with public attitudes towards and treatment of the disabled in society, with gradual movement towards accommodation for different types of disability accompanying greater understanding of the complexity of disability and disability issues. For much of Canada's history, persons with physical, behavioural, or cognitive disabilities have tended to be stigmatized, marginalized, or left as dependants subject to the predilections of family or private caregivers. Throughout much of the twentieth century, disability issues came to be framed increasingly through a medical model in which disabilities were regarded as pathologies or forms of impairment that required management and treatment by health-care professionals and other experts (Titchkosky, 2003). Medical approaches to disability continue to prevail, often for legitimate reasons, but sometimes with consequences that are highly contested or disturbing, as in the extensive prescription of mood-altering drugs to children and youth diagnosed with behavioural or learning disabilities (Maté, 1999). More recently, crystallized around the successful quest to include disability rights within the 1982 Canadian Charter of Rights and Freedoms, persons with disability and their advocates have focused on the rights of the disabled, including provision for equity, autonomy, and participation in all spheres of social life.

In education, extensive debate has focused on the extent to which students should be included or integrated into regular programs and classes as opposed to having specially designated programs. This focus has recently shifted to acknowledge the need for educational institutions to provide more extensive services and programs to ensure that students with disabilities have viable options to participate fully in education at all levels where they are eligible. In the process, educational participation and attainment levels among persons with disabilities have improved, but remain below national averages. For Canadians ages 16 to 64, persons with disabilities are about 1.5 to 2 times more likely to have less than high school, and about half as likely to have a university degree, than those without a disability, but much of this gap disappears for those in the 15–24 cohort (Canadian Council on Learning, 2007a). About 6 per cent of students who graduated from Canadian universities in 2006 reported having a disability, which is more than twice the level reported in 1995 but below age-adjusted rates of disability in the population as a whole (CAUT, 2007: 21; Statistics Canada, 2007e). The importance of educational equity is underscored by observations discussed throughout this chapter and elsewhere in the book of the strong associations between educational prospects and economic and social well-being.

Close to 175,000 school-age children were reported in 2006 to have some form of disability, representing 4.6 per cent of all children aged 5–14 years in Canada, compared to 4.0 per cent in 2001 (Statistics Canada, 2007e: 23–5). These include various forms of disability, including difficulties with hearing, sight, speech, and mobility, although learning disabilities and chronic health conditions account for the majority of cases. There is considerable variation across provinces and disability categories in the levels of success and the kinds of services and programs available for students with disabilities. All but about 4 per cent of school-age children in Canada attend schools, with about 60 per cent of elementary school-age children with mild or moderate disabilities in Canada integrated in regular school classes, ranging from about half of those in Quebec and British Columbia to close to three-quarters of those in Prince Edward Island and New Brunswick (Canadian Council on Learning, 2007a; Kohen et al., 2007). Children and youth with more severe disabilities or limited physical or cognitive activity are more likely to be placed in special programs or educated in other ways.

These trends highlight the continuing need to improve educational services for students with disabilities as well as the complex arrangements that these improvements can sometimes entail. Without special funding agreements or collaboration with other agencies, for instance, it can be prohibitively expensive for many school districts to provide expensive equipment, tutors, or aides required to meet the needs of relatively small numbers of students. Educational institutions, often driven by legal rulings and human rights challenges, have begun recently to implement more comprehensive policies and services guided by principles of **reasonable accommodation**, which seek to ensure that, except in cases that would cause undue hardship to the organization, appropriate physical arrangements, supports, and practices are in place to ensure that each individual with a disability will be able to participate fully in educational programs and activities. Such initiatives can contribute to environments more conducive to educational participation by students with disabilities but, as Frazee (2003: 13) cautions, without full appreciation for what these measures mean in the context of real learning situations, they can also perpetuate disadvantage 'by imposing conditions upon inclusion, once again holding out the offer of equal participation as contingent upon their capacity to emulate valued social norms.' Accessible buildings and appropriate services and supports are important preconditions to address needs of students with disabilities, but these represent only part of a broader social environment. Many students with disabilities continue to encounter both attitudinal and physical barriers in and out of educational settings that restrict their prospects to function fully on a day-to-day basis or compel them to lower their educational aspirations.

REGIONAL INEQUALITY

Canadians receive unequal amounts of and returns from education on the basis of where they live. These differences reflect disparities between urban and rural settings, provincial and regional diversity, and inequalities within a single geographical site such as a city or metropolitan area.

Educational indicators are generally more favourable for persons living in cities in comparison with those who reside in rural areas. Rural residents have less formal education, on average, than urban residents do. There is a declining, but persistent, gap in educational attainment between rural and urban populations. Data from the 2006 census reveal that, among persons aged 25 to 64, just over one-quarter (26 per cent) of urban residents, compared to 11 per cent of those in rural communities, had university degrees (Statistics Canada, 2008d: 25). Conversely, one-fifth of the urban population and over one-third of persons living in predominantly rural regions had less than high school (Rothwell and Turcotte, 2006: 6). Some of these differences can be accounted for by the fact that educational institutions, especially at the post-secondary level, are concentrated in urban areas, as are jobs and services associated with higher levels of education, as well as recent immigrants, who are typically more highly educated than the Canadian-born population.

Rural/urban disparities, however, also appear among the school-age population. Dropout rates, overall, are higher among rural than urban residents, and rural students who drop out of school tend to leave earlier. Despite declining dropout rates across Canada (between 2001 and 2005, an average of 10.1 per cent of 20–4-year-olds were not in school and did not have a high school diploma, compared to 15.7 in the early 1990s), the dropout rate in rural areas remains, at 17.2 per cent, higher even than national levels were in the previous decade (Bowlby and McMullen, 2005). Rural residents typically have lower university participation rates than those from urban areas but slightly higher rates of participation in community colleges and CEGEPS. Analysis of a national cohort of youth who were 18 to 20 in 1999 reveals that by 2005 (at ages 24–6), 52 per cent of those from urban communities had attended university and 32 per cent had attended colleges, while participation rates in both university and college were 40 per cent among those from rural communities (Shaienks and Gluszynski, 2007: 9).

Patterns of educational inequality are evident in comparisons across provinces and territories, as the data in Tables 8.1 and 8.2 illustrate. Levels of educational attainment fall below national averages in regions that tend to be poorer, including most Atlantic provinces, Quebec, Manitoba, and Saskatchewan (as well as Nunavut, for which tabulated data are not available). Close to one-quarter of the populations in each of these provinces or regions have not completed high school, and in nearly all of them the proportion of the population with a post-secondary diploma, certificate, or degree is below the national average of 55.6 per cent. The converse is true for the 'have' provinces of Ontario, Alberta, and British Columbia (as well as the one exception, the Yukon Territory), which meet or exceed the national average levels of educational attainment. Comparative studies of reading skills and adult literacy reveal broadly similar trends, with lower scores more prevalent among rural populations in Newfoundland and Labrador, New Brunswick, Québec, and Nunavut (Statistics Canada and CMEC, 2007: 104–6).

Some levelling out occurs, however, when current levels of educational participation are considered, reflecting the increasingly high overall proportions of young people engaged in basic and continuing education. The data in Table 8.2 reveal relatively little variation across provinces in levels of educational participation among youth. Between 75 and 85 per cent of the 15–19 age cohort were in school in 2005–6, while rates of university participation among 20–4-year-olds were below the national average of 25 per cent in only three provinces (Alberta, British Columbia, and Prince Edward Island). Labour market prospects for youth have some impact on these rates, particularly in western Canada where there tend to be higher dropout rates, slightly lower university participation rates, and lower youth unemployment rates.

There are also regional differences in people's attitudes towards schooling and educational performance. Ironically, persons living in regions with the lowest levels of education tend to have more positive views of schooling than those with higher levels. Various surveys of public opinion typically reveal that people in the Prairie provinces and Atlantic Canada tend to have more favourable attitudes about schools and improved quality of education than those from provinces with the highest urban concentrations of population (Williams and Millinoff, 1990: 37–8; Canadian Education Association, 2007: 7, 10). Such poll results reflect, at times, public reaction to unpopular educational reforms in specific provinces, such as Ontario in the late 1990s. They also reveal, though, strong convictions that education is important to the future of rural communities and to options for individuals from those communities. Rural communities face a perpetual challenge to address the reality that many of their youth look to education as a channel for educational, economic, and social opportunities that exist in cities or other regions (Knight, 1993: 306–7; Wotherspoon, 1998: 138).

Observed differences in educational attainment and attitudes towards schooling reflect several important dimensions of Canadian social reality. To a large extent, education systems in Canada have emerged and developed amid debates

Table 8.1   Educational Attainment, by Province and Territory, 2006 (% of Population Aged 25–64)

	Less Than High School	Graduated from High School	Apprenticeship or Trades Certificate or Diploma	Post-Secondary Certificate or Diploma (College or University)	University Degree
Canada	15.4	23.9	12.4	25.3	22.9
Newfoundland and Labrador	25.6	19.6	14.8	25.9	14.0
Prince Edward Island	18.7	23.7	11.8	28.4	17.5
Nova Scotia	18.6	20.9	13.9	26.4	20.2
New Brunswick	21.0	25.7	12.4	24.8	16.1
Quebec	17.1	21.1	18.1	22.9	20.8
Ontario	13.6	25.0	8.8	26.7	26.0
Manitoba	20.4	25.4	11.3	23.5	19.4
Saskatchewan	19.4	26.7	13.7	23.2	17.1
Alberta	15.4	24.1	12.4	26.1	22.0
British Columbia	12.4	25.9	12.0	25.7	24.1
Yukon	15.3	21.2	13.1	28.1	22.2
Northwest Territories	23.0	18.5	11.5	26.9	20.0
Nunavut	46.0	10.3	9.4	21.5	12.8

Source: Compiled from Statistics Canada, *2006 Census of Population*, Catalogue no. 97-560-XCB2006007.

Table 8.2 Dimensions of Educational Participation, by Provinces

	Education Participation Rate (% of 15–19 age cohort enrolled in secondary or post-secondary studies, 2005–6)	College Participation Rate (% of 20–4 age cohort, 2005–6)	University Participation Rate (% of 20–4 age cohort, 2005–6)	High School Dropout Rate, 2002–3 to 2004–5*	Unemployment Rate (% of labour force, 15–24 year age cohort, 2006)	Percentage of the School-age Population (ages 5–24) in Low Income, 2004
Canada	81	11	25	10.1	11.6	15
Newfoundland and Labrador	85	11	26	8.0	22.9	17
Prince Edward Island	84	6	23	9.7	14.4	7
Nova Scotia	84	5	29	9.3	13.7	11
New Brunswick	82	6	26	9.2	13.7	10
Quebec	80	9	26	11.9	13.6	13
Ontario	85	13	28	9.1	13.1	14
Manitoba	80	8	27	13.0	8.8	13
Saskatchewan	78	5	26	10.7	8.6	16
Alberta	75	12	17	12.0	6.8	16
British Columbia	78	16	21	7.5	8.2	18

*Percentage of 20–4-year-olds without a high school diploma and not in school.
Sources: Compiled from Statistics Canada and CMEC (2007: 185, 339–42); Bowlby and McMullen (2005); Statistics Canada, CANSIM Table 2820002.

over the degree to which competing economic and social considerations should drive educational planning and programs. On the one hand, imperatives such as economies of scale, efficiency, and cost considerations have led to consolidation of schools and school districts and centralization of programs and resources. Regions with stronger economic bases are in a better position than poorer regions to provide both the resources to finance a strong educational system and employment opportunities for people with educational credentials. Similarly, smaller provinces and rural or isolated areas with limited populations are less likely to be able to offer a complete range of educational programs and services than are city schools or larger school districts. On the other hand, educational institutions are under pressure to be responsive to local concerns and to provide meaningful services. Schools with low enrolments may not be cost-efficient, but they may be able to offer several advantages to students and community members—greater opportunities for teacher–student interaction, sensitivity to parental concerns, higher morale, and benefits for students with educational difficulties or from disadvantaged backgrounds—that tend not to be found in larger school settings (Leithwood and Jantzi, 2007). In rural areas and smaller communities, especially, schools are essential for more than their educational offerings, serving as focal points for sports and recreation, social organizations, and cultural events that contribute to an enhanced quality of life within the community. Nonetheless, such schools often remain at risk through an absence of adequate resources and stability (Bolaria et al., 1995: 433–5).

The structure of educational finance in Canada has been shaped by efforts to compensate for some of the most severe consequences of regional inequalities. Until the end of the twentieth century, funding for elementary and secondary education in nearly all provinces (except New Brunswick and Prince Edward Island) came predominantly from tax revenue generated at the school board or district level, augmented by grants from provincial governments to equalize school spending between poorer and wealthier districts. Federal–provincial arrangements generally have operated on a similar principle, with equalization payments and special funding programs for post-secondary education based on the transfer of funds from the federal government to ensure that the 'have-not' provinces are able to provide comparable services to those available in the 'have' provinces (Dibski, 1995: 69–70). Such programs have sought to ensure that a basic range and level of educational services, along with health care and other social services, are available to residents in all provinces and regions.

Recent changes to cost-sharing formulas and funding arrangements, however, have tended to shift the burden of funding downward, while centralizing fiscal constraints, thereby heightening fears that inequalities among districts will increase (Barlow and Robertson, 1994: 12). The federal government provides provinces and territories with educational support through the Canada Social Transfer and other 'investment' programs that transfer funding to assist in such areas as early childhood development, childhood learning, job training, and post-secondary education. Nonetheless, these kinds of arrangements remain unstable and inadequate for several reasons, including the shifting terrain of federal–provincial relations, rising costs and demand for education of various kinds, federal initiatives to contain social spending and co-ordinate programs, and the pre-eminence that health care (in addition to policy areas like security) has gained over education and other social programs on the policy agenda. The pace of parallel measures taken by provincial governments, especially in the 1990s, to restrain education spending, centralize control over many educational decision-making matters, eliminate or place limits on local school district discretionary spending and taxation powers, and reduce the numbers of school boards has recently slowed but has not entirely been reversed (Young et al., 2007: 41–7, 148ff.). In Manitoba and Saskatchewan, the only remaining provinces to maintain significant local education taxation supported by equalization arrangements, controversy exists over issues related to education funding and school district size. While it is likely that these developments may produce some long-overdue innovations in educational organization and programming—especially as attention has come to be refocused in the twenty-first century on the importance of strategic educational investment and promotion of a knowledge economy—they also increase the likelihood that programs and services for selected groups, such as people with special educational needs or residents in smaller communities, will be reduced or cut out altogether.

CONCLUSION

This chapter has examined several dimensions and consequences of educational inequality in Canada. The expansion of the education system and broadening of conceptions of educational opportunity over the past century have resulted in substantial gains in educational attainment among nearly all segments of the population. This expansion has been especially important for many women, as well as for some members of visible minority and Aboriginal populations, providing access to educational programs and subsequent social and economic positions reliant on advanced educational credentials, which traditionally have not been open to them. Considerable evidence indicates that not only does education contribute to social mobility but it also limits the extent to which social inequalities simply are reproduced from one generation to the next. There is a real basis to claims that educational gains can lead to increased social and economic opportunities and that individuals can benefit from education regardless of their social background.

However, substantial obstacles continue to stand in the way of full equality of access to and benefit from education for many segments of the population. Gender equity has been achieved in participation rates at most levels of formal education, but gender segregation remains in areas of study concentration and in the ability to translate educational credentials into subsequent educational and career advancement. Similarly, visible minorities and people with physical disabilities have demonstrated considerable gains in levels of educational participation and attainment, but their ability to translate those advances into socio-economic success also depends on such factors as personal experiences of discrimination and their structural location in Canadian society. With a few notable exceptions, persons of Aboriginal ancestry, in particular, remain a considerable distance away from education and employment equity with the population as a whole. Such problems as sexism, racism, poverty, and regional disparities often compound one another, contributing to distinctly different probabilities that people from diverse social backgrounds will achieve educational and social success.

In summary, then, there is a contradictory relationship between formal education and social and economic opportunity. Education is a vital ingredient in most recipes for success, sometimes as a contributing factor but more often as part of an overall package associated with relative privilege or disadvantage. Several policy and organizational changes, such as improved educational access for minorities, education equity initiatives, multiculturalism, teacher training for greater sensitivity to the educational needs of distinct categories of learners, and inclusive curricula, have enhanced opportunities for people who have been typically disadvantaged. However, schooling, both actively, in terms of how it responds to and rewards people on a differential basis, and tacitly, in terms of the gaps, silences, and failures to confront socio-economic disparities on a systematic basis, also contributes to the ongoing reproduction of social inequality.

To be sure, there will be new opportunities for some individuals as jobs are created that reward intelligence, initiative, and technical proficiency as opposed to socio-economic background. Nonetheless, recent policy and program changes in the direction of funding cutbacks, restrictions on or deletion of support services for students, greater individual responsibility for educational costs and options, and realignment of educational priorities in conjunction with wider fiscal planning are likely to minimize the chances that those from less privileged social backgrounds will receive equitable access to and benefits from formal education. Significant challenges, debates, and reforms surrounding contemporary education are the focus of the next chapter.

ANNOTATED FURTHER READINGS

Alladin, Ibrahim. 1996. *Racism in Canadian Schools.* Toronto: Harcourt Brace. The author demonstrates that, contrary to ideologies that emphasize equity and opportunity, Canadian schooling is infused with various racist practices.

Castellano, Marlene Brant, Lynne Davis, and Louise Lahache, eds. 2000. *Aboriginal Education: Fulfilling the Promise.* Vancouver: University of British Columbia Press. The authors highlight several promising developments, as well as crucial challenges, that characterize education for Canada's Aboriginal people in the wake of the 1996 report of the Royal Commission on Aboriginal Peoples.

Curtis, Bruce, D.W. Livingstone, and Harry Smaller. 1992. *Stacking the Deck: The Streaming of Working-Class Kids in Ontario Schools.* Toronto: Our Schools/Our Selves Education Foundation. This is one of the few detailed Canadian accounts of streaming and its impact on children from different social backgrounds.

Curtis, James, Edward Grabb, and Neil Guppy, eds. 2004. *Social Inequality in Canada: Patterns, Problems, and Policies*, 4th edn. Toronto: Pearson Education. This collection incorporates theoretical and analytical chapters that explore major dimensions and consequences of social inequality in Canada. Both historical and contemporary issues are addressed, covering such themes as gender, age, socio-economic and regional inequality, as well as education.

Fennell, Shailaja, and Madeleine Arnot, eds. 2008. *Gender Education and Equality in a Global Context: Conceptual Frameworks and Policy Perspectives*. London: Routledge. Contributors from several nations examine the meaning and nature of gender and equality as social and economic relations shift in a global context. Research and theoretical discussions are framed around diverse educational forms, challenges, and possibilities.

Shalla, Vivian, and Wallace Clement, eds. 2007. *Work in Tumultuous Times: Critical Perspectives*. Montreal and Kingston: McGill-Queen's University Press. Several authors examine how Canadian society is being restructured by significant social and economic transformations, leading to extensive instability and uncertainty in working and domestic relationships. Contributors highlight the ways in which class, gender, and racial inequalities intersect with differences in how people experience and manage them.

Willms, J. Douglas, ed. 2002. *Vulnerable Children: Findings from Canada's National Longitudinal Survey of Children and Youth*. Edmonton: University of Alberta Press and Human Resources Development Canada. This book summarizes findings from the comprehensive National Longitudinal Survey of Children and Youth. It covers crucial causes, consequences, and dimensions of negative life experiences associated with vulnerability, including racial and ethnic discrimination, parenting concerns, family violence, poverty, and learning and behavioural disorders.

KEY TERMS

Class A social grouping based on social and economic relations, defined in terms of people's position with respect to ownership and control of assets that contribute to the production of new goods and services.

Equality of opportunity The view that all persons should have the same chance to succeed or fail on their own merits, regardless of their social background.

Equality of results The notion that intervention by the state or other agencies is necessary to guarantee that all persons will achieve at least minimum agreed-upon standards of living and access to other essential resources and opportunities.

Gender segmentation The concentration of males and females within distinct and separate jobs, education programs, and other social sites, often associated with differential status and benefits.

Meritocratic The principle that persons are selected for social positions based on merit, or achievement in accordance with universal standards and criteria.

Reasonable accommodation The requirement that an institution or service provider will make arrangements or provisions to remove barriers that discriminate against an individual or group protected under human rights legislation. Based on the recognition that equal treatment can sometimes be discriminatory towards particular individuals or groups, such as persons with disability or cultural minorities, there is also acknowledgement that accommodation cannot be extended to the point of causing undue hardship on the service provider.

Social Darwinism A view that societies change through their internal evolutionary processes, commonly employed to justify existing social inequalities to reflect 'survival of the fittest'.

Socially disadvantaged Those who are unable to attain important social and economic resources as a result of barriers or inadequate opportunities relative to standards that prevail among a nation or social group as a whole.

Social reproduction The process by which social structures and systems of inequality are maintained over time.

Socio-economic status (SES) A measure of the relative social and economic position of a person or group, determined by such factors as income, wealth, occupation, education level, family background, and prestige accorded an occupation.

Visible minority A term used in Canada to refer to non-Caucasian persons of specified racial or ethnic origins other than Aboriginal.

STUDY QUESTIONS

1. To what extent is educational achievement the outcome of individual effort as opposed to social factors? Explain your answer.
2. Discuss the extent to which education contributes to or restricts opportunities for social and economic success among diverse racial and ethnic groups in Canada.
3. Explain why, despite efforts to ensure that schooling is inclusive and responsive to all students, strong educational inequalities persist among social groups.
4. Which groups have benefited the most from educational expansion over the past five decades? Explain your response.
5. To what extent is there a gender bias in contemporary schooling that favours either girls or boys? Discuss and explain.
6. Discuss the importance of university education in the context of a knowledge society. To what extent is university open to and able to provide equitable opportunities for students from diverse social backgrounds? To what extent should people look to universities as opposed to other forms of education in order to improve these prospects?
7. How has the expansion of educational opportunities and attainment levels across the population affected the level of social and economic inequality in Canada?

Chapter 9

Contemporary Educational
Challenges and Reforms

INTRODUCTION

Previous chapters have emphasized the need to understand education as a dynamic and often contradictory endeavour. While education systems have been remarkably resilient over time (to the point that some critics consider them obsolete), formal educational institutions and their participants are continually challenged to rethink and reshape themselves to keep pace with important social, economic, and political transformations. Posed another way, the uneven pace at which transformations occur across three levels (the context, content, and structure of schooling) has fuelled periodic tensions and uncertainty over the role and relevance of education in a changing world. The social and economic contexts in which education systems operate are being rapidly transformed by significant shifts in technologies, knowledge forms, social relationships, and personal identities and life courses. The content of schooling is also changing, although typically in a more gradual manner. Educational participants are becoming increasingly more diverse, bringing with them desires and capacities to modify programs, curricula, knowledge, and resources for appropriate educational practices. Finally, while the institutional structure and organization of educational services are also being transformed, these changes have tended to be much less dramatic than changes in socio-economic contexts and educational processes. These relationships have contributed to a proliferation of alternative educational venues and forms at the same time that existing institutional arrangements are being reconfigured, challenged, or defended by various groups.

The first two chapters identified sociology as a discipline concerned with an understanding of relations between individuals and societies, and formal education as a social institution that contributes to the development of individual capacities and social competencies. One of the defining characteristics of life in advanced capitalist societies has been the dramatic reconfiguration of individual experiences, institutional arrangements, and social relationships to the extent that notions of individuality, society, and social organization are undergoing fundamental reassessment. We are influenced by, and able to interact with, persons, organizations, and processes that extend far beyond the sites in which we conduct most of our face-to-face daily encounters. We have access to levels and forms of knowledge, technological devices and applications, and consumer products well beyond what could likely be imagined by sociologists and educators in the late nineteenth and early twentieth centuries. However, just as early sociologists struggled with the mixed promises and dangers inherent to the development of industrial capitalism and liberal democracies, so do contemporary sociologists wrestle with the direction and consequences of current social and economic trajectories.

These tensions, which are expressed in varied and sometimes conflicting ways, are captured in notions of a 'risk society' in which the products and consequences of human intervention in nature and society have created serious threats—climate change, environmental devastation, nuclear and chemical weapons, technological dependency, public health epidemics, and large-scale violent conflict—that may exceed our capacity to control them (Beck, 1992; Giddens, 1990). In such a context, not only does the individual bear an increasing degree of responsibility to engage in strategies and actions to compensate for the insecurity and uncertainty of life, but the institutions and mechanisms designed to foster social protection and rational planning or certainty carry potential dangers of their own (Baumann, 1989). Previous chapters have pointed to various ways in which these dynamics are being experienced and played out in and around education, including heightened involvement in education and training initiatives in response to volatile labour markets, intensification of work and stresses that accompany overload and uncertainty across various spheres of life, changing life course patterns, **marketization**, i.e., the extension of market relations in education, and aggressive patterns of commodification and consumption. Education is expected to equip people to develop capacities by which to identify and confront the major challenges of the day at the same time that it supplies qualified personnel and knowledge to those social and economic systems that contribute to many of those problems.

This chapter draws together major themes and issues highlighted throughout the book by exploring key issues and challenges that continue to drive educational reform in Canada and other nations. At the heart of contemporary debates over education are concerns about how best to accommodate the demands and uncertainties associated with a globalizing world. The transformations that accompany what is often characterized as a knowledge society convey promises of advanced levels of prosperity and enhanced conditions of life, but they also carry with them high levels of risk and uncertainty in personal and collective circumstances and deep inequalities in resources, capacities, and opportunities. Beginning with a brief discussion of the dynamics associated with educational change, the chapter explores how these relationships intersect with three contemporary educational issues: calls for increased **accountability** and rational planning in education; the impact of new technologies on education; and the implications of social diversity for education.

UNDERSTANDING CONFLICTING VISIONS OF EDUCATIONAL REFORM

Education systems have benefited in some ways from the re-emergence of discourses that place human capital development and knowledge at the centre of strategies to build a highly skilled labour force. Educational expansion is a key component in the quest to adapt to a knowledge-based economy governed by advanced technologies, accelerated information-processing capacities, innovation, and flexibility. This approach coincided with de-emphasis on fiscal restraint and renewed government spending on social and economic programs, or at least it did until the diversion of state policy and resources throughout most of North America and Europe to issues related to security and the military following the 11 September 2001 terrorist attacks in the United States. Education systems have also attempted to reshape themselves to capture new resources and ameliorate criticism from public, government, and corporate interests.

Previous chapters have revealed that, despite being held in generally high regard, education systems have not been immune to a general crisis of confidence in government and public institutions while attracting unique critiques along the way. Critics continue to level serious charges against existing education systems— our education system has not maintained competitiveness with educational outputs in the most advanced nations; students are not learning essential skills and performing as well as they must to succeed in the global economy; schools are too costly to maintain in their present form; too much attention is placed on frivolous programs to the neglect of the basics; there is not enough discipline and respect for traditional values in the schools; education systems and personnel need to be more open and accountable to the public; schools need to be more responsive to market forces; taxpayers (or 'consumers') who are paying for education require a wider array of educational choices. The catalogue of criticisms is long.

Defenders of public education assert that the critics are creating a distorted portrayal and offering misguided proposals for educational reform that may be even more damaging than the alleged problems. By way of rebuttal, critics respond that many of the people who speak out on behalf of education systems are teachers, bureaucrats, and others whose self-interest lies in preserving the educational status quo. Governments have followed suit by implementing a variety of reforms to constrain and reallocate educational costs, expand public and parental choice, and address issues of accountability, openness, and public participation.

Overriding the aforementioned specific concerns, a new hegemony has arisen to suggest that existing education systems must undergo more fundamental changes to align themselves with new social and economic realities. This vision advances beyond an earlier notion of basic education, combined with selection mechanisms to ensure that the most capable persons gain the capacities they require for higher-level jobs and social positions, by placing a reformed general education system into a broader continuum of ongoing training, innovation, and skill development (United Nations Development Programme, 2001: 84–5). The OECD (2002: 21) poses the dilemma as a significant area of concern for contemporary societies:

> A democratic society, genuinely committed to the encouragement of lifelong learning for all its people, is faced with a great challenge in the system of education it inherits from the antecedent meritocratic society. Can a system designed to sort and reward the most able be reformed in such a way as to help everyone fulfil their (very diverse) potential? Or, if reform is impossible, is a kind of educational revolution on the agenda for learning?

The vehemence with which contending views about educational reform are expressed signifies the importance of education to both public and personal life. As Chapter 3 has emphasized, many of these debates are not new—the history of public education is riddled with an ongoing litany of critiques, defences, and counter-critiques about education systems and their efficacy. Whatever positions are advocated, widespread concern clearly exists over the necessity to maintain an accessible, equitable system of quality education in the face of significant social and economic changes.

Education debates tend to be characterized by diverse strands that emerge around fundamental contradictions between what Carnoy and Levin (1985) term capitalist and democratic imperatives in education, as discussed in Chapter 7. Apple (2000: 17–18), following Gintis (1980), argues that these tensions are indicative of underlying contention over **property rights**, where individual rights and liberties are governed by market relations, contracts, and the possession of private property, and **person rights**, in which people's rights and freedoms are granted on the basis of citizenship and moral claims. Support for initiatives such as market-based education reforms, reduction of state funding for education, and an emphasis on standardized curricula exemplify some of the ways in which capitalist imperatives and property rights have begun to influence educational decision-making. On the other hand, movements to broaden public access to education, to foster **inclusive schooling** that represents and serves the full range of diversity within communities, and to develop curricula and programs oriented to social justice issues are indicative of approaches to educational reform guided by democratic considerations and human rights.

RATIONAL PLANNING AND EDUCATIONAL ACCOUNTABILITY

Debate over how to measure and interpret educational quality and outcomes has accompanied strongly divergent views about how to reform the education system to improve its performance. One set of issues in which competing educational interests and ideologies have become highly visible is debate over accountability and choice, and related emphasis on market-driven alternatives such as **charter schools**, educational voucher systems, and parental choice models. Some proponents of reform have argued that educational competition and accountability can be increased by implementing merit pay for teachers, basing their salaries or providing incentive bonuses in accordance with student performance or test results. Others see reform as a matter of continuous monitoring and critical reflection by educators, sometimes as a professional responsibility and in other cases in collaboration with other groups, including administrators and community members.

Wilkinson (1994: 17) summarizes the three main factors normally involved in such debates—concern over the declining quality of education in Canada in the face of increasing international competitiveness; concern over the kinds of values transmitted through schooling; and frustration over the lack of responsiveness to change within the educational bureaucracy. Ungerleider (2003: 221–2) points to the need for decisive leadership at all levels to guide public schooling, informed by a solid foundation of knowledge and understanding of the complexities of schooling.

Some of these arguments have been outlined in previous chapters. The issues of concern illustrate how various groups—such as business and neo-liberal interests calling for competitiveness in education and religious organizations seeking the promotion of faith-based values in schooling—come to be aligned within the New Right. By contrast, many other segments of the population, including education and teachers' organizations, organized labour, coalitions to promote social justice, and people who subscribe to more inclusive notions of social equality, have expressed considerable opposition to proposals for market-driven educational reforms.

Fundamental to these debates are competing conceptions about what the goals and purposes of education are and whose interests schooling should serve. Advocates of varying positions agree that public education requires some reform to meet the needs of diverse groups of learners in a rapidly changing social and economic context. Many critics, however, argue that extensive changes reaching beyond the current system are necessary to compensate for a lack of quality, imagination, choice, and effective outcomes in public education.

Proponents of property rights and market-based educational choice make their case by highlighting, in part, relationships between educational and economic indicators to demonstrate the deficiencies of the present system. Demands for drastic educational reform were bolstered in the early 1990s by data suggesting that Canada was receiving poor returns on its education investments, as signified by its relatively poor or 'mediocre' ranking on labour market activity, economic performance, and student rankings in comparative scores on standardized mathematics, science, and literacy tests (Economic Council of Canada, 1992: 40; Schweitzer, 1995: 47). This critique has been tempered somewhat by more recent findings that Canadian students, both in general and within many provinces, are faring relatively better than those in most other comparable nations—and much better than in the United States.

In part, the emphasis on test scores and other indicators of educational performance reveals a desire by educators, policy-makers, and parents for systematic feedback on education activities. In terms of assessment of and reporting on individual student performance, for instance, school jurisdictions across the country have sought compromises between those parents and teachers who want test scores that produce a numerical or letter grade purporting to show exactly where one student stands in relation to others and those who feel that anecdotal reporting and commentary about educational processes provide a truer reflection of a student's ability and progress (Lewington, 1995: A1).

In education, following innovations in the health-care domain, there has been growing emphasis on the application of **evidence-based decision-making**. The principle of exchanging and drawing upon a solid foundation of research-based findings in order to guide educational practice has widespread support among educators, policy-makers, and other groups, although there is less agreement as to how best to implement such a process (Levin and Seward, 2003). Just as parents wish to know how well their children are doing in comparison with others, educators and other interested groups want information about how well different education systems and their outputs measure up against one another. Teachers now spend considerable amounts of their time engaging in critical reflection and planning based on various forms of assessment and indicators from test scores and other types of feedback. On a broader scale, the Canadian Council on Learning was initiated in 2004 as an independent organization, funded by the federal government, as a mechanism to promote lifelong learning, facilitate and exchange research on different dimensions of learning, and foster the application of research evidence in educational decision-making. Among its varied activities, the council has focused attention on the development of strategies to address serious data gaps, particularly with respect to post-secondary education, that have made it difficult to draw meaningful comparisons and implement effective changes (Canadian Council on Learning, 2007d: 8).

Educators and education bodies have shed much of their initial reluctance to engage in comparative testing, driven both by political pressures and by genuine desire for a knowledge base that may contribute to improved educational performance. Nonetheless, the results from various comparative databases remain highly volatile, especially when they are used to promote the agendas of particular bodies, such as the Fraser Institute, which has published school-by-school 'report cards' on educational performance in Alberta, British Columbia, Ontario, and Quebec in its pursuit of market-driven education reform. De Broucker and Sweetman (2002: 8), noting the potential that comparative educational indicators have to be employed in narrow ways by specific groups, stress that 'It is all too common to focus on problems, and they certainly exist, but problems are in fact "news" (and often covered by the news media), whereas the "un-newsworthy" is mostly good compared to that experienced by other countries.'

Since the 1990s, Canada (through various federal government departments, provincial governments, and the Council of Ministers of Education Canada) has participated in recurrent cycles of initiatives like the Trends in International Mathematics and Science Study, the Progress in International Reading Literacy Study, the Program for International Student Assessment, and the Pan-Canadian Assessment Program. These programs, which variously employ standardized tests to compare mathematics, reading, writing, literacy, and science skills at particular age or grade levels across jurisdictions, signify a growing desire for data to provide a comparative baseline for guiding educational assessment and decision-making. Parallel to these developments are movements towards a national curriculum and core curricula in several provinces that provide specified areas of study and learning materials for all learners at particular stages of their studies. Government inquiries conducted over the past two decades, including commissions on learning and education undertaken in Alberta, Ontario, and Newfoundland and Labrador, have acknowledged that issues surrounding problems of assessment, evaluation, and reporting are highly complex. At the same time, consistent with the prevailing trends, their recommendations pointed to the implementation of more systematic procedures for testing and assessing both students and education system performance that reduce these issues to quantifiable outcomes.

Debates over testing in Canada have also been somewhat muted in comparison to the United States. Legislation in the US, notably the federal No Child Left Behind Act, has generated extensive controversy and skewed educational pathways for many students by linking funding allocation to student outcomes (Irons and Harris, 2007; Meier and Wood, 2004). More generally, in both jurisdictions, numerous critics have pointed out that standardized tests, curricula, and perform-ance indicators do not reflect the true nature and quality of education and tend to discount socio-economic background and other factors that can influence out-comes. For standardized tests that compare student performance in different provinces and countries to be valid and fair, there must be some assurance that students in each jurisdiction have had an opportunity to cover the material or acquire the skills being tested. Consequently, testing tends to be restricted to a nar-row range of all material that is likely to be covered in a subject area. It remains highly debatable as to how accurately test scores reflect student ability either with-in a given subject area or in more general terms. This is further limited by the fact that testing and evaluation, particularly when they are oriented to empirical or 'objective' measures, generally focus on relatively discrete bits of information rather than on critical thinking and wider, more complex activities usually regard-ed as essential within educational practices. Given that the school day consists of both formal curricular expectations and social and other dimensions of the 'hid-den' curriculum, there is no necessary correlation between the number of school days and the amount or quality of education in a given school jurisdiction.

Test data must be carefully presented and interpreted to be meaningful. Media and political commentary often ignores the fact that most international and interprovincial comparisons of test results draw on different populations or sub-groups of students. Some jurisdictions with lower 'average' test scores often include a wider range of students than other jurisdictions that draw from more selective student bodies that would be expected to produce higher score results (Gilliss, 1995: 121–3). Some rethinking of comparative test results has accompa-nied findings that demonstrate the impact of specific factors—notably socio-eco-nomic inequality—on overall performance. In particular, especially within Canada, jurisdictions that have the most favourable outcomes tend to be those in which the participants from the lowest socio-economic categories do well, and which reveal the least difference among learners from the top and bottom socio-economic categories (Willms, 1997: 20; Bussière et al., 2001: 32–3; Bussière et al., 2007: 41).

Testing and assessment procedures can often generate a unique logic apart from the outcomes they are overtly intended to measure. Ball (2004) refers to many recent processes employed by governments and education administrators to report on school activities as 'performativity', which can serve a dual function of reporting and impression management. The use of performance indicators and other standards to measure educational effectiveness provides decision-makers with a wide range of information that may be used to gauge and compare different individuals, institutions, or units. In the process, it creates a significant amount of new work in gathering information, meeting to discuss reporting and decision-making procedures, reporting, and debriefing, which, in turn, can take time away from teaching and learning processes themselves. At the same time, akin to dangers that teachers may respond to standardized testing by 'teaching to the text' in order to generate the best results rather than focusing on other activities, the staff and schools being assessed learn to be proficient in how they highlight the best results and minimize limitations, presenting themselves in the most favourable way possible. The impetus for much evidence-based practice in education is viewed by some critics as an attack on teacher professionalism driven by technical agendas in which knowledge is reduced to limited bits of factual information devoid of a clear understanding of social contexts and human relationships (Clegg, 2005: 417–18). Lessard (2004: 34, 48) uses the case of educational reforms in Quebec to illustrate the tensions and contradictions carried by a 'logic of indicators' driven by mechanical applications of enterprise culture in contrast with efforts to pursue effective pedagogical innovations grounded in classroom practice.

As has been noted throughout this book, schooling and learning are about much more than simply acquiring and repeating information. Many critics ignore the more indeterminate human and social dimensions of education as they seek to generate standardized achievement test scores and quantitative measures of educational accountability for specific ends. Evidence from New Zealand, Australia, the United Kingdom, and several American states in which educational measurement and accountability have been key elements of market-based school reforms indicates that these measures have been employed more fully to control education, discipline teachers, and appease parents than to contribute to more effective teaching and learning (Smyth et al., 2000). Discourses of accountability and measurement are often silent on the cultural and political dimensions to learning. Persons from distinct social backgrounds have varying degrees of access to information deemed as valuable or valid from the dominant cultural perspective. In many educational settings, not high test scores but the extent to which all students can gain access to meaningful social opportunities and experiences is the mark of student and school success. Bacon (1995: 87), expressing the concerns of many Canadian teachers, emphasizes that:

> Outcomes are not just things that are measurable. For example, appreciation of cultural diversity, adaptability to change, values clarification, a sense of personal worth and responsibility, and character development are all important outcomes but are difficult to measure. Nor are these things the sole responsibility of the school. These responsibilities are shared with parents and others in society.

Box 9.1 Social and Economic Imperatives and School Ratings

Interest in issues of school choice and accountability has paralleled the desires by many parents to ensure that their children receive a solid educational foundation that ensures they will be competitive for further education and employment opportunities in an information society. One of the best-known and most controversial mechanisms devoted to fostering school choice and to providing parents with information about school performance is a report card on schools in several provinces, including Alberta, British Columbia, Ontario, and Quebec, issued periodically by the Fraser Institute. The report cards rank schools at particular levels in each province according to a composite index composed of provincial test score results and patterns from particular grades in such areas as reading, writing, and numeracy. Proponents of the reporting initiative point to the benefits it offers to educators and parents in providing useful information that can drive educational improvement over time, though this is typically expressed in language framed around notions of educational consumers and marketplaces, as Peter Cowley (2007: 6), one of the authors of the report cards, reveals:

It was in the context of this rather dismal educational landscape [of government policies that discouraged expansion of private schooling] that The Fraser Institute initiated the school performance measurement project. Its main product—report cards on individual school performance—would, to the extent possible, establish one of the conditions necessary for a free market in education; namely, the availability to consumers, in this case parents, of reliable information on the comparative value of services provided by competing suppliers, in this case schools.

These annual audits of school performance would assist parents in two ways.

First, they would enable parents to make more informed decisions when choosing a school for their children. Second, they would enable parents to advocate more effectively for improvement at their children's schools. These two purposes would be served by bringing together in the report cards a variety of objective data on student results at individual schools in such a way as to make comparisons among schools easy. The results would then be published in an understandable format and made available to the widest possible audience.

Critics, by contrast, point to serious bias and deficiencies in both the aims and the methodology employed in the report cards, ignoring social dimensions in favour of economic imperatives. A British Columbia teacher (Waber, 2006: 6–7) identifies several specific internal flaws and wider omissions in the reporting procedures—including ranking schools on a provincial level rather than by the characteristics the report seeks to highlight, confusing **educational governance** (especially public versus private) with other factors that influence performance, ignoring class size, ignoring budgetary factors, and obscuring demographic factors related to students' social backgrounds—and condemns the reports more broadly:

> The focus of the *Report Card* is exceedingly narrow. To identify schools that effectively meet the expectations of the larger community, parents should have access not only to their academic results but also to objective information regarding their success in nurturing non-academic, behavioral, attitudinal and social skills. But even the formula that [report authors] Cowley and Easton use to calculate academic ratings is questionable. Their weighting of the scores for reading, writing, numeracy, gender differences, and meeting expectations exaggerates the differences between schools and school systems.
>
> The shortcomings of the *Report Card* are glaring. It glosses over, or fails to consider, some of the influences that others have found responsible for large differences in academic achievement. Until its authors take into account the numbers of students who require ESL and special needs instruction in each school, the effect of selective admission, the vagaries of the gender gap and the differences in per-pupil cost, a ranking that includes both public and independent schools lacks validity.

One former business executive, commenting on his reversal of an earlier assessment that schools should be governed more like businesses, stresses that he has since 'learned that a school is not a business. Schools are unable to control the quality of their raw material, they are dependent upon the vagaries of politics for a reliable revenue stream, and they are constantly mauled by a howling horde of disparate, competing customer groups that would send the best CEO screaming into the night' (Vollmer, 2003: 42). Posed another way, the determination of educational quality is a highly contested process that involves several levels of human judgement:

> the common denominator among all attempts to judge educational quality is the imposition of human judgement with all of its complex and conflicted assumptions, values, biases, cultural predispositions, and so forth. In this respect, the narrowest of quality evaluation schemes founded purely on standardized tests is no more objectively valid than the most uncomplicated of holistic quality judgements. All parties to the educational process do the same thing in this matter, they impose—or attempt to impose—their ideas about the knowledge, beliefs, values, and attitudes the schools ought to foster. (Paquette, 1989: 23)

EDUCATION AND NEW TECHNOLOGIES

The revolutionizing possibilities and imperatives associated with the 'information age' are integral to contemporary educational reform processes. The rapid pace of innovation in new information and communications technologies (ICTs) has been accompanied by greater levels of adoption of computer and digital technologies at work and school, and in the home and daily life. Computers, advanced data-processing systems, technology transfer programs, and electronic information networks, notably the Internet and World Wide Web, have affected our expectations about education in the same way that they have altered many general patterns of living and working. Educational institutions encounter rising expectations about their ability both to incorporate information technologies into their own activities and to train persons who have the capacity to master and develop new technologies in innovative ways. Like most educational issues, there are contradictory dimensions to how people view these developments and what their implications are for education systems.

Technological innovations have been eagerly embraced by some segments of education communities and resisted or regarded with disdain by others. It is important to distinguish, in these varied responses, between the use and impact of technologies as they relate to individual learners and educators, and those associated with education systems or processes as a whole. Individuals may use computers or network systems, for instance, to conduct research and write term papers, to organize attendance records or grade reports, to introduce graphic presentations or simulations to classes, or to exchange information with people in other educational settings. These applications may be used as resources to facilitate administrative, teaching, or learning practices for individuals without substantially altering teaching or learning processes. Technological innovations may also be applied in a slightly more engaged manner involving changes that apply both to individuals and to education systems, such as the teaching of courses in computers or data-processing or the introduction of distance education courses by television, teleconferencing, or computers, but which still are combined with more traditional educational practices.

Technological change can alter education in more fundamental ways. In the extreme, information and communications technologies suggest an imperative for new paradigms based on drastic alterations to our whole way of thinking, learning, interacting, and living. Information technologies are commonly posed as inescapable realities that set the pace and standard for work and socio-economic survival in the emergent global scheme of things. Schooling, if it is to be relevant, must ensure that students become familiar with the operation of computers and other new technologies, which means that the infrastructure must be sufficiently equipped with these technologies—and be able to adapt and innovate within ongoing processes of change. Spurred by varying forms of government support and corporate funding, several initiatives have emerged in recent years to promote the introduction and use of new technologies and information-based learning systems at virtually all levels of education and training.

Box 9.2 Internet Skills among Canadian Youth

Educators and education systems are struggling to keep pace with a world in which Internet use is a taken-for-granted phenomenon in the lives of children and youth. A survey of over 5,000 Canadian students in Grades 4 to 11 reveals the growing confidence that boys and girls alike have with some computer-related skills (ERIN Research, 2005: 57, 59):

> Kids rated their own skill level in ten common areas of their lives. Most of the skills, listed in [the following table], relate to the world of schools and friends— only two are specifically computer-based (skill using the Internet and skill playing computer games). The rating scale runs from 0 to 100 with 50 as the midpoint. If people rate their skills accurately, the average rating would be 50. If most people thought that they were better than average, then the mean rating would be higher than 50.
>
> In fact most of the ratings exceed 50, meaning that students as a group tend to be rather confident in their abilities. 'Using the Internet' is, by a slight margin, the top-ranked skill. Both girls and boys feel confident in their Internet abilities.

Table 9.1 Girls' and Boys' Self-Ratings of 10 Skills

(Skill rating: 0 = Not as good; 50 = about the same; 100 = better)

Skill	Girls	Boys	Total
Using the Internet*	62	68	65
Making friends	66	62	64
Telling jokes, making people laugh	60	65	63
Reading*	66	58	62
Playing computer games*	50	71	61
Sports*	51	64	58
Math and science*	52	57	54
Visual arts*	55	47	51
Shopping*	62	33	47
Playing a musical instrument or singing	51	42	47

*Statistically significant gender difference accounting for 1 per cent or more of the variance.

It is no surprise that heavy Internet use is associated with skill using the Net and skill playing computer games. But what about shopping or making friends or making people laugh? One hypothesis is that kids who are good shoppers recognize that the Internet is one tool of the trade and they spend time online to advance their interest in shopping. Likewise, the Net is a medium for making new friends (e.g., via MSN), and it is a huge source of humorous material (several of the top-ranked 'favourite sites' deal primarily in jokes).

Kids who are interested in making new friends will use the Net as one channel of social interaction and will therefore increase the time they spend online. On the other hand, those who are interested in math, science, reading and the arts may find less to advance their interests on the Net and spend less time online. What the hypothesis states is that shopping, making friends and being funny are skills that, for today's youth, are embedded in electronic communications. The Internet is an extension of everyday social life and an integral part of these skill sets.

Source: © Media Awareness Network, *Young Canadians in a Wired World*, Ottawa, Canada, 2008, http://www.media-awareness.ca, quoted with permission.

Educational innovations now in place or underway include the delivery of entire educational programs by computer-based curricular modules, the transformation of classrooms into fully 'wired' learning centres, and electronic networks that provide for 'virtual' campuses or schools. There is growing official support to integrate new technologies more comprehensively into education. In the mid-1990s, Ontario's Royal Commission on Learning (1994: 26–7) stressed that 'it is crucial that every classroom in every school be part of the information highway', driven by the conviction 'that information technology is one of the engines needed to drive the necessary transformation of the education system.' By the end of the decade, initiatives like SchoolNet, organized through Industry Canada in conjunction with provincial and territorial governments, were promoted as vehicles that would link all public schools and libraries through the Internet with the aim to prepare learners for the knowledge-based society. Some of these initiatives have not been as successful as initially anticipated, but they have been supplanted by an immense range of alternatives at local, national, and international levels. The most common types of developments have included:

- purchase and action plans to incorporate computers and other electronic devices, programs, software, and communication networks into the ongoing activities of educational institutions;
- the establishment of computer-assisted learning and computer-based training programs, especially for students with special needs and other targeted groups;
- the introduction of hands-on learning technologies in classrooms and technology support programs for educators;
- use of information networks for distance learning and modular learning programs; and
- electronic linkages among new institutional networks of participants and partners in education and other fields.

The introduction of new technologies and information networks has wide-spread appeal because of the advantages they offer to both educators and learners. Routine tasks can sometimes be integrated into computer programs in an effi-cient, cost-effective manner that may both benefit and enhance the interest of the learner, teacher, or administrator. Information and materials previously beyond the reach of many educational institutions, particularly in remote areas or those with limited supporting resources, are now often readily available to all partici-pants who have access to computer facilities or advanced communications tech-nology. Information and service networks, learning packages in CD- or DVD-ROM form, multi-media kits, distance education programs, and on-line, wireless, or satellite transmission of information enable educators, students, and even parents to access an unprecedented range of resources. The digitization of library resources, journals and books, and other materials provides unprecedented access to important learning and research resources. Students who acquire computer and programming skills and gain facility with information transmission and retrieval processes have favourable access to competitive job markets driven by technolog-ical change. Moreover, computer-literate students and school personnel con-tribute to the pool of highly qualified people required to advance further technological progress. Information technology and the networks it fosters also promote co-operation and innovation among educational institutions and between education and other sectors of the economy.

There are, however, several limiting factors to how far education can and should be modified by technological change. Tran (1995: 50–1) poses a number of fundamental questions that continue to be relevant as educators contend with how best to integrate ICTs into the classroom. These include:

- What is the goal of education and how do computer systems contribute to this goal?
- What are the best approaches to teaching students, training teachers, and evaluating programs?
- How is computer technology related to various subject areas?
- How far can new technology be incorporated without damaging major learning objectives?

Some proponents of the expansion of computer technology in the classroom tend to portray teachers and other school personnel as uninformed or rigid detractors who resist changes that have already been embraced by students and employers (Lewington and Orpwood, 1993: 100). However, in many cases, computers and new information systems are introduced into schools without a thorough assess-ment of how they will be incorporated into daily school routines, how they affect teachers' work, and what kinds of training and support resources are available. Even when school systems and personnel are firmly committed to the expansion of new technologies, for instance, deficiencies in areas such as in-service training, techni-cal support, and access to hardware and software will undermine the potential contributions these technologies can make to educational practices. Cuban (2001: 177–8) observes that, even as computer use has become ubiquitous in North American schools, there have been no clear advances in educational outcomes related to academic achievement and efficiency, no clearly defined agreement on what constitutes computer literacy, and no technological revolution in teaching and learning in most classrooms.

From the perspective of learners, new technologies constitute additional forms of cultural and fiscal capital that differentially affect opportunities for success or failure. Increasing numbers of people have access to computers and Internet connections at home, school, workplaces, and public sites such as libraries and wireless access points. New technologies tend to be adopted more widely over time once their utility is established and basic start-up costs drop. At the same time, differential means and opportunities possessed by families, communities, and institutions to keep abreast of up-to-date, compatible forms of information technology and support contribute to the persistence of gaps in technological access and use.

The explosion of computer technology over the past two decades has fostered considerable interest in a phenomenon widely described as the **digital divide** with reference to the inequitable nature of information technology access, use, and returns. The digital divide separates people with ready access to computer technology and Internet connections from those without such access. Sciadis (2002: 4–5) emphasizes several variants of digital divides, based on two main sets of factors. One set of issues concerns the unequal distribution of access to information and communications technologies across significant sociological and demographic categories including age, gender, class, and geography. Data from 2000 reveal that about 85 per cent of 15-year-olds in Canada, compared to an average of 70 per cent of those the same age in all OECD nations, had access to a computer at home on a daily basis or several times per week (Statistics Canada, 2002). Some evidence suggests that the widespread penetration of computer technologies throughout much of the world has closed some of these gaps. Rates of Internet access in the developed world remained six times those in developing nations in 2006, although these had been 10 times higher in 2002 (UNCTAD, 2007: 25). Sciadis (2002: 18) suggests that more people in all categories are employing computer technologies with increasing frequency, but the divide between the top and bottom income groups has persisted or even widened since the mid-1990s (ibid., 5).

A second area of concern is related to differences in access and capabilities with respect to specific technologies, including analogue and digital devices. One dimension of uneven levels of skill associated with ICTs is a generational divide in application, capabilities, and attitudes related to new technologies. A cross-Canada survey (Ipsos Reid, 2007: 2), comparing responses of persons aged 55 and over with those between ages 18 and 55, for instance, reveals that:

Behaviourally, older Canadians lag behind the younger groups in each of 20 common online activities Canadians have ever participated in. The gap is largest for listening to Internet radio (34 per cent), downloading free MP3 files (32 per cent), visiting blogs (23 per cent), conducting online banking (21 per cent), researching courses and schools (21 per cent), comparison shopping (20 per cent), searching for real estate (18 per cent), researching trips (17 per cent), using the Internet at work for personal reasons (17 per cent), and purchasing online (14 per cent). These divides are evident in surveys of Canadian school-age youth.

These trends are significant to relationships at work, school, and other social spheres as children and youth become increasingly immersed in and adept with a wide range of technologies and applications beyond capacities held by their parents, teachers and supervisors. Educational institutions, including universities that have often been at the cutting edge of new technologies, are scrambling to expand technologies and programs that incorporate ICTs as ever-emerging technologies emerge. Consequently, by the time the 'established' order begins to incorporate or respond to favourite networking sites and devices, youth who are the most 'connected' have already moved on to new ones.

Source: The Canadian Interactive Reid Report, © Ipsos Reid.

These issues have significant implications for schooling. Educational activity, in general, tends to facilitate computer use both directly and indirectly. Data from Statistics Canada reveal that students, especially in younger age cohorts, are more engaged than non-students in Internet use for both educational and other purposes (McKeown and Underhill, 2007). By contrast, despite the promise that computers may hold for expanding education and training possibilities, students' use of computers for personal enjoyment, gaming, and communications tends to match or prevail over word processing and other activities related to schoolwork (Corbett and Willms, 2002: 14). Results from an international survey show that for three-quarters of Canadian 15-year-old students, computers were available in school on a regular basis, though just under two out of five of them used computers at school frequently, with girls reporting both less frequent use of computers and less certainty about the importance of computers than boys (Statistics Canada, 2002).

Educational applications of technology can also be undermined by the inability of educators to appreciate the potential held by digital technologies because of their own lack of understanding and facility with ongoing changes. Clifford (2005: 15) portrays graphically the gap between 'cyberkids' and technologically illiterate educators:

Many young people spend a lot of time online and gaming, yet educators have very little understanding of the intellectual skills they actually use there. Cyberkids multitask, plugged into ipods, MSN and their cell phones all at once. They send text messages and video clips wherever, whenever. Writing, they'd rather hunker down crosslegged in a busy hallway than sit quietly, straightbacked, with feet flat on the floor in the ergonomically approved positions most of us were taught in Grade 10 typing classes. They pull their laptops out of backpacks and connect to the wireless network in their favorite coffee shop. Talking about it as old fogies, we chuckle together about the generation gap and how we know that we just don't get it. If there are young people nearby, they generally keep their mouths shut. 'How do you listen to those headphones and actually concentrate on what you are supposed to be doing?' we ask them, like anthropologists trying to win our way into the exotic rituals of a jungle tribe.

Gender-related differences extend to how computers are used and the kinds of computer-related training undertaken in schooling. Males remain much more actively involved than females in computer studies and computer use at all levels of education, particularly in fields that involve computer programming and advanced applications, as opposed to data entry, word processing, or clerical uses (Collis, 1991; Dryburgh, 2002). In many educational settings, women's positions are undermined by tendencies to privilege technical knowledge over social skills and by masculinist cultural assumptions and social practices associated with information technologies (Butterwick et al., 2007: 286; Rose and Jenson, 2007: 66–7). Among Canadian teens, half or more of all males, compared to just over one-third of females, identify their computer and the Internet as a source of enjoyment, with males substantially more likely to identify video and computer gaming as a major source of enjoyment. Females, on the other hand, are slightly more likely than males to designate e-mail communications as a source of enjoyment (Bibby, 2001: 24). Differences in computer use and applications tend to be associated, in turn, with gender-differentiated labour market and employment patterns (Taylor, 2005).

Much of the discussion over the implementation of new technologies in education concerns the specific advantages or disadvantages of technology while ignoring wider political and pedagogical considerations. Among the most ardent promoters of computer and advanced technological innovations in education are business interests, corporations, specialists, or government personnel whose profits or career advancement are linked with prospects for widespread adoption of their products or services in educational settings, or parents who seek competitive advantage for their children (Mangan, 1994). Education poses a highly lucrative market for business and commercial interests both directly and indirectly, through sales of information and communications technology and related products to educational institutions, broader influence over educational decision-making, and cultivation of product identification and marketing to students and their families.

The rhetoric associated with new technologies sometimes helps to foster a misleading sense of urgency in which it appears imperative for us to master technology or else become doomed to failure. As funding and program priorities shift towards an emphasis on computer technology, other programs and services may be cut or undermined. Some critics point out that it is easy to become mesmerized by graphics, simulations, and other technical capabilities, as well as imagery related to technological revolutions and information highways, to such an extent that fundamental moral and human dimensions of education are forgotten (Beattie, 1996: 104–5). In its most extreme forms, technology can decontextualize education, reduce knowledge to isolated bits or fragments of information, and undermine the kinds of face-to-face contact and social interaction that are vital to many learning processes (Nelsen, 1997).

Computers and other new technologies, as with many other factors associated with teaching and learning, play a contradictory role in educational relationships. Information technology can stimulate interest, increase access to resources and programs, enhance innovation and flexibility, facilitate connections among educational participants, and ensure that education is attuned to emergent global trends. It can also work to the disadvantage of educators and learners who do not have access to or are unable to master technological developments. It may democratize access to information, but it can also contribute to centralized control, increased monitoring of individual activity, and limits to freedom. It can open up new employment and creative possibilities, but it can also contribute to the reproduction of existing social inequalities and the emergence of new dimensions by which more privileged groups come to distance themselves from the underprivileged. Underlying all of these concerns is the recognition that schooling, by nature, tends to be highly nuanced and complex because it involves social as well as technical relationships.

EDUCATION AND SOCIAL DIVERSITY

As educational institutions struggle to remain relevant and viable, they must contend with the ongoing challenge of how best to define their mandates and serve the students and communities they intend to reach. One of the most prominent characteristics of contemporary educational institutions is the tremendous range of diversity among students and other participants. This phenomenon reflects the changing composition of populations, the recognition that more people are attending and staying in school for longer periods of time, the integration of previously excluded groups into educational settings, and more fluid boundaries between different forms of schooling and other social and educational sites. In all of these regards, internal and external transformations are challenging and reconfiguring the educational landscape. In addition to the array of choices created by new institutional arrangements and programs, increased attention is being paid to various kinds of lifelong learning and informal learning that occur in community and work settings and other sites beyond formal educational institutions. These initiatives, at the same time, have exerted new pressures on public schooling and traditional modes of educational delivery to remain open, accessible, and meaningful to a diverse range of learners and their communities. Diversity can be one of the major strengths of democratic public institutions, but it also poses practical challenges in how it is best accommodated.

The educational world has also gained complexity as educational constituencies have broadened. Education is beginning earlier in life, with expanded preschool and early childhood initiatives, and continuing well beyond high school and post-secondary levels for most people. Demographic changes, immigration, increasing Aboriginal populations, changes in families and workplaces, modifications to the life course, and broader concerns about personal, community, and social security are altering the nature of student bodies and the attitudes and

Box 9.3 Roots of Empathy

Educational reform is often accused of being susceptible to emerging fads, jargon, and innovations that have little sustained impact on educational outcomes. Sometimes the most straightforward approaches that address fundamental social relationships work best, as evident in the highly successful development of a program called Roots of Empathy founded by Canadian educator and parent/child advocate Mary Gordon in 1996. The program, which is endorsed by provincial education ministries and school boards across the country, pairs elementary school students with parents and infants from within the community, enabling participants to develop close interpersonal connections while learning about human development, positive parenting skills, and activities linked to core curricular areas. Roots of Empathy (2005) summarizes the program's main features:

> During a typical Roots of Empathy family visit, the baby, parent and Roots of Empathy Instructor gather on a special blanket on the classroom floor. Students sit in a circle around the blanket and are taken through guided observations of the baby. Students observe, ask questions, and discuss the infant's behaviour, vocalization, temperament, and overall responses. Students have an opportunity to observe the growing attachment of the baby to the parent, which provides them with a working model of responsive parenting.
>
> Each of the family visits focuses on a different theme related to infant development, such as crying, sleep, or language. Babies are between 2 and 4 months old at the beginning of the Roots of Empathy program and about one year old at its conclusion, a period of incredible growth and development in a baby's life. Over this time, children in the program can learn how to see and feel things as others see and feel them, understand how babies develop, and observe the healthy acquisition of language. Children also learn important safety issues, such as Shaken Baby Syndrome, Fetal Alcohol Spectrum Disorder (FASD), the perils of second-hand smoke, and the recommended way to put babies to sleep to protect against Sudden Infant Death Syndrome (SIDS).
>
> As the program progresses, the students become attached to 'their' baby as they observe the continuum of the infant's development, celebrate milestones, interact with the baby, learn about an infant's needs and witness the baby's growth and development. The program also has links to the school curriculum of the grade level to which it is being offered. With the Instructor, students use math skills to measure and weigh their baby and chart the development. They write poems or create raps for the baby. They read stories that tap emotional literacy, such as fear, sadness, anger, shyness. Children learn to relate to their own feelings, as well as recognize these same emotions in others.

When children understand how others feel, they are less likely to victimize them through bullying. Information on infant safety and development also helps children to be more thoughtful when dealing with infants. Ultimately, they become more competent parents who will be less likely to abuse their children. Roots of Empathy builds social and human capital.

At the same time, parents involved with the program acquire new insight into the powerful role their love and stimulation plays in the development of their baby's brain. The value provided by the Roots of Empathy Instructors home-visiting and direct parent education has a ripple effect in the community where the program is being implemented.

expectations they carry with them. Educational institutions and participants are positioning themselves to respond to admonitions that the stakes of getting an education—and getting the proper kinds of education—are growing.

Various educational programs and services have also emerged in response to the needs of diverse educational constituencies. These include:

- adult education, university degree programs for mature students, and integration programs for persons who return to school later in life;
- ESL, heritage language, cultural education, and anti-racism education programs;
- programs for Aboriginal students and educational institutions and initiatives under First Nations control;
- educational programs and services for the visually or hearing-impaired, or for persons with other physical or mental disabilities;
- alternative schools or classes for intellectually gifted, emotionally impaired, or learning-disabled students;
- expansion of distance education, Web-based courses, and other options for students who cannot attend classes in person as a result of geography, time, work, mobility, or other restrictions;
- increased acknowledgement and recognition of alternative forms of knowledge, including indigenous knowledge, knowledge acquired on the job or in other social settings, and assessment and recognition mechanisms for prior learning;
- co-operative education and other learning programs that combine formal schooling with vocational training or community or work experience;
- scholarship or mentoring programs to encourage female students to complete studies in fields like natural sciences and computers and to promote male literacy and reading skills;
- internationalization of education, exchange programs, and co-operative arrangements between educational institutions in different nations.

Many of these changes are positive insofar as they expand educational opportunities and provide options for education and training appropriate to people's circumstances and needs. Expanded educational services may provide particular benefits for segments of the population that typically have been excluded from all but the most basic levels of education. It is crucial, at the same time, to analyze and not take for granted issues like sponsorship, control, funding, accessibility, and delivery of programs and services in order to gain a full understanding of the nature and implications of educational change and innovation.

This is especially true of reforms that are fiscally or politically motivated, or those that treat education in an abstract way as an industry or business. Economically, it often makes sense to close community or neighbourhood schools with low enrolments, to increase class sizes or tuition fees, or to prioritize education programs that contribute to high student achievement and employment. However, other, sometimes less tangible, social, pedagogical, and ethical dimensions are also crucial to educational practice and decision-making. Educators, administrators, and policy-makers, in the process, need to keep a strong perspective on the questions and limitations that surround the appropriateness and applicability of such indicators.

Education reform and decision-making are much more complex matters than commonly assumed. A vast literature, spanning several fields, has emerged to explain or move beyond questions about why schooling appears impervious to so many reform initiatives (Rowan and Miskel, 1999; Sarason, 1996; Fullan, 2007). There are few absolute or readily agreed-upon answers to questions about such issues as the optimal class size for teaching and learning at different levels, the impact of mainstreaming of special-needs students within regular classrooms on different groups of students, the extent to which decisions over school closures should consider community interests as well as cost factors, the amount of formal recognition that should be given to different education credentials, and the relative merit of training workers as opposed to educating citizens. It is likely that debates over these kinds of issues will intensify as the role of education in a globally changing society comes under further public scrutiny.

CONCLUSION

This book has emphasized the insight that an essential starting point from which to base an understanding of educational issues lies in the observation that education and schooling are complex, multi-dimensional, and contradictory endeavours. Each chapter has pointed to instances in which educational structures and practices intersect with and resemble other social institutions as well as instances in which education contains unique and sometimes conflicting dimensions. These observations can be confusing and sometimes frustrating to students, participants, and researchers, but they also contribute to possibilities to generate essential understandings and changes. Education is a social activity concerned with the development and transformation of human beings. As education is converted into various informal and institutional forms, it both reflects and modifies the social

Box 9.4 Core Educational Challenges in the Twenty-First Century

Education systems are undergoing substantial modification as they come to be aligned in accordance with fundamental social, economic, and cultural transformations. Education is positioned as a central driver of social and economic change, but it is also being realigned to adjust to various external pressures. A growing body of literature offers numerous descriptions, analyses, and prescriptions for emerging educational directions, many of which have been discussed in this chapter and other places throughout the book. Many of the core trends and pressures facing education are summarized succinctly by Peters and Besley (2006: 172):

Main Trends and Pressures Facing Education

1. *Globalization and increasing competition*
   - Increased globalization (as world economic integration).
   - Increased levels of national and international competition.
   - Increased power and importance of global and multinational corporations.
   - Increased importance of research to global multinationals.
   - Importance of regional and international trade and investment agreements.
   - The growing economic and political importance of the Asian economies, including China.
2. *Public-sector changes*
   - Declining socio-political priority of education as an entirely state-funded activity.
   - Corporatization and privatization of the public sector.
   - Greater interpenetration of public and private enterprises.
   - Growth of managerialism (New Public Management) and new contractualism.
   - Localization and autonomy: decentralization, devolution, and delegation of authority to local communities and government agencies.
   - Demands for increased efficiency and accountability.
3. *Increasing importance of knowledge*
   - Increasing economic, social, and cultural importance of knowledge.
   - Commodification and mercantilization of knowledge.
   - Increasing role and importance of telecommunications and information technologies.
   - New political, legal, and ethical problems of 'information economy' (e.g., intellectual property, copyright, plagiarism).
4. *Employment*
   - Changing nature of advanced economies to knowledge-based industries.
   - Changing structure of the labour market (e.g., casualization, feminization of the workforce).

- Demand for highly skilled, technically competent workforce, with an emphasis on generic and transferable 'core' skills.

5. *Education policy*
   - Increasing multicultural and international nature of societies and education institutions.
   - Increased demand from a highly diversified, 'massified' student population.
   - Need for lifelong learning and 'second-chance' education.
   - The vocationalization of education through partnerships with business and the promotion of entrepreneurial culture.
   - Erosion of state education by non-traditional providers.
   - Individualization and customization of programs for learners.

Source: Peters, Michael A. and A.C. Tina Besley. 2006. *Building Knowledge Cultures: Education and Development in the Age of Knowledge Capitalism.* Lanham, Md: Rowman and Littlefield.

world of which it is a part. Consequently, education has personal and social importance, as well as wider economic and political significance.

These issues, in turn, point to important questions linked to social policy formulation and research in education. Some of these, as we have seen, have been addressed by research and analysis, but because all of them involve conflicting choices and interpretations, they require much more intensive scrutiny. A sampling of these questions is listed below:

- What is really meant by quality education?
- Who should pay for education? To what extent, and at what levels, should the state cover education costs as opposed to leaving responsibility with individuals, families, employers, or other agencies?
- To what extent should learners be segregated from, or integrated with, other learners according to ability and special needs?
- To what extent should specific groups or communities, defined by such factors as religion, cultural values, political beliefs, or economic interests, be able to establish and control their own educational institutions? If such schools are established, who should pay for them and what kinds of guidelines, if any, should be in place to ensure their consistency with federal or provincial standards?
- How should we define and measure educational success?
- To what extent should educational priorities and programs be determined by labour markets?
- How do education systems need to change in order to provide effective knowledge and sustainable actions related to environmental issues and planetary concerns?
- How much should public education be focused on local concerns as opposed to global issues?

- How much autonomy should educators and education specialists, as opposed to parents and community members, have to plan and deliver educational services?

While sociological analysis, in conjunction with other forms of inquiry, can help provide a foundation and tools from which to assess these issues, it cannot provide absolute answers. This book began with an overview of key debates central to sociological inquiry that must be taken into consideration when addressing questions such as the ones posed here. Our analysis should be guided by a recognition that social structures and institutions, which give shape to our experiences and provide definition for social issues, also are constructed and can be changed through human activity.

Sociology enables us to gain insights about our lives by examining the relationships between individuals and social forces. In sociological research and analysis, as with all other dimensions of human social life, we must make decisions about what to study, how to examine it, and what to do about our findings. The answers we come up with emerge only from the choices made by people as they interact with one another and their social circumstances. Education, in this sense, is a critical process in our ability to broaden our basis of social understanding, increase our ability to make meaningful life decisions, and transform our world in ways that can be beneficial to all of us.

This chapter has highlighted emergent debates and issues associated with contemporary demands for educational reform. There is a broad range of positions about what education should be about and how it should be organized. These tend to be focused on divergent views that stress, on the one hand, an understanding of education as a commodity that can be marketed like other goods and services and, on the other hand, an emphasis on the personal, transformative characteristics of education for social justice. The centrality of the diverse forms of education to human life suggests that education will continue to be contested, leaving open questions about how to ensure that all people are able to develop and use their capacities in meaningful ways.

ANNOTATED FURTHER READINGS

Cuban, Larry. 2000. *Oversold and Underused: Computers in the Classroom.* Cambridge, Mass.: Harvard University Press. The author investigates the claims made by proponents and critics of computers in education systems, providing strong evidence about the limits and prospects associated with the integration of new technologies within existing classroom settings.

de Broucker, Patrice, and Arthur Sweetman, eds. 2002. *Towards Evidence-Based Policy for Canadian Education.* Montreal and Kingston: McGill-Queen's University Press. Contributors from diverse academic and policy perspectives highlight relevant issues, advances, and concerns related to educational measurement and research oriented to the improvement of educational practices and outcomes.

Jenson, Jennifer, Chloë Brushwood Rose, and Brian Lewis, with Richard Smith, Stan Shapson, Penny Milton, and Robert Kennedy. 2007. *Policy Unplugged: Dis/Connections between Technology Policy and Practices in Canadian Schools.* Montreal and Kingston: McGill-Queen's University Press. Researchers and educators offer an overview and assess the impact of federal and provincial policies, programs, and funding practices for technology in K–12 schools. The authors highlight in particular the existence and consequences of a gap between high-level policies and specific practices.

Portelli, John P., and R. Patrick Solomon, eds. 2001. *The Erosion of Democracy in Education: From Critique to Possibilities.* Calgary: Detselig. This collection draws on examples from different Canadian contexts to highlight serious concerns arising from recent educational reforms and to work towards an alternative, progressive vision for education.

Repo, Satu, ed. 1998. *Making Schools Matter: Good Teachers at Work.* Toronto: James Lorimer. Contributors present examples from a variety of teaching contexts and jurisdictions in Canada to demonstrate the broad range of effective and innovative educational possibilities.

Robertson, Heather-Jane. 1998. *No More Teachers, No More Books: The Commercialization of Canada's Schools.* Toronto: McClelland & Stewart. The author offers a pointed critique of the ways in which powerful lobby groups and business interests are attacking and reshaping schools in order to expand opportunities for commercialization and ensure stronger alignment with market forces.

Ungerleider, Charles. 2003. *Failing Our Kids: How We Are Ruining Our Public Schools.* Toronto: McClelland & Stewart. The author, drawing on extensive experience as an educational researcher, administrator, and policy-maker, examines conflicting challenges that are posing dangers for public schools. He makes a highly informed case for the development of strong schools that can contribute effectively to economic development and informed citizenship.

KEY TERMS

Accountability The expectation that public education, like other state-provided services, has clearly defined objectives that members of the public can identify and assess as to how well and how cost-effectively they are being met.

Charter schools Schools based on a contract or charter that outlines specific arrangements and performance commitments, made between school representatives and school boards or government bodies.

Digital divide The gap between individuals, groups, and regions based on differential access to and use of computers and information communications technologies.

Educational governance The laws, procedures, regulations, and institutional arrangements that outline how education systems are organized and operated within a specific jurisdiction.

Evidence-based decision-making The systematic assessment and application of comprehensive research-based knowledge to inform decision-making and practice in education, health care, and other realms.

Inclusive schooling A concept that emphasizes schools as agencies that actively incorporate and respond to diverse student needs, regardless of social, physical, or cultural characteristics.

Marketization A process in which social relationships are transformed by defining people as consumers and social services such as education are considered as profit-making endeavours or commodities that are produced, bought, and sold in a market environment.

Person rights The basis for a vision of democracy in which all people are assured specific social entitlements and opportunities for meaningful participation in social, political, and economic life by virtue of their residence or citizenship within a jurisdiction.

Property rights The notion that social, economic, and political participation are based on market relations, private property, and contractual arrangements.

STUDY QUESTIONS

1. Considerable recent controversy has been generated over the issue of whether there should be an overarching public system of education or a variety of educational alternatives that allow parents optimal choice for their children's schooling. Discuss whether the provision of education should be a public or private matter, critically assessing the strengths and limitations of the main positions within this debate.

2. Critically discuss the extent to which educational practices have been affected by, and should be modified to adapt to, computerization and new developments in information and communications technologies.

3. Discuss the role of formal educational institutions in a context that places increasing emphasis on lifelong learning. To what extent should the role and mandate of school be broadened, relative to alternatives that place greater emphasis on learning at home, on the job, and in other sites?

4. Discuss the extent to which parents and other community members should be involved in decision-making within local schools. Should schools respond primarily to local interests or address broader concerns?

5. Discuss the extent to which, and the ways in which, educational reform is necessary in order to fulfill contemporary social and economic expectations.

6. Describe and explain major directions in recent educational reform, indicating which groups have had the strongest influence on those reforms.

Websites

www.afneducation.ca
The Assembly of First Nations website includes policies, position papers, research, and resources related to education and other matters of importance to First Nations across Canada.

www2.asanet.org/soe/
This site, maintained by the Sociology of Education section of the American Sociology Association, is directed primarily to professionals and researchers engaged in the field. It contains a summary description of the sociology of education and emerging issues, as well as many useful links to other databases and relevant sites.

www.caut.ca/
The Canadian Association of University Teachers, which represents academic staff at Canadian universities, reports on its website major developments, issues, and analyses relevant to post-secondary education.

www.policyalternatives.ca/welcome/index.cfm
The Canadian Centre for Policy Alternatives is an independent organization that conducts research and fosters public dialogue on a variety of issues related to social and economic justice. Its activities include widespread coverage of issues concerning and relevant to education in Canada, including publication of the quarterly journal *Our Schools/Our Selves*.

www.ccl-cca.ca/ccl
The Canadian Council on Learning was established in 2004 to foster and exchange knowledge about all aspects of learning relevant to Canada. It brings together and facilitates research and research and policy networks relevant to lifelong learning, organized through five knowledge centres based in different regions of Canada—Aboriginal learning, adult learning, early childhood learning, health and learning, and work and learning.

www.cfs-fcee.ca/html/english/home/index.php
The Canadian Federation of Students provides a student voice and perspective on postsecondary issues, policies, and relevant matters of concern to its membership (drawn from university and college students in institutions across Canada) and others interested in educational matters. The CFS site includes position papers, research and analysis, and links to other major education information sites.

www.cdnsba.org/
The Canadian School Boards Association represents school boards and school board associations across Canada. The association's website includes information and links on issues of educational policy and governance, research, and other important developments related to elementary and secondary education.

www.cmec.ca/
The home page for the Council of Ministers of Education Canada provides access to major databases and reports and studies conducted through that organization, as well as links to each of the provincial and territorial ministries of education and other important Canadian and international education bodies.

www.eric.ed.gov/
ERIC, the Educational Resources Information Center, contains a comprehensive database of information (mostly abstracts of journal articles and reports) on various aspects and fields related to education, including sociology of education. It is a valuable reference tool and starting point for research into both contemporary and historical educational issues.

www.hrdc-drhc.gc.ca/common/home.shtml
Human Resources and Social Development Canada provides information on jobs, education and training initiatives, children and youth, Aboriginal people, persons with disabilities, and other factors relevant to workplace and community participation. The website contains extensive research and reports in addition to basic information about government programs and employment in Canada.

www.oecd.org/home/
The website of the Organization for Economic Co-operation and Development provides useful and up-to-date information for international comparisons and developments. It includes report summaries, statistics, and links to major documents on education and related thematic areas that highlight significant trends and issues for 30 member countries and several dozen other nations.

www.wallnetwork.ca/
The site for the Work and Lifelong Learning national research network includes information and links relevant to an understanding of how work and learning are changing in a global economy. It presents definitions, discussion papers, and research findings that document the nature and extent of learning that takes place in various forms and contexts, including informal learning and other forms of learning that occur outside of formal educational institutions.

www.fnh.utoronto.ca/indigenousEducation.html
The Indigenous Education Network was started in 1989 by Aboriginal students at the Ontario Institute for Studies in Education/University of Toronto, and includes both Aboriginal and non-Aboriginal students, faculty, alumni, community members, and others who organize events, foster collaborative work, and provide support for and public information related to Aboriginal education. Its website, now housed within First Nations House at the University of Toronto, is oriented primarily to post-secondary education but includes links to numerous sites for those interested in historical and contemporary dimensions of indigenous people and their education.

www.sosig.ac.uk/roads/subject-listing/World-cat/soceduc.html
The Social Science Information Gateway, based in the United Kingdom, offers a substantial and useful set of links to significant reports, databases, journals, publishers, government bodies, and other organizations pertinent to the sociology of education in numerous national settings.

www.statcan.ca/
Statistics Canada provides the most comprehensive body of data and information on education and numerous related areas on its website and through its links with other sites. The site includes census data, diverse databases and reports on both current and historical dimensions of Canadian social and economic life, and learning resources for students and educators.

www.tcrecord.org/
The website for *Teachers' College Record* offers an on-line journal, discussion groups, and other items of interest to educators, educational researchers, and students. Free registration is required for access to numerous items that are relevant to many significant dimensions of teaching and learning.

portal.unesco.org/en/ev.php-URL_ID=29008&URL_DO=DO_TOPIC&URL_SECTION= 201.html
The United Nations Educational, Scientific and Cultural Organization seeks to foster dialogue, mutual respect, and improved living conditions for people on a global scale. Its website includes useful resources and information relevant to education as well as related social and cultural issues, including reports and programs on education in specific nations and on a comparative level.

References

Abboud, Rida, Jennifer Chong, Darcy Gray, Rizwana Kaderdina, Mark Masongsong, and Kajori Monika Rahman. 2002. *The Kit: A Manual by Youth to Combat Racism through Education*. Ottawa: United Nations Association in Canada.

Acker, Sandra. 1999. *The Realities of Teachers' Work: Never a Dull Moment*. London: Cassell.

Addams, Jane. 1999 [1910]. *Twenty Years at Hull House: with autobiographical notes*, ed. and intro. Victoria Bissel Brown. Boston: Bedford St Martin's.

Albas, Daniel, and Cheryl Albas. 1993. 'Disclaimer Mannerisms of Students: How To Avoid Being Labelled as Cheaters', *Canadian Review of Sociology and Anthropology* 31, 4: 422–45.

Alladin, Ibrahim. 1996. *Racism in Canadian Schools*. Toronto: Harcourt Brace.

Altenbaugh, Richard J. 1995. 'The Irony of Gender', in Mark B. Ginsburg, ed., *The Politics of Teachers' Work and Lives*. New York: Garland Publishing, 73–90.

Althusser, Louis. 1971. 'Ideology and Ideological State Apparatuses', in Althusser, ed., *Lenin and Philosophy and Other Essays*. New York: Monthly Review Press, 172–86.

Anderson, James G. 1968. *Bureaucracy in Education*. Baltimore: Johns Hopkins University Press.

Andres, Lesley, and E. Dianne Looker. 2001. 'Rurality and Capital: Educational Expectations and Attainment of Rural, Urban/Rural and Metropolitan Youth', *Canadian Journal of Higher Education* 31, 2: 1–45.

Andres Bellamy, Lesley. 1993. 'Life Trajectories, Action, and Negotiating the Transition from High School', in Anisef and Axelrod (1993: 137–57).

———. 1994. 'Capital, Habitus, Field, and Practice: An Introduction to the Work of Pierre Bourdieu', in Erwin and MacLennan (1994: 120–36).

Angus Reid Group. 1999. 'Canadians' Assessment and Views of the Education System', press release, Toronto, 22 June.

Anisef, Paul, and Paul Axelrod, eds. 1993. *Transitions: Schooling and Employment in Canada*. Toronto: Thompson Educational Publishing.

———, ———, Etta Baichman-Anisef, Carl James, and Anton Turritin. 2000. *Opportunity and Uncertainty: Life Course Experiences of the Class of '73*. Toronto: University of Toronto Press.

——— and Norman Okihiro. 1982. *Losers and Winners: The Pursuit of Equality and Social Justice in Higher Education*. Toronto: Butterworths.

Apple, Michael W. 1986. *Teachers and Texts: A Political Economy of Class and Gender Relations in Education*. New York: Routledge & Kegan Paul.

———.1995. *Education and Power*, 2nd edn. New York: Routledge.

———. 1999. *Power, Meaning, and Identity: Essays in Critical Educational Studies*. New York: Peter Lang.

———. 2000. *Official Knowledge: Democratic Education in a Conservative Age*. New York: Routledge.

———. 2004. *Ideology and Curriculum*, 3rd edn. New York: RoutledgeFalmer.

———. 2006. 'Rhetoric and Reality in Critical Educational Studies in the United States', *British Journal of Sociology of Education* 27, 5: 679–87.

Arbus, Judith. 1990. 'Grateful To Be Working: Women Teachers during the Great Depression', in Frieda Forman, Mary O'Brien, Jane Haddad, Dianne Hallman, and Philinda Masters, eds, *Feminism and Education: A Canadian Perspective*. Toronto: Centre for Women's Studies in Education, 169–90.

Armstrong, Pat, and Hugh Armstrong. 2001. *The Double Ghetto: Canadian Women and Their Segregated Work*, 3rd edn. Toronto: Oxford University Press.

Arnot, Madeleine, and Jo-Anne Dillabough. 1999. 'Feminist Politics and Democratic Values in Education', *Curriculum Inquiry* 29, 2: 159–89.

—— and Mairtin Mac An Ghaill, eds. 2006. *The RoutledgeFalmer Reader in Gender and Education*. London: Routledge.

—— and Kathleen Weiler, eds. 1993. *Feminism and Social Justice in Education: International Perspectives*. London: Falmer.

Aronowitz, Stanley, and Henry A. Giroux. 1993. *Education Still Under Siege*, 2nd edn. Toronto: OISE Press.

Ashton, David, and Graham Lowe. 1991. 'School-to-work Transitions in Britain and Canada: A Comparative Perspective', in Ashton and Lowe, eds, *Making Their Way: Education, Training and the Labour Market in Canada and Britain*. Toronto: University of Toronto Press, 1–14.

Ashton, David N., and Johnny Sung. 1997. 'Education, Skill Formation, and Economic Development: The Singaporean Approach', in Halsey et al. (1997: 207–18).

Assembly of First Nations. 1988. *Tradition and Education: Towards a Vision of Our Future*, National Review of First Nations Education, vol. 1. Ottawa: Assembly of First Nations.

——. 2005. *First Nations Education Action Plan*. Ottawa: Assembly of First Nations, 31 May.

Association of Universities and Colleges of Canada (AUCC). 2007a. *Trends in Higher Education. Volume 1. Enrolment*. Ottawa: AUCC.

——. 2007b. *Trends in Higher Education. Volume 2. Faculty*. Ottawa: AUCC.

Aurini, Janice, and Scott Davies. 2005. 'Choice without Markets: Homeschooling in the Context of Private Education', *British Journal of Sociology of Education* 26, 4: 461–74.

Axelrod, Paul. 1997. *The Promise of Schooling: Education in Canada, 1800–1914*. Toronto: University of Toronto Press.

——. 2002. *Values in Conflict: The University, the Marketplace and the Trials of Liberal Education*. Montreal and Kingston: McGill-Queen's University Press.

Bacon, Allan. 1995. 'The Teachers' Perspective on Accountability', *Canadian Journal of Education* 20, 1: 85–91.

Baez, Javier Eduardo, and Indhira Vanessa Santos. 2007. *Children's Vulnerability to Weather Shocks: A Natural Disaster as a Natural Experiment*. New York: Social Science Research Network.

Baldwin, John R., and Desmond Beckstead. 2003. *Knowledge Workers in Canada's Economy, 1971–2001*. Ottawa: Minister of Industry, Analytical Paper, Statistics Canada Catalogue no. 11-624-MIE No. 004 (Oct.).

Ball, Stephen J. 2004. 'Performativities and Fabrications in the Education Economy: Towards the Performative Society', in Ball, ed, *The RoutledgeFalmer Reader in Sociology of Education*. New York: RoutledgeFalmer, 143–55.

Ballantine, Jeanne H., and Joan Z. Spade, eds. 2008. *Schools and Society: A Sociological Approach to Education*, 3rd edn. Thousand Oaks, Calif.: Pine Forge Press.

Barlow, Maude, and Heather-Jane Robertson. 1994. *Class Warfare: The Assault on Canada's Schools*. Toronto: Key Porter Books.

Battiste, Marie. 2000. 'Introduction: Unfolding the Lessons of Colonization', in Battiste, ed., *Reclaiming Indigenous Voice and Vision*. Vancouver: University of British Columbia Press, xvi–xxx.

Bauer, Gabrielle. 2001. 'Why Boys Must Be Boys: Is Your Son's School Giving Him What He Needs To Succeed?', *Canadian Living* (Nov.).

Bauman, Zygmunt. 1989. *Modernity and the Holocaust*. Ithaca, NY: Cornell University Press.

Beattie, Catherine. 1996. 'The Computer in Schools: Visions, Illusions, and Mistakes', in Geoffrey Milburn, ed., *'Ring Some Alarm Bells in Ontario': Reactions to the Report of the Royal Commission on Learning*. London, Ont.: Althouse Press, 95–107.

Beaujot, Roderic, and Don Kerr. 2007. *Emerging Youth Transition Patterns in Canada: Opportunities and Risks: Discussion Paper*. Ottawa: Government of Canada Policy Research Initiative.

Beck, Ulrich. 1992. *Risk Society: Towards a New Modernity*. London: Sage.

Becker, Howard S. 1952. 'Social Class Variations in the Teacher–Pupil Relationship', *Journal of Educational Sociology* 25: 451–65.

———. 1953. 'The Teacher in the Authority System of the Public School', *Journal of Educational Sociology* 26: 128–41.

———. 1996. 'School Is a Lousy Place To Learn Anything In', in Robert G. Burgess, ed., *Howard Becker on Education*. Buckingham, UK: Open University Press, 99–112. Originally published in *American Behavioral Scientist* (1972): 85–105.

Bell, Daniel. 1973. *The Coming of Post-Industrial Society*. New York: Basic Books.

Bellas, Marcia L. 1999. 'Emotional Labour in Academia: The Case of Professors', *Annals, American Academy of Political and Social Science* 561: 96–110.

Berger, Joseph, Anne Motte, and Andrew Parkin. 2007. *The Price of Knowledge: Access and Student Finance in Canada*, 3rd edn. Montreal: Canada Millennium Scholarship Foundation.

Bernhard, Judith K., and Joyce Nyhof-Young. 1994. 'Towards Increased Participation of Women in Science and Technology: Social Theory and Interventions for Girls in Ontario Elementary Schools', in Erwin and MacLennan (1994: 397–416).

Bernier, Rachel. 1996. 'The Labour Force Survey: 50 Years Old in 1996', in Statistics Canada, *Labour Force Annual Averages 1995*. Ottawa: Minister of Industry, Science and Technology, A33–50.

Bernier, Suzanne. 1995. 'Youth Combining School and Work', *Education Quarterly Review* 2, 4: 10–23.

Bernstein, Basil. 1977. 'Class and Pedagogies: Visible and Invisible', in Jerome Karabel and A.H. Halsey, eds, *Power and Ideology in Education*. New York: Oxford University Press, 511–34.

Berthelot, Jocelyn. 2006. *Une école pour le monde, une école pour tout le monde. L'éducation québécoise dans le contexte de la mondialisation*. Montréal: VLB Éditeur.

Bibby, Reginald W. 2001. *Canada's Teens: Today, Yesterday, and Tomorrow*. Toronto: Stoddart.

Bills, David B. 2004. *The Sociology of Education and Work*. Malden, Mass.: Blackwell.

Birchard, Karen. 2002. 'European Report Compares Student Conditions in Eight Countries', *University Affairs* (Dec.): 24.

Black Learners Advisory Committee. 1994. *BLAC Report on Education. Redressing Inequity— Empowering Black Learners*. Halifax: Black Learners Advisory Committee.

Blackmore, Jill. 1999. *Troubling Women: Feminism, Leadership and Educational Change*. Buckingham, UK: Open University Press.

Blau, Peter M., and Otis Dudley Duncan. 1967. *The American Occupational Structure*. New York: John Wiley and Sons.

Blau, Peter M. 2006. 'A Profile of Elementary and Secondary School Principals in Canada: First Results from the 2004–2005 Survey of Principals', *Education Matters: Insights on Education, Learning and Training in Canada* 3, 2 (June), Statistics Canada Catalogue no. 81-004-XIE. At: <www.statcan.ca/english/freepub/81-004-XIE/81-004-XIE2006002.htm>.

Blouin, Patric, and Marie-Josée Courchesne. 2007. *Summary Public School Indicators for the Provinces and Territories, 1998/1999 to 2004/2005*. Ottawa: Minister of Industry. Statistics Canada Culture, Tourism and the Centre for Education Statistics Research Papers, Aug. Catalogue no. 81-595-MIE2007050.

Bohatyretz, Sandra, and Garth Lipps. 1999. 'Diversity in the Classroom: Characteristics of Elementary Students Receiving Special Education', *Education Quarterly Review* 6, 2: 7–19.

Bolaria, B. Singh. 2000. 'An Introduction to Social Issues and Contradictions: Sociological Perspectives', in Bolaria, ed., *Social Issues and Contradictions in Canadian Society*, 3rd edn. Toronto: Harcourt Brace & Company, 1–19.

———, Harley D. Dickinson, and Terry Wotherspoon. 1995. 'Rural Issues and Problems', in Bolaria, ed., *Social Issues and Contradictions in Canadian Society*, 2nd edn, 419–43.

Boothby, Daniel, and Torben Drewes. 2006. 'Postsecondary Education in Canada: Returns to University, College and Trades Education', *Canadian Public Policy* 32, 1: 1–22.

Bosetti, Lynn. 2001. 'The Alberta Charter School Experience', in Claudia R. Hepburn, ed., *Can the Market Save Our Schools?* Vancouver: Fraser Institute, 101–20.

Bouchard, Brigitte, and John Zhao. 2000. 'University Education: Recent Trends in Participation, Accessibility and Returns', *Education Quarterly Review* 6, 4: 24–32.

Bourdieu, Pierre. 1977. 'Cultural Reproduction and Social Reproduction', in Jerome Karabel and A.H. Halsey, eds, *Power and Ideology in Education.* New York: Oxford University Press, 487–511.

——. 1984 [1979]. *Distinction: A Social Critique of the Judgement of Taste.* Cambridge, Mass.: Harvard University Press.

—— and Jean-Claude Passeron. 1979. *The Inheritors: French Students and Their Relations to Culture.* Chicago: University of Chicago Press.

Bourgon, Lyndsie. 2008. 'MAS Are Becoming the New BA', *The Sheaf* (Saskatoon, University of Saskatchewan), 3 Jan., A4

Bowers, Norman, Anne Sonnet, and Laura Bardone. 1999. 'Background Report: Giving Young People a Good Start: The Experience of OECD Countries', in Organization for Economic Co-operation and Development, *Preparing Youth for the 21st Century: The Transition from Education to the Labour Market.* Proceedings of the Washington, DC, Conference, 23–4 Feb. 1999. Paris: OECD, 7–86.

Bowlby, Geoff. 1996. 'Relationship between Postsecondary Graduates' Education and Employment', *Education Quarterly Review* 3, 2: 35–44.

—— and Kathryn McMullen. 2005. 'Provincial Dropout Rates—Trends and Consequences', *Education Matters* 2, 4, Statistics Canada Catalogue no. 81-004-XIE. At: <www.statcan.ca/english/freepub/81-004-XIE/2005004/drop.htm>.

Bowles, Samuel, and Herbert Gintis. 1976. *Schooling in Capitalist America: Educational Reform and the Contradictions of Economic Life.* New York: Basic Books.

Braithwaite, Max. 1979. *Why Shoot the Teacher?* Toronto: McClelland & Stewart.

Braverman, Harry. 1974. *Labor and Monopoly Capital: The Degradation of Work in the Twentieth Century.* New York: Monthly Review Press.

British Columbia. 1875. *Annual Report of the Public Schools, 1875.* Victoria: Province of British Columbia.

——. 1904. *Annual Report of the Public Schools, 1904.* Victoria: Province of British Columbia.

——. 1988. *A Legacy for Learners: The Report of the Royal Commission on Education.* Victoria: Province of British Columbia.

British Columbia School Trustees' Association. 1980. 'Rules Required for Teachers in Revelstoke Area, 1915', *BCSTA Reports*, 17 Oct.

Brookes, Anne-Louise. 1992. *Feminist Pedagogy: An Autobiographical Approach.* Halifax: Fernwood.

Brown, Phillip, and Hugh Lauder. 2006. 'Globalisation, Knowledge and the Myth of the Magnet Economy', *Globalisation, Societies and Education* 4, 1: 25–57.

——, Andy Green, and Hugh Lauder. 2001. *High Skills: Globalization, Competitiveness, and Skill Formation.* Oxford: Oxford University Press.

Bruce, Christopher J., and Arthur M. Schwartz. 1997. 'Education: Meeting the Challenge', in Bruce, R.D. Kneebone, and K.J. McKenzie, eds, *A Government Reinvented: A Study of Alberta's Deficit Elimination Program.* Toronto: Oxford University Press, 383–416.

Burman, Erica. 2005. 'Childhood, Neo-liberalism and the Feminization of Education', *Gender and Education* 17, 4: 351–67.

Bushnik, Tracey. 2003. *Learning, Earning and Leaving: The Relationship between Working While in High School and Dropping Out.* Ottawa: Minister of Industry, Education, Skills and Learning, Research Paper. Catalogue no. 81-595-MIE, No. 004.

Bussière, Patrick, Fernando Cartwright, Robert Crocker, Xin Ma, Jillian Oderkirk, and Yanhong Zhang. 2001. *Measuring Up: The Performance of Canada's Youth in Reading, Mathematics and Science.* Ottawa: Minister of Industry Canada.

————, Tamara Knighton, and Dianne Pennock. 2007. *Measuring Up: Canadian Results of the OECD PISA Study. The Performance of Canada's Youth in Science, Reading and Mathematics. 2006 First Results for Canadians Aged 15.* Ottawa: Minister of Industry. Statistics Canada Catalogue no. 81-590-XIE2007001.

Butlin, George. 2000. 'Determinants of University and Community College Leaving', *Education Quarterly Review* 6, 4: 8–23.

Butterwick, Shauna, Kaela Jubas, and Hong Zhu. 2007. 'Gender Matters in IT and Skills Hierarchies and Women's On the Job Learning', in Lesley Farnell and Tara Fenwick, eds, *Educating the Global Workforce: Knowledge, Knowledge Work and Knowledge Workers.* Abingdon, UK: Routledge, 278–88.

Campaign 2000. 2007. *It Takes a Nation to Raise a Generation: Time for a National Poverty Reduction Strategy,* 2007 Report Card on Child and Family Poverty. Toronto: Campaign 2000, 26 Nov. At: <www.campaign2000.ca/rc/>.

Canadian Association of University Teachers (CAUT). 2007. *CAUT Almanac of Post-Secondary Education in Canada, 2007.* Ottawa: CAUT.

Canadian Council on Learning. 2006a. *Canadian Attitudes on Post-secondary Education.* Ottawa: Canadian Council on Learning.

————. 2006b. 'School Enrolment Trends in Canada', *Lessons in Learning* (26 Sept.). Ottawa: Canadian Council on Learning.

————. 2007a. 'Canada Slow To Overcome Limits for Disabled Learners', *Lessons in Learning* (26 Feb.). Ottawa: Canadian Council on Learning.

————. 2007b. *Redefining How Success Is Measured in First Nations, Inuit and Métis Learning.* Ottawa: Canadian Council on Learning.

————. 2007c. *Report on Learning in Canada 2007, Post-Secondary Education in Canada - Strategies for Success.* Ottawa: Canadian Council on Learning.

————. 2007d. *The State of Learning in Canada: No Time for Complacency, Report on Learning in Canada 2007.* Ottawa: Canadian Council on Learning.

————. 2007e. *2007 Survey of Canadian Attitudes toward Learning: Results for Elementary and Secondary School Learning.* Ottawa: Canadian Council on Learning.

Canadian Council on Social Development. 2003. 'Census Analysis: Census Shows Growing Polarization of Income in Canada'. Ottawa: Canadian Council on Social Development. At: <www.ccsd.ca/pr/2003/censusincome.htm>.

————. 2007. 'CCSD's Stats and Facts: Economic Security—Poverty'. At: <www.ccsd.ca/factsheets/>.

Canadian Education Association. 2007. *Public Education in Canada: Facts, Trends and Attitudes 2007.* Toronto: Canadian Education Association.

Canadian Federation of Humanities and Social Sciences. 2007. 'Post-Secondary Pyramid— Equity Audit 2007'. Ottawa: Canadian Federation of Humanities and Social Sciences. At: <www.fedcan.ca/equityaudit>.

Canadian Institute of Public Opinion. 1976. 'One-in-Three Believe Education Has Slipped', *The Gallup Report,* 27 Mar.

Canadian Labour Congress. 2008. *Women in the Workforce: Still a Long Way from Equality.* Ottawa: Canadian Labour Congress (Mar.).

Canadian Millennium Scholarship Foundation (CMSF). 2005. *Changing Course: Improving Aboriginal Access to Post-Secondary Education in Canada.* Montreal: CMSF, Research Notes #2. At: <www.millenniumscholarships.ca/images/Publications/mrn-changing-course-en.pdf>.

Canadian Race Relations Foundation. 2000. *Racism in Our Schools: What To Know about It; How To Fight It.* Ottawa: Canadian Race Relations Foundation.

Canadian Teachers' Federation. 1993. *Progress Revisited: The Quality of (Work) Life of Women Teachers.* Ottawa: Canadian Teachers' Federation.

————. 1997. *Behind the Charter School Myths.* Ottawa: Canadian Teachers' Federation.

———. 2005. 'Canadian Teachers Face Longer Hours of Work and More Challenging Working Conditions Compared to Four Years Ago: National Survey', news release, 15 July. At: <www.ctf-fce.ca/archive/docs/en/PRESS/2005/pr05-14.htm>.

———. 2006. 'Beyond the Bake Sale: Exposing the Many Faces of Commercialization in Canada's Schools', news release, 15 May. At: <www.ctf-fce.ca/archive/docs/en/PRESS/2006/pr06-12.htm>.

———. 2007. *Teaching in Canada*. Ottawa: Canadian Teachers' Federation. At: <www.ctf-fce.ca/e/teaching_in_canada/teachers_%20associations.asp>.

Canadian Women's Foundaton. 2005. *Girls in Canada 2005*. Toronto: Canadian Women's Foundation, Sept.

Carnoy, Martin. 1974. *Education as Cultural Imperialism*. New York: D. McKay Co.

——— and Henry M. Levin. 1985. *Schooling and Work in the Democratic State*. Stanford, Calif.: Stanford University Press.

Carpay, John. 2004. 'Why Teachers Should Not Be Allowed To Strike', *Let's Talk Taxes*. Edmonton: Canadian Taxpayers' Federation, 8 June. At: <www.taxpayer.com/main/news.php?news_id=723>.

Carr-Saunders, A.M. 1966. 'Professionalism in Historical Perspective', in H.M. Vollmer and D.L. Mills, eds, *Professionalization*. Englewood Cliffs, NJ: Prentice-Hall, 2–9.

Castellano, Marlene Brant, Lynne Davis, and Louise Lahache, eds. 2000. *Aboriginal Education: Fulfilling the Promise*. Vancouver: University of British Columbia Press.

Central Advisory Council for Education (The Plowden Report). 1967. *Children and Their Primary Schools*, 2 vols. London: Her Majesty's Stationery Office.

Chabbott, Colette, and Francisco O. Ramirez. 2000. 'Development and Education', in Maureen T. Hallinan, ed., *Handbook of the Sociology of Education*. New York: Kluwer Academic/Plenum Publishers, 163–87.

Chafe, J.W. 1969. *Chalk, Sweat, and Cheers: A History of the Manitoba Teachers' Society*. Winnipeg: Manitoba Teachers' Society.

Chalmers, John W. 1968. *Teachers of the Foothills Province: The Story of the Alberta Teachers' Association*. Toronto: University of Toronto Press.

Charland, Jean-Pierre. 2000. *L'entreprise éducative au Québec, 1840–1900*. Québec: Les presses de l'Université Laval.

Chomsky, Noam. 2003. 'The Function of Schools: Subtler and Cruder Methods of Control', in Kenneth J. Saltman and David A. Gabbard, eds, *Education as Enforcement: The Militarization and Corporatization of Schools*. New York: RoutledgeFalmer, 25–35.

Chubb, John E., and Terry M. Moe. 1990. *Politics, Markets, and America's Schools*. Washington: Brookings Institution.

Cicourel, Aaron V., and John J. Kitsuse. 1963. *The Educational Decision-Makers*. Indianapolis: Bobbs-Merrill.

Clairmont, Don, and Richard Apostle. 1997. 'Work: A Segmentation Perspective', in Axel Van den Berg and Joseph Smucker, eds, *The Sociology of Labour Markets: Efficiency, Equity, Security*. Scarborough, Ont.: Prentice-Hall Allyn and Bacon, 388–404.

Clark, Burton R. 1962. *Educating the Expert Society*. San Francisco: Chandler.

Clark, Warren. 1991. *The Class of '86: A Compendium of Findings of the 1988 National Graduates Survey of 1986 Graduates with Comparisons to the 1984 National Graduates Survey*. Ottawa: Employment and Immigration Canada.

———. 2000. '100 Years of Education', *Canadian Social Trends* 59 (Winter): 3–7.

Clegg, Sue. 2005. 'Evidence-based Practice in Educational Research: A Critical Realist Critique of Systematic Review', *British Journal of Sociology in Education* 26, 3: 415–28.

Clement, Wallace. 1974. *The Canadian Corporate Elite: An Analysis of Economic Power*. Toronto: McClelland & Stewart.

——— and Leah F. Vosko, eds. 2003. *Changing Canada: Political Economy as Transformation*. Montreal and Kingston: McGill-Queen's University Press.

────── and Glenn Williams. 1989. *The New Canadian Political Economy*. Montreal and Kingston: McGill-Queen's University Press.

Clifford, Pat. 2005. 'CYBER Kids', *Education Canada* 45, 2: 14–16.

──────. 2008. 'End Notes: An Edutainment Version of "No Child Left Behind"', *Education Canada* 48, 4: 76.

Cohen, Stanley. 1972. *Folk Devils and Moral Panics*. London: MacGibbon and Kee.

Coleman, James S. 1968. 'The Concept of Equality of Educational Opportunity', *Harvard Educational Review* 38, 1: 7–22.

────── et al. 1966. *Equality of Educational Opportunity*. Washington: US Government Printing Office.

Collard, John, and Cecilia Reynolds, eds. 2005. *Leadership, Gender and Culture in Education: Male and Female Perspectives*. New York: Open University Press.

Collins, Patricia Hill. 2006. 'Going Public: Doing the Sociology That Had No Name', in Dan Clawson, Robert Zussman, Joya Misra, Naomi Gerstel, Randall Stokes, Douglas L. Anderton, and Michael Burawoy, eds, *Public Sociology: Fifteen Eminent Sociologists Debate Politics and the Profession in the Twenty-first Century*. Berkeley: University of California Press, 101–13.

Collins, Randall. 1971. 'Functional and Conflict Theories of Educational Stratification', *American Sociological Review* 36, 6: 1002–19.

──────. 2000. 'Comparative and Historical Patterns of Education', in Maureen T. Hallinan, ed., *Handbook of the Sociology of Education*. New York: Kluwer Academic/Plenum Publishers, 213–39.

Collis, Betty. 1991. 'Adolescent Females and Computers: Real and Perceived Barriers', in Gaskell and McLaren (1991: 147–61).

Connell, R.W., D.J. Ashenden, S. Kessler, and G.W. Dowsett. 1982. *Making the Difference: Schools, Families and Social Division*. Sydney: George Allen & Unwin.

Contenta, Sandro. 1993. *Rituals of Failure: What Schools Really Teach*. Toronto: Between the Lines.

Corbett, Bradley A., and J. Douglas Willms. 2002. 'Information and Communication Technology: Access and Use', *Education Quarterly Review* 8, 4: 8–15.

Corman, June, and Meg Luxton. 2007. 'Social Reproduction and the Changing Dynamics of Unpaid Household and Caregiving Work', in Shalla and Clement (2007: 262–88).

Corporation des Enseignants du Québec (CEQ). 1974. 'Our Schools Serve the Ruling Class', in George Martell, ed., *The Politics of the Canadian Public School*. Toronto: James Lorimer, 172–85.

Corrigan, Philip, Bruce Curtis, and Robert Lanning. 1987. 'The Political Space of Schooling', in Wotherspoon (1987: 21–43).

Côté, James E., and Anton Allahar. 2006. *Critical Youth Studies: A Canadian Focus*. Toronto: Pearson Prentice-Hall.

Cottingham, Mollie E. 1958. 'The Canadian Conference on Education', *The B.C. Teacher* 37, 8: 398–9, 407–8.

Coulter, Rebecca Priegert. 1993. 'Schooling, Work and Life: Reflections of the Young in the 1940s', in Coulter and Ivor F. Goodson, eds, *Rethinking Vocationalism: Whose Work/Life Is It?* Toronto: Our Schools/Our Selves, 69–86.

Council of Ministers of Education Canada. 2001. *The Development of Education in Canada*. Toronto: Council of Ministers of Education Canada.

Cowley, Peter. 2007. 'Bringing Education into the Market Place: Part I—The Report Cards on Schools', *Fraser Forum* (Sept.): 6–9.

Craig, Wendy M., and Yossi Harel. 2004. 'Bullying, Physical Fighting and Victimization', in Candace Currie, Chris Roberts, Antony Morgan, Rebecca Smith, Wolfgang Settertobulte, Oddrun Samdal, and Vivian Barnekow Rasmussen, eds, *Young People's Health in Context: Health Behaviour in School-aged Children (HBSC) Study: International Report from the 2001/2002 Survey*. Geneva: World Health Organization, 133–44.

Crawley, Mike. 1995. *Schoolyard Bullies: Messing with British Columbia's Education System*. Victoria: Orca Book Publishers.

Creese, Gillian, Neil Guppy, and Martin Meissner. 1991. *Ups and Downs on the Ladder of Success: Social Mobility in Canada*. Ottawa: Minister of Industry, Science and Technology, Statistics Canada Catalogue no. 11-612.

Crompton, Susan. 2002. 'I Still Feel Overqualified for My Job', *Canadian Social Trends* 67 (Winter): 23–6.

Crysdale, Stewart, Alan J.C. King, and Nancy Mandell. 1999, *On Their Own? Making the Transition from School to Work in the Information Age*. Montreal and Kingston: McGill-Queen's University Press.

——— and Harry MacKay. 1994. *Youth's Passage Through School to Work: A Comparative Longitudinal Study*. Toronto: Thompson Educational Publishing.

Cuban, Larry. 2001. *Oversold and Underused: Computers in the Classroom*. Cambridge, Mass.: Harvard University Press.

Currie, Jan, and Janice Newson, eds. 1998. *Universities and Globalization: Critical Perspectives*. Thousand Oaks, Calif.: Sage.

Curtis, Bruce. 1988. *Building the Educational State: Canada West, 1836–1871*. Barcombe, Lewes: Falmer.

———, D.W. Livingstone, and Harry Smaller. 1992. *Stacking the Deck: The Streaming of Working-Class Kids in Ontario Schools*. Toronto: Our Schools/Our Selves Education Foundation.

Curtis, James, Edward Grabb, and Neil Guppy, eds. 2003. *Social Inequality in Canada: Patterns, Problems and Policies*, 4th edn. Toronto: Pearson Education Canada.

Danylewycz, Marta, Beth Light, and Alison Prentice. 1991. 'The Evolution of the Sexual Division of Labor in Teaching: Nineteenth Century Ontario and Quebec Case Study', in Gaskell and McLaren (1991: 33–60).

——— and Alison Prentice. 1986. 'Teachers' Work: Changing Patterns and Perceptions in the Emerging School Systems of Nineteenth and Early Twentieth Century Central Canada', *Labour/Le Travail* 17: 59–80.

Darder, Antonia, Maria Baltodano, and Rodolfo D. Torres. 2003.'Critical Pedagogy: An Introduction', in Darder, Baltodano and Torres, eds, *The Critical Pedagogy Reader*. New York: RoutledgeFalmer, 1–21.

Davey, Ian E. 1978. 'The Rhythm of Work and the Rhythm of School', in McDonald and Chaiton (1978: 221–53).

Davies, Scott. 1995. 'Leaps of Faith: Shifting Currents in Critical Sociology of Education', *American Journal of Sociology* 100, 6: 1448–78.

——— and Neil Guppy. 2006. *The Schooled Society: An Introduction to the Sociology of Education*. Toronto: Oxford University Press.

———, Linda Quirke, and Janice Aurini. 2006. 'Institutional Theory Goes to the Market: The Challenge of Rapid Growth in Private K–12 Education', in Heinz Meyer and Brian Rowan, eds, *The New Institutionalization and the Study of Education*. Albany, NY: SUNY Press, 103–22.

de Broucker, Patrice, and Arthur Sweetman. 2002. 'Introduction', in de Broucker and Sweetman, eds, *Towards Evidence-Based Policy for Canadian Education*. Kingston: John Deutsch Institute for the Study of Economic Policy/Statistics Canada, 1–14.

de Graaf, Nan Dirk, Paul M. De Graaf, and Gerbert Kraaykamp. 2000. 'Parental Cultural Capital and Educational Attainment in the Netherlands: A Refinement of the Cultural Capital Perspective', *Sociology of Education* 73, 2: 92–111.

Dehli, Kari. 1993. 'Subject to the New Global Economy: Power and Positioning in Ontario Labour Market Policy Formation', in Rebecca Priegert Coulter and Ivor F. Goodson, eds, *Rethinking Vocationalism: Whose Work/Life Is It?* Toronto: Our Schools/Our Selves Education Foundation, 113–41.

Dei, George J. Sefa. 1996. *Anti-Racism Education: Theory and Practice*. Halifax: Fernwood.

———. 2006. 'Black-Focused Schools: A Call for Re-visioning', *Education Canada* 46, 3: 27–31.

——— and Agnes Calliste, eds. 2000. *Power, Knowledge and Anti-Racism Education: A Critical Reader*. Halifax: Fernwood.

———, Irma Marcia James, Leeno Luke Karumanchery, Sonia James-Wilson, and Jasmin Zine. 2000. *Removing the Margins: The Challenges and Possibilities of Inclusive Schooling*. Toronto: Canadian Scholars' Press.

———, Leeno Luke Karumanchery, and Nisha Karumanchery-Luik. 2004. *Playing the Race Card: Exposing White Power and Privilege*. New York: Peter Lang.

de Janvry, Alain, Elisabeth Sadoulet, Pantelis Solomon, and Renos Vakis. 2006. *Uninsured Risk and Asset Protection: Can Conditional Transfer Programs Serve as Safety Nets?* Social Protection Discussion Paper No. 0604. Washington: World Bank.

Denis, Wilfrid B. 1995. 'The Meech Lake Shuffle: French and English Language Rights in Canada', in B. Singh Bolaria, ed., *Social Issues and Contradictions in Canadian Society*, 2nd edn. Toronto: Harcourt Brace & Company, 161–92.

Dennison, John D. 1981. 'The Community College in Canada: An Educational Innovation', in J. Donald Wilson, ed., *Canadian Education in the 1980's*. Calgary: Detselig, 213–30.

Dewey, John. 1966. *Democracy and Education*. New York: Free Press.

Dibski, Dennis. 1995. 'Financing Education', in Ratna Ghosh and Douglas Ray, eds, *Social Change and Education in Canada*, 3rd edn. Toronto: Harcourt Brace & Company, 66–80.

Dillabough, Jo-Anne. 2004. 'Class, Culture, and the "Predicaments of Masculine Domination": Encountering Pierre Bourdieu', *British Journal of Sociology of Education* 25, 4: 489–506.

Dolby, Nadine, and Greg Dimitriadis, eds. 2004. *Learning to Labor in New Times*. New York: Routledge.

Dominion Bureau of Statistics. 1924. *The Canada Year Book 1922–23*. Ottawa: King's Printer.

———. 1963. *Survey of Higher Education 1954–1961*. Ottawa: Queen's Printer.

Downie, Bryan M. 1978. *Collective Bargaining and Conflict Resolution in Education: The Evolution of Public Policy in Ontario*. Kingston: Queen's University Industrial Relations Centre, Research and Current Issues Series No. 36.

Dreeben, Robert. 1968. *On What Is Learned in School*. Reading, Mass.: Addison-Wesley.

Drolet, Marie. 2005. *Participation in Post-secondary Education in Canada: Has the Role of Parental Income and Education Changed over the 1990s?* Ottawa: Minister of Industry. Statistics Canada Analytical Studies Branch Working Paper Series No. 243, Catalogue no. 11F0019MIE.

Drucker, Peter F. 1993. *Post-Capitalist Society*. New York: HarperCollins.

Dryburgh, Heather. 2002. 'Learning Computer Skills', *Education Quarterly Review* 8, 2: 8–18.

Dubois, Julie. 2006. *Trends in Student Borrowing and Pathways: Evidences from the 1990, 1995 and 2000 Classes. Final Report*. Ottawa: Human Resources Skills and Development Canada.

Durkheim, Émile. 1933 [1893]. *The Division of Labor in Society*. New York: Free Press.

———. 1956 [1922]. *Education and Society*. Glencoe, Ill.: Free Press.

Duxbury, Linda, and Chris Higgins. 2003. *Work–Life Conflict in Canada in the New Millennium: A Status Report*. Final Report, Oct. Ottawa: Health Canada.

Easton, Stephen T. 1988. *Education in Canada: An Analysis of Elementary, Secondary and Vocational Schooling*. Vancouver: Fraser Institute.

Economic Council of Canada. 1991. *Employment in the Service Economy*. Ottawa: Minister of Supply and Services Canada.

———. 1992. *A Lot to Learn: Education and Training in Canada. A Statement by the Economic Council of Canada*. Ottawa: Minister of Supply and Services Canada.

Education International. 2007. 'October 5th World Teachers Day', news release. Brussels: WTD Campaigns Team, Education International. At: <www.ei-ie.org/worldteachersday/en/index.php>.

Edwards, R. Gary, and Josephine Mazzuca. 1999. 'Armed Forces Top Institutional List for Respect and Confidence', *The Gallup Poll* 59, 31 (20 May).

Ellsworth, Elizabeth. 1992. 'Why Doesn't This Feel Empowering? Working Through the Repressive Myths of Critical Pedagogy', in Carmen Luke and Jennifer Gore, eds, *Feminisms and Critical Pedagogy*. New York: Routledge, 90–119.

ERIN Research Inc. 2005. *Young Canadians in a Wired World. Phase II Student Survey*. Ottawa: Media Awareness Network.

Erwin, Lorna, and David MacLennan, eds. 1994. *Sociology of Education in Canada: Critical Perspectives on Theory, Research & Practice*. Toronto: Copp Clark Longman.

Eyre, Linda. 1991. 'Gender Relations in the Classroom: A Fresh Look at Coeducation', in Gaskell and McLaren (1991: 193–219).

Fahmy-Eid, Nadia. 2003. 'The History of Women's Education: Assessment and New Perspectives for the Future', *Historical Studies in Education/Revue d'histoire de l'éducation* 15, 1: 18–36.

Fennell, Shailaja, and Madeleine Arnot, eds. 2008. *Gender Education and Equality in a Global Context: Conceptual Frameworks and Policy Perspectives*. London: Routledge.

Fine, Sean. 2001. 'Schools Told to Fix Boys' Low Grades', *Globe and Mail*, 27 Aug., A1, A7.

Finnie, Ross. 2000. 'Holding Their Own: Employment and Earnings of Postsecondary Graduates', *Education Quarterly Review* 7, 1: 21–37.

———. 2001. 'Graduates' Earnings and the Job Skills–Education Match', *Education Quarterly Review* 7, 2: 7–21.

——— and Gaetan Garneau. 1996. 'Student Borrowing for Postsecondary Education', *Education Quarterly Review* 3, 2: 10–34.

———, Eric Lascelles, and Arthur Sweetman. 2005. *Who Goes? The Direct and Indirect Effects of Family Background on Access to Post-secondary Education*. Ottawa: Minister of Industry. Statistics Canada Analytical Studies Research Paper Series No. 237, Catalogue no. 11F1109MIE.

Fischer, Claude S., Michael Hout, Martin Sanchez Jankowski, Samuel R. Lucas, Ann Swindler, and Kim Voss. 1996. *Inequality by Design: Cracking the Bell Curve Myth*. Princeton, NJ: Princeton University Press.

Fiske, Edward B., and Helen F. Ladd. 2000. *When Schools Compete: A Cautionary Tale*. Washington: Brookings Institution Press.

Fleming, Thomas. 1986. '"Our Boys in the Field": School Inspectors, Superintendents and the Changing Character of School Leadership in British Columbia', in Nancy M. Sheehan, J. Donald Wilson, and David C. Jones, eds, *Schools in the West: Essays in Canadian Educational History*. Calgary: Detselig, 285–303.

Fleras, Augie, and Jean Leonard Elliott. 1992. *Multiculturalism in Canada: The Challenge of Diversity*. Scarborough, Ont.: Nelson Canada.

——— and ———. 2003. *Unequal Relations: An Introduction to Race and Ethnic Dynamics in Canada*, 4th edn. Toronto: Prentice-Hall.

Floud, Jean, A.H. Halsey, and F.M. Martin. 1956. *Social Class and Educational Opportunity*. London: Heinemann.

Forcese, Dennis. 1997. *The Canadian Class Structure*, 4th edn. Toronto: McGraw-Hill Ryerson.

Fournier, Elaine, George Butlin, and Philip Giles. 1995. 'Intergenerational Change in the Education of Canadians', *Education Quarterly Review* 2, 2: 22–33.

Fraser, Steven, ed. 1995. *The Bell Curve Wars: Race, Intelligence, and the Future of America*. New York: Basic Books.

Frazee, Catherine. 2003. *Thumbs Up! Inclusion, Rights and Equality as Experienced by Youth with Disabilities*. Toronto: Laidlaw Foundation, Working Paper Series, Perspectives on Social Inclusion.

Freedman, Joe. 1995. *The Charter School Idea: Breaking Educational Gridlock*. Red Deer, Alta: Society for Advancing Educational Research.

Freire, Paulo. 1970. *Pedagogy of the Oppressed*. New York: Herder and Herder.

———. 1985. *The Politics of Education: Culture, Power and Liberation*. South Hadley, Mass.: Bergin and Garvey.

Frempong, George, and J. Douglas Willms. 2002. 'Can School Quality Compensate for Socioeconomic Disadvantage?', in Willms, ed., *Vulnerable Children: Findings from Canada's National Longitudinal Survey of Children and Youth*. Edmonton: University of Alberta Press and Human Resources Development Canada, 277–303.

Frenette, Marc. 2005a. *Is Post-secondary Access More Equitable in Canada or the United States?* Ottawa: Statistics Canada Analytical Studies Branch Research Paper Series Number 244, Catalogue no. 11F00019MIE.

———. 2005b. *The Impact of Tuition Fees on University Access: Evidence from a Large-scale Price Deregulation in Professional Programs*. Ottawa: Statistics Canada Analytical Studies Branch Research Paper Series Number 263, Catalogue no. 11F0019MIE.

———. 2007. *Why Are Youth from Lower-income Families Less Likely To Attend University? Evidence from Academic Abilities, Parental Influences, and Financial Constraints*. Ottawa: Statistics Canada Analytical Studies Branch Research Paper Series Number 295, Catalogue no. 11F0019MIE.

——— and Simon Coulombe. 2007. *Has Higher Education among Young Women Substantially Reduced the Gender Gap in Employment and Earnings?* Ottawa: Minister of Industry, Statistics Canada Analytical Studies Branch Research Paper Series Number 301, Catalogue no. 11F0019MIE.

Fullan, Michael. 2007. *The New Meaning of Educational Change*, 3rd edn. New York: Teachers College Press.

Fuller, Bruce. 2000. 'Introduction: Growing Charter Schools, Decentering the State', in Fuller, ed., *Inside Charter Schools: The Paradox of Radical Decentralization*. Cambridge, Mass.: Harvard University Press, 1–11.

Fuller, Steve. 2006. *The New Sociological Imagination*. London: Sage.

Gaffield, Chad. 1982. 'Schooling, the Economy, and Rural Society in Nineteenth-Century Ontario', in Joy Parr, ed., *Childhood and Family in Canadian History*. Toronto: McClelland & Stewart, 69–92.

Galarneau, Diane, Howard Krebs, René Morissette, and Xuelin Zhang. 2001. *The Quest for Workers: A New Portrait of Job Vacancies in Canada*. Ottawa: Minister of Industry, The Evolving Workplace Series, Statistics Canada Catalogue no. 71-584-MPE No. 2.

Gallen, Verna, Bruce Karlenzig, and Isobel Tamney. 1995. 'Teacher Workload and Work Life in Saskatchewan', *Education Quarterly Review* 2, 4: 49–58.

Gaskell, Jane. 1992. *Gender Matters from School to Work*. Toronto: OISE Press.

——— and Arlene McLaren. 1991. 'Women as Mothers, Women as Teachers', in Gaskell and McLaren (1991: 19–32).

——— and ———, eds. 1991. *Women and Education*, 2nd edn. Calgary: Detselig.

———, ———, and Myra Novogrodsky. 1989. *Claiming an Education: Feminism and Canadian Schools*. Toronto: Our Schools/Our Selves.

Gerth, H.H., and C. Wright Mills. 1946. *From Max Weber: Essays in Sociology*. New York: Oxford University Press.

Giddens, Anthony. 1987. *Sociology: A Brief but Critical Introduction*, 2nd edn. San Diego: Harcourt Brace Jovanovich.

———. 1990. *The Consequences of Modernity*. Stanford, Calif.: Stanford University Press.

Gilbert, Sid, and Jeff Frank. 1998. 'Educational Pathways', in Human Resources Development Canada and Statistics Canada, *High School May Not Be Enough: An Analysis of Results from the School Leavers Follow-up Survey, 1995*. Ottawa: Minister of Public Works and Government Services Canada, Catalogue no. 81-585-XBE, 9–20.

Gilliss, Geraldine. 1995. 'The Grade Is Made If One Looks at the Data Carefully', in Thomas T. Schweitzer, Robert K. Crocker, and Gilliss, *The State of Education in Canada*. Montreal: Institute for Research on Public Policy, 119–26.

Gintis, Herbert. 1980. 'Communication and Politics', *Socialist Review* 10 (Mar./June): 189–232.

——— and Samuel Bowles. 1980. 'Contradiction and Reproduction in Educational Theory', in Len Barton, Roland Meighan, and Stephen Walker, eds, *Schooling, Ideology and the Curriculum*. Barcombe, Lewes: Falmer, 51–65.

Giroux, Henry A. 1983. *Theory and Resistance in Education*. South Hadley, Mass.: Bergin and Garvey.

———. 1988. *Teachers as Intellectuals*. Westport, Conn.: Bergin and Garvey.

——— and Peter McLaren, eds. 1989. *Critical Pedagogy, the State, and Cultural Struggle*. Albany: State University of New York Press.

Goffman, Erving. 1961. *Asylums*. Garden City, NY: Doubleday.

Gorbutt, David. 1972. 'The New Sociology of Education', *Education for Teaching* 89 (Autumn): 3–11.

Government of Canada. 2001. *Achieving Excellence: Investing in People, Knowledge and Opportunity*. Ottawa: Industry Canada, Catalogue no. C2-596/2001.

———. 2002. *Knowledge Matters: Skills and Learning for Canadians: Canada's Innovation Strategy*. Ottawa: Minister of Industry.

Government of Saskatchewan. 2003. *School Plus: Well-being and Educational Success for ALL Children and Youth*. Regina: Saskatchewan Learning (Spring).

Gracey, Harry L. 1977. 'Learning the Student Role: Kindergarten as Academic Boot Camp', in Dennis H. Wrong and Gracey, eds, *Readings in Introductory Sociology*, 3rd edn. New York: Macmillan, 215–26.

Gramsci, Antonio. 1971. 'The Intellectuals', in Quintin Hoare and Geoffrey Nowell Smith, eds and trans, *Selections from the Prison Notebooks of Antonio Gramsci*. London: Lawrence and Wishart, 13–23.

Grayson, J. Paul. 1997. *Who Gets Jobs? Initial Labour Market Experiences of York Graduates*. Toronto: Institute for Social Research, York University.

Grieshaber-Otto, Jim, and Matt Sanger. 2002. *Perilous Lessons: The Impact of the WTO Services Agreement (GATS) on Canada's Public Education System*. Ottawa: Canadian Centre for Policy Alternatives.

Guppy, Neil, and Scott Davies. 1998. *Education in Canada: Recent Trends and Future Challenges*. Ottawa: Statistics Canada.

——— and ———. 1999. 'Understanding Canadians' Declining Confidence in Public Education', *Canadian Journal of Education* 24, 3: 265–80.

———, Robert Crocker, Scott Davies, Claire LaPointe, and Larry Sackney. 2005. *Parent and Teacher Views on Education: A Policy-maker's Guide*. Kelowna, BC: Society for the Advancement of Excellence in Education.

Gurria, Angel. 2007. 'Launch of PISA 2006', speech of the OECD Secretary-General, Japan Press Club, Tokyo, 4 Dec. At: <www.oecd.org/document/35/0,3343,en_2649_37455_39722787_1_1_1_37455,00.html>.

Hall, Christine. 2004. 'Theorizing Changes in Teachers' Work', *Canadian Journal of Educational Administration and Policy* 32, 1 (1 July). At: <www.umanitoba.ca/publications/cjeap/articles/noma/theorising.change.html>.

Hall, E.M., and L.A. Dennis. 1968. *Living and Learning: The Report of the Provincial Committee on Aims and Objectives of Education in the Schools of Ontario* (Hall-Dennis Report). Toronto: Ontario Department of Education.

Hamilton, Roberta. 2005. *Gendering the Vertical Mosaic: Feminist Perspectives on Canadian Society*, 2nd edn. Toronto: Pearson Prentice-Hall.

Hango, Darcy, and Patrice de Broucker. 2007. *Education-to-Labour Market Pathways of Canadian Youth: Findings from the Youth in Transition Survey*. Ottawa: Minister of Industry, Statistics Canada Catalogue no. 81-515MIE2007054.

Hargreaves, Andy. 2003. *Teaching in the Knowledge Society: Education in the Age of Insecurity*. New York: Teachers College Press.

Hargreaves, David H. 1967. *Social Relations in a Secondary School*. London: Routledge & Kegan Paul.

Harrison, Trevor W., and Jerrold L. Kachur, eds. 1999. *Contested Classrooms: Education, Globalization and Democracy in Alberta*. Edmonton: University of Alberta Press.

Hart, Doug, and D.W. Livingstone. 2007. *Public Attitudes towards Education in Ontario 2007: The 16th OISE/UT Survey*. Toronto: Ontario Institute for Studies in Education of the University of Toronto.

Health Canada. 1999. *Healthy Development of Children and Youth: The Role of the Determinants of Health*. Ottawa: Minister of Health Canada.

Heisz, Andrew. 2007. *Income Inequality and Redistribution in Canada: 1976-2004*. Ottawa: Minister of Industry, Statistics Canada Analytical Studies Branch Research Paper Series No. 298 (May).

———, A. Jackson, and G. Picot. 2002. *Winners and Losers in the Labour Market of the 1990s*. Ottawa: Statistics Canada Analytical Studies Branch Research Paper Series No. 184 (Feb.).

Henchey, Norman. 1977. 'Pressures for Professional Autonomy and Public Controls', in Hugh A. Stevenson and J. Donald Wilson, eds, *Precepts, Policy and Process: Perspectives on Contemporary Canadian Education*. London, Ont.: Alexander, Blake Associates.

Henry, Frances, and Carol Tator. 2005. *The Colour of Democracy: Racism in Canadian Society*, 3rd edn. Toronto: Thomson Nelson.

Hepburn, Claudia Rebanks. 1999. 'The Case for School Choice: Models from the United States, New Zealand, Denmark, and Sweden'. Vancouver: Fraser Institute Critical Issues Bulletin (Sept.).

Herrnstein, Richard J. 1973. *IQ in the Meritocracy*. Boston: Little Brown.

——— and Charles Murray. 1994. *The Bell Curve: Intelligence and Class Structure in American Life*. New York: Free Press.

Hochschild, Arlie Russell. 1983. *The Managed Heart: Commercialization of Human Feeling*. Berkeley: University of California Press.

Hoff Sommers, Christina. 2000. *The War against Boys: How Misguided Feminism Is Harming Our Young Men*. New York: Simon and Schuster.

Holt, John. 1964. *How Children Fail*. New York: Pitman.

hooks, bell. 2000. *Feminist Theory: From Margin to Center*, 2nd edn. Cambridge, Mass.: South End Press.

Houston, Susan E. 1982. 'The "Waifs and Strays" of a Late Victorian City: Juvenile Delinquents in Toronto', in Joy Parr, ed., *Childhood and Family in Canadian History*. Toronto: McClelland & Stewart, 129–42.

——— and Alison Prentice. 1988. *Schooling and Scholars in Nineteenth-Century Ontario*. Toronto: University of Toronto Press.

Hughes, Karen D., and Graham S. Lowe. 2000. 'Surveying the "Post-Industrial" Landscape: Information Technologies and Labour Market Polarization in Canada', *Canadian Review of Sociology and Anthropology* 37, 1: 28–53.

Hull, Jeremy. 2000. *Aboriginal Post-Secondary Education and Labour Market Outcomes: Canada, 1996*. Ottawa: Indian and Northern Affairs Canada Research and Analysis Directorate.

Human Resources Development Canada. 1996. 'Labour Market Polarization . . . What's Going On?', *Applied Research Bulletin* 2, 2: 5–7.

————. 2000. *Profile of Canadian Youth in the Labour Market*, Second Annual Report to the Forum of Labour Market Ministers. Ottawa: Human Resources Development Canada, Catalogue no. RH61-1/2000E.

Hunter, Alfred J., and Jean McKenzie Leiper. 1993. 'On Formal Education, Skills and Earnings: The Role of Educational Certificates in Earnings Determination', *Canadian Journal of Sociology* 18, 1: 21–42.

Hurst, Charles E. 1992. *Social Inequality: Forms, Causes, and Consequences*. Boston: Allyn and Bacon.

Illich, Ivan. 1970. *Deschooling Society*. New York: Harper and Row.

Industry Canada. 1992. *A Lot to Learn: Education and Training in Canada*. Ottawa: Industry Canada.

Indian and Northern Affairs Canada. 2004. 'Backgrounder: Aboriginal Workforce Participation Initiative', news release, 18 Nov. At: <www.ainc-inac.gc.ca/nr/prs/s-d2004/02525abk_e.html>.

————. 2005. *Basic Departmental Data 2004*. Ottawa: Minister of Public Works and Government Services Canada.

Ipsos Reid. 2003. 'A Good Understanding of the Basics (91%) Tops 7 Goals As To What Parents Say Their Children Need for a Successful Education—But Only Half (51%) Are Satisfied with Their Child's Progress towards This Goal', press release, Toronto, 23 Feb.

————. 2007. '"Digital Divide" Remains Wide—Only Six-In-Ten Canadians Aged 55+ Have Access to the Internet Canadians Aged 55+ Have Not Integrated the Internet into Their Daily Lives', news release. Vancouver: IPSOS Reid, 15 Feb.

Irons, E. Jane, and Sandra Harris. 2007. *The Challenges of No Child Left Behind: Understanding the Issues of Excellence, Accountability, and Choice*. Lanham, Md: Rowman and Littlefield.

Isenbarger, Lynn, and Michalinos Zembylas. 2006. 'The Emotional Labour of Caring in Teaching', *Teaching and Teacher Education* 22, 1: 120–34.

Jackson, Nancy S. 1987. 'Ethnicity and Vocational Choice', in Young (1987: 165–82).

————. 1993. 'Rethinking Vocational Learning', in Rebecca Priegert Coulter and Ivor F. Goodson, eds, *Rethinking Vocationalism: Whose Work/Life Is It?* Toronto: Our Schools/Our Selves Education Foundation, 166–80.

————. 1994. 'Rethinking Vocational Learning: The Case of Clerical Skills', in Erwin and MacLennan (1994: 341–51).

Jackson, Philip W. 1968. *Life in Classrooms*. New York: Holt, Rinehart and Winston.

Jaenen, Cornelius J. 1986. 'Education for Francization: The Case of New France in the Seventeenth Century', in Jean Barman, Yvonne Hébert, and Don McCaskill, eds, *Indian Education in Canada*, vol. 1: *The Legacy*. Vancouver: University of British Columbia Press, 45–63.

Jaine, Linda, ed. 1993. *Residential Schools: The Stolen Years*. Saskatoon: University Extension Press.

James, Carl E. 1993. 'Getting There and Staying There: Blacks' Employment Experience', in Anisef and Axelrod (1993: 3–20).

————. 2003. *Seeing Ourselves: Exploring Race, Ethnicity and Culture*, 3rd edn. Toronto: Thompson Educational Publishing.

Jencks, Christopher, et al. 1972. *Inequality: A Reassessment of the Effect of Family and Schooling in America*. New York: Basic Books.

Jenks, Chris. 1998. 'Introduction', in Jenks, ed., *Core Sociological Dichotomies*. London: Sage, 1–7.

Jensen, Arthur. 1973. *Educability and Group Difference*. New York: Harper and Row.

Johnson, F. Henry. 1968. *A Brief History of Canadian Education*. Toronto: McGraw-Hill.

Kailin, Julie. 2002. *Antiracist Education: From Theory to Practice*. Lanham, Md: Rowman and Littlefield.

Kanagarajah, Sri. 2006. *Business Dynamics in Canada 2003*. Ottawa: Minister of Industry, Statistics Canada Catalogue no. 61-534-XIE2006 (Mar.).

Kanpol, Barry. 1992. *Towards a Theory and Practice of Teacher Cultural Politics: Continuing the Postmodern Debate*. Norwood, NJ: Ablex Publishing.

Karabel, Jerome, and A.H. Halsey. 1977. 'Educational Research: A Review and an Interpretation', in Karabel and Halsey, eds, *Power and Ideology in Education*. New York: Oxford University Press, 1–85.

Katz, Joseph. 1969. *Society, Schools and Progress in Canada*. Toronto: Pergamon Press.

Kazemipur, Abdolmohammad, and Shiva S. Halli. 2001. 'The Changing Colour of Poverty in Canada', *Canadian Review of Sociology and Anthropology* 38, 2: 217–38.

Kelly, Jennifer. 1998. *Under the Gaze: Learning to Be Black in White Society*. Halifax: Fernwood.

Kenway, Jane, and D. Langmead. 1998. 'Governmentality, the "Now" University and the Future of Knowledge Work', *Australian Universities' Review*, 41, 2: 28–31.

—— and Helen Modra. 1992. 'Feminist Pedagogy and Emancipatory Possibilities', in Luke and Gore (1992: 138–66).

—— and Sue Willis. 1998. *Answering Back: Girls, Boys and Feminism in Schools*. London: Routledge.

Kerckhoff, Alan C. 2000. 'Transition from School to Work in Comparative Perspective', in Maureen T. Hallinan, ed., *Handbook of the Sociology of Education*. New York: Kluwer Academic/Plenum Publishers, 453–74.

Kerr, Kevin. 1997. *Labour Market Developments*, Library of Parliament Research Branch Current Issue Review. Ottawa: Minister of Supply and Services Canada.

Kincheloe, Joe L. 2007. 'Critical Pedagogy in the Twenty-first Century: Evolution for Survival', in Peter McLaren and Joe L. Kincheloe, eds, *Critical Pedagogy: Where Are We Now?* New York: Peter Lang, 9–42.

King, Alan J.C., William F. Boyce, and Matthew A. King. 1999. *Trends in the Health of Canadian Youth*. Ottawa: Health Canada.

—— and Marjorie J. Peart. 1992. *Teachers in Canada: Their Work and Quality of Life*. Ottawa: Canadian Teachers' Federation.

Kirkness, Verna, and Sheena Selkirk Bowman. 1992. *First Nations and Schools: Triumphs and Struggles*. Toronto: Canadian Education Association.

Knight, Doug. 1993. 'Understanding Change in Education in Rural and Remote Regions of Canada', in Earle Newton and Knight, eds, *Understanding Change in Education: Rural and Remote Regions of Canada*. Calgary: Detselig, 299–310.

Knighton, Tamara, and Sheba Mirza. 2002. 'Postsecondary Participation: The Effects of Parents' Education and Household Income', *Education Quarterly Review* 8, 3: 25–32.

Kohen, Dafna, Sharanjit Uppal, Anne Guevremont, and Fernando Cartwright, 2007. 'Children with Disabilities and the Educational System: A Provincial Perspective', *Education Matters* 4, 1 (May). At: <www.statcan.ca/english/freepub/81-004-XIE/2007001/childis.htm>.

Kozol, Jonathan. 1967. *Death at an Early Age: The Destruction of the Hearts and Minds of Negro Children in Boston Public Schools*. New York: Houghton Mifflin.

Krahn, Harvey, and Alison Taylor. 2007. '"Streaming" in the 10th Grade in Four Canadian Provinces in 2000', *Education Matters* 4, 2 (June). At: <www.statcan.ca/english/freepub/81-004-XIE/2007002/stream.htm>.

Lacey, Colin. 1970. *Hightown Grammar: The School as a Social System*. Manchester: Manchester University Press.

Lambert, Mylène, Klarka Zeman, Mary Allan, and Patrick Bussière, 2004. *Who Pursues Postsecondary Education, Who Leaves and Why? Results from the Youth in Transition Survey*. Ottawa: Minister of Industry. Culture, Tourism and the Centre for Education Statistics Research Paper no. 026, Statistics Canada Catalogue no. 81-595-MIE2004026.

Lapointe, Mario, Kevin Dunn, Nicolas Tremblay-Côté, Louis-Philippe Bergeron, and Luke Ignaczak. 2006. *Looking Ahead: A 10-Year Outlook for the Canadian Labour Market*

(2006–2015). Ottawa: Human Resources and Social Development Canada, Labour Market and Skills Forecasting and Analysis Unit Strategic Policy Research Directorate Report (Oct.), Catalogue no. HS28-23/2006E.

Lareau, Annette. 1989. *Home Advantage: Social Class and Parental Intervention in Elementary Education.* London: Falmer.

———— and Erin McNamara Horvat. 1999. 'Moments of Social Inclusion and Exclusion: Race, Class, and Cultural Capital in Family-School Relationships', *Sociology of Education* 72, 1: 37–53.

———— and Elliott B. Weininger. 2003. 'Cultural Capital in Educational Research: A Critical Assessment', *Theory and Society* 32, 5/6: 567–606.

Lauder, Hugh, Phillip Brown, Jo-Anne Dillabough, and A.H. Halsey. 2006. 'The Prospects for Education: Individualization, Globalization, and Social Change', in Lauder, Brown, Dillabough, and Halsey, eds, *Education, Globalization & Social Change.* Oxford: Oxford University Press, 1–70.

Lauwerys, Joseph. 1973. *The Purposes of Education: Results of a CEA Survey.* Toronto: Canadian Education Association.

Lawr, Douglas, and Robert Gidney, eds. 1973. *Educating Canadians: A Documentary History of Public Education.* Toronto: Van Nostrand Reinhold.

Lawson, Robert F., and Roger R. Woock. 1987. 'Policy and Policy Actors in Canadian Education', in Ratna Ghosh and Douglas Ray, eds, *Social Change and Education in Canada.* Toronto: Harcourt Brace Jovanovich, 133–42.

Lawton, Stephen B. 1995. *Busting Bureaucracy to Reclaim Our Schools.* Montreal: Institute for Research on Public Policy.

Leacy, F.H. 1983. *Historical Statistics of Canada*, 2nd edn. Ottawa: Statistics Canada.

LeBlanc, Jules. 1974. 'Becoming Political: The Growth of the Quebec Teachers' Union', in Martell (1974: 151–64).

Lee, Mark. 2004. 'Socio-Economic Inequalities', in William Boyce, ed., *Young People in Canada: Their Health and Well-being.* Ottawa: Health Canada, 9–15.

Lehmann, Wolfgang. 2007. 'I Just Didn't Feel Like I Fit In': The Role of Habitus in University Drop-out Decisions', *Canadian Journal of Higher Education* 37, 2: 89–110.

Leithwood, Kenneth, and Doris Jantzi. 2007. *Review of Empirical Evidence about School Size Effects: A Policy Perspective.* Report prepared for the Board of Education (Aug.). Regina: Regina School Division.

Lessard, Claude. 1995. 'Equality and Inequality in Canadian Education', in Ghosh and Ray (1995: 178–95).

————. 2004. 'L'Obligation de Résultats en Éducation: De Quoi s'agit-il? Le contexte Québecoise d'une Demande Sociale, un rhétorique du changement et une extension de la recherche', in Claude Lessard and Philippe Meirieu, eds, *L'Obligation de Résultats en Éducation.* Saint-Nicolas, Québec: Les Presses de l'Université Laval, 23–49.

Lévesque, M. 1979. *L'égalité des chances en éducation, considérations théoriques et approches empiriques.* Québec: Conseil Supérieur de l'Education.

Levin, Benjamin. 1990. 'Tuition Fees and University Accessibility', *Canadian Public Policy* 16, 1: 51–9.

———— and Shirley Seward. 2003. *Consultations on the Government of Canada's Proposal to Establish a Canadian Learning Institute*, Summary Report. Ottawa: Human Resources and Development Canada Strategic Policy, Canadian Learning Institute Project (Feb.).

Levinson, David L., and Alan R. Sadovnik. 2002. 'Education and Sociology: An Introduction', in Levinson, Peter W. Cookson Jr, and Sadovnik, eds, *Education and Sociology: An Encyclopedia.* New York: RoutledgeFalmer, 1–16.

Lewington, Jennifer. 1995. 'Report Cards Get a New Twist', *Globe and Mail*, 13 Nov., A1.

———— and Graham Orpwood. 1993. *Overdue Assignment: Taking Responsibility for Canada's Schools*. Toronto: John Wiley & Sons.

Leydesdorff, Loet, and Henry Etkowitz. 1997. 'A Triple Helix of University–Industry–Government Relations', in H. Etkowitz and L. Leydesdorff, eds, *Universities and the Global Knowledge Economy: A Triple Helix of University–Industry–Government Relations*. London: Pinter, 155–62.

Li, Chris, Ginette Gervais, and Aurélie Duval. 2006. *The Dynamics of Overqualification: Canada's Underemployed University Graduates*. Ottawa: Minister of Industry, Analytical Paper, Statistics Canada Catalogue no. 11-621-MIE2006039.

Li, Peter S. 1988. *Ethnic Inequality in a Class Society*. Toronto: Wall and Thompson.

————. 1996. *The Making of Post-War Canada*. Toronto: Oxford University Press.

————. 2003. *Destination Canada: Immigrant Debates and Issues*. Toronto: Oxford University Press.

Lin, Jane. 2006. 'The Teaching Profession: Trends from 1999 to 2005', *Education Matters* 3, 4 (Dec.), Statistics Canada Catalogue no. 81-004-XIE. At: <www.statcan.ca/english/freepub/81-004-XIE/81-004-XIE2006004.htm>.

Livingstone, D.W. 1983. *Class, Ideologies and Educational Futures*. London: Routledge.

————. 1985. *Social Crisis and Schooling*. Toronto: Garamond Press.

————. 1987. 'Crisis, Classes and Educational Reform in Advanced Capitalism', in Wotherspoon (1987: 57–67).

————. 1994. 'Searching for Missing Links: Neo-Marxist Theories of Education', in Erwin and MacLennan (1994: 55–82).

————. 2004. *The Education–Jobs Gap: Underemployment or Economic Democracy*. Toronto: Garamond Press.

———— and Doug Hart. 2005. *Public Attitudes towards Education in Ontario 2004: The 15th OISE/UT Survey*. Toronto: Ontario Institute for Studies in Education of the University of Toronto.

———— and Antonie Scholtz. 2007. 'Contradictions of Labour Processes and Workers' Use of Skills in Advanced Capitalist Economies', in Shalla and Clement (2007: 131–62).

Lockhart, Alexander. 1979. 'Educational Opportunities and Economic Opportunities—the "New" Liberal Equality Syndrome', in John A. Fry, ed., *Economy, Class and Social Reality: Issues in Contemporary Canadian Society*. Toronto: Butterworths, 224–37.

————. 1991. *School Teaching in Canada*. Toronto: University of Toronto Press.

Lortie, Dan C. 1975. *Schoolteacher: A Sociological Study*. Chicago: University of Chicago Press.

Love, James. 1978. 'The Professionalization of Teachers in Mid-Nineteenth Century Upper Canada', in McDonald and Chaiton (1978: 109–28).

Lowe, Graham S. 2000. *The Quality of Work: A People-Centred Agenda*. Toronto: Oxford University Press.

————. 2002. 'Leveraging the Skills of Knowledge Workers', *Isuma Canadian Journal of Policy Research* 3, 1: 79-86.

————. 2007. *21st Century Job Quality: Achieving What Canadians Want*. Ottawa: Canadian Policy Research Networks Research Report W37 Work and Learning.

Luffman, Jacqueline, and Deborah Sussman. 2007. 'The Aboriginal Labour Force in Western Canada', *Perspectives on Labour and Income* 8, 1: 13–27. Ottawa: Statistics Canada Catalogue no. 75-001-XIE.

Luke, Carmen, and Jennifer Gore, eds. 1992. *Feminisms and Critical Pedagogy*. New York: Routledge.

Lynch, Kathleen. 1989. *The Hidden Curriculum: Reproduction in Education, an Appraisal*. London: Falmer.

McAndrew, Marie. 1995. 'Ethnicity, Multiculturalism, and Multicultural Education in Canada', in Ghosh and Ray (1995: 165–77).

Macdonald, Doune. 1999. 'Teacher Attrition: A Review of Literature', *Teaching and Teacher Education* 15, 8: 835–48.

McDonald, Neil, and Alf Chaiton, eds. 1978. *Egerton Ryerson and His Times: Essays on the History of Education*. Toronto: Macmillan.

McKeown, Larry, and Cathy Underhill. 2007. 'Learning Online: Factors Associated with Use of the Internet for Educational Purposes', *Education Matters* 4, 4 (30 Oct.). At: <www.statcan.ca/english/freepub/81-004-XIE/2007004/internet-en.htm>.

McLaren, Arlene, and Jim Gaskell. 1995. 'Now You See It, Now You Don't: Gender as an Issue in School Science', in Jane Gaskell and John Willinsky, eds, *Gender Informs Curriculum: From Enrichment to Transformation*. New York: Teachers College Press, 136–56.

McLaren, Peter. 2007. *Life in Schools: An Introduction to Critical Pedagogy in the Foundations of Education*, 5th edn. New York: Addison-Wesley Longman.

McNeil, Linda M. 1986. *Contradictions of Control: School Structure and School Knowledge*. New York: Routledge & Kegan Paul.

McRobbie, Angela. 1978. 'Working Class Girls and the Culture of Femininity', in Women's Studies Group, Centre for Contemporary Cultural Studies, *Women Take Issue*. Birmingham: University of Birmingham, Centre for Contemporary Cultural Studies, 96–108.

Mandell, Nancy, and Stewart Crysdale. 1993. 'Gender Tracks: Male-Female Perceptions of Home–School–Work Transitions', in Anisef and Axelrod (1993: 19–41).

Mangan, J. Marshall. 1994. 'The Politics of Educational Computing in Ontario', in Erwin and MacLennan (1994: 263–77).

Mann, Jean. 1980. 'G.M. Weir and H.B. King: Progressive Education or Education for the Progressive State', in J. Donald Wilson and David C. Jones, eds, *Schooling and Society in 20th Century British Columbia*. Calgary: Detselig, 91–118.

Mannheim, Karl. 1936. *Ideology and Utopia: An Introduction to the Sociology of Knowledge*. New York: Harcourt, Brace and World.

Manzer, Ronald. 1994. *Public Schools and Political Ideas: Canadian Educational Policy in Historical Perspective*. Toronto: University of Toronto Press.

Martel, Denis, Jocelyn Gagnon, Joanne Pelletier-Murphy, and Johanne Grenier. 1999. 'Pygmalion en éducation physique: un mythe bien réel', *Canadian Journal of Education* 24, 1: 42–56.

Martell, George, ed. 1974. *The Politics of the Canadian Public School*. Toronto: James Lorimer.

Martin, Wilfred. 1976. *The Negotiated Order of the School*. Toronto: Macmillan.

———. 1982. *Teachers' Pets and Class Victims*. St John's: Publications Committee, Faculty of Education, Memorial University of Newfoundland.

——— and Allan J. Macdonell. 1982. *Canadian Education: A Sociological Analysis*, 2nd edn. Scarborough, Ont.: Prentice-Hall.

Marx, Karl. 1963 [1869]. *The Eighteenth Brumaire of Louis Bonaparte*. New York: International Publishers.

———. 1977 [1862–3]. *Capital: A Critique of Political Economy*, vol. 1. New York: Vintage Books.

——— and Friedrich Engels. 1965 [1848]. *Manifesto of the Communist Party*. Peking: Foreign Languages Press.

Maté, Gabor. 1999. *Scattered Minds: A New Look at the Origins and Healing of Attention Deficit Disorder*. Toronto: Alfred A. Knopf.

Meier, Debra, and George Wood, eds. 2004. *Many Children Left Behind: How the No Child Left Behind Act is Damaging Our Children and Our Schools*. Boston: Beacon Press.

Miller, James R. 1996. *Shingwauk's Vision: A History of Native Residential Schools*. Toronto: University of Toronto Press.

Mills, C. Wright. 1951. *White Collar: The American Middle Classes*. New York: Oxford University Press.

————. 1956. *The Power Elite*. New York: Oxford University Press.

Monture-Angus, Patricia. 1995. *Thunder in My Soul: A Mohawk Woman Speaks*. Halifax: Fernwood.

Morissette, René, Xuelin Zhang, and Marie Drolet. 2002. 'Are Families Getting Richer?', *Canadian Social Trends* 66 (Autumn): 15–19. Statistics Canada Catalogue no. 11-008.

Moscovitch, Allan, and Glenn Drover. 1987. 'Social Expenditures and the Welfare State: The Canadian Experience in Historical Perspective', in Allan Moscovitch and Jim Albert, eds, *The 'Benevolent' State: The Growth of Welfare in Canada*. Toronto: Garamond Press, 13–43.

Moss, Gemma, and Dena Attar. 1999. 'Boys and Literacy: Gendering the Reading Curriculum', in Jon Prosser, ed., *School Culture*. Thousand Oaks, Calif.: Sage, 133–44.

Muir, J. Douglas. 1968. *Collective Bargaining by Canadian Public School Teachers*. Task Force on Labour Relations Study No. 11. Ottawa: Information Canada.

Murphy, Raymond. 1994. 'A Weberian Approach to Credentials: Credentials as a Code of Exclusionary Closure', in Erwin and MacLennan (1994: 102–19).

Myers, Douglas. 1973. 'Introduction', in Myers, ed., *The Failure of Educational Reform in Canada*. Toronto: McClelland & Stewart, 11–13.

Myles, John, and Gail Fawcett. 1990. *Job Skills and the Service Economy*. Ottawa: Economic Council of Canada, Working Paper No. 4.

Nakhaie, M. Reza. 1996. 'The Reproduction of Class Relations by Gender in Canada', *Canadian Journal of Sociology* 21, 4: 523–58.

National Council of Welfare. 2007. 'Persistence of Poverty by Highest Level of Education, 1999–2004', *Poverty Statistics 2004*. Ottawa: National Council of Welfare. At: <www.ncwcnbes.net/documents/researchpublications/ResearchProjects/PovertyProfile/2004/Persistence-EducationENG.pdf>.

Nayak, Anoop. 2003. *Race, Place and Globalization: Youth Cultures in a Changing World*. New York: Berg Publishers.

Naylor, Charlie. 2002. 'Teacher Workload and Stress: An International Perspective on Human Costs and Systemic Failure', *Our Schools/Our Selves* 11, 3: 125–50.

———— and Anne C. Schaefer. 2002. 'Teacher Workload and Stress: A British Columbia Perspective', *Education Quarterly Review* 8, 3: 33–6.

Neatby, Hilda. 1953. *So Little for the Mind*. Toronto: Clarke, Irwin.

Nelsen, Randle W. 1997. 'Reading, Writing and Relationships among the Electronic Zealots: Distance Education and the Traditional University', in Nelsen, ed., *Inside Canadian Universities: Another Day at the Plant*. Kingston, Ont.: Cedarcreek Publications, 184–210.

————. 2007. *Fun and Games and Higher Education: The Lonely Crowd Revisited*. Toronto: Between the Lines.

———— and David Nock, eds. 1978. *Reading, Writing, and Riches: Education and the Socio-Economic Order in North America*. Kitchener, Ont.: Between the Lines.

Ng, Roxanna. 1991. 'Teaching against the Grain: Contradictions for Minority Teachers', in Gaskell and McLaren (1991: 99–115).

Ngo, Hieu Van, and Barbara Schleifer. 2004. 'Immigrant Children and Youth in Focus', *Canadian Issues* (Spring): 29–33. At: <canada.metropolis.net/pdfs/Van_ngo_e.pdf>.

Nikiforuk, Andrew. 1993. *School's Out: The Catastrophe in Public Education and What We Can Do About It*. Toronto: Macfarlane Walter & Ross.

Nolan, Kathleen, and Jean Anyon. 2004. 'Learning To Do Time: Willis's Model of Cultural Reproduction in an Era of Postindustrialism, Globalization, and Mass Incarceration', in Nadine Dolby and Greg Dimitriadis, eds, *Learning to Labor in New Times*. New York: Routledge, 133–50.

Nugent, Becky, and Diana Calhoun Bell. 2006. *Toward Deprivatized Pedagogy*. Cresskill, NJ: Hampton Press.

O'Haire, Noreen. 2005. *CTF Survey on Gender and Leadership*. Ottawa: Canadian Teachers' Federation. At: <www.ctf-fce.ca/e/programs/pd/gender_issues/SurveyOnGenderIdentity_PDP_Fall2004_4-4_EN.pdf>.

Oderkirk, Jillian. 1996. 'Computer Literacy—A Growing Requirement', *Education Quarterly Review* 3, 3: 9–29.

Ogbu, John. 1994. 'Racial Stratification and Education in the United States: Why Inequality Persists', *Teachers College Record* 96: 264–98.

Ogle, Jennifer Paff, and Molly Eckman. 2002. 'Dress-Related Responses to the Columbine Shootings: Other-Imposed and Self-Designed', *Family and Consumer Sciences Research Journal* 31, 2: 155–94.

Olson, Paul. 1995. 'Poverty and Education in Canada', in Ratna Ghosh and Ray, eds, *Social Change and Education in Canada*, 3rd edn. Toronto: Harcourt Brace, 196–208.

Ontario Human Rights Commission. 2003. *The Ontario Safe Schools Act: School Discipline and Discrimination*. Consultation Paper prepared by Ken Bhattacharjee, 8 July. Toronto: Ontario Human Rights Commission. At: <www.ohrc.on.ca/en/resources/discussion_consultation/SafeSchoolsConsultRepENG>.

Organization for Economic Co-operation and Development (OECD). 2001. *OECD Economic Outlook* 70 (Dec.). Paris: OECD.

———. 2002. *Understanding the Brain: Towards a New Learning Science*. Paris: OECD.

Ornstein, Allan. 2007. *Class Counts: Education, Inequality, and the Shrinking Middle Class* Lanham, Md: Rowman and Littlefield.

Ornstein, Michael, Penni Stewart, and Janice Drakich. 1998. 'The Status of Women Faculty in Canadian Universities', *Education Quarterly Review* 5, 2: 9–29.

Osberg, Lars. 2006. 'Pulling Apart—The Growing Gulfs in Canadian Society', *Policy Options* 27, 4: 8–11.

——— and Andrew Sharpe. 2004. 'Has Economic Well-being Improved in Canada and the United States?', in Edward N. Wolffe, ed., *What Has Happened to the Quality of Life in the Advanced Industrialized Nations?* Cheltenham, UK: Edward Elgar, 123–52.

———, Fred Wien, and Jan Grude. 1995. *Vanishing Jobs: Canada's Changing Workplaces*. Toronto: James Lorimer.

Ouellette, Sylvie. 2006. *How Students Fund Their Postsecondary Education: Findings from the Postsecondary Education Participation Survey*. Ottawa: Minster of Industry. Culture, Tourism and the Centre for Education Statistics Research Paper No. 042 (Apr.), Statistics Canada Catalogue no. 81-595-MIE2006042.

Ozga, Jennifer, and Martin Lawn. 1981. *Teachers, Professionalism and Class: A Study of Organized Teachers*. London: Falmer.

Pacholik, Barb. 2007. 'Size Matters in Schools, Study Says', *Regina Leader-Post*, 5 Sept., A1–2.

Paquette, Jerry. 1989. 'The Quality Conundrum: Assessing What We Cannot Agree On', in Stephen B. Lawton and Rouleen Wignall, eds, *Scrimping or Squandering? Financing Canadian Schools*. Toronto: OISE Press, 11–28.

Parelius, Robert James, and Ann Parker Parelius. 1987. *The Sociology of Education*, 2nd edn. Englewood Cliffs, NJ: Prentice-Hall.

Parsons, Talcott. 1959. 'The School Class as a Social System: Some of Its Functions in American Society', *Harvard Educational Review* 29: 297–318.

Paton, J.M. 1962. *The Role of Teachers' Organizations in Canadian Education*. Toronto: W.J. Gage.

Pendakur, Ravi. 2000. *Immigrants and the Labour Force: Policy, Regulation, and Impact*. Montreal and Kingston: McGill-Queen's University Press.

Peters, Michael A., and A.C. Tina Besley. 2006. *Building Knowledge Cultures: Education and Development in the Age of Knowledge Capitalism*. Lanham, Md: Rowman and Littlefield.

Phillips, Charles E. 1957. *The Development of Education in Canada*. Toronto: W.J. Gage.

Pierson, Paul. 2001. 'Coping with Permanent Austerity: Welfare State Restructuring in Affluent Democracies', in Paul Pierson, ed, *The New Politics of the Welfare State*. Oxford: Oxford University Press, 410–56.

Piore, Michael J. 1979. *Birds of Passage: Migrant Labour in Industrial Societies*. New York: Cambridge University Press.

Poelzer, Irene. 1990. *Saskatchewan Women Teachers, 1905–1920: Their Contributions*. Saskatoon: Lindenblatt and Hamonic.

Popkewitz, Thomas S. 1991. *A Political Sociology of Educational Reform: Power/Knowledge in Teaching, Teacher Education, and Research*. New York: Teachers College Press.

Portelli, John P., and R. Patrick Solomon, eds. 2001. *The Erosion of Democracy in Education*. Calgary: Detselig.

Porter, John. 1965. *The Vertical Mosaic: An Analysis of Social Class and Power in Canada*. Toronto: University of Toronto Press.

———, Marion Porter, and Bernard R. Blishen. 1982. *Stations and Callings: Making It Through the School System*. Toronto: Methuen.

Prentice, Alison. 1977. *The School Promoters: Education and Social Class in Mid-Nineteenth Century Upper Canada*. Toronto: McClelland & Stewart.

——— and Susan E. Houston, eds. 1975. *Family, School and Society in Nineteenth Century Canada*. Toronto: Oxford University Press.

——— and Marjorie R. Theobald. 1991. 'The Historiography of Women Teachers: A Retrospect', in Prentice and Theobald, eds, *Women Who Taught: Perspectives on the History of Women and Teaching*. Toronto: University of Toronto Press, 3–33.

Press, Harold, Gerald Galway, and Eldred Barnes. 2002. 'Teacher Labour Market Conditions in Canada: Balancing Demand and Supply', *School Business Affairs* (Nov.): 28-32.

———. 1996. 'Revitalizing Public Education in Canada: The Potential of Choice and Charter Schools', *Fraser Forum* (Aug.), special issue.

Priesnitz, Wendy. 2008. *Challenging Assumptions in Education*, 2nd edn. Toronto: Alternate Press.

Pupo, Noreen, and Ann Duffy. 2007. 'Blurring the Distinction between Public and Private Spheres: The Commodification of Household Work—Gender, Class, Community, and Global Dimensions', in Shalla and Clement (2007: 289–325).

Randhawa, B.S. 1991. 'Inequities in Educational Opportunities and Life Chances', in Terry Wotherspoon, ed., *Hitting the Books: The Politics of Educational Retrenchment*. Toronto and Saskatoon: Garamond Press and the Social Research Unit, 139–58.

Raptis, Helen. 2005. 'A Tale of Two Women: Edith Lucas, Mary Ashworth, and the Changing Nature of Educational Policy in British Columbia, 1937–1977', *Historical Studies in Education/Revue d'histoire de l'éducation* 17, 2: 293–319.

Ray, Brian D. 2001. 'Homeschooling in Canada', *Education Canada* 41, 1: 28–31.

Rees, Ruth. 1990. 'Gender Distribution in Canada's Schools: It's Still as Bad as You Think', *Our Schools/Our Selves* 2, 3: 20–2.

Regnier, Robert, and Brian D. MacLean. 1987. 'Hegemony in Education: The Nuclear Industry in Northern Schools', in Wotherspoon (1987: 165–79).

Reitz, Jeffrey G. 2001. 'Immigrant Skill Utilization in the Canadian Labour Market: Implications of Human Capital Research', *Journal of International Migration and Integration* 2, 3: 347–78.

Repo, Satu. 1974. 'BC Teachers Turn Political', in Martell (1974: 200–17).

———. 1998. *Making Schools Matter: Good Teachers at Work*. Toronto: James Lorimer.

Reynolds, Cecilia. 1990. 'Too Limiting a Liberation: Discourse and Actuality in the Case of Women Teachers', in Frieda Forman, Mary O'Brien, Jane Haddad, Dianne Hallman, and Philinda Masters, eds, *Feminism and Education: A Canadian Perspective*. Toronto: Centre for Women's Studies in Education, 145–68.

———. 2002. 'Introduction: New Questions about Women and School Leadership', in Reynolds, ed., *Women and School Leadership: International Perspectives*. Albany: State University of New York Press, 1–8.

———, Robert White, Carol Brayman, and Shaun Moore. 2008. 'Women and Secondary School Principal Rotation/Succession: A Study of the Beliefs of Decision Makers in Four Provinces', *Canadian Journal of Education* 31, 1: 32–54.

Rice, James R. 2002. 'Being Poor in the Best of Times', in G. Bruce Doern, ed., *How Ottawa Spends 2002–2003: The Security Aftermath and National Priorities*. Toronto: Oxford University Press, 102–20.

——— and Michael J. Prince. 2000. *Changing Politics of Canadian Social Policy*. Toronto: University of Toronto Press.

Rist, Ray C. 1970. 'Student Social Class and Teacher Expectations: The Self-Fulfilling Prophecy in Ghetto Education', *Harvard Educational Review* 40 (Aug.): 411–50.

Ritzer, George. 2008. *Classical Sociological Theory*, 5th edn. New York: McGraw-Hill.

Roberge, Roger, Jean-Marie Berthelot, and Michael Wolfson. 1995. 'Health and Socio-Economic Inequalities', *Canadian Social Trends* 37 (Summer): 15–19.

Robertson, Heather-Jane. 1998. *No More Teachers, No More Books: The Commercialization of Canada's Schools*. Toronto: McClelland & Stewart.

———. 2007. *Great Expectations: Essays on Schools and Society*. Ottawa: Canadian Centre for Policy Alternatives.

———, David McGrane, and Erika Shaker. 2003. *For Cash and Future Considerations: Ontario Universities and Public–Private Partnerships*. Ottawa: Canadian Centre for Policy Alternatives.

Robertson, Susan. 2000. *A Class Act: Changing Teachers' Work, the State, and Globalisation*. London: Falmer.

Rockhill, Kathleen, and Patricia Tomic. 1995. 'Situating ESL between Speech and Silence', in Jane Gaskell and John Willinsky, eds, *Gender In/forms Curriculum: From Enrichment to Transformation*. New York: Teachers College Press, 209–29.

Roots of Empathy. 2005. *Roots of Empathy in Action*, program summary. Toronto: Roots of Empathy. At: <www.rootsofempathy.org/infopackage.html>.

Rose, Chloë Brushwood, and Jennifer Jenson. 2007. 'Gender Inequality and Professional School Culture: Teachers at Work with Technology', in Jenson, Rose, and Brian Lewis, with Richard Smith, Stan Shapson, Penny Milton, and Robert Kennedy, *Policy Unplugged: Dis/Connections between Technology Policy and Practices in Canadian Schools*. Montreal and Kingston: McGill-Queen's University Press, 48–67.

Rosenthal, Robert, and Lenore Jacobson. 1968. *Pygmalion in the Classroom: Teacher Expectation and Pupils' Intellectual Development*. New York: Holt, Rinehart and Winston.

Rothwell, Neil, and Martin Turcotte. 2006. 'The Influence of Education on Civic Engagement: Differences across Canada's Rural–Urban Spectrum', *Rural and Small Town Canada Analysis Bulletin* 7, 1 (July), Statistics Canada Catalogue no. 21-006-XIE. At: <www.statcan.ca/english/freepub/21-006-XIE/21-006-XIE2006001.pdf>.

Rowan, Brian, and Cecil G. Miskel. 1999. 'Institutional Theory and the Study of Educational Organizations', in Joseph Murphy and Karen Seashore Louis, eds, *Handbook of Research on Educational Administration: A Project of the American Educational Research Association*, 2nd edn. San Francisco: Jossey-Bass, 359–83.

Royal Commission on Aboriginal Peoples. 1996a. *Report of the Royal Commission on Aboriginal Peoples*, vol. 1, *Looking Forward, Looking Back*. Ottawa: Minister of Supply and Services Canada.

———. 1996b. *Report of the Royal Commission on Aboriginal Peoples*, vol. 3, *Gathering Strength*. Ottawa: Minister of Supply and Services Canada.

Royal Commission on Learning. 1994. *For the Love of Learning*, vol. 4, *Making It Happen*. Toronto: Queen's Printer for Ontario.

Royal Commission on the Relations of Capital and Labour in Canada. 1889. *Report of the Royal Commission on the Relations of Capital and Labour in Canada*. Ottawa: Government of Canada.

Rubenson, Kjell, Richard Desjardins, and Ee-Seul Yoon. 2007. *Adult Learning in Canada: A Comparative Perspective. Results from the Adult Literacy and Life Skills Survey*. Ottawa: Minister of Industry, Statistics Canada Catalogue no. 89-552-XIE no. 17 (Oct.).

Runté, Robert. 1998. 'The Impact of Centralized Examinations on Teacher Professionalism', *Canadian Journal of Education* 23, 2: 166–81.

Rushton, Philippe, and Anthony Bogaert. 1987. 'Race Differences in Sexual Behavior: Testing an Evolutionary Hypothesis', *Journal of Research on Personality* 21: 529–51.

Samuelson, Les. 1991. 'The Neo-Conservative Sacrifice of Youth: Quality of Youth Employment and Its Consequences', in Terry Wotherspoon, ed., *Hitting the Books: The Politics of Educational Retrenchment*. Toronto and Saskatoon: Garamond Press and the Social Research Unit, 119–38.

Sarason, Seymour B. 1996. *Revisiting 'The Culture of the School and the Problem of Change'*. New York: Teachers College Press.

Saskatchewan Association of University Teachers. 2006. *Submission to the Review of Post-Secondary Education*. Regina: Saskatchewan Association of University Teachers (Nov.). At: <www.aeel.gov.sk.ca/aar/submissions/SAUT-URFA%20.pdf>.

Saskatchewan Education. 1996. *Building Communities of Hope: Best Practices for Meeting the Learning Needs of At-Risk and Indian and Métis Students*. Regina: Saskatchewan Education.

Saskatchewan Teachers' Federation. 1995. *The Workload and Worklife of Saskatchewan Teachers: Full-Time Teachers 1994–95*. Saskatoon: Saskatchewan Teachers' Federation Research Report No. 1.

Satzewich, Vic, and Terry Wotherspoon. 2000. *First Nations: Race, Class, and Gender Relations*. Regina: Canadian Plains Research Centre.

Schecter, Stephen. 1977. 'Capitalism, Class, and Educational Reform in Canada', in Leo Panitch, ed., *The Canadian State: Political Economy and Political Power*. Toronto: University of Toronto Press, 373–416.

Schissel, Bernard. 2006. *Still Blaming Children: Youth Conduct and the Politics of Child Hating*. Black Point, NS: Fernwood.

——— and Terry Wotherspoon. 2003. *The Legacy of School for Aboriginal People: Education, Oppression, and Emancipation*. Toronto: Oxford University Press.

Sciadas, George. 2002. *The Digital Divide in Canada*. Ottawa: Statistics Canada Research Paper, 1 Oct., Catalogue no. 56F0009XIE.

Schweitzer, Thomas T. 1995. *The State of Education in Canada*. Montreal: Institute for Research on Public Policy.

Sears, Alan. 2003. *Retooling the Mind Factory: Education in a Lean State*. Aurora, Ont.: Garamond Press.

Sewid-Smith, Daisy. 1991. 'In Time Immemorial', in Dorothy Jensen and Cheryl Brooks, eds., *In Celebration of Our Survival: The First Nations of British Columbia*. Vancouver: University of British Columbia Press, 16–32.

Shack, Sybil. 1973. *The Two-Thirds Minority: Women in Canadian Education*. Toronto: Guidance Centre, University of Toronto.

Shaienks, Danielle, and Thoasz Gluszynski. 2007. *Participation in Postsecondary Education: Graduates, Continuers and Drop Outs, Results from YITS Cycle 4*. Ottawa: Minster of Industry. Culture, Tourism and the Centre for Education Statistics Research Paper no. 059. Statistics Canada Catalogue no. 81-595-MIE2007059.

Shalla, Vivian, and Wallace Clement, eds. 2007. *Work in Tumultuous Times: Critical Perspectives.* Montreal and Kingston: McGill-Queen's University Press.

Shor, Ira. 1980. *Critical Teaching and Everyday Life.* Boston: South End Press.

Siedule, Tom. 1992. *The Influence of Socioeconomic Background on Education.* Ottawa: Economic Council of Canada, Working Paper No. 34.

Silver, Jim, and Kathy Mallett, with Janice Greene and Freeman Simard. 2002. *Aboriginal Education in Winnipeg Inner-City Schools.* Winnipeg: Canadian Centre for Policy Alternatives and Winnipeg Inner-City Research Alliance.

Simon, Roger. 2001. 'Now's the Time: Foreword', in Portelli and Solomon (2001: 11–13).

Sims, Jinny. 2004. 'Open Letter to Don Wright, Commissioner, Commission to Review Teacher Collective Bargaining', 27 Sept. Vancouver: British Columbia Teachers' Federation Negotiations. At: <bctf.ca/BargainingAndContracts.aspx?id=4920>.

Skolrood, Arthur Harold. 1967. 'The British Columbia Teachers' Federation: A Study of Its Historical Development, Interests and Activities from 1916 to 1963', Ed.D. thesis, University of Oregon.

Smaller, Harry, Rosemary Clark, Doug Hart, David Livingstone, and Zahra Noormohammed. 2000. 'Teacher Learning, Informal and Formal: Results of a Canadian Teachers' Survey', New Approaches to Lifelong Learning Working Paper 14-2000. At: <www.oise.utoronto.ca/depts/ sese/csew/nall/res/index.htm>.

Smyth, John. 2001. *Critical Politics of Teachers' Work: An Australian Perspective.* New York: Peter Lang.

———, Alastair Dow, Robert Hattam, Alan Reid, and Geoffrey Shacklock. 2000. *Teachers' Work in a Globalizing Economy.* London: Falmer.

Srivastava, Sarita. 2007. '"Let's Talk": The Pedagogy and Politics of Anti-racist Change', in Mark Coté, Richard J.P. Day, and Greig de Peuter, eds, *Utopian Pedagogy: Radical Experiments against Neoliberal Globalization.* Toronto: University of Toronto Press, 294–313.

Standing Committee on Aboriginal Affairs and Northern Development. 2007. *No Higher Priority: Aboriginal Post-Secondary Education in Canada: Report of the Standing Committee on Aboriginal Affairs and Northern Development.* Ottawa: House of Commons.

Standing Committee on Public Accounts. 2005. *Education Program and Post-Secondary Student Support. Report of the Standing Committee on Public Accounts.* Ottawa: House of Commons, June.

Statistics Canada. 1973. *Education in Canada 1973.* Ottawa: Information Canada.

———. 1984. *Education in Canada 1983.* Ottawa: Minister of Supply and Services Canada.

———. 1993. *Schooling, Work and Related Activities, Income, Expenses and Mobility: 1991 Aboriginal Peoples' Survey.* Ottawa: Minister of Industry, Science and Technology, Catalogue no. 89-534.

———. 2001a. *Education in Canada, 2000.* Ottawa: Minister of Industry, Catalogue no. 81-229.

———. 2001b. 'Trends in the Use of Private Education', *The Daily*, 4 July.

———. 2002. 'Computer Access at School and at Home', *The Daily*, 29 Oct.

———. 2003. *Education in Canada: Raising the Standard* (2001 Census, Analysis Series). Ottawa: Statistics Canada, Catalogue no. 96-F0030-X1E2001012.

———. 2007a. *Immigration in Canada: A Portrait of the Foreign-born Population, 2006 Census.* Ottawa: Minister of Industry (Mar.), Statistics Canada Catalogue no. 97-557-XIE2006

———. 2007b. 'Labour Force Survey Estimates (LFS), by Educational Attainment, Sex and Age Group, Annually', Table 2820004, CANSIM multidimensional database. At: <dc2.chass. utoronto.ca/cgi-bin/cansimdim/c2_getArrayDim.pl>.

———. 2007c. 'Labour Force Survey Estimates (LFS), by National Occupational Classification for Statistics (NOC-S) and Sex', CANSIM multidimensional database. At: <dc2.chass. utoronto.ca/cgi-bin/cansimdim/c2_seriesCart.pl>.

———. 2007d. 'Labour Force Survey', *The Daily*, 7 Dec.

————. 2007e. *Participation and Activity Limitation Survey 2006: Analytical Report*. Ottawa: Minister of Industry, Social and Aboriginal Statistics Division Analytical Paper (Dec.). Catalogue no. 89-628-XIE2007002. At: <dc2.chass.utoronto.ca.cyber.usask.ca/cgi-bin/cansimdim/c2_getArrayDim.pl>.

————. 2007f. 'Shopping for Back to School', *Back to school . . . by the numbers*. Ottawa: Statistics Canada media Release, 13 Sept. At: <www42.statcan.ca/smr08/smr08_088_e.htm>.

————. 2008a. *Aboriginal Identity, Sex, and Age Groups for the Population of Canada*. Ottawa: Statistics Canada, 2006 Census of Canada, Catalogue no. 97-558-XCB2006007 (15 Jan.).

————. 2008b. *Canada's Changing Labour Force, 2006 Census*. Ottawa: Minister of Industry (Mar.). Statistics Canada Catalogue no. 97-559-XIE2006001.

————. 2008c. *Earnings and Income of Canadians over the Past Quarter Century, 2006 Census*. Ottawa: Minister of Industry (May), Statistics Canada Catalogue no. 97-563-XIE2006001.

————. 2008d. *Educational Portrait of Canada, 2006 Census*. Ottawa: Minister of Industry (Mar.). Statistics Canada Catalogue no. 97-560-XIE2006001.

————. 2008e. Labour Force Activity, Highest Certificate, Diploma or Degree, Aboriginal Identity, Age Groups and Sex for the Population 15 Years and Over, 2006 Census. Ottawa: Minister of Industry, Statistics Canada Catalogue no. 97-559-XCB2006019. At: <www12.statcan.ca/english/census06/data/topics/ListProducts.cfm?Temporal=2006&APATH=3&THEME=7>.

———— and Council of Ministers of Education Canada (CMEC). 2007. *Education Indicators in Canada: Report of the Pan-Canadian Education Indicators Program 2005*. Ottawa: Canadian Education Statistics Council, Catalogue no. 81-582-XPE.

———— and Organization for Economic Co-operation and Development (OECD). 2005. *Learning a Living: First Results of the Adult Literacy and Life Skills Survey*. Ottawa and Paris: Statistics Canada and OECD, Statistics Canada Catalogue no. 89-603XIE2005001.

Stebbins, Robert A. 1971. 'The Meaning of Disorderly Behavior: Teacher Definition of a Classroom Situation', *Sociology of Education* 44, 2: 217–36.

————. 1975. *Teachers and Meaning: Definitions of Classroom Situations*. Leiden: E.J. Brill.

Steering Group for the Situational Analysis of Canada's Education Sector Human Resources. 2002. *The ABCs of Educational Demographics: Report of the Findings of a Situational Analysis of Canada's Education Sector Human Resources*. Ottawa: Canadian Alliance of Education and Training Organizations, Jan.

Steinberg, Shirley R., and Joe L. Kincheloe, eds. 1997. *Kinderculture: The Corporate Construction of Childhood*. Boulder, Colo.: Westview Press.

Stelmach, Bonnie. 2004. 'Unlocking the Schoolhouse Doors: Institutional Constraints on Parent and Community Involvement in a School Improvement Initiative', *Canadian Journal of Educational Administration and Policy* 31 (18 June). At: <www.umanitoba.ca/publications/cjeap/articles/stelmach.html>.

Stonechild, Blair. 2006. *The New Buffalo: The Struggle for Aboriginal Post-Secondary Education in Canada*. Winnipeg: University of Manitoba Press.

Strategic Council. 2007. *Attitudes and Perceptions of Higher Education: A Summary Report to the Association of Canadian Universities and Colleges of Canada*. Toronto: Gregg, Kelly, Sullivan, and Woolstencraft: The Strategic Council, Mar.

Strathdee, Rob. 2005. 'Globalization, Innovation, and the Declining Significance of Qualifications-Led Social and Economic Change', *Journal of Educational Policy* 20, 4: 437–56.

Stromquist, Nelly P., and Karen Monkman. 2000. 'Defining Globalization and Assessing Its Implications on Knowledge and Education', in Stromquist and Monkman, eds, *Globalization and Education: Integration and Contestation across Cultures*. Lanham, Md: Rowman and Littlefield, 3–26.

Sullivan, Alice. 2002. 'Bourdieu and Education: How Useful Is Bourdieu's Theory for Researchers?', *Netherlands Journal of Social Sciences* 38, 2: 144–66.

Sutherland, Neil. 1976. *Children in English-Speaking Canada: Framing the Twentieth-Century Consensus*. Toronto: University of Toronto Press.

Sweet, Robert, and Paul Gallagher. 1999. 'Private Training Institutions in Canada: New Directions for a Public Resource', *Journal of Educational Administration and Foundations* 13, 2: 54–77.

——— and Nancy Mandell. 2005. 'Exploring Limits to Parental Involvement in Their Children's Homework', in Sweet and Paul Anisef, eds, *Preparing for Post-Secondary Education: New Roles for Governments and Families*. Montreal and Kingston: McGill-Queen's University Press, 273–88.

Tanner, Julian, Harvey Krahn, and Timothy F. Hartnagel. 1995. *Fractured Transitions from School to Work: Revisiting the Dropout Problem*. Toronto: Oxford University Press.

Tardif, Maurice, and Claude Lessard. 1999. *Le Travail Enseignant au Quotidien: Contribution à l'étude du travail dans les métiers et les professions d'interactions humaines*. Saint-Nicolas, Que.: Les Presses de L'Université Laval.

——— and ———. 2004. 'Introduction', in Maurice Tardif et Claude Lessard, eds, *La profession d'enseignant aujourd'hui: Évolutions, perspectives et enjeux internationaux*. St Nicolas, Que., and Bruxelles: Les Presses de l'Universié Laval et De Boeck, 1–18.

Taylor, Alison. 2001. *The Politics of Educational Reform in Alberta*. Toronto: University of Toronto Press.

———. 2005. 'Finding the Future That Fits', *Gender and Education* 17, 2: 165–87.

———. 2007. *Pathways for Youth to the Labour Market: An Overview of High School Initiatives*. Ottawa: Canadian Policy Research Network and Canadian Council on Learning.

Titchkosky, Tanya. 2003. *Disability, Self and Society*. Toronto: University of Toronto Press.

Titley, E. Brian. 1982. 'Tradition, Change and Education in French Canada', in Titley and Miller (1982: 45–56).

——— and Peter J. Miller, eds. 1982. *Education in Canada: An Interpretation*. Calgary: Detselig.

Tomkins, George S. 1977. 'Canadian Education and the Development of a National Consciousness: Historical and Contemporary Perspectives', in Alf Chaiton and Neil McDonald, eds, *Canadian Schools and Canadian Identity*. Toronto: Gage, 6–28.

———. 1981. 'Stability and Change in the Canadian Curriculum', in J. Donald Wilson, ed., *Canadian Education in the 1980's*. Calgary: Detselig, 135–58.

Torres, Carlos Alberto, and Theodore R. Mitchell, eds. 1998. *Sociology of Education: Emerging Perspectives*. Albany: State University of New York Press.

Tran, Dien. 1995. 'Communication Technology and Education in Canada', in Ghosh and Ray (1995: 45–53).

Tran, Kelly. 2004. 'Visible Minorities in the Labour Force: 20 Years of Change', *Canadian Social Trends* 73 (Summer): 7–11.

Ungerleider, Charles S. 1994. 'Power, Politics, and the Professionalization of Teachers in British Columbia', in Erwin and MacLennan (1994: 370–9).

———. 2003. *Failing Our Kids: How We Are Ruining Our Public Schools*. Toronto: McClelland & Stewart.

UNICEF Innocenti Research Centre. 2002. 'A League Table of Educational Disadvantage in Rich Nations', *Innocenti Report Card* No. 4 (Nov.). Florence: United Nations Children's Fund.

United Nations Conference on Trade and Development (UNCTAD). 2007. *Science and Technology for Development: The New Paradigm of ICT*. Information Economy Report 2007–2008. New York and Geneva: United Nations.

United Nations Development Programme. 2001. *Human Development Report 2001: Making New Technologies Work for Human Development*. New York: Oxford University Press.

———. 2007. *Human Development Report 2007/2008. Fighting Climate Change: Human Solidarity in a Divided World*. New York: Palgrave Macmillan.

United Nations Educational, Scientific and Cultural Organization (UNESCO). 2007. *Education for All by 2015: Will We Make It?* EFA Global Monitoring Report, 2008. Paris: UNESCO.

Veltmeyer, Henry. 1986. *The Canadian Class Structure.* Toronto: Garamond Press.

Vinken, Henk. 2007. 'New Life Course Dynamics?', *Young* 15, 1: 9–30.

Vollmer, Jamie Robert. 2003. 'The Blueberry Story: The Teacher Gives the Businessman a Lesson', *Our Schools/Our Selves* 12, 3: 41–2.

Vosko, Leah F. 2003. 'Gender Differentiation and the Standard/Non-Standard Employment Distinction: A Genealogy of Policy Interventions in Canada', in Danielle Juteau, ed., *Social Differentiaton: Patterns and Processes.* Toronto: University of Toronto Press, 25–80.

———. 2007. 'Gendered Labour Market Insecurities: Manifestations of Precarious Employment in Different Locations', in Shalla and Clement (2007: 52–97).

Waber, Dietmar. 2006. 'Examining the Examiners: Reflections on Non-Partisanship, the Fraser Institute and the Report Card on Schools', *Education Canada* 46, 3: 4–8.

Walford, Geoffrey, and W.S.F. Pickering, eds. 1998. *Durkheim and Modern Education.* London: Routledge.

Walkerdine, Valerie. 1998. *Counting Girls Out: Girls and Mathematics,* new edn. London: Falmer.

Waller, Willard. 1965. *The Sociology of Teaching.* New York: John Wiley & Sons.

Warburton, Rennie. 1986. 'The Class Relations of Public School Teachers in British Columbia', *Canadian Review of Sociology and Anthropology* 23, 2: 210–29.

Weber, Sandra, and Claudia Mitchell. 1999. 'Teacher Identity and Popular Culture', in Jon Prosser, ed., *School Culture.* Thousand Oaks, Calif.: Sage, 145–60.

Weiler, Kathleen. 1988. *Women Teaching for Change: Gender, Class and Power.* New York: Bergin and Garvey.

Weis, Lois. 1990. *Working Class without Work: High School Students in a De-industrializing Economy.* New York: Routledge.

———, Cameron McCarthy, and Greg Dimitriadis, eds. 2006. *Ideology, Curriculum and the New Sociology of Education: Revisiting the Work of Michael Apple.* New York: Routledge.

White, Patrick. 2008. 'Afrocentric: Bad Word, Good Idea', *Globe and Mail,* 18 Jan., L1, L3.

Whitty, Geoff. 1997. 'Marketization, the State, and the Re-Formation of the Teaching Profession', in Halsey et al. (1997: 299–310).

Wickstrom, Rod A. 1994. 'Educational Change: Can We Make Sense of Reality?', *Education Canada* 34, 4: 4–10.

Wilkinson, Bruce W. 1994. *Educational Choice: Necessary But Not Sufficient.* Montreal: Institute for Research on Public Policy.

Willard, Doug. 2001. 'Keeping Canada's Teaching Profession Alive and Well', *Hill Times,* 8 Oct.

Williams, Tom R., and Holly Millinoff. 1990. *Canada's Schools: A Report Card for the 1990s: A CEA Opinion Poll.* Toronto: Canadian Education Association.

Willis, Paul. 1977. *Learning to Labor: How Working Class Kids Get Working Class Jobs.* New York: Columbia University Press.

Willms, J. Douglas. 1997. *Literacy Skills of Canadian Youth.* Ottawa: Minister of Industry, Statistics Canada Catalogue no. 89-552-MIE no. 1.

———. 2002. 'The Prevalence of Vulnerability', in Willms, ed., *Vulnerable Children: Findings from Canada's National Longitudinal Survey of Children and Youth.* Edmonton: University of Alberta Press and Human Resources Development Canada, 45–69.

Wilson, J. Donald. 1981. 'Religion and Education: The Other Side of Pluralism', in Wilson, ed., *Canadian Education in the 1980's.* Calgary: Detselig, 97–113.

———. 1991. '"I Am Ready To Be of Assistance When I Can": Lottie Bowron and Rural Women Teachers in British Columbia', in Alison Prentice and Marjorie R. Theobald, eds, *Women Who Taught: Perspectives on the History of Women and Teaching.* Toronto: University of Toronto Press, 202–29.

————, Robert M. Stamp, and Louis-Philippe Audet, eds. 1970. *Canadian Education: A History.* Scarborough, Ont.: Prentice-Hall.

Wolfe, David A. 2002. 'Innovation Policy for the Knowledge-Based Economy: From the Red Book to the White Paper', in G. Bruce Doern, ed., *How Ottawa Spends 2002–2003: The Security Aftermath and National Priorities.* Toronto: Oxford University Press, 137–56.

Woods, Peter. 1983. *Sociology and the School: An Interactionist Viewpoint.* Boston: Routledge & Kegan Paul.

Worth, W.H. 1972. *A Future of Choices—A Choice of Futures: A Report of the Commission on Educational Planning* (Worth Report). Edmonton: Queen's Printer.

Wotherspoon, Terry. 1984. 'Ideals and Sausage Factories: Schools in Capitalist Society', in John A. Fry, ed., *Contradictions in Canadian Society: Readings in Introductory Sociology.* Toronto: John Wiley & Sons, 207–18.

————, ed. 1987. *The Political Economy of Canadian Schooling.* Toronto: Methuen.

————. 1989. 'Immigration and the Production of a Teaching Force: Policy Implications for Education and Labour', *International Migration* 27, 4: 543–62.

————. 1991. 'Educational Reorganization and Retrenchment', in Wotherspoon, ed., *Hitting the Books: The Politics of Educational Retrenchment.* Toronto and Saskatoon: Garamond Press and Social Research Unit, 15–58.

————. 1993. 'From Subordinate Partners to Dependent Employees: State Regulation of Public School Teachers in Nineteenth Century British Columbia', *Labour/Le Travail* 31 (Spring): 75–110.

————. 1995a. 'The Incorporation of Public School Teachers into the Industrial Order: British Columbia in the First Half of the Twentieth Century', *Studies in Political Economy* 46 (Spring): 119–51.

————. 1995b. 'Multiculturalism and the Management of Race and Ethnic Relations in Canadian Schooling', in Wotherspoon and Paul Jungbluth, eds, *Multicultural Education in a Changing Global Economy: Canada and the Netherlands.* Munster: Waxmann, 41–60.

————. 1998. 'Education, Place, and the Sustainability of Rural Communities in Saskatchewan', *Journal of Research in Rural Education* 14, 3: 131–41.

————. 2003. 'Aboriginal People, Public Policy, and Social Differentiation in Canada', in Danielle Juteau, ed., *Social Differentiation: Patterns and Processes.* Toronto: University of Toronto Press, 155–204.

————. 2006. 'Teachers' Work in Canadian Aboriginal Communities', *Comparative Education Review* 50, 4: 672–94.

Wyn, Johanna, Sandra Acker, and Elisabeth Richards. 2000. 'Making a Difference: Women in Management in Australian and Canadian Faculties of Education', *Gender and Education* 12, 4: 435–47.

Young, Jon, ed. 1987. *Breaking the Mosaic: Ethnic Identities in Canadian Schooling.* Toronto: Garamond Press.

————, Benjamin Levin, and Dawn Wallin. 2007. *Understanding Canadian Schools: An Introduction to Educational Administration,* 4th edn. Scarborough, Ont.: Nelson.

Young, Michael F.D., ed. 1971. *Knowledge and Control: New Directions for the Sociology of Education.* London: Collier-Macmillan.

Younghusband, Lynda. 2006. 'Teacher Stress and Working Environments: Implications for Teaching and Learning', *Newfoundland Quarterly* 98, 4: 8–11.

Zeman, Klarka. 2007. 'A First Look at Provincial Differences in Educational Pathways from High School to College and University', *Education Matters* 4, 2 (19 June), Statistics Canada Catalogue no. 81-004-XIE.

Zietsma, Danielle. 2007. *The Canadian Immigrant Labour Market in 2006: First Results from Canada's Labour Force Survey.* Ottawa: Minister of Industry, Immigrant Labour Force Analysis Series Research Paper, Statistics Canada Catalogue no. 71-606-XIE2007001.

Index

Aboriginal Learning Knowledge Centre, 128–9
Aboriginal peoples: colonial education and, 57–60; educational authorities of, 79; educational opportunity and, 240, 247–54; frameworks for success and, 128–9; population of, 233; residential schools and, 58–60, 114–15, 248; silencing and, 133; social inequality and, 225; perceptions of school and, 113; teachers and, 150–1; as teachers, 167–8
access: equality of, 226
accountability, 280–6, 301
Acker, Sandra, 165, 176
Addams, Jane, 26
adult and continuing education, 78, 102, 107, 209, 233
Afrocentric schooling, 133–4
agency, human, 7, 18
Albas, Daniel, and Cheryl Albas, 31
Alladin, Ibrahim, 274
allocation: as school function, 22, 23
Altenbaugh, Richard J., 160–1
amalgamation, 107
analysis: guidelines for, 50–1
Anisef, Paul, et al., 221
anti-racism education, 15, 18, 46–7, 231, 241–2, 246–7; barriers to, 123–4; impact of, 132–3
appearance, 30, 136
Apple, Michael W., 17, 39, 41, 42, 135, 176, 195; on intensification, 170, 173–5; on New Right, 97–8; on textbooks, 126–7
apprenticeships, 81
aptitude tests, 132
Armstrong, Pat, and Hugh Armstrong, 214
Arnot, Madeleine, 44, 52
Ashworth, Mary, 56–7
Assembly of First Nations, 232
assessment: school, 282–6; student, 281–4; teacher, 169–70, 175
associations, teachers', 151, 177
attainment: see educational attainment
attendance, compulsory, 65–6, 230
Axelrod, Paul, 75

Bacon, Allan, 284
Ball, Stephen J., 283–4
Ballantine, Jeanne H., and Joan Z. Spade, 17
Barlow, Maude, and Heather-Jane Robertson, 101
Beaujot, Roderic, and Don Kerr, 209
Becker, Howard, 31
Bellamy, Lesley Andres, 196
Bernstein, Basil, 39, 127, 130
Bills, David, 222
biology: gender and, 121
BLAC (Black Learners Advisory Committee), 134
Blau, Peter M., and Otis Dudley Duncan, 25
Boothby, Daniel, and Torbin Drewes, 238
Bourdieu, Pierre, 39–40, 132, 196
Bourgon, Lyndsie, 193
Bowers, Norman, et al., 206, 208
Bowlby, Geoff, 210
Bowles, Samuel, and Herbert Gintis, 35–6, 37–8, 52
boys: bullying and, 140–1; Internet and, 288; performance of, 119–22; see also gender; men
British Columbia Teachers' Federation, 154–5
Brown, Phillip, et al., 222
bullying, 135–6, 140–1
bureaucracy, 29; educational, 67
business: education and, 66–7, 191–2, 197

Campaign 2000, 262–3
Canada Student Loan Program, 265
Canadian Association of University Teachers, 147
Canadian Council on Learning, 13, 86, 140–1, 182–3, 186, 232–3, 282
Canadian Education Association, 99, 101, 200
Canadian Taxpayers' Federation, 154
Canadian Teachers' Federation, 147, 152, 171
capitalist imperative, 199–201, 222, 280
Carnoy, Martin, and Henry M. Levin, 27, 199, 280
Castellano, Marlene Brant, et al., 274
CEGEP, 79

centralization: schools and, 84
Chafe, J.W., 149
Chalmers, John W., 149
Charter of Rights and Freedoms, 267
charter schools, 91–2, 280, 301
Chicago School, 26, 31
Chubb, John E., and Terry M. Moe, 90
class, social, 12, 15, 275; educational
    opportunity and, 255–66; performance
    and, 121
class size, 87–8
Clement, Wallace, 38
Clifford, Patricia, ix, 292–3
climate change, 229
Cohen, Stanley, 137
Coleman Report, 25–6
collective bargaining, 149, 155, 177
Collins, Patricia Hill, 5–6
Collins, Randall, 29–31, 102, 192
Columbine High School, 30
commercialization, 95–6
community: involvement of, 100–1
community colleges, 81–2; see also
    post–secondary education
computers, 287–94
Comte, Auguste, 5, 8
Conference on Education (1958), 71–2
conflict: stability and, 7–8
conflict theories, 29
Connell, R.W., et al., 139
Contenta, Sandro, 143
Cooley, C.H., 31
correspondence principle, 35–6, 37–8, 52
Corrigan, Philip, et al., 199
Côté, James E., and Anton Allahar, 143
Coulter, R.P., 200
Council of Ministers of Education Canada,
    86
Cowley, Peter, 285
credentials, 29–31, 68, 111, 143; Aboriginal
    peoples and, 252; 'creep' in, 193;
    immigration and, 243; teachers', 148;
    work and, 188, 189, 192–3, 209
credential inflation, 40, 192–3
critical analysis, 12, 14–16, 33–50, 112
'critical functionalism', 36
critical pedagogy, 14–15, 18, 47–50
critical progressivism, 27
critical sociology, 130–1
Crysdale, Stewart, et al., 222
Cuban, Larry, 291, 300

cultural capital, 31, 52, 127, 130, 196
cultural reproduction, 39–40, 52
cultural theory, 228
curriculum, 61, 73, 76; bias of, 131–2;
    educational opportunity and, 230–1;
    elementary, 69, 79; hidden, 22, 112, 114,
    144, 188, 195; official knowledge and,
    125–30; secondary, 69; standardized,
    169–70; work and, 194
Curtis, Bruce, et al., 76, 257, 264, 274, 275
'cyberkids', 292–3

Danylewycz, Marta, and Alison Prentice, 157
Darder, Antonia, et al., 52
data, research, 13–14
Davies, Scott, 17–18, 107, 256
de Broucker, Patrice, and Arthur Sweetman,
    282, 300
decision-making, evidence-based, 13, 281–6,
    301
'definition of the situation', 31–2, 53
Dei, George J. Sefa, et al., 18, 133, 134
democratic imperative, 199–201, 222, 280
demographics: enrolment and, 81
deskilling, 211, 222
development, human, 112–16
deviant behaviour, 135–6
Dewey, John, 26
digital divide, 291–3, 301
Dillabough, Jo-Anne, 44
disabilities: students with, 234, 266–8
discipline: school, 116, 137; work, 195
diversity: challenges of, 294–9
division of labour, 159, 166–7, 177
dress, 30, 135
dropout, 119–20, 144
Durham District School Board, 120
Durkheim, Émile, 6–7, 13, 20–1, 28, 52

earnings, 208, 210; gender and, 208, 237–9
education: black-focused, 133–4; Canadian
    history of, 54–77; Canadian structure of,
    78–108; central questions in, 1–3;
    colonial period of, 57–67; contemporary
    challenges and, 277–302; definition of, 1,
    18; denominational, 58, 86; economic
    contributions of, 189–98, 196–8; as
    employment, 54, 196–8; funding of, 54,
    69, 81–5, 89, 94–7, 272–3; governance of,
    94–101, 286, 301; household spending
    on, 95; inclusive, 132–3, 142, 280, 301;

international growth in, 101–6; multicultural, 46, 246; private, 79, 86, 89–90, 92–3, 108; private funding of, 89, 95–6; process of, 109–44; public, 54, 76; public system development and, 61–6; secular, 61; social significance of, 3; 20th-century period of, 66–74; *see also* anti-racism education; post-secondary education

educational attainment, 3, 68, 69–70, 107, 208; Aboriginal peoples and, 248–9, 253–4; parents and, 255, 256–7; provinces and, 270

educational choice, 78, 88–93, 280

educational marketplace, 88–93

educational opportunity, 224–76; meanings of, 226; other countries and, 260; politics of, 230–3

educational progressivism, 26–7, 66–7, 76

elementary schooling, 69, 79

employability, 188, 222

employment, 179–223; education, 54, 196–8; growth in, 184–6; immigration and, 242–4; reports on, 181–6; trends in, 202–21; *see also* labour market; work

English as a second language (ESL), 246–7

enrolment, 54, 62, 68, 69, 233; Aboriginal, 247–8, 250; gender and, 234–7; patterns of, 81–2

equality of opportunity, 231, 275

equality of results, 226–7, 275

ethics, 4

ethnic minorities: educational opportunity and, 240–7; performance and, 122; streaming and, 122, 125; *see also* visible minorities

evidence-based decision-making, 13, 281–6, 301

expenditures, 54, 69, 81–5 94–7; educational opportunity and, 272–3; private, 89, 95–6

Eyre, Linda, 119

feminism, 12, 14; liberal, 42; radical, 42–3; socialist, 43

feminist pedagogy, 15, 18, 119, 231

feminist theory, 42–6

feminization, 157–68, 177

Fennell, Shailaja, and Madeleine Arnot, 275

Finnie, Ross, et al., 250, 256–7

First Nations: *see* Aboriginal peoples

First Nations educational authorities, 79

First Nations Holistic Lifelong Learning Model, 128–9

Fischer, Claude S., et al., 228

Fleras, Augie, and J.L. Elliott, 246

Forcese, Dennis, 256

Fraser Institute, 282, 285–6

Frazee, Catherine, 268

Freedman, Joe, 91

Freire, Paul, 49, 125

Frenette, Marc, 259

Friesen, John W., and Virginia Lyons Friesen, 107

Fuller, Steve, 6

fundraising, school, 95–6

Galarneau, Diane, et al., 211–12

Gaskell, Jane, 39, 44, 119, 236

gender, 15; computer use and, 288, 293; earnings and, 208, 212; education and, 42–6; educational opportunity and, 229, 234–40; international goals and, 103, 104–5; streaming and, 119–22; teachers and, 117, 153–68; work and, 213–17; *see also* boys; girls; men; women

gender segmentation, 236–7, 275

genetics: gender and, 121

Giddens, Anthony, 7

girls: bullying and, 140–1; Internet and, 288; performance of, 119–22; *see also* gender; women

Giroux, Henry A., and Peter McLaren, 49

globalization, 16, 179–81, 278

Goffman, Erving, 114

Gordon, Mary, 295

governance, educational, 94–101, 286, 301

government: federal, 84–6; funding and, 94; levels of, 79, 84–5; official knowledge and, 126; *see also* provinces

Gracey, Harry L., 115

Gramsci, Antonio, 130

guidelines: research and, 50–1

Guppy, Neil, 17–18, 101, 107, 245

Guss, Lois, 59

habitus, 40, 196, 222

Hall, Christine, 170

Hall-Dennis Report, 72–3

Hango, Darcy, and Patrice de Broucker, 218–19

Hargreaves, Andy, 176

Hart, Doug, and D.W. Livingstone, 94, 96–7

hegemony, 117, 130–1, 144
Henry, Frances, and Carol Tator, 122–4, 246
Hepburn, C.R., 98
Herrnstein, Richard J., and Charles Murray, 228
hidden curriculum, 22, 112, 114, 144, 188, 195
historical materialism, 34; *see also* critical analysis
Hochschild, Arlie Russell, 31
Hoff Summers, Christina, 234
home-based schooling, 90
hooks, bell, 43
Hughes, Karen D., and Graham S. Lowe, 211
Hull, Jeremy, 252
human agency, 7, 18, 110, 114
human capital theory, 25, 53, 190–2, 278–80
human development, 112–16
Hunter, Alfred J., and Jean McKenzie Leiper, 261

Illich, Ivan, 72
immigration: educational opportunity and, 233, 242–5
inclusive education, 132–3, 142, 280, 301
'Indian Control of Indian Education', 250
Indian and Northern Affairs Canada, 254
indigenous knowledge, 47, 57, 76
individualism, 112–14, 131
individuals: schooling and 12–14, 117; society and, 6–7
individuation, 112, 144
industry: education and, 66–7, 191–2, 197
informal learning, 78, 107, 292
information and communications technologies (ICTs), 287–94
information society, 1; *see also* knowledge economy/society
institutions, 9
intelligence: race and, 228; tests of, 132
intensification, 168, 170, 173–5, 177
Internet, 287, 288–9, 291
interpretive analysis, 8–9, 11–12, 18, 28–33, 110
Inuit, 129, 248; *see also* Aboriginal peoples
Inuit Holistic Lifelong Learning Model, 129

Jackson, Nancy S., 245
Jaenen, Cornelius J., 58
James, Carl E., 245
Jencks, Christopher, 37

Jenks, Chris, 18
Jenson, Jennifer, 301
Juvenile Delinquents Act, 65

Kanagarajah, Sri, 204
Kanpol, Barry, 136
Karabel, Jerome, and A.H. Halsey, 33
Kazemipur, A. and S.S. Halli, 244
Kenway, Jane, and Sue Willis, 120–1, 237
Kerckhoff, Alan C., 187
Kincheloe, Joe L., 48–9
'kinderculture', 137
Kirkness, Verna, and S.S. Bowman, 57, 115, 252
knowledge: high-/medium-/low-, 204–6; indigenous/traditional, 47, 57, 76; official, 117, 125–30; production of, 125
knowledge economy, 1, 179–81, 204–6, 278–9
knowledge societies, 78
knowledge workers, 210–11, 222
Krahn, Harvey, and Alison Taylor, 121

labelling, 32, 110, 118
labour: division of, 159, 166–7, 177
labour market: polarization in, 211–12; segmented, 212–14; trends in, 202–21; *see also* employment; work
Lapointe, Mario, et al., 184–6
Lauder, Hugh, et al., 18
Lawr, Douglas A., and Robert D. Gidney, 76
Lawton, Stephen B., 98
legislation: safety, 137–8; teachers and, 162; in United States, 13, 283
Lessard, Claude, 226, 284
Lévesque, M., 226
liberal theory, 20–8
lifelong learning, 78, 188, 206, 220–1, 223, 282, 292
literacy, international, 103, 106
Little Poplar, Alphonse, 59–60
Livingstone, D.W., 36, 106, 209, 220, 222
Lockhart, Alexander, 176
'looking-glass self', 31
Lortie, Dan C., 145
Lowe, Graham, 222
Lucas, Edith, 56–7

McAndrew, Marie, 246
Mac An Ghaill, Mairtin, 52
Macdonald, Doune, 171

McLaren, Arlene, and Jim Gaskell, 119
McLaren, Peter, 49, 143, 245
McNeil, Linda M., 139
Mannheim, Karl, 29
Manzer, Ronald A., 76
marketization, 278, 302
Martell, George, 38
Martin, Wilfred, 110, 143
Marx, Karl, 7, 34–5
Marxism, 12, 14
Marxist educational theory, 34–42, 110
Mead, G.H., 26, 31
media: moral panic and, 137
men: earnings and, 208, 212; education and, 42; educational attainment and, 70; educational opportunity and, 234–40; as teachers, 153–68; work and, 202, 213–17, 237–40; see also boys; gender
meritocracy, 240, 255
Métis, 248; see also Aboriginal peoples
Métis Holistic Lifelong Learning Model, 129
microsociology, 11
Mills, C. Wright, 29
morality, 198–9
moral panics, 137, 144
moral regulation, 61, 76, 175, 177
multicultural education, 46, 246
multiculturalism, 75, 246
municipal government, 84
Murphy, Raymond, 31

National Occupational Classification (NOC), 184
nature-nurture controversy, 121
Nayak, Anoop, 42
Neatby, Hilda, 69
Nelsen, Randle, and David Nock, 38–9
neo-Weberian analysis, 29–31
new economy, 181, 191, 223
New Right, 97–8, 101, 281
'new' sociology of education, 32–3
New Zealand: charter schools in, 91
Nikiforuk, Andrew, 98, 152
'No Child Left Behind', 13, 283
non–formal education, 78
normal schools, 163, 165, 177
Nova Scotia: Afrocentric school in, 134

official knowledge, 117, 125–30
Ogle, J.P., and M. Eckman, 30
Olson, Paul, 264

Ontario: 'zero tolerance' in, 137–8
opportunity, equality of, 231; see also educational opportunity
order perspective, 9
organic analogy, 10
Organization for Economic Co-operation and Development (OECD), 102, 180–1, 279
Ornstein, Allan, 256
Osberg, Lars, et al., 217

Pacholik, Barb, 87–8
Paquette, Jerry, 286
Parelius, R.J., and A.P. Parelius, 20
parents: educational attainment of, 255, 256–7; influence of, 255, 256–9; involvement of, 100–1
Parsons, Talcott, 21–2, 23–4
partnerships, university-industry-government, 191–2, 197
Paton, J.M., 148–9
patriarchy, 12, 43
pedagogy, 53; critical, 14–15, 18, 47–50; feminist, 15, 18, 119, 231; 'visible' and 'invisible', 127, 130
Penfield, Wilder, 71–2
person rights, 280, 302
Peters, M.A., and A.C. Tina Besley, 298
Phillips, Charles E., 149, 163
Plowden Report, 25–6
political economy approach, 15–16, 18, 34–42
Portelli, John P., and R. Patrick Solomon, 301
Porter, John, 25, 240, 255
positivism, 8–9, 18
post-industrial society, 179, 223
postmodernism, 14
post-secondary education, 69–70, 76, 79, 81–2; Aboriginal peoples and, 250–1; class and, 256–8, 265–6; female teachers and, 155–6; gender and, 234–6; significance of, 3, 81–2
poverty: child, 233, 262–3; educational opportunity and, 229, 261–5
practice: critical pedagogy and, 47–50
pressure group theory, 148, 149
primary education, international, 103, 105
private education, 79, 86, 108; public education and, 86, 92–3; types of, 89–90
privatization, 93, 95–6, 108

professionalism: gender and, 165–6; teachers and, 148–53; theories of, 148–9
professionalization, 67, 174–5, 177
professional trait theory, 148
Program of International Student Assessment, 259
progressivism: critical, 27; educational, 26–7, 66–7, 76
proletarianization, 152, 168–75, 177
property rights, 280, 281, 302
provinces: education and, 79, 84; educational opportunity and, 269–73; responsibilities of, 126; teachers' organizations and, 147
public education, 54, 76; development of, 61–6; private education and, 86, 92–3
public opinion, 99, 101, 200; moral panic and, 137; teachers and, 152

Quebec: post-secondary education in, 79

race, 46–7; alternative schools and, 133–4; educational opportunity and, 240–7; intelligence and, 228; performance and, 121
racialization, 46–7
racism, 15, 46–7; discourses of, 123–4; *see also* anti-racism education
Rapti, Helen, 56–7
rationalization, 29
rational planning, 280–6
reasonable accommodation, 268, 275
reform: market-driven, 97–101, 88–93, 280–6; models of, 99; teachers and, 150–1
reform movements, 65, 66–7, 70–4
regimentation, 115–16
regional inequalities, 225–6, 268–73
regulations: early, 64–5; moral, 61, 76, 175, 177; resistance and, 116–17; teachers and, 161–3, 169–70
Reitz, Jeffrey G., 243–4
religion: education and, 58, 60, 86, 198–9
Repo, Satu, 301
research: guidelines for, 50–1; sociological, 4, 13–14; status attainment, 25, 69; theory and, 20
residential schools, 58–60, 114–15, 248
resistance: regulations and, 116–17; student, 135–7, 139; theory of, 41–2, 53
results: equality of, 226–7, 275

rights: 'to learn', 199–201; person, 280, 302; property, 280, 281, 302
'risk society', 278
Robertson, Heather-Jane, 107, 301
Robertson, Susan, 176, 177
Rockhill, Kathleen, and Patricia Tomic, 247
Roots of Empathy, 295–6
Rosenthal, Robert, and Lenore Jacobson, 31
Royal Commission on Aboriginal Peoples, 76, 115, 133, 251, 253–4
Royal Commission on Education (BC), 200
Royal Commission on Learning (ON), 289
Royal Commission on the Relations of Capital and Labour, 192
Runté, Robert, 170

Safe Schools Act (ON), 137–8
safety, school, 137–8, 142
Saskatchewan Association of University Teachers, 248
Schissel, Bernard, and Terry Wotherspoon, 143
schools: alternative, 133–4; boarding, 114–15; charter, 91–2, 280, 301; common, 159; grammar, 159; normal, 163, 165, 177; private, 89–90, 108; ratings of, 282, 285–6; residential, 58–60, 114–15, 248; size of, 67, 87–8; specialized, 90; student conceptions of, 111, 113
school boards, 79
school choice, 78, 88–93, 280
schooling, 2, 18; process of, 109–44; theory and, 110–12
SchoolNet, 289
'School Plus', 251
Sciadis, George, 291
scientific management, 26–7, 66
Sears, Alan, 107
secondary schooling, 79
self-fulfilling prophecies, 31, 53, 118
service sector, 202
Shalla, Vivian, and Wallace Clement, 275
silencing, 117, 131–5, 144
skills, workplace, 189–94
'skills challenge', 182–3
Skolrood, A.H., 149
'social action', 6
social change, 5, 7–8, 12
Social Darwinism, 227–8, 276
social equality, 224

'social facts', 6
social identities, 110, 112–16
social inequality, 224–76; determinants of,
    232–76; explanations of, 227–30
socialization, 110, 144; as school function,
    22, 23
socially disadvantaged, 227, 276
social reproduction, 237–8, 276
social sciences, 4–5
social structures, 7, 19
society: individual and, 6–7
socio-economic status, 259, 276
sociology: critical, 12, 14, 130–1; definition
    of, 2, 4, 5, 6, 19; 'new', 32–3; other
    disciplines and, 4–5; perspectives of,
    9–14; as term, 5; theories of, 20–53
Spencer, Herbert, 227
stability, social, 5, 7–8
state apparatus, 62, 76
status attainment research, 25, 69
Steinberg, S.R., and J.L. Kincheloe, 137
streaming, 117–25, 144; ethnic minorities
    and, 122, 125
strikes: teachers and, 154–5
structural analysis, 110
structural determination, 7
structural functionalism, 9–11, 20–8, 53
structuralism: social inequality and, 228–30
students: categories of, 110; conceptions of
    school and, 111, 113; loans/debt and,
    265–6; resistance and, 135–7, 139;
    responses of, 135–7, 139, 142; teachers
    and, 139; work choice and, 195–6
subemployment, 220
Sutherland, Neil, 194
symbolic interactionism, 11, 31, 53
Symth, John, et al., 177

teachers, 145–178; Aboriginal, 150–1, 167–7;
    assessment of, 169–70, 175; duties of,
    63–4; early, 62, 63–4; expectations of, 31;
    gender and, 64, 153–68; 'ideal', 160;
    number of, 147, 158; organizations of,
    74, 147–8, 149, 151, 152, 154–5, 166, 177;
    other countries and, 164; part-time, 147;
    pay of, 149, 156–7, 159, 160–1; as
    professionals, 67, 148–53; regulation of,
    161–3, 169–70; stress and, 150, 170–1;
    training of, 149, 162–3, 165, 168–9;
    visible minority, 167–8; work conditions
    of, 164, 170–4, 177

teaching: historical accounts of, 148–9;
    sociology of, 145
technological functionalism, 25, 190–1, 223
technologies, new, 287–94
tests: intelligence, 132; standardized, 281–4
textbooks, 126–7
Thomas, W.I., 31
Toronto District School Board, 133–4
Torres, Carlos Alberto, and Theodore R.
    Mitchell, 52
total institution, 114–15, 144
traditional knowledge, 47, 57
Tran, Dien, 290
Tran, Kelly, 244
transitions, 188, 201, 206, 223; school-to-
    work, 187
treatment: equality of, 226
'Triple Helix', 191
tuition fees, 265–6

underemployment, 220, 223
unemployment, 183, 186
Ungerleider, Charles, 152, 280–1, 301
unions, teachers', 147–8
United Nations: education goals of, 103–6,
    224
United Nations Association in Canada, 241–2
United States: charter schools in, 91
university, 81–2; partnerships and, 191–2,
    197; women managers at, 45–6; see also
    post-secondary education
urban/rural inequalities, 268–9

victimization, 140–1
violence, 137–8; see also bullying
visible minorities, 47, 276; silencing and,
    133–4; social inequality and, 225; see also
    ethnic minorities
vocational and technical training, 81, 190,
    194, 223
Vosko, Leah F., 213–14
vouchers, school, 91, 280

Walkerdine, Valerie, 120
Waller, Willard, 31, 52, 145
Weber, Max, 6–7, 29
websites, 303–4
Weis, Lois, 139
welfare state, 68, 76
'whiteness', 47
Wickstrom, Rod A., 99

Wilkinson, Bruce W., 280
Willis, Paul, 39, 40–1, 52
Willms, J. Douglas, 275
women: earnings and, 208–212; education
    and, 42–6, 55; educational attainment
    and, 70; educational opportunity and,
    234–40; labour force participation and,
    75; social inequality and, 225; as teachers,
    64, 153–68, 173; work and, 202, 213–17,
    237–40; see also gender; girls
Woods, Peter, 136
work, 179–223; discipline of, 195; 'mismatch'
    with education and, 180–7; trends in,
    202–21; see also employment; labour force

World Education Forum, 103
World Health Organization, 141
World Teachers' Day, 164
Worth Report, 72–3
Wyn, Johanna, Sandra Acker, and Elizabeth
    Richards, 45–6

Young, Jon, Benjamin Levin, and Dawn
    Wallin, 107
youth: work and, 206–9, 218–19, 221
youth cultures, 137–42

'zero tolerance', 137–8